Multilateral Negotiations

Multilateral Negotiations

Lessons from Arms Control, Trade, and the Environment

by Fen Osler Hampson

with Michael Hart

The Johns Hopkins University Press

Baltimore and London

© 1995 The Johns Hopkins University Press
All rights reserved. Published 1995
Printed in the United States of America on acid-free paper
04 03 02 01 00 99 98 97 96 95   5 4 3 2 1

The Johns Hopkins University Press
2715 North Charles Street
Baltimore, Maryland 21218-4319
The Johns Hopkins Press Ltd., London

ISBN 0-8018-4999-3

Library of Congress Cataloging-in-Publication Data will be found at the end
of this book.
A catalog record for this book is available from the British Library.

Contents

Preface

The nature of international relations has undergone fundamental changes in the last few decades, brought on by, among other things, the emergence of new political actors, the development of new technologies, and the increase in interdependence. Accordingly, the demands and practices of diplomacy have been fundamentally altered. Political, military, economic, environmental, and social problems are often no longer limited to the realm of domestic politics or to a few countries. Today, many of the most pressing problems are global in scope, requiring large coalitions of actors to tackle them.

As a result, a plethora of institutions and organizations has been created for dealing with the new diplomatic issues directly resulting from these fundamental changes. Year after year, more and more actors become increasingly involved in the creation and development of such multilateral regimes and forums. This, in turn, requires new strategies and approaches for cooperation and coordination.

One such area of diplomatic practice that has undergone significant change has been the exercise of international negotiations. While bilateral negotiations are still commonplace, international negotiations are increasingly multilateral, involving more than just two actors, and quite frequently tens of actors, as for example in the negotiations of the European conventional arms control regime or the ozone protection regime. Also more commonplace in diplomacy is the handling of more than one specific issue in the context of multilateral negotiations, as seen in the negotiations pertaining to the General Agreement on Tariffs and Trade (GATT).

Multilateral negotiations are therefore significant because solutions to the problems that these complex negotiations seek to address require different forms of coordination and bargaining than those traditionally practiced in diplomacy. Less prevalent are the days of unilateral and bilateral solutions. Modern negotiations are extremely complicated, often involving many parties, each with the need to act in self-interest. However, unlike bilateral negotiations or negotiations in which hegemons dictate the conditions, most multilateral negotiations exhibit the practice of coalition building, which serves to overcome the complexity of a multiparty bargaining environment. As such, multilateral negotiations produce unique bargaining patterns that need to be understood, given that multilateral negotiations are a regular and constant feature of diplomacy.

While a lot of attention has been paid recently to the new types of global problems and issues that cross national borders and affect international relations—as well as to the actual components and functions of the institutions and regimes established to deal with such matters—relatively little has been written on the process of negotiation itself. This leaves a void in the literature on international negotiations and bargaining strategies, which this book attempts to fill.

It is in pursuit of this objective—adding to our understanding of multilateral negotiations—that this book is written. It attempts to explain the process of international negotiation and the strategies pertaining to bargaining in a multilateral setting. It also seeks to show the concrete connection between the theory and practice of multilateral negotiations by examining several cases of multilateral negotiations that fall under one of the three different issue-areas of great concern to diplomats: arms control, trade, and the environment.

The following friends and colleagues volunteered valuable information and insights to the researching and writing of this book: Alexander Akalovsky, Lorraine Eden, Alexander George, James Goodby, Lloyd Jensen, Louis Klarevas, Brian Mandell, Christopher Maule, Dean Pruitt, Judith Reppy, Brian Tomlin, Saadia Touval, Lawrence Weiler, and William Zartman. In particular, Alexander Akalovsky, James Goodby, and Lawrence Weiler were kind enough to take time from their busy schedules to discuss the negotiation of the Limited Test Ban treaty, and in the process provided valuable new information on its negotiation. Various portions of the book were also presented at seminars at the Paul Nitze School of Advanced International Studies, Johns Hopkins University, and the Peace Studies Program at Cornell University.

The chapters on trade negotiations reflect the advantages available to someone with daily, unrestricted access to the negotiations. Wittingly or unwittingly, therefore, many of Michael Hart's colleagues in the Canadian Department of Foreign Affairs and International Trade contributed to the information and analysis on which his chapters are based. In particular, Michael Hart wishes to thank John Curtis, John Weekes, Bill Dymond, Brian Morrisey, and Doug Waddell for their comments and help in preparing these chapters. The chapter on the GATT/International Trade Organization negotiations had its origins in a project that Michael started with the late Frank Stone, who provided unfailing encouragement and advice, and who had a key understanding of the critical role of the past in conditioning day-to-day policy decisions. Other veterans of that era who deserve special thanks for their wisdom and invaluable insights are Simon Reisman and Rodney Grey. Michael would also like to thank his wife Mary Virginia who, in his words, "played her usual stellar role in helping translate ideas into felicitous prose." Both Michael and I also appreciate the fact that our students at Carleton gave us the opportunity to test various ideas and explanations, thus sharpening our arguments.

A special note of thanks is also due to the Research and Writing Grant Program of the John D. and Catherine T. MacArthur Foundation, without whose assistance this project might never have come to fruition. We also want to thank Pauline Adams who proofread the entire book under a tight deadline. Finally, Henry Tom and the reviewers at the Johns Hopkins University Press deserve special thanks for their helpful suggestions, their courteous patience, and their unending enthusiasm for this project. To all mentioned, and to those who unintentionally may have been omitted, we are grateful.

I   Introduction

1   Multilateral Negotiations

Multilateral negotiations and their management are increasingly important manifestations of international politics. In recent years, an extraordinary array of issues dealing with the environment, international economics, and international security has become the focus of multilateral negotiations. Whether the issue is climate change, ozone depletion, conventional arms control, nuclear proliferation, or international trade and monetary relations, all are the subjects of intensive international discussions and negotiations involving multiple actors and interests, highly complex agendas, and differentiated international settings. This reflects a more general trend toward multilateralism. As Robert Keohane writes, "since the end of World War II, multilateralism has become increasingly important in world politics, as manifested in the proliferation of multilateral conferences on a bewildering variety of themes and an increase in the number of multilateral intergovernmental organizations from fewer than 100 in 1945 to about 200 in 1960 and over 600 in 1980."[1]

The concept of multilateralism is somewhat vague and elusive, however. John Ruggie suggests that at its core "multilateralism refers to coordinating relations among three or more states in accordance with certain principles." But he goes on to point out that those principles have had widely different forms of expression throughout history, ranging from collective security schemes intended to coordinate security relations among states to rules of nondiscrimination in trading relations between countries. Ruggie thus suggests that "multilateralism is an institutional form which coordinates relations among three or more states on the bases of 'generalized' principles of conduct—that is, principles which specify appropriate conduct for a class of actions, without regard to particularistic interests of the parties or the strategic exigencies that may exist in any specific occurrence."[2] This definition is useful because it draws our attention to the importance of generalized principles in the conduct and management of relations among states. But Ruggie's definition may still be restrictive insofar as it fails to discuss the diplomatic bargaining and negotiation processes through which the international community confers political legitimacy or comes to accept such principles.

Multilateral literally means "many sided." As such, it is a label that can be used to describe not only a variety of activities ranging from international negotiations to the actual structure and performance of specific international institutions, but also a variety of actors ranging from states to transnational businesses and other nongovernmental actors. Our concern in this book is with multilateralism defined as a process of international negotiation involving primarily, though by no means exclusively, state actors and at least three parties, although, as William Zartman notes, the distinguishing feature of multilateral negotiations in post–World War II international relations is that they have involved "tens of parties."[3] The principal characteristic of these negotiations is complexity, involving not just large numbers of players but multiple interests, roles, issues, and hierarchies, all of which may vary over the duration of such negotiations.

Some observers argue that the increasing trend toward multilateral diplomacy and negotiations reflects the growth of interdependence in economic, political, and cultural ties between states and the declining utility of force in international politics, that is, the rise of soft power.[4] Others suggest that international negotiations are extensions of national policy-making processes in an attempt to manage and maintain control over increasingly complex problems that cross state boundaries.[5] Still others have adopted a contractual line of argument to explain the growing demand for international institutions and the changing patterns of international cooperation generally.[6] Although international-relations scholars will continue to debate the reasons,[7] it is unquestionably true, as Gilbert Winham observes, that "we are entering an era in which international negotiation appears to be the predominant mode of relations between states, and conditions in the international system are likely to maintain this mode for some time to come."[8]

Multilateral negotiations are fundamentally different from bilateral negotiations. Large numbers do in fact introduce a qualitatively different kind of diplomacy in international politics. The hallmark of this diplomacy is that it occurs between groups or coalitions of state actors, which "magnifies the difficulties of the bilateral forum by 200–500 percent."[9] A second characteristic of multilateral diplomacy on collective action problems involving public goods is the increasing involvement of a variety of nonstate actors, including epistemic or expert communities, nongovernmental organizations, and public-interest groups who bring issues to the attention of policy makers, raise public consciousness and awareness, and set the negotiating agenda. A third feature of this diplomacy is that it often takes place under the aegis of international organizations, giving them special power and leverage to shape prenegotiation processes and influence the terms of subsequent negotiations. A fourth factor, due to the protracted nature of such negotiations, is the variance in levels of commitment to negotiation and certain outcomes, often due to changes in national leaderships and priorities over time.

This book is a study of multilateral negotiations in a specifically comparative context, focusing on a number of cases dealing with security, economic, and environmental negotiations. These negotiations have been directed at the creation (or strengthening) of international regimes, defined here as "sets of principles, norms, rules, and decision-making procedures around which actors' expectations converge."[10] The central issue that concerns this study is how agreements are reached when there are many parties and issues involved in negotiations. This general question can be broken down into several interrelated questions or subthemes:

- How do issues get to the table in multilateral negotiations, and are prenegotiation processes similar or different for different kinds of issues?
- Once issues get to the table, who sits at the table and who are the "tiers" of relevant stakeholders? Are there common rules or procedures for representation and decision making in multilateral forums?
- What are the procedures and institutional mechanisms (formal and informal) for managing complexity in multilateral negotiations (for both issues and parties)? Do these mechanisms differ significantly from one issue area to another, especially in the setting of agendas?
- What are the obstacles (strategic and psychological) to reaching agreement or closure in multilateral negotiation? Are they similar or different for different issue areas?
- What are the factors that facilitate agreement (and the process of negotiation itself) in multilateral negotiations? Are the apparent conditions or requirements for success similar or different across different issue areas?

This book argues that the hallmark of multilateral diplomacy is that it occurs between groups or coalitions. Coalitions help to simplify and facilitate the bargaining process in the complex setting of multiparty, multiissue diplomacy. However, the formation of coalitions can also hinder the prospects of reaching an agreement if interests are incompatible and rival coalitions deadlock. Thus, one of the principal challenges to multilateral diplomacy is to design the negotiation in such a way that the creation of cooperative or "winning" coalitions is enhanced, while the formation of conflictual or "blocking" coalitions is minimized. This is achieved by negotiating strategies and tactics that decompose complex issues, sequence the negotiations in such a way as to maximize the realization of joint gains, and encourage parties to eschew comprehensive agreements in favor of more modest or partial settlement packages.

At the same time, agency—defined in terms of actor behavior and roles —is also crucial to the negotiating process. As Zartman explains, to the question "how to explain outcomes?" we must first ask the question: "How did/do the parties manage the characteristic complexity of their encounter in order to produce outcomes?"[11] The answer to this question is that complexity is managed when the parties take on various roles and perform certain functions that not only simplify the daunting complexity of the multilateral setting but also lessen the formidable strategic and positional impediments to bargaining that often exist. As Alexander Wendt observes, "the process of creating new institutions is one of internalizing new understandings of self and other, *of acquiring new role identities,* not just of creating external constraints on the behavior of exogenously constituted actors."[12] Thus, for example, the role of leadership is crucial to the advancement of negotiations, as is the designation of representatives who can assume responsibility for bargaining on each group's behalf. Brokers and mediators who can devise bridging and other solutions to otherwise intractable problems may also be necessary for negotiations to succeed. Politically mobilized communities of experts armed with specialized knowledge can also play an important role in defining the boundaries of the negotiating problem and identifying the kinds of actions that are needed to deal with it.

In advancing the argument that actor roles and negotiation design are crucial factors in multilateral diplomacy, this study first reviews the current theoretical literature on multilateral negotiations. Based on a review of this literature, the study identifies a series of propositions or working hypotheses about the nature and processes of multilateral negotiations and how these two sets of variables influence bargaining behavior and negotiation outcomes. These hypotheses are then explored in a series of historical cases of multilateral negotiation involving instances of both failure and success in reaching international agreement.

Contending Approaches to Multilateral Negotiations

Although multilateral negotiations have been one of the hallmarks of international diplomacy since the end of World War II, it is only recently that scholars have begun to pay attention to them as management tools in international politics. Moreover, it was not until recently that scholars began developing conceptual models to explain the processes of multilateral negotiations. In a review of the literature, conducted in 1987, William Zartman noted that, "although some significant case studies of multilateral negotiation have occurred . . . and some excellent studies of them have been written, the study of negotiations is still as far as ever from having a handle on the multilateral phenomenon."[13]

Since Zartman's review, the theoretical and empirical literature on multilateral negotiations has grown.[14] Students of international negotiation and bargaining, as well as students of international relations more generally, have underscored the importance of multilateral negotiation processes in international politics. Much of the earlier work on international regimes stressed the role of market failures and shared interests in explaining the origins of international cooperation.[15] This literature tended to assume that once shared interests were realized, international regimes would form more or less automatically, thus playing down the role of international negotiation as a factor in regime formation.[16] However, recent work has stressed the importance of international negotiation as a crucial intervening variable between structural (or market) failures and governance outcomes, on the grounds that even rational utility maximizers will regularly experience difficulties in realizing joint gains and that international cooperation may be thwarted by strategic behavior, intraparty bargaining, and issue linkage.[17]

Although it is generally recognized that multilateral negotiations are fundamentally different from bilateral negotiations and that the greater complexity of multilateral negotiations (in terms of both parties and issues) poses greater barriers to closure and the arrival of meaningful international agreements than might occur in the bilateral setting, there is little consensus in the literature as to the conditions or factors that may foster or hinder multilateral negotiations and facilitate or thwart agreement and closure. Whether multilateral-negotiation processes in different issue areas are similar or different is also a matter for further investigation. It is often assumed, for example, that international security issues are different from international economic and environmental issues. One obvious difference is that concerns about compliance and defection are usually more acute in security issues than in economic and environmental issues. However, an observation like the following, that "security negotiations are often motivated by a desire to defend existing realities in international relations [whereas] economic negotiations often spring from an effort to create new realities in the international environment,"[18] is debatable. One of the hallmarks of recent multilateral arms control initiatives, within the framework of both the Conference on Security and Cooperation in Europe (CSCE) and the United Nations Conference on Disarmament (UNCD), is that they have been directed at changing the status quo and creating new security structures. Conversely, it is readily apparent that the international trade negotiations in the Uruguay Round of the General Agreement on Tariffs and Trade (GATT) stalled because some parties preferred the status quo to further reductions in trade barriers.

The growing literature on multilateralism is in some ways as unruly as the phenomenon it seeks to analyze and explain. There are obviously different ways to classify the literature, and all schemes are somewhat arbitrary.[19] However, for the purposes of simplification, a threefold categorization of the different approaches to multilateral negotiation is offered here: *structural analysis,* defined as power-oriented explanations of international negotiation; *decisional analysis,* approaches that rely on formal, that is, utility-maximization, models of decision making; and *process analysis,* which addresses the context of international negotiation and how it affects actors' choices and decision making. Each approach, as we see below, offers different insights into the nature of the bargaining process as well as the factors and forces that may promote or hinder agreement in the multilateral setting.

Structural Analysis

Structural approaches typically treat international bargaining problems in terms of the power resources and capabilities of the parties to a negotiation. In the international relations literature, this approach is most commonly identified with the realist school, which emphasizes the impact of the international distribution of power on the behavior of states and the role of power in deciding political outcomes.[20] Realist theory leads one to believe that strong states will prevail in international negotiations because they can use their superior resources to coax and cajole weaker parties into submission. The outcome of international negotiations—be they bilateral or multilateral—will thus tend to represent the preferences of the more powerful actors in the international system, that is, outcomes are predetermined. To the extent that weaker actors do become involved in negotiations with more powerful ones, such as in North-South negotiations, they will be motivated by a desire to change the rules of the game in favor of more authoritative regimes that will increase their own wealth and control or, at least, prevent a further deterioration of control and autonomy.[21] Such efforts will be thwarted by more powerful states unless redistributive measures are seen to be in their own long-term interest. From a realist standpoint, therefore, international negotiations are not especially interesting phenomena or worthy of special study, because they merely reflect broader, systemic processes and the exercise or denial of structural power in international politics.

More recently, some international relations scholars have sought to reformulate realist tenets in order to explain why international cooperation in the multilateral setting may be difficult to achieve and why international regimes may be difficult to negotiate in the absence of hegemony or may erode over time. These scholars argue that states are constantly worried about cheating and the relative gains of other states and will, therefore, be constantly attuned to the impact of any relationship on their defensive (relative or positional) power capabilities. These same barriers pose a major challenge to international negotiations and may frustrate agreement. As Joseph Grieco explains in his own study of negotiations in the Uruguay Round of the GATT, "a state will decline to join, or leave, or will sharply limit its commitment to a cooperative arrangement if it believes that gaps in otherwise mutually positive gains favor partners."[22] Implicit in Grieco's analysis is the presupposition that state concerns about positional gains may, in fact, be heightened by international bargaining and negotiation processes such that international cooperation is thwarted by the very processes that seek to enhance it. In this respect, international negotiation is an important intervening variable in explaining the salience of relative or positional gains in international politics.

In contrast to the realist school of international relations, some students of international negotiations have focused on the ways weaker parties can overcome structural impediments and asymmetries in power capabilities to achieve bargaining outcomes favorable to themselves. These approaches start with the observation that the strong do not always necessarily prevail over the weak—international politics is more often like the story of Gulliver and the Lilliputians. Instead of viewing power capabilities and resources as immutable, these approaches identify ways weaker parties can manipulate bargaining situations to their advantage when the initial power balance is not tipped in their favor. It is therefore assumed that power relationships are likely to fluctuate over time because of tactical maneuvering and that the successful acquisition of power at one point in time does not assure its continuation.[23] In these approaches, bargaining and negotiation are all-important intervening variables between structural power and outcome in international politics. Weak actors will react to asymmetries in structural power by adopting bargaining tactics and strategies that change the status quo and raise their own security points.[24] For example, it is argued that weak parties will seek more formal negotiating forums to strengthen their hand in negotiations, especially if decisions are based on majority voting rules. Weak states may also resort to "erratic or irresponsible behavior" to strengthen their moral claims—what some call "coercive deficiency" and define as the persuasive tactic of the weak. Weaker parties may also refuse to make concessions or make unreasonably high demands at the outset of negotiations until they are convinced that the stronger party is willing to make concessions.[25] By manipulating deadlines, asking for mediators, withholding signatures, splitting coalitions, and pairing demands with more powerful actors, weak states may also increase their bargaining leverage.[26] Effective use of linkage strategies across different issues may also be a source of power for the weak.[27]

Some studies suggest that parties do best in negotiation when they feel equal and when either side can exercise a veto over the other's unilateral achievement of goals.[28] Thus, symmetry may be crucial for negotiation success, and parties intent on negotiation may do best to wait until structural symmetry has emerged. Coalition behavior may also affect bargaining strategies and outcomes. Robert Rothstein argues that a coalition of the weak can affect regime creation provided that the coalition remains unified and develops a bargaining strategy appropriate to the context of the decision. Understanding correctly the countervailing sources of the group's negotiating power and the importance of placing intergroup needs for agreement ahead of intragroup needs for unity are accordingly important ingredients for successful bargaining.[29]

As Zartman notes, structural analysis has moved away from its "initial post hoc formulation that outcomes are determined by the power position of the parties" toward a "tactical analysis" based on a definition of power as "a way of exercising a causal relation."[30] Tactical analysis thus treats power as a responsive or situational characteristic of negotiations, where outcomes depend not just on absolute capabilities but on bargaining skills and knowledge and on the way such resources are organized and utilized.

There are, however, a number of problems with structural analysis, not only as a theoretical tool but also in its application to multilateral negotiations. First, although structural analysis is essential to understanding the basic form of any political relationship, the concept of power defined as resources, skill, knowledge, and so forth, is notoriously ambiguous and highly context specific. As Jacob Bercovitch and others have noted, qualities that are valuable in one bargaining setting may have contrary value in others, and we therefore need "better tools—concepts, ideas, and propositions—to examine real-life situations of bargaining and negotiation."[31] Second, structural analysis is more amenable to cases of bilateral negotiation, where questions about symmetry or asymmetry can be posed more easily, than to multilateral negotiations, where encounters are more likely to be rule-oriented than power-oriented because of the number of parties involved.[32] Although some multilateral negotiations are, in essence, bilateral dealings between two large coalitions or blocs, for example, North-South negotiations, parties are likely to form shifting alliances for bargaining purposes, and there may well be more than two camps as other coalitions form during the negotiation process.[33] Third, to the extent that nongovernmental actors, international organizations, and transgovernmental coalitions or groupings are directly or indirectly involved in international negotiations, structural approaches that focus on state actors and their capabilities may be deficient in explaining the fundamental nature of bargaining processes and outcomes of international negotiation.[34] Moreover, Robert Putnam notes, international negotiations are typically two-level games involving domestic constituencies and coalitions and the controlled exchange of partial information.[35] Structural analysis may, therefore, present an overly reified and simplistic image of international bargaining and negotiation processes, particularly in the multilateral setting.

Decisional Analysis

In contrast to structural analysis, which emphasizes the role of power in bargaining relationships, formal decisional analysis treats bargaining as a preference-revelation problem among parties with competing interests, where, once relative linkages and trade-offs are identified, Pareto-optimal and other bargaining solutions can be assembled. These models assume that all individuals are utility maximizers and that bargaining payoffs can be quantified and subjected to formal analysis once utility preferences are known and ordered accordingly. These approaches seek to prescribe the best course of action and the best outcome for each party in a disruptive bargaining relationship.

Game Theory. In game-theoretic approaches, bargaining situations are distinguished by the number of parties involved, whether the conflicts are zero-sum or non-zero-sum, and whether the game is iterated or not. The concept of strategic rationality is central to game theory, because it recognizes that individual egoistic rational actors cannot pursue their own interests independently of the choices of other actors. Actors' choices and preferences may result in different kinds of games, for example Chicken versus Prisoners' Dilemma. Iteration may change not only the outcome of the game but also the structure of the situation. The prospects for cooperation may also be enhanced or diminished in iterated games.[36]

In N-person games, preference-revelation problems are compounded by the large number of actors and by strategic complexity. Game-theoretic approaches have dealt with complexity in terms of a number of simplifying assumptions. When N is very large, it is assumed that each actor's actions will go unnoticed and, therefore, each actor will behave on the assumption that other actors will not react, hence the problem of collective action and free riders. In smaller groupings, when actors can monitor each other's behavior, strategic relations between actors are generally assumed to be symmetric. Models of public-goods provision, for example, work on this assumption—although some models do allow for asymmetry. It is also assumed that actors can pursue discriminatory policies toward other actors, thus linking good behavior with rewards and bad or undesirable behavior with sanctions.[37] In some models, N-person games are treated as essentially linked two-person games, thus allowing for the evolution of cooperative relationships even when N is large.[38] Others deal with multilateral complexity by assuming that issues are unidimensional and that alternatives can be arrayed in a continuum, that is, that some alternatives are valued more highly than others.[39] Still other approaches deal with complexity in multiparty games through coalition analysis focusing on the strategic problems players may face in deciding whether or not to join particular coalitions and how they can share different units of reward.[40] However, the simplifying assumptions that are often called for to model coalitional behavior are difficult to sustain when the number of players involved is large, coalitions do not have a monolithic structure, and noneconomic and nonobjective tradeoffs between different issues are involved.

In one sense, game-theoretic approaches are useful for understanding the structural problems associated with cooperation in large numbers and the mechanisms that can diminish transaction and information costs. These approaches underscore the importance of reducing large multilateral negotiations to smaller numbers (through coalitions), although strategies to reduce the number of players will impose costs on third parties and reduce the overall magnitude of the gains from cooperation.[41] Game theory is also useful for identifying payoff structures in different kinds of games and the kinds of strategies that will elicit cooperative versus noncooperative behavior among players. However, the virtues of parsimony and elegance prove to be their principal weaknesses in trying to explain negotiation processes in complex multilateral settings when multiple actors and interests are involved and N is large. As Knut Midgaard and Arild Underdal observe, "as conference size increases, there will be more values, interests, and perceptions to be integrated or accommodated. . . . This suggests the general proposition that *conference size tends to make it more difficult to decide one's own moves and to find satisfactory solutions to the problems involved.*"[42]

Many of the assumptions upon which game-theoretic models are based —that all actors are utility maximizers and enjoy perfect or near-perfect information concerning their opponents' preferences; that the rules of interaction are fixed; that the actors are single players representing only themselves—are either untested or unprovable.[43] Finally, although game-theoretic approaches are useful for identifying different trade-offs and Pareto-optimal packages, they have next to nothing to say about actual bargaining processes and how actors will negotiate to arrive at an outcome. It is simply assumed that once actors identify the relevant payoff structure they will automatically seek the optimal solution, even though there is little direct evidence to support this contention.

Linkage Analysis. Somewhat different from formal game theory but in the same theoretical tradition is linkage analysis, which seeks to use analysis to identify ways in which parties can realize joint gains or achieve an integrative solution in situations characterized by differences in valuation or preferences, probability assessments, risk aversion, and time preferences.[44] Adding or subtracting issues or parties can significantly enhance or diminish the zone of an agreement in multiparty, multi-issue settings, depending upon the preferences of the players. Formal modeling techniques have been applied to actual instances of multilateral negotiation in order to identify appropriate trade-offs and linkage strategies.[45] In a comprehensive study of the Law of the Sea negotiations, James Sebenius finds that adding differentially valued, unrelated issues and offering side payments can increase the zone of agreement, whereas adding a very divisive issue to a negotiation may destroy the possibilities for an agreement on otherwise tractable issues.[46]

Many of the same criticisms of game theory are applicable to linkage analysis and other formal modeling techniques of negotiation. Rarely are preferences known at the outset of a negotiation. The fact that preferences may well change during the course of a protracted and lengthy negotiation as new information comes to light, learning occurs, values change, and policies shift as a result of changes in government and shifting domestic coalitions further complicates concession strategies and the identification of meaningful zones of agreement.[47] Furthermore, formal modeling techniques may actually overstate the importance of strategic impediments to bargaining. As Howard Raiffa notes, "to some extent, the complexity of the real situation softens the intensity of the bargaining dynamics. The parties are not clear about what is in their own interests, and their knowledge about the interests of others is likewise vague. Compromise is often easier to arrange in a situation of ambiguity. In this perverse sense, the complexity of reality yields simplicity; many real-world negotiations are happily not as divisive as starkly simple laboratory games, because in the real world it is difficult to see clearly what is in one's own best interest."[48]

Concession Analysis. Making concessions is central to any negotiation situation, and it is generally recognized that parties will not be able to reach a common position without incurring some costs. Concession analysis attempts to explain how parties can move to an agreement that maximizes their own return by manipulating initial offers and the rate and size of concessions.[49] Concession theory is derived largely from game theory, and most models are based on two-person games. Different strategies of concession making are identified in the literature. These include tough strategies, moderately tough or intermediate strategies, soft strategies, and fair strategies. The effectiveness of different bargaining strategies usually depends on the characteristics of the bargainers and the bargaining situation, and there is little evidence to suggest that any one strategy is inherently superior to another.[50]

In situations of multilateral bargaining, however, research indicates that negotiators rarely pursue conscious or deliberate concession strategies. High levels of uncertainty and information overload in the multilateral setting encourage negotiators to develop simplified cognitive structures to facilitate bargaining such that there is little direct monitoring of individual behavior and concessions by other players. Concession strategies and concession analysis may, therefore, be inapplicable (or inappropriate) to multilateral negotiations because of the special cognitive and communication burdens placed on decision makers. Simulation research also suggests that leadership, bureaucratic management, and information control—variables that have traditionally not received much attention in the negotiation literature—may be more important to negotiation practices in the multilateral diplomatic setting than concession tactics and behavior.[51]

Process Analysis

Process-oriented models of international negotiation can be distinguished from formal decision-making models according to Herbert Simon's definition of "substantive" versus "procedural" rationality.[52] As noted above, formal models of decision making and negotiation generally assume that all individuals, regardless of their beliefs, will be utility maximizers. Simon argues that this assumption is highly questionable, because it fails to distinguish between the "real world" and the decision maker's perception of the world. Simon argues that if we accept the proposition that the knowledge and computational power of the decision maker are severely restricted or limited, then we must distinguish between the real world and the actor's perception and reasoning about it. That is to say, we must construct a theory of the processes of decision making and then test it empirically, identifying not only the reasoning processes of the decision maker but his or her subjective frame of reference and representation of the problem. For rational-choice theorists, "rationality is often viewed in terms of the choices it produces."[53] To others, like Simon, rationality is viewed in terms of the processes it employs to arrive at a decision—that is, there is an important distinction to be made between procedural and substantive rationality. The former draws our attention to the circumstances under which alternatives are chosen by the decision maker, including the cognitive and evaluative frame of reference, the organizational or bureaucratic setting, and even cultural or other institutional factors that can affect decision-making strategies and the latitude for choice.

What are called here "process-oriented" explanations of international negotiation all share, following Simon, a procedural notion of rationality, that is, they eschew narrower, expected utility maximization notions about human behavior while seeking to address the broader environmental context of negotiation and the cognitive and social milieu of decision making. These approaches typically view the negotiation process in terms of phases where different situational pressures, cognitive influences, personality factors, and interactional factors (e.g., the nature of communications, tactics strategies, phases, and concessions) may impinge on negotiation behavior and influence outcomes. Many of these approaches attempt to integrate historical and institutional analysis with sociopsychological insights into the negotiation process. Instead of viewing bargaining outcomes and payoffs as fixed and as a distributive form of negotiation (i.e., zero-sum), these approaches treat negotiation as an integrative or positive-sum game and as an exercise in value and norm creation where the evolution of trust and reciprocity and the creation of new values may be more crucial to negotiation success or failure than the way payoffs are arranged or structured.[54] Newly created norms and values may also produce a more desirable kind of success than outcomes that produce agreements with no change in norms and values. Some of these approaches are mentioned briefly below.

Institutional Bargaining. Institutional bargaining approaches treat multilateral negotiation as an exercise in integrative bargaining characterized by high levels of uncertainty, Pareto-inferior bargaining outcomes, and nonstrategic behavior.[55] Transnational alliances among interest groups and governmental actors supportive of particular kinds of institutional arrangements may play a significant role in shaping the agenda of negotiations. Bargaining is characterized by linkages across a complex array of issues, shifting involvement of actors and interests, and logrolling behavior. Institutional bargaining also operates on the basis of unanimity rules or consensus instead of majority rules or rules that favor the development of winning coalitions.[56] Success in institutional bargaining situations will depend on the extent to which issues lend themselves to contractual interactions, the salience of the issues, arrangements that all participants can accept as equitable, clear-cut and effective compliance mechanisms, and effective leadership.[57] In one sense, all process-oriented explanations of international negotiations treat multilateral negotiations as exercises in institutional bargaining, including the approaches discussed below. However, the emphasis placed on particular variables or factors in negotiations varies, with some analysts paying greater attention to the intranegotiatory environment, and others to extranegotiatory influences and factors.

Staging and Sequencing. Staging and sequencing analysis pays special attention to the diagnostic, formula, and detail stages of negotiations, viewing negotiation as a problem-solving art where outcomes are explained by the performance of behaviors at specifically appointed phases of negotiation. It underscores the complexity of actors and issues where the possibilities of reaching a mutually agreeable solution depend on the dynamics of the negotiation process itself and on the ability of negotiations to move from one phase to another.

Daniel Druckman and William Zartman, for example, argue that international negotiation can be conceived as a process of unfolding stages or turning points that mark the passage of negotiation from one stage to another. Interactions and patterns of mutual responsiveness between the parties to a bargaining relationship will be influenced by key events that either break bargaining impasses and move negotiations through to accommodation or lead to stalemate and no settlement. Zartman treats negotiation as a process of "ripening," where parties' willingness to reach a negotiated settlement will depend on the existence of a hurting stalemate, a looming catastrophe, valid representatives, and mutual recognition that a negotiated settlement represents a way out of the conflict.[58] Druckman suggests that negotiation is a process of "building a package" consisting of four stages: "defining the scope of, or agenda for, the negotiation; a search for formulas or principles; flushing out the issues; and a search for the implementation of details."[59]

Both Druckman and Zartman emphasize the relation between the negotiatory and extranegotiatory environments. Zartman addresses the structural dynamics of the extranegotiatory environment and the way parties' changing perceptions of the continuing costs of conflict versus the costs of settlement will influence their desire to seek a negotiated solution. Druckman underscores the importance of what he calls "turning points" and shocks or "crises," which may prevent or promote movement through the successive stages of negotiation and are generally external to the negotiation process itself and beyond the control of negotiators.[60]

Cognitive Analysis. Cognitive approaches to bargaining and negotiation stress the limits of rational choice, that is, substantive rationality, while emphasizing the role of perceptions and expectations of the parties to the negotiation and their experience from previous interactions (i.e., learning) as determinants of choice.[61] Cognitive psychologists demonstrate that heuristics and biases can constrain negotiating choices, whereas motivational psychologists stress the role of human needs and motivations in negotiating strategies. In the complex setting of multilateral negotiations, cognitive processes that manage complexity, simplify perceptions, and achieve cognitive consistency may be crucial to structuring choices and dealing with uncertainty.[62] Psychological theories of attribution also suggest that "normal" biases, like the failure to consider the intended decision of one's negotiating partners, nonrational escalation of commitments, overconfidence in the validity of one's own estimates, and the assumption that the opponent is a unitary actor, are likely to be aggravated in large bureaucratic settings characterized by high levels of uncertainty.[63] Differences in interpretations of past history may also block recognition of future gains from agreements in areas of mutual interest.[64]

Learning models on international negotiations in the international relations literature (as distinct from the literature on negotiations) stress the role of epistemic communities in the development of convergent cognitive frames of reference and expectations that may be crucial to the successful negotiation of new international regimes. Ernst Haas defines epistemic communities as "composed of professionals (usually recruited from several disciplines) who share a commitment to a common causal model and a common set of political values." These professionals are also committed to translating their model into public policy by monopolizing "access to strategic decision-making positions."[65] In his work on international environmental issues, Peter Haas has emphasized the importance of "like-minded" associations of scientific experts in the negotiation of new multilateral environmental agreements.[66] International negotiations are thus part of a broader phenomenon of social learning trying to "manage interdependence."[67] Decision makers are involved in understanding a complex set of causal connections in a new problem and the interdependence between trends, events, and consequences—what Joseph Nye calls "complex learning." Although it is recognized that international regimes themselves may contribute to learning processes, relatively little attention, aside from the recent work on epistemic communities, has been paid by international relations scholars to the role of negotiation itself as an independent variable in learning.[68]

Mediation. In the extensive literature on third-party mediation, mediation is generally viewed as an activity that can facilitate movement toward a negotiated settlement, especially in situations where parties are at loggerheads and view their conflict in zero-sum terms. Third parties can facilitate conflict resolution by restructuring issues, identifying alternatives, modifying adversaries' perspectives, packaging and sequencing issues, building trust, offering side payments, or threatening penalties and sanctions.[69] The intervention of a third party will transform dyadic bargaining into a three- or multi-cornered relationship in which the third party effectively becomes one of the negotiators in a now transformed multilateral negotiating system.[70] The tasks of the third-party mediator typically involve meeting with stakeholders to assess their interests, helping to choose spokespeople or team leaders, identifying missing groups, stakeholders, and strategies for representing diffuse interests, drafting protocols and setting agendas, suggesting options, identifying and testing possible trade-offs, writing and ratifying agreements, and monitoring and facilitating implementation of agreements.[71] Such functions can be performed by states, international organizations, or various nongovernmental organizations and actors.[72] Impartiality is not necessarily a requirement for mediation success, although, generally speaking, a mediator must be acceptable to the parties concerned and capable of delivering what the parties cannot achieve themselves through self-help.[73]

Process-oriented models of negotiation seek to move beyond the restrictive assumptions about rationality inherent in game-theoretic and other formal models of decision making. They allow for greater empirical richness and consider a wider array of variables in international negotiation processes. Given the complexity of multilateral negotiation processes and the fact that such negotiations are not particularly amenable to formal decisional analysis unless a number of highly simplifying assumptions are introduced, inductive, as opposed to deductive, methods of analysis may prove more useful in understanding the processes and methods of reaching agreement in the multilateral setting. At the same time, these approaches focus on the process of negotiation, seeking to explain why decision makers do not always pursue Pareto-optimal strategies in bargaining situations, why they forego key windows of opportunity or accept an agreement later that they could have had much earlier. Unlike formal models of negotiation, process models do not treat actors as monoliths or unitary actors. Actors are multidimensional, and decision making will have an internal or domestic component as well as an external one.[74] These approaches also stress the integrative (versus distributive) aspects of negotiation and the construction of positive-sum agreements around a formula that will guide the implementation process. In order to resolve divergent interests and positions, leadership, imagination, and incremental or trial-and-error methods of negotiation are often needed. Mediators may also play a crucial role acting as go-betweens and bringing parties and issues together.[75]

However, what these approaches gain in empirical richness they lose in analytic elegance and simplicity. Whereas more formal models of negotiation and decision making seek to develop hypotheses and generalizations that are invariant across space and time, contingency models of negotiation are necessarily locked into a series of historically grounded propositions that may be unique to the case in question. As Geoffrey Martin notes, "practical scholars are reluctant to make sweeping generalizations about the nature of negotiation because of their lack of confidence in the predictability of negotiation and because they often indulge in the case study approach. On the other hand, the theoretical scholars believe that the lessons drawn from negotiations are generalizable, perhaps because many of them conduct experimental research."[76]

Approach of This Study

There are clearly a variety of different theoretical approaches to the study of multilateral negotiations, all of which contain important theoretical insights into the negotiation process. No single approach is inherently superior to another, although there are clear trade-offs between the level of generality and the degree of empirical relevance or historical accuracy of each model. However, all approaches recognize that multilateral negotiations are qualitatively different from bilateral negotiations insofar as greater complexity in terms of parties, interests, and issues fundamentally changes the nature of bargaining processes and the norms and rules of interaction.

Starting with the insight that multilateral negotiation is essentially a bargaining process that occurs between different coalitions—coalitions being a predominant defining characteristic of multilateral diplomacy—this study explores the conditions that not only give rise to coalitions but also allow competing coalitions to reach a consensus and arrive at an agreement, merging into a winning coalition. Because our concern here is to describe how integrative bargaining solutions are reached in the multilateral setting, we have adopted an approach focused on process. At the same time, we argue that there is a relationship between process and structure, insofar as the parties to the negotiation must develop mechanisms (tactical, procedural, and institutional) in order to surmount the numerous barriers (structural and positional) that all too frequently stand in the way of cooperation. They do this by taking on specialized roles and resorting to specific bargaining strategies and techniques that reduce complexity and organize interests and issues in a way that facilitates the prospects of reaching an agreement.[77] The formation of issue-based coalitions among rallying interests is thus critical to reducing the inherent complexity of the multilateral setting. At the same time, if negotiations are to move forward, coalition structures must be sufficiently flexible to allow for issue trading and linkage. Such flexibility is achieved by structuring the negotiation in such a way that it is amenable to logrolling and the identification of bargaining solutions that satisfy the major interests of the parties to the negotiation. Exactly how this process is managed is the subject of the next chapter, where we argue that multilateral negotiation is essentially a coalition-building, coalition-bridging, and sometimes, when interests clash, a coalition-breaking exercise. The critical players in this process are experts, international bureaucrats, and coalitions of small states or lesser powers who help to define prenegotiation possibilities and the subsequent structure and agenda of the negotiations.

Following Alexander George, the study is designed as a disciplined configurative or controlled comparison that employs a variety of general hypotheses or probability statements to explain outcomes in a series of historical cases of multilateral negotiation.[78] In the next chapter, we review a number of theories about the nature of multilateral negotiations in greater detail. Various conditions identified in the literature as necessary for or conducive to reaching agreement in the multilateral setting are assessed. Several aspects of these theories are singled out for refinement and elaboration in order to develop a number of working hypotheses, which are then explored in a number of actual cases of multilateral negotiation for the purposes of a controlled comparison.

All of the cases represent instances of multilateral negotiation, the principal actors in each case are states, and, although different issues are the subject of negotiation, all involve efforts to devise new multilateral institutions and rules of cooperation or international regimes. In some instances, negotiations were successful and resulted in agreement; in others, they did not. Thus, our task is to try to explain the variance in outcomes by looking for similarities and differences in the negotiating processes. Using the method of a controlled comparison, we seek to identify a variety of different causal patterns and the conditions under which each distinctive causal pattern—represented in the case in question—occurred.[79]

The cases of multilateral negotiation examined in this book are the negotiations leading to the Limited Test Ban Treaty (1963), the Stockholm Conference on Confidence- and Security-Building Measures and Disarmament in Europe (CCSBMDE) and negotiations leading to a Cooperative Security System for Europe (1986), negotiations on conventional forces that eventually led to the CFE (Conventional Forces, Europe) Treaty (1990), the origins of the GATT (General Agreement on Tariffs and Trade) versus the failure of the ITO (International Trade Organization), the Uruguay Round of the GATT, negotiations leading to the United Nations Convention and Montreal Protocol on Substances That Deplete the Ozone Layer (1985,

1987), negotiations leading to the Basel Convention on Transboundary Movement of Hazardous Wastes and Their Disposal (1989), and negotiations directed at an international convention on global warming and climate change. These cases vary considerably with regard to whether or not negotiations were successful in devising new international regimes (or partial regimes) to address collective action problems.

Several criteria informed our selection of cases. In comparing negotiations from the early postwar period with more recent experience, we sought to examine how the nature and conduct of multilateral diplomacy has changed over the years, not only within a given issue area but also across issue areas. A second consideration was that the negotiations in each issue area fulfill the criteria for multilateral diplomacy in terms of both issues and parties, as stated above—that is, that they involve more than three parties, preferably more than ten, and more than a single issue. A third consideration was that there be an identifiable and assessable outcome (did the negotiation fail within the time frame set by the parties, or did it succeed?). This ruled out the inclusion of certain arms control treaties in the study (e.g., CTB negotiations or those involving chemical weapons, which are still ongoing—or were too close to call in terms of an outcome at the time the study was initiated). Where possible, we also tried to control for certain variables in order to reduce some of the natural variance in the selection of cases. Hence, the selection of environmental negotiations that took place under UNEP auspices; the selection of trade negotiations under the GATT; the selection of arms control negotiations that involved the two superpowers along with their allies and the neutral or nonaligned bloc of nations.

It should be noted at the outset that in any study of this kind there is an obvious difficulty in deciding which combination and sequence of variables are most important in explaining the origins of a particular set of negotiations and subsequent outcomes. This is especially true in the absence of direct or firsthand evidence about the thoughts and motivations of key negotiators who were involved. Moreover, anecdotal information, personal recollections based on interviews and memoirs, and such may contain incomplete or inaccurate information about the motivations of the players and the actual course of events. The historical case-study method employed here has obvious limitations, which derive from the inherent limitations of circumstantial inference. Where possible, we have used firsthand accounts and recollections of the prenegotiation and negotiation period. In the absence of such information, we have relied on secondary sources and tried to reconstruct the choices and consequences of political action in an attempt to judge the motivations of the players involved and the context and forces pressing on them. This method explores both ends of a causal chain—context →motive →choice—to determine the characteristic of the intermediate link, motive. Accordingly, it inclines us to think in terms of individuals constrained by outer circumstances rather than individuals acting under internal compulsion. Historical events, rather than instincts, appear as the starting point of behavior, and actions are often interpreted as reactions.

2 Barriers to Negotiation and Requisites for Success

It is generally recognized that the presence of a large number of participants in a venture does not necessarily pose insurmountable barriers to cooperation.[1] Although Mancur Olson argues that the provision of collective
goods is inversely related to the size of the group (because of increasing organizational costs, declining individual benefits, and declining possibilities of strategic interaction as group size increases), others have challenged
this relationship on the grounds that economies of scale, iterated and
small-group interactions, and institutionalization (e.g., the formation of
regimes) can help overcome barriers to cooperation in large groups.[2] Many
international relations scholars have stressed the importance of regimes,
in particular, on the grounds that they lend transparency, lower transactions costs, and allow sanctions or penalties to be imposed on defectors or
those who otherwise refuse to cooperate. In other words, regimes allow for
the use of selective incentives to encourage or foster cooperation.[3] But
where regimes themselves do not exist, such options typically are not
available. Many of the dilemmas of collective action therefore remain.

The logic of collective action thus has some relevance to the problems
of multilateral negotiations, especially when negotiations are directed at
the formation or construction of international regimes. The chief obstacles
to multilateral negotiations are complexity and uncertainty: complexity
created by the large number of parties to the negotiation and issues on the
table, uncertainty heightened by the difficulties of communicating preferences and exchanging information among a large number of participants. One response to this problem is what Miles Kahler calls "minilateralism" (the functional equivalent to Duncan Snidal's privileged "k" group,
which provides for the public good in the absence of a hegemon).[4] However, as Kahler notes, this response is inadequate "for creating and extending regimes to incorporate larger numbers of participants." Large-number
cooperation thus requires "new institutional devices that [combine] the
hierarchical structure of many issue-areas with the need for wider participation."[5]

At one level, coalition building is critical to handling the complexities
of multilateral negotiations, and it is the principal distinguishing feature

of these negotiations.[6] However, coalitions do not spring up automatically on their own. The process of coalition building is aided and abetted by role differentiation among parties and the emergence of leaders, mediators, supporters, and blockers in the negotiation process. At another level, the design of the negotiation also affects the outcome. Issue sequencing and the use of tactics like "agenda packaging," "placement," and "stalking horse" proposals can be used to influence the climate of discussions, forge coalitions, and build momentum toward agreement.[7] What happens around the conference table is not the only thing that can drive negotiations forward. In addition to institutional devices and procedures, circumstantial factors (e.g., domestic politics) and contingency factors (e.g., unexpected events like crises) can play an important role in fostering or thwarting cooperation and facilitating or impeding the coalition-building process.[8]

Multilateral negotiations are, in essence, coalition-building enterprises involving states, nonstate actors, and international organizations. Leadership, negotiating strategies and tactics, and formulas are all directed at and related to the process of building coalitions and achieving a consensus that will carry negotiations forward. As discussed below, the critical players in this process are experts, who define prenegotiation possibilities and the subsequent agenda of negotiations; coalitions of smaller states or lesser powers, who devise bridging solutions to seemingly intractable problems; and the bureaucrats, who staff international organizations and use their position to forge strategic alliances with their counterparts in national bureaucracies in order to advance negotiations.

A number of variables may affect the multilateral negotiation process, and the task of sorting out causal relationships is a formidable one. By viewing the negotiation process in terms of stages, however, it is possible to delineate the potential independent effects of these variables on the negotiation process. To the extent that some factors are present in more than one stage of negotiation, we may be able to arrive at some preliminary judgments about their relative importance to the negotiation process.

One of the challenges to any theory of negotiation is to identify the causal sequence of a series of independent variables in order to understand better the role of underlying or deep causal factors versus more proximate or immediate influences in bargaining and negotiation.[9] Hence the purpose of the study is not to test formally all matter and varying theories of negotiation. Rather, it is more akin to a "plausibility probe," where the goal is to test the explanatory significance of several different clusters of independent variables. Thus, the study is directed at saying something about the causal sequence and relative importance of those variables that different studies (mostly inductive) have identified as interesting or noteworthy in the multilateral negotiation process. In the discussion that follows we try to (1) define these variables as carefully as possible; (2) suggest that there is a causal sequence related to different phases of the negotiation process; and (3) indicate that different independent variables may have differing levels or degrees of importance depending upon the phase of negotiation under consideration. The study therefore offers the functional equivalent of a periodic table of elements for the multilateral negotiation process. It tries to demonstrate, in a systematic way, the relationship among different variables along the negotiation spectrum and the explanatory weight that should be given to each.

Phases of Negotiation

All negotiations, whether bilateral or multilateral, typically move through several phases. These phases are described in the negotiation literature as prenegotiation, negotiation, and agreement and implementation (see fig. 2.1). Each of these phases has different functions in relation to the overall process of negotiation, as well as different characteristics or features. Negotiations are therefore marked by "turning points," defined as "events or processes that mark the passage of a negotiation from one state to the next, signaling progress from earlier to later phases."[10]

Prenegotiation

In recent years, students of bargaining and negotiation have paid increasing attention to the prenegotiation phase of the negotiation process. Prenegotiation has been variously described as (1) the period where parties define the problem, develop a commitment to negotiate, and arrange negotiations;[11] (2) the "diagnostic phase," when parties recognize "that new solutions have to be invented" and that "a new order must be created or problems managed in its absence";[12] (3) the "de-escalation phase" of a conflict, when parties seek to redefine their relationship and reevaluate the means to achieving that end;[13] and (4) the period "when one or more parties considers negotiation as a policy option and communicates this intention to other parties," ending "when the parties agree to formal negotiations (an exchange of proposals designed to arrive at a mutually acceptable outcome in a situation of interdependent interests) or when one party abandons the consideration of negotiation as an option."[14] All of these definitions center on the notion that prenegotiation is the prelude to formal negotiations, marked by a decision by one or more parties to consider negotiation as a behavioral option.[15]

The prenegotiation phase itself can be disaggregated further into several stages: (1) the *identification of problems,* where problems that deserve collec-

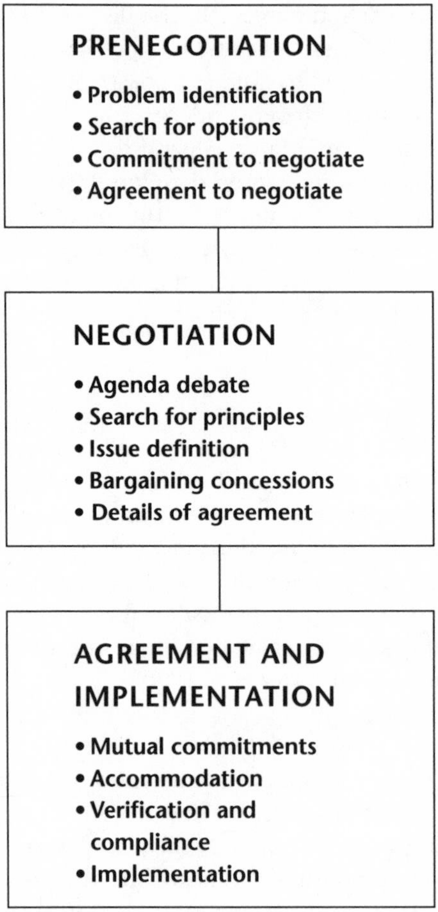

PRENEGOTIATION

- Problem identification
- Search for options
- Commitment to negotiate
- Agreement to negotiate

NEGOTIATION

- Agenda debate
- Search for principles
- Issue definition
- Bargaining concessions
- Details of agreement

AGREEMENT AND IMPLEMENTATION

- Mutual commitments
- Accommodation
- Verification and compliance
- Implementation

Fig. 2.1 Phases of Negotiation

tive attention are noted and values are restructured such that negotiation is added to the array of options being considered by the parties for dealing with the problems; (2) the *search for options,* when parties begin to "think the unthinkable" and "come to terms with the need to negotiate"; (3) the *commitment to negotiate,* when parties begin to decide upon the initial substance or agenda of negotiations; and (4) the *agreement to negotiate,* where the parties agree to enter into formal negotiations.[16]

The prenegotiation phase is useful to parties because it promises lower exit costs than do formal negotiations, should prenegotiation fail. In a multilateral setting, prenegotiation may be especially useful for managing complexity when many potential parties and issues are involved and the risks of formal negotiation are high. Prenegotiation can serve a variety of critical functions in developing the appropriate institutional structures for subsequent negotiations. These include the specifications of boundaries to formal negotiations, including the basic principles and rules that will guide the negotiations themselves; the identification and selection of participants; and the setting and delimiting of the negotiation agenda, that is, deciding what issues will be on or kept off the negotiating table.[17] Even if leaders are not interested in a formal agreement, prenegotiation may bring additional benefits, such as building public support for government policies, satisfying allies, or avoiding potential crises.[18]

Negotiation

There is little disagreement in the literature as to what constitutes the negotiation phase, although analysts have treated the actual phases of formal negotiations somewhat differently, developing their own special typologies to describe the negotiation process. The formal negotiation phase is characterized by "the exchange of information and the negotiation proper over the detailed terms of an agreement."[19] During this phase, the participants will exchange information, discuss alternative negotiation packages, and move from a general formula to the actual details of an agreement. Druckman describes the passage of negotiation from one phase to another as involving the following elements: an agenda debate, a search for guiding principles, definition of the issues, bargaining for favorable concessions, and a search for implementation details.[20] William Zartman and Maureen Berman describe negotiations in terms of a "formula phase," where the parties move toward a "shared perception or definition" of the problem that "establishes terms of trade, the cognitive structure of referents for a solution, or an applicable criterion of justice," followed by a "detail phase" where the parties, having already established a general formula for agreement, work out the precise details of the agreement.[21]

P. H. Gulliver identifies eight stages: (1) the search for an arena; (2) the composition of the agenda and the definition of the issues; (3) the establishment of maximal limits to the issues in dispute; (4) the narrowing of the differences; (5) the preliminaries to final bargaining; (6) the final bargaining; (7) the ritual affirmation; and (8) the execution of the agreement.[22] Key to all discussions about the negotiation process, however, is the notion that talks must pass from one phase to another in order for there to be progress and that the passage of talks may be disrupted or derailed at any one of these key junctures. In each phase, the negotiators will engage in different kinds of activities, ranging from monitoring, information gathering, and coordinating activities in the early stages of negotiation to debate and bargain over the actual details of the agreement in later rounds.

Agreement and Implementation

At the agreement phase, parties will reach a preliminary settlement and seek to translate that settlement into a concrete package of mutual commitments and undertakings. In multilateral negotiations, this process may be prolonged and difficult as efforts are made to accommodate the varying interests and concerns of the various parties to the final settlement. Furthermore, verification and compliance considerations have to be taken into account. Even at this final stage, there is the danger that some participants may introduce last-minute reservations or proposals into the discussions. These can delay and sometimes even prevent a final settlement. Finally, once the parties have actually signed the final agreement, there is the question of implementation and how the agreement is to be enforced. Occasionally, new or unanticipated problems will crop up in the implementation phase. Sometimes this requires further negotiations or discussions among the original participants. New parties may also enter the discussions if they are affected by the agreement or have the power to block or negatively affect its implementation.

Obstacles to Multilateral Negotiation

As discussed in chapter 1, there are clearly a variety of structural impediments that make multilateral negotiations more difficult to sustain than bilateral negotiations. But there are also a number of procedural elements associated with a multilateral setting that may pose additional obstacles to agreement, including process-generated stakes and the provisions governing decision-making procedures in a multilateral setting.

Multiple Parties and Interests

There is almost an inverse relation between the number of participants and issues in multilateral negotiations and the likelihood of reaching an agreement that accommodates each participant's interests. Saadia Touval explains this relation as follows: "The larger the number of participants, the greater the likelihood of conflicting interest and positions, and the more complex the interconnections among the parties."[23] However, increasing numbers and difficulties in negotiation are related to heterogeneity of interests and perceptions; large numbers need not pose an insurmountable barrier if participants' preferences are homogeneous or convergent. Moreover, not all parties will enjoy the same amount of bargaining power, although the ability of more powerful actors to direct the negotiation process will diminish if there are more than two of them and if they have conflicting goals and objectives.[24] As N increases, the likelihood of encountering diverse preferences within the population also increases, negatively affecting the possibilities of reshaping those interests into a mutually satisfactory settlement. In this respect, "uncertainty as to the exact preferences of others implies uncertainty as to which criteria should be met if a solution is to be satisfactory. And even if the criteria are clear, the wider the range of interests, the harder it is to generate solutions that satisfy them all."[25] When the numbers are large, it becomes more difficult for negotiators to identify potential trade-offs and relevant concessions.

Complexity also increases communication and information-processing difficulties. Parties are required to manage large amounts of information and to respond to a complex and competing array of interests. Signals can become confused or mixed, generating distrust or leading to misinterpretation. Parties may overestimate the extent to which their own preferred solution meets the concerns of other groups. This can lead to a reassessment of relationships. Concessions that are granted may not be reciprocated, or, in the confusion of multilateral conference diplomacy, parties may simply lose track of important information and other players' interests. Instead of following a process of convergence, negotiations become an exercise in "puzzle-solving," where "the trick is for parties to find a solution that will accommodate their overlapping and conflicting interests."[26]

Blocking Coalitions

Coalitions are defined as "the unification of the power or resources (or both) of two or more parties so that they stand a better chance of obtaining a desired outcome or of controlling others not included in the coalition."[27] Most negotiations when N is large have a tendency to break down into negotiations between different bargaining sets or coalitions. Participants will join a coalition if the costs of coalition membership are lower than the costs of individual membership in the negotiation or if the perceived benefits and potential gains of joining a coalition are seen to be greater than going it alone. Coalitions can also compensate for structural weakness in asymmetric bargaining situations, especially if weaker actors can band together and pool scarce resources.[28] A coalition, though, must be perceived as an effective bargaining unit that will achieve its purpose and increase each member's share of net benefits. Otherwise, members will opt out of the coalition to join another or to form a new coalition. Thus, two of the conditions for successful bargaining are: (1) bargains must allow for side payments to key coalition members; and (2) intracoalition bargaining is simplified (particularly in loose coalitions) if what is received in the bargain has "something in it for everybody."[29]

Although integrative bargaining possibilities in the multilateral setting typically depend upon the formation of crosscutting coalitions,[30] opposing interests—what James Sebenius calls "blocking coalitions"—may act to "prevent agreement on or implementation of an otherwise desirable treaty."[31] Such coalitions are generally comprised of actors who enjoy sufficient structural power that their defection from a cooperative solution or refusal to participate in a negotiated settlement will be sufficient to prevent agreement. Depending on the actual rules of procedure, however, smaller actors without structural power can also block agreement if negotiations are governed by unanimity rules or consensus procedures.

Intracoalition dynamics and behavior can also frustrate negotiations and adversely affect the possibilities of reaching an agreement. Coalitions are unwieldy entities and typically arrive at a negotiating position only after hard bargaining among the members of the group has taken place. Having developed a position, a coalition may be reluctant to change or modify it, since doing so may lead to conflict within the coalition, perhaps even causing the coalition's breakup. Similarly, coalitions held together by ideology or adherence to a narrow set of principles may also be inflexible negotiators. Although toughness and unyielding behavior increase the probability of an agreement close to that party's social-preference function, they also increase the chances of no agreement at all—what is sometimes referred to as the "toughness dilemma."[32] In settings where successful bargaining depends upon compromise and a willingness to make concessions, unyielding behavior may work to the coalition's disadvantage by increasing the chances that no agreement will be reached.[33]

Intrinsic Interests, Belief Systems, and Ideology

Blocking coalitions are usually based on shared intrinsic interests and commitment to a particular set of values and beliefs. David Lax and James Sebenius define intrinsic interests as follows: "One's interest in an issue is intrinsic if one values favorable terms of settlement on the issue independent of any subsequent dealings."[34] Intrinsic interests are, therefore, usually independent of bargaining outcomes but can affect the possibilities of settlement. For example, negotiators may place emphasis on particular standards of justice that provide the basis for choice when there is a range of possible outcomes. Since shared principles often serve as focal points for choosing a settlement, agreement is more difficult when they differ.[35]

Intrinsic interests can also influence expectations about the purpose and value of the negotiation process itself. As Helmut Sonnenfeldt observes about Soviet as against American attitudes toward arms negotiations in the 1970s, "Americans often feel uneasy if a negotiation does not conclude with a completed document, signed, sealed, and delivered. This is not the case with the Soviets. They have often been prepared to engage in endless talk and negotiations without conclusion and still attempt to promote their interests through that process."[36]

Multiparty, multi-issue negotiations also tend to promote ideologically motivated strategies, which can adversely affect the bargaining process more than when parties and issues are fewer in number. As Gilbert Winham notes, "complexity encourages negotiators to develop simplified and sometimes unrealistic cognitive structures that facilitate bargaining and decision-making." Furthermore, "as complexity reduces the possibility that governments will comprehend the issues before a negotiation, it increases the possibility that ideological position will influence the attitude of governments toward the negotiation . . . [and] the probability that governments will become committed to simplified, overriding goals."[37] Although ideology can promote the development of convergent expectations and value structures that are conducive to agreement, to the extent that value and belief systems diverge they can have the opposite effect and harden bargaining positions via the formation of ideologically motivated blocs or what could be called coalitions of the like-minded.

Issues marked by high levels of uncertainty and risk also tend to reinforce ideologically motivated, as opposed to problem-solving, approaches in multilateral negotiations. For example, Steve Rayner argues that international discourse about global environmental change has been infused by conflicting "moral" and "nature myths," each of which points to a completely different set of response strategies and policy instruments. The success of these negotiations may therefore turn on the ability of negotiators and other interested parties to create new myths that accommodate (or synthesize) competing visions of nature and establish new terms of discourse.[38]

Conflicting cultural values create their own special obstacles and barriers to negotiation. Culture can be conceived of as a system or entity "consisting of interrelated parts, each of which only can be understood with reference to the context in which it occurs" or as "a set of antecedent factors that can be analyzed and measured separately."[39] Culture can color the behavior of individuals and negotiators in a wide range of situations. Culture-bound aspects of behavior, including language, forms of communication, and customs, as well as the individual traits or psychological characteristics of members of a delegation, can also affect the ways issues are handled to reach an agreement. In large-scale multilateral negotiations, when many different countries, and hence cultures, are represented at the bargaining table, the likelihood that cultural differences will hinder communications and negatively affect the provision of a public good through the conflicting desires and strategies of the actors increases.[40]

Process-Generated Stakes

Negotiations typically acquire their own political and psychological dynamic such that the negotiation process itself generates gains and losses that can affect outcomes. This can happen in several ways. Negotiators may define gains and losses not just on the basis of the final outcome but also by how they play the game. As Arild Underdal explains, "clients back home will frequently like to see their representatives 'put up a real fight' on their behalf. A delegation may try to maneuver so as to disassociate itself from unfavorable outcomes and at the same time try to claim credit for positive achievement. . . . A government may be reluctant to sign, let alone propose, a solution it considers unfair but nonetheless marginally better than the best available noncooperative alternative . . . [because] the act of *signing* or *proposing* implies a positive approval and commitment that would make it more vulnerable to domestic criticism."[41]

Negotiators may also be locked in by previous moves and decisions; for example, rejecting a proposed solution early in negotiations may make it harder to accept later on. Yielding to blunt threats may be seen as a sign of political weakness. Highly visible conference structures typical of large-scale conference diplomacy encourage political grandstanding and reflexive position taking that could be avoided in more informal gatherings and off-the-record workshops.[42] Thus, the process of negotiation generates its own incentives and disincentives, which can affect the possibilities of agreement and accommodation.[43]

Rules and Procedures

Decision-making rules differ from one international forum to another, but the provisions governing negotiating processes can enhance or weaken the likelihood, content, and form of agreements. There are essentially three different kinds of mechanisms: traditional, consensus, and mixed rules of procedure.[44] In the traditional system, decisions are taken by simple majority vote or some variation thereof. In the U.N. General Assembly, for example, decisions are taken on the basis of two-thirds majority of the members present and voting in the assembly. However, in many international forums, decisions are made on the basis of consensus without formal voting or according to a mixed system of decision making involving a combination of formal voting and informal consensus procedures. International forums involving large numbers of participants where highly complex scientific and technical issues are the focus of discussion have lent themselves to consensus decision-making procedures.

Although consensus procedures strengthen the bargaining position of coalitions that do not enjoy structural power, they can also be abused by those who seek to delay, hold up, or block agreement.[45] Decisions arrived at via consensus may also be more ambiguous in order to mask underlying disagreements between parties. Consensus or mixed rules of procedure, therefore, have a tendency to increase the risks of suboptimal outcomes in large groups where collective goods are concerned.[46]

Facilitating Factors in Multilateral Negotiations

Students of international negotiations have identified several factors that can facilitate bargaining processes and increase the prospects of success in reaching international agreement. Whereas some factors are crucial to moving negotiations from one stage to another, others may be experienced in more than one stage. Some factors may bring an issue to the negotiating table over and above the functional requirements of prenegotiation (i.e., prenegotiation as a strategy that offers a way to manage complexity at lower levels of commitment than formal negotiations). Others may facilitate bargaining processes within the multilateral forum itself. Although the concept of success in multilateral negotiations is treated here as being related to the concept of closure, that is to say, formal agreement among the parties to the negotiation, success is also considered in relation to the process of negotiation itself and the ability of negotiations to move from one stage to another. Although the fact that prenegotiation leads to the onset of formal negotiation is no guarantee of ultimate success, it is readily apparent that without successful prenegotiation the likelihood of reaching agreement would be nil. In this respect, it is important to examine the underlying or "deep" causes of negotiation, the factors that bring an issue to the negotiating table, along with "proximate" or more immediate causes of negotiation success or closure.

Most discussions about prenegotiation and negotiation processes are linked to the concept of social learning. Learning is often described in terms of greater understanding about means-ends relationships, efforts to reduce uncertainty and improve predictability in the decision-making environment, rejection of old stereotypical images and creation of new forms of discourse, new understandings about old problems, or reframing of old conceptions and terms of reference.[47] However, as Stein notes, "cognitive psychology cautions . . . against overly optimistic estimates of the capacity to learn. It identifies serious obstacles to learning at the individual level. Generally, people assimilate new information to existing beliefs; they are 'cognitive misers.'"[48]

Some theories of learning emphasize the role of persuasive communication in learning processes; others stress the role of discontinuous events or "forced compliance"; and still others emphasize the role of personality, self-perception, and cognitive schema in attitude change.[49] It is outside the scope of this study to review these theories here. Instead, we offer a number of propositions drawn from the negotiation literature about formal triggers that not only bring issues to the negotiating table but also move negotiations forward after they begin. These explanations emphasize, in varying degrees, the role of crisis and consensual knowledge, although all note an important link between prenegotiation, negotiation, and learning in which a combination of continuous and discontinuous events may prompt a change in attitudes and lead to corresponding new behaviors.

Crises

Crises are situations where a grave threat is perceived, which usually develops suddenly and poses a direct challenge to the vital interests or core values and beliefs of the decision maker. Charles Hermann defines a crisis as "a situation that (1) threatens high-priority goals of the decision-making unit, (2) restricts the amount of time available for response before the decision is transformed, and (3) surprises the members of the decision-making unit by its occurrence." A crisis may not lead to severe conflicts of interest between states but may set up a conflict of values within the state.[50] Crises therefore present new costs and risks (or magnify existing ones) by underscoring the need to take remedial action. But they also challenge core values, attitudes, and beliefs, thereby fundamentally altering the decision-making context and established patterns of thinking and action. For this reason, crises are usually associated with learning, and according to Stein, when learning occurs in prenegotiation "it is a sporadic response to crisis, not a smooth incremental process of structural adaptation." For this reason, crises have a tendency to provoke "important and far-reaching changes in fundamental beliefs which . . . [permit] a reframing of the problem and the active consideration of negotiation."[51]

The role of crises is stressed in other accounts, not just of prenegotiation processes but of negotiation, too. Oran Young, for instance, argues that "even in negotiations that allow considerable scope for integrative bargaining under a veil of uncertainty, institutional bargaining exhibits a natural tendency to bog down into a kind of sparring match in which participants jockey for positional advantage. . . . Given this background, it will come as no surprise that exogenous shocks from crises frequently play a significant role in breaking these logjams and propelling the parties toward agreement on the terms of institutional arrangements."[52] In his classic study of negotiations, Arthur Lall notes that "if certain negotiations are extremely protracted, generally the main reason is that an awareness of impending crisis has either not developed or has not been operative long enough to produce a sense of urgency."[53] Richard Haass also maintains that a "crisis or near-crisis can contribute to diplomacy if there is a shared recognition that steps must be taken to avoid developments that will be costly to all concerned," provided that "it leaves the parties believing that accord is in their interest."[54]

But crises can also break the normal rhythms and patterns of a negotiation by creating logjams and thwarting progress. In a study of negotiations over military-base rights in Spain, Druckman notes that impasses or "downturns" in negotiations were prompted by political crises that threatened a breakdown in talks.[55] Other studies have also documented how domestic or international crises can check the momentum of ongoing negotiations or cause delays in prenegotiation.[56]

These different understandings about the role of crises in prenegotiation and negotiation are not just semantic but illustrate the fact that crises can play different roles in different bargaining situations and present different payoffs to the parties concerned. A *distributive* crisis is a crisis that threatens unequal or asymmetric distributions of gains and losses as a result of the crisis itself and reinforces the perception that the attainment of one party's goals (or a collectivity's) will be at the exclusion of another side's goals.[57] These crises typically have a negative effect on negotiations by transforming the bargaining relationship into a zero-sum relationship.[58] An *integrative* crisis tends to have the opposite effect: it enhances perceptions of mutual vulnerability or joint losses while reinforcing the perception that potential costs to all parties can only be reduced or eliminated via cooperative measures and solutions. Integrative crises thus encourage parties to define a problem as a common concern when the nature of the problem permits solutions that benefit all parties or when the gains of one party do not represent equal sacrifices by others. Conversely, distributive crises weaken the possibilities of formal cooperation by creating clear winners and losers.

Perceptions about the nature, meaning, and consequences of a crisis may, of course, change over time; there may be a cross-over effect: as new information comes to light, there is further communication between parties, and previous areas of uncertainty about cause-effect relationships and the distribution of costs and benefits are reduced or eliminated. Crises previously understood in distributive terms can therefore come to be viewed as shared or integrative, thereby facilitating prenegotiation and negotiation processes. But it should be noted that even if the parties come to recognize that the pie is an expanding one—that there are joint gains to be realized from cooperation—there still remains the question of how the pie should be divided. As Sebenius notes, "integrative bargains engender distributive ones. If interests make up a negotiation's basic data and alternatives place limits on it, then joint gains from agreement, regardless of how they are shared, constitute its potential."[59]

Crises can also be distinguished by the number of actors or players affected. *Specific* crises affect a discrete number of actors or a particular subset of a group, whereas *general* crises are indiscriminate in terms of the parties they affect. A specific integrative crisis may bring a party to the negotiating table if the gains of negotiation are perceived to outweigh the costs of the "best alternative to a negotiated agreement" (BATNA).[60] However, a specific integrative crisis is unlikely to sustain the negotiation process through to the agreement phase unless other parties to the negotiation (who, by definition, have not experienced the crisis themselves) see important gains to be achieved from a negotiated agreement for other reasons. Conversely, a specific distributive crisis will usually cause a party to walk away from the table and reject negotiation as an alternative to BATNA because the costs of negotiation are deemed to outweigh the gains of non-negotiation. Similarly, distributive crises with general consequences may frustrate the negotiation process in a multilateral setting because one group's gains are necessarily at the expense of another (unless the consequences are indeterminate, i.e., so diffuse that it is impossible to predict who the winners and losers are, in which case cooperation will be made easier), whereas general integrative crises, where losses are widespread and, on average, the perceived gains from cooperation outweigh the costs of noncooperation, will tend to enhance the possibilities for negotiation.

The importance of crises to prenegotiation and negotiation is also linked to the temporal aspects of crises. An impending, just passed, or ongoing crisis is far more likely to have a direct impact on behavior than a crisis that lies far off in some distant future (or past) where normal discounting rules apply. The proximity of the crisis in time to the actual prenegotiation or negotiation itself is, therefore, also likely to be an important determinant of its impact on the behavior of the parties concerned.

Thus, one of the questions to be asked about any multilateral negotiation is whether the course of prenegotiation (and subsequent negotiations) was influenced either positively or negatively by (1) a mutual or nonmutual sense of crisis, that is, whether the crisis was specific or general in terms of its consequences; (2) whether the crisis engendered joint perceptions about losses and gains and thus facilitated the formation of coalitions, that is, whether the crisis was viewed as having *shared* distributive or integrative consequences; and (3) whether the crisis was seen as impending, immediate, or long-term.

Epistemic Communities and Consensual Knowledge

Prenegotiation and negotiation processes typically involve not just communication and exchanges of information but also cognition and learning, in which expert advice may play a crucial role in both defining the negotiation agenda and helping to develop a consensus among the potential parties to a negotiation that there is a genuine problem warranting a cooperative solution. Gulliver describes the learning process in negotiation as follows:

> Received information is interpreted and evaluated by a party and added to what he already knows or thinks he knows. Thus a party may be able to learn more about his own expectations and preferences about those of his opponent, and about their common situation and possible outcomes. Learning may also induce changes in the party's preference set and his strategies or it may reinforce his existing position. Learning may raise the need to give further information to him so that he may be induced to learn and therefore be persuaded to shift his position to something more favorable to the party. Depending on the kind of learning, the party makes a tactical choice concerning the purpose and content of his next message, which is then proffered to his opponent. In turn, the other party goes through the same procedure and then offers his information to the first party . . . and so on. Thus, one might say, the wheels turn and the vehicle moves.[61]

The importance of consensual knowledge as a prenegotiation trigger and a factor that facilitates learning and the development of convergent preferences is stressed in a number of different accounts of multilateral negotiation. Robert Rothstein argues that in multilateral settings where power is dispersed and fragmented and no state is sufficiently powerful to command agreement, "consensual knowledge may be the best means of providing a stable foundation for agreements, especially agreements that require active cooperation (not merely isolated national actions) to succeed." This is especially true in situations marked by high levels of uncertainty, where "the complexities of the issues themselves, doubts about the wisdom of extrapolating from even recent experience in a rapidly changing environment, and the problems attendant upon the need to reach agreements among so many states with so many differing interests and levels of development [will] render a quest for consensual knowledge appropriate and even mandatory."[62]

Peter Haas carries the argument about consensual knowledge one step further, arguing that international regimes may be initiated or stem from the actions of "communities of shared knowledge"—what he and others call "epistemic communities." These groups can change state interests and practices by acquiring and sustaining control over a substantive policy domain, introducing new policy alternatives to governments, and relating shared norms and principles to codified conventions. As governments themselves "learn" more about a given problem, they will accept the need for more comprehensive and coordinated policies and look to epistemic communities for advice and information.[63]

Cognitive approaches, as Steven Haggard and Beth Simmons note, are important in explaining the substantive content of regime rules and approaches, but their predictive value is problematic, "particularly when they emphasize the importance of consensual knowledge . . . since future knowledge is, by definition, impossible to foresee." In the case of "knowledge-oriented" cognitivism, Haggard and Simmons point out that scientific evidence is often resisted or ignored by other social groups and interests; thus, cognitive theory "needs to specify more clearly the types of issues and conditions under which consensual knowledge is likely to drive cooperation."[64]

Arguably, policy makers are more likely to seek epistemic or expert advice on public policy issues characterized by high levels of risk and uncertainty.[65] Policy makers will be more disposed to look to experts for advice and to take that advice into account in making decisions when the potential costs and risks of new policies (or policy inaction) are deemed to be high than when costs are low and the level of uncertainty associated with a given problem is negligible. Consensual knowledge is, therefore, more likely to affect prenegotiation processes on issues characterized by high levels of risk and uncertainty than on issues where costs and risks are readily identifiable or already known to policy makers themselves.

To the extent that experts can reduce or establish boundaries to uncertainty and provide formal risk assessments that identify the costs and benefits associated with different policy options, their influence will be felt not only in the prenegotiation stage of multilateral diplomacy but also in the negotiation, agreement, and implementation stages. However, one of the paradoxes of epistemic knowledge is that on issues where politicians turn to the experts for advice, the experts themselves may know little or may be unable to provide clear-cut answers and policy solutions. Moreover, as Ernst Haas notes, on any given issue there may well be rival epistemic communities that do not share beliefs about cause and effect or ends and means; the experts themselves may be divided.[66]

Because the epistemology of scientific discourse—the concepts and language of probability statements, hypothesis formulation and testing, and so forth—is generally alien to the kind of discourse that takes place in the political arena, public opinion serves as an important bridge between the epistemic and policy-making communities. Peter Morrisette argues that dread, familiarity, and exposure are the key factors that can be used to evaluate whether the public will be motivated to respond to a problem and lobby their politicians, protest against industry or government, or participate in programs designed to mitigate or avert disaster.[67] *Dread* is the degree to which the public sees a problem as globally catastrophic, threatening current and future generations, and preventable or reducible through involuntary or personal means. *Familiarity* involves the degree to which phenomena are understood by the public. *Exposure* is the degree to which risks are avoidable or unavoidable.

According to Morrisette, issues that are high in dread, low in familiarity, and high in exposure have the greatest likelihood of motivating the public, whereas issues that are low in dread, high in familiarity, and low in exposure are least likely to motivate the public. This is because people are more likely to be troubled by contradictory theories and the complexity of scientific debates when their information is acquired from scientific sources than when it is acquired from the media. Thus, heightened public concern about an issue may in fact be more important than the presence of a consensus within the epistemic community in determining whether or not politicians decide to take an issue seriously. However, media overemphasis of opposing points of view within the scientific community and suggestions that debate is more polarized than in fact it is can engender confusion and lead to policy paralysis or inaction.[68]

The connection between epistemic communities, consensual knowledge, and prenegotiation and negotiation processes is an extraordinarily complex one. However, epistemic communities and consensual knowledge are more likely to be important factors in prenegotiation where issue areas are characterized by high levels of risk and uncertainty, than when uncertainty is low for the reasons noted above. The extent to which scientists and experts are able to garner broader public support may also be crucial in determining whether or not issues reach the negotiating table. When public perceptions are infused with a heightened sense of what Morrisette calls the "dread factor," policy makers are more likely to react and more willing to look for solutions than when public and media interest in a problem is low.

None of the above should imply that parties armed with expert advice and consensual knowledge will automatically reach agreement once they take up the negotiation option. Unless parties have similar criteria for evaluating policy options or an equally precise concept of bargaining power—axioms that are not found even in formal bargaining theory—negotiations may still fail.[69] Additionally, as noted by Edward Parsons and Richard Zeckhauser, multiparty international negotiations are typically asymmetric insofar as negotiators "differ sharply in the tradeoff each perceives between the benefit of the collective good being provided and their costs in providing it themselves. . . . Such asymmetries can obstruct agreements by putting the nations at odds over which negotiated solutions are desirable."[70] Epistemic theories are insensitive to the distributive implications of negotiated agreements intended to provide collective goods.

The interaction between science and policy making may also be characterized by (1) a misleading faith in the ability of scientific analysis to resolve questions that are value laden; (2) a tendency to elevate trends to destiny and assume that policy choices are predetermined; (3) the questionable assumption that rival epistemic communities share similar beliefs about cause and effect; and (4) the assumption that the epistemology of science and policy making are similar, when, in fact, they are not. Nonetheless, experts can play a crucial role in defining prenegotiation possibilities, providing a knowledge basis for coalitions to form, and delimiting the scope of the agenda of subsequent negotiations. In this respect, epistemic knowledge may be a necessary condition for prenegotiation on issues characterized by high levels of risk and uncertainty, even though subsequent possibilities for reaching agreement are likely to depend on factors other than consensual knowledge and learning.

Once parties have actually committed themselves to formal negotiations, what are the factors that tend to promote convergence and closure within the arena of multilateral negotiation itself? There is no easy answer to this question, and the negotiation literature suggests that we are a long way from a general theory, or, for that matter, even general understanding, of the nature of the multilateral negotiation processes. Nonetheless, the findings and results of a number of empirically based studies point to the salience of a number of key variables that can facilitate bargaining processes among competing coalitions in the multilateral setting.

Crosscutting Coalitions and Bridging

As noted above, the formation of coalitions is a general characteristic of most multiparty bargaining situations, especially the kind of large-scale negotiations that take place at the global level. Although coalitions may form to compensate for structural weaknesses in asymmetric bargaining situations, they also help to reduce cognitive complexity, facilitate communications and exchanges of information, and simplify bargaining procedures by structuring multilateral conferences into manageable groups "which can then form common positions and negotiate through group chairpersons."[71] Relevant examples include the Group of 77, representing developing countries in the North-South dialogue, the twelve members of the European Community, which negotiate as a common entity in trade talks, and the neutral and nonaligned nations, which work together as a bloc in the Conference on Security and Cooperation in Europe (CSCE). The coalescence of states into groups is generally essential to facilitating negotiations in any multilateral conference setting, even though "the complexities of intra-group negotiations and the problems of maintaining group cohesion and preventing defections to rival coalitions" renders the bargaining process far more complex and cumbersome than it is in bilateral negotiations.[72]

Nonetheless, too much group cohesion and inflexibility hinders bargaining processes; therefore what is often called for is the formation of crosscutting coalitions or "bridging" solutions that can bring competing interests together into a mutually agreeable framework for settlement. Crosscutting coalitions typically emerge when two or more competing parties change their positions such that interests between two or more groups now overlap. When bargaining involves multiple issues, it may be possible to arrange an exchange of concessions such that when one party concedes on issues A, B, and C and the other on issues D, E, and F, part of each party's proposal is accepted and part of each party's proposal is rejected. Such an arrangement will work if the concessions involved are minimally costly to the parties making the concession but yield considerable benefits to the parties who are recipients of the concession. This process is sometimes known as logrolling,[73] but it is likely to lead to a series of crosscutting and interlocking ties and agreements that reduce the confrontational elements of bargaining and make a collapse of negotiations more costly to the parties who have been able to reach an agreement.[74]

Bridging occurs not by trading concessions but through the identification of a new formula or set of options that satisfies the principal needs of the parties concerned. For example, two people are in a room: one wants the window open for fresh air, but the other wants to avoid a draft by keeping the window closed. A bridging solution is one where they decide to open a window in an adjacent room, which brings in fresh air but avoids a draft, thus offering a third mutually satisfactory alternative.[75]

Bridging occurs when groups or individuals use a combination of imagination and technical skill to invent new solutions and identify new institutional options in bargaining situations where the major actors are deadlocked and unable to arrive at a cooperative agreement. These actors provide a "middle way" between major protagonists, not by "difference splitting" but by providing "a genuine alternative middle ground upon which the major actors [can] meet."[76] Typically, bridging solutions are offered by smaller states or middle powers who do not have structural power, that is, are not capable of providing a collective good on their own, but can compensate for a lack of structural power through the exercise of bargaining and negotiation skills directed at bringing competing interests together.[77] Bridging solutions can also be devised by other actors, such as the leaders of international organizations, who have injected themselves into the negotiating process in order to provide public goods and who may seek other rewards from mediation (e.g., prestige, bureaucratic influence).[78]

Representation

Coalitions will generally choose representatives to bargain for the group if sufficient trust has developed among the members of the coalition. Representation is crucial to simplifying and restructuring multilateral negotiations so that issues are amenable to logrolling and bridging. Representatives can be chosen on the basis of (1) power relationships (the most powerful state or states having the greatest stake and interest in an issue); (2) technical expertise (states with special knowledge, expertise, or understanding about an issue); and (3) diplomatic and bargaining skills (states whose diplomats are known to be persuasive advocates and good negotiators). In some instances, representation can help to build coalitions or serve as an alternative to coalitions when large groups are unwieldy and inflexible. Effective representation depends upon a number of conditions being fulfilled, including close links between the plenary group and the units being represented; shared interests between representatives and their constituencies so that the representative is not just a spokesperson or mouthpiece for the groups; and delegated authority, so that the representative has some leeway to make independent decisions during the actual course of negotiations that will be subsequently binding on the group as a whole.[79] Nonetheless, patterns of authority and participation can vary enormously from one coalition to another. Comparing Western and Eastern-bloc coalitions in the mutual and balanced force reduction (MBFR) talks, Jonathan Dean remarks: "Where negotiation is among a coalition of allies . . . the coalition cannot make the slightest move in negotiation, cannot make a single statement, without agreement of all participants. On the Western side, a coalition negotiation is a confederation in action. Given the more dominant position of the Soviet Union within the Warsaw Pact and the relative weakness of restrictions on its decision-making power stemming from the presence of allies, the difficulty of reaching decisions within the Warsaw Pact alliance is not identical."[80]

Entrepreneurial Leadership

Leadership is widely recognized as an important ingredient in integrative institutional bargaining processes, especially when large numbers are involved. Oran Young defines an entrepreneurial leader as "an individual who relies on negotiating skill to frame issues in ways that foster integrative bargaining and to put together deals that would otherwise elude participants endeavoring to form international regimes through institutional bargaining." The entrepreneurial leader's role is related to "the existence of a bargainer's surplus coupled with more or less severe collective action problems plaguing efforts on the part of the principals to strike the bargain necessary to capture the surplus." Innovative thinking is often required to break through bargaining deadlocks arising from positional bargaining and the operation of unanimity or consensus rules in multiparty conferences so that the participants reap the bargainer's surplus. Young defines these functions as follows: (1) setting and shaping agendas; (2) drawing attention to the issues at stake; (3) inventing novel solutions to overcome bargaining impediments; and (4) brokering and making deals.[81] Such leadership can be exercised by the chairperson of international meetings, by members of bridging coalitions of the kind mentioned above, by individual delegates, by heads or representatives of international organizations, or by heads of government.

A key requisite of leadership, beyond problem-solving skills, is effective communication skills. In order to be successful, a leader must be able to create the conditions, through his formula and presentation, that address the communication needs of the parties to the negotiation and their mutual interest in lowering barriers to communication, increasing the supply and control of information, and reducing transactions costs.[82] Communication, "whether directed at joint problem solving or issue confrontation, can be as effective as conclusion of agreements in improving international relationships."[83]

Effective leadership also demands successful management of policy-making processes at the domestic level, in order to ensure that negotiations move forward and are not undermined by interagency disagreements or domestic political squabbles. In international arms control negotiations, for example, Alexander George notes that effective presidential leadership includes the ability to set agenda priorities and deal with competing policy goals and trade-offs, discipline domestic advisers and bureaucratic actors, develop a domestic consensus and adequate policy coalition in support of a decision, and ensure policy legitimacy and support for decisions in the Congress.[84] Leaders' effectiveness in international negotiations is also likely to turn on their power, authority, and influence within their own state, their interest in foreign affairs, and the importance of the foreign policy issue to the domestic politics of their state.[85]

Simple Solutions or Focal Points

The search for a formula that satisfies competing interests represents the main activity of negotiation and is the key basis for any agreement. Zartman and Berman define a formula as "a shared perception or definition of the conflict that establishes terms of trade, the cognitive structure of referents for a solution, or an applicable criterion of justice," on grounds that a formula is more than just a concession or compromise based on a series of fixed moves or positions. To be effective, a formula or agreed solution must be "framed by a relatively simple definition or conception of an outcome" that encompasses the essential demands of the parties concerned. The formula is balanced insofar as it brings together competing interests in a way that is considered fair while meeting certain standards or criteria of justice. These criteria can be substantive, procedural or impartial, equitable, compensatory, or subtractive.[86]

Young also notes the importance of simplicity and clarity in finding formulas that contribute to success in institutional bargaining. Arrangements based on considerations of equity, where all parties "can come away with the sense that their primary concerns have been treated fairly," are more important than the achievement of allocative efficiency.[87] His conception of justice is largely procedural, although there may be other relevant criteria as well.

Finding the right formula is a creative, problem-solving process. According to Zartman, there is no single way to go about it: "Combining and bridging competing proposals is one way. . . . Another involves finding proposals that go less far in the desired direction than the other party might wish but that are nonetheless better than the status quo. The land between reality and perfection is strewn with measures that can improve one side's lot without being offensive to the other."[88] Nonetheless, the success of the negotiation process depends on the ability of actors to reduce complexity into a simple resolving formula that establishes clear terms of trade and is based on shared principles of justice.

Clear-Cut Compliance Mechanisms

All collective action problems are typically plagued by problems of cheating and defection. Game theorist Kenneth Oye remarks that "as the number of players increases, the likelihood of autonomous defection and recognition and control problems increases. Cooperative behavior rests on calculations of expected utility. . . . Discount rates and approaches to calculation are likely to vary across actors, and the prospects for mutual cooperation may decline as the number of players and the probable heterogeneity of actors increases." Thus, one of the challenges in N-person games is to devise collective enforcement mechanisms that will discourage the likelihood of defection and permit the "selective punishment" of violators of established norms.[89]

International negotiations directed at establishing arrangements that yield benefits to parties who do not trust each other must, therefore, devise mechanisms to ensure compliance with the terms of an agreement when it goes into effect. Generally speaking, agreements will be more attractive to parties, and thus easier to negotiate, when clear-cut and effective verification and compliance mechanisms are available. The ability to include verification and compliance mechanisms into the negotiation formula may be crucial to overall success of the negotiation.

But the negotiation challenge does not stop here. Most, though by no means all, international agreements rely on the ability of their individual members to ensure compliance within their own territorial jurisdiction. According to Young, international regimes are more likely to succeed "when the participants can rely on relatively simple, nonintrusive compliance mechanisms" that do not violate national sovereignty or "expend scarce political resources."[90] Agreements that are not verifiable not only are more difficult to negotiate but are also likely to become embroiled in controversy later on. Furthermore, every agreement is imperfect and is likely to contain substantial ambiguities that can be exploited by the parties should they choose to do so. The availability of institutional mechanisms to which disputing parties can turn when such conflicts arise may be crucial to ensuring the continuing success and viability of agreement.[91]

Issue Decomposition, Sequencing, and Incrementalism

International negotiations on complex issues characterized by high levels of uncertainty are more likely to succeed when parties demonstrate flexibility and comprehensive agreements are eschewed in favor of partial or limited settlements on specific issues. Such an approach maximizes substantive desirability and the realization of joint gains while minimizing the likelihood that opposing interests will rally to form a blocking coalition. In addition, careful sequencing of issues in the bargaining process and incremental—as opposed to comprehensive—bargaining strategies can also reduce bargaining pressures and generate momentum in the direction of an agreement.

Sebenius argues that large-scale conference diplomacy on complex issues like the Law of the Sea or climate change is more likely to succeed when issues are dealt with sequentially, via a series of limited, strategically chosen protocols that generate momentum in the direction of more encompassing agreements. Similarly, framework protocols that contain no formal commitments and rely instead on voluntary actions and compliance can help create new international norms, foster new research and the spread of information, and speed up the process of formal framework and protocol negotiations. As new information is acquired, coordination improves, and monitoring mechanisms are strengthened, agreements can be ratcheted up and new targets and obligations established that strengthen and improve upon existing treaty commitments.[92]

The argument for incremental approaches to negotiations is that half a loaf is better than none. Incremental approaches to negotiations allow parties "to test their solutions and get used to them." Participant incrementalism may be especially useful in asymmetrical multiparty conflicts, allowing weaker actors the options of buying in, buying out, or buying off the stronger members of the coalition. In the first, weaker actors can join the agreement but use accession "against new concessions that preserve the nature of the agreement." In the second, the weaker side can use accession to "buy out" the majority "by negotiating a new agreement between the two groups of parties." In the third, the weaker coalition tries "to woo away" members of the more powerful coalition "into a counteragreement" with the weaker members.[93] Members of the more powerful coalition may extend the offer of side payments and other benefits to get parties outside the agreement to join in.

Partial agreements and incremental strategies may also be useful when ideological divisions and basic value orientations are such that they do not permit comprehensive solutions and approaches to problem solving. For example, at least until relatively recently and perhaps still, "a comprehensive security regime, one that would deal with all or most aspects of the competition and rivalry affecting the security interface of the two superpowers, [was] not feasible." Nonetheless, as Alexander George, Philip Farley, and Alexander Dallin go on to explain, this situation did not prevent the two superpowers from "working out viable, mutually useful arrangements for some of their security problems." Although the security dimension of the U.S.-Soviet relationship embraced many issues, by decoupling issues from each other they were able to focus on their efforts on contriving mutually cooperative security arrangements in a number of areas, which turned out to be "mutually reinforcing" in regulating competition and facilitating cooperation.[94]

Although issue and participant incrementalism can create or enhance a possible zone of agreement, they can also block the possibilities for further agreement or more comprehensive settlements because parties are reluctant to move beyond the status quo. What was initially conceived as a "stepping stone" may in fact become a "stopping place."[95] Thus, one of the challenges of incremental negotiation approaches is how to sustain the political momentum behind negotiations once an agreement to negotiate has been reached. The use of a single negotiating text spelling out areas of agreement and disagreement (usually in bracketed text) can facilitate the negotiating process by indicating what must be bargained over. As Ian Bellany explains, "in its *very* earliest, perhaps pre-treaty form, treaty documentation may have an almost uncontentious quality and be heavily slanted towards technical or scientific matters. It thus becomes an accept-able—because neutral—starting point, or single negotiating text, for the veto powers to bargain over and subsequently flesh out."[96]

William Pendergast argues that packaging and sequencing of the negoti-ation agenda are crucial to building momentum in any negotiation. Agenda scrutiny is the argument for letting sleeping dogs lie as part of an effective negotiating strategy. These are issues that will reopen the negoti-ating agenda or generate controversy and deadlock, for example, linking progress in arms control in U.S.-Soviet relations to controversial issues of human rights. Agenda packing "is the deliberate proliferation of issues— often of a symbolic or procedural nature—to consume time and energy." If negotiations are to move forward, these issues must be excluded from the agenda or deferred to the end of an agenda," thereby limiting the scrutiny accorded them." Building momentum can be achieved by dealing with the easy issues first, recognizing (1) that "it is easier to move from agreement to disagreement than [from] disagreement to agreement"; (2) that "a 'soft' opening enables the parties to gain experience working together" and to "build an escalating commitment to agreement"; and (3) the acquisition of "equity in agreement."[97] The use of stalking-horse proposals, that is, ex-aggerated demands on dispensable items that can be traded for conces-sions on more important matters later on, can also propel negotiations for-ward, provided they are used sparingly and introduced at the right moment.

Related to issue sequencing and staging is the use of working groups to deal with specific questions. Milgaard and Underdal distinguish between horizontal and vertical working groups: the former involve all parties and deal with specific issues or subissues in the negotiation, whereas the latter consist of a smaller number of delegates who work together on one or more issues and report to plenary.[98] The advantage of working groups is that they promote flexibility and are more conducive to discussion and de-liberation than large-scale, plenary forums. Working groups may be infor-mal or formal, and their deliberations kept secret or accountable to the conference as a whole—although the effectiveness of such groupings may diminish if key groups feel that they are being left out of the decision-mak-ing process.

Conclusion

This chapter has discussed the principal obstacles to negotiation in multi-lateral conference diplomacy and identified a number of factors that inter-national negotiation scholars single out as potentially helpful to the bar-

PRENEGOTIATION

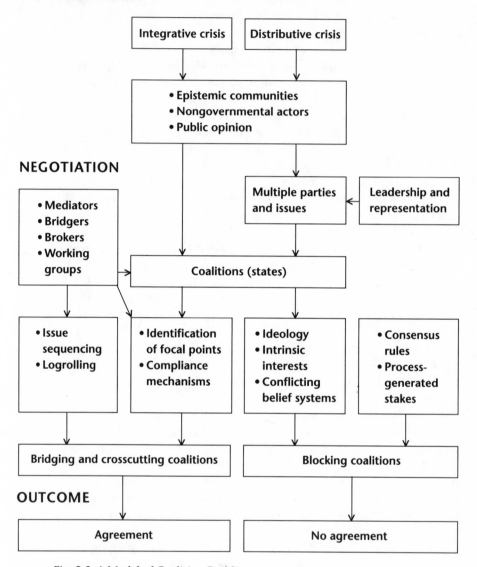

Fig. 2.2. A Model of Coalition Building

gaining process (see fig. 2.2). These variables have different degrees of importance at different stages of the negotiation process. In the prenegotiation phase, crises and consensual knowledge are viewed as important variables in fostering consensus, allowing coalitions to form, and bringing issues to the negotiating table. However, crises can differ in terms of their potential distribution of gains and losses, and it is hypothesized that it usually takes a mutual or integrative sense of crisis to transform a bargaining relationship into one where the parties recognize that there are joint gains to be achieved through cooperation. The connection between consensual knowledge, expert advice, and negotiation is also extremely complex, but these factors are more likely to make their presence felt on issues characterized by high levels of risk and uncertainty, where growing public pressure demands solutions from policy makers. Although consensual knowledge is no guarantee of agreement in multilateral negotiations, experts can nonetheless play a crucial role in defining prenegotiation possibilities and the subsequent agenda of negotiations.

Once a set of issues reaches the negotiating table, the main challenge is to organize complexity, which is experienced at the level of both parties and issues. Coalitions simplify the bargaining process at one level, even though they lead to further subnegotiations at the intracoalition level. Moreover, to the extent that coalitions are based on shared intrinsic interests, belief systems, or values, bargaining positions can harden across coalitions and hinder the prospects for agreement. The creation of crosscutting or bridging coalitions, the designation of bargaining representatives, and the presence of leadership can greatly facilitate bargaining processes within and across coalitions. Similarly, the identification of simple resolving formulas, clear-cut compliance mechanisms, and the use of decomposition, sequencing, and incremental negotiation tactics can maximize the likelihood of cooperation while minimizing the possibility that opposing interests will rally to form blocking coalitions.

There are also clear linkages between the external and internal environment of negotiations, between contingency (or context) and agent behavior. Integrative crises, for example, can attenuate the divisive tendencies of blocking coalitions by reshaping perceptions about the desirability of pursuing negotiating strategies that will maximize joint gains. Crises can also create opportunities for leadership to emerge where none existed before. Similarly, effective leadership, as noted above, usually depends on a leader's ability not just to break bargaining deadlocks but also to manage policy-making processes at the domestic level so that international negotiations are not undermined by political division at home. These variables draw our attention to the roles different parties take on for themselves during negotiations and the tactics negotiators adopt to reduce the inherent complexity of a multilateral setting into workable coalitions.

In the chapters that follow, we explore the independent influences of these different variables or influences on multilateral negotiation in order to better understand the potential requirements for success. Our purpose is not to test theories but to follow what Harry Eckstein, Alexander George, and others call a "disciplined-configurative" mode of analysis that identifies relevant variables on the basis of existing theories in order to explain outcomes in a given set of cases.[99] The results cannot prove or disprove any given hypothesis about bargaining relationships, but one can determine whether the hypothesis is useful to explain the evidence in these cases.[100] To provide a common focus for comparison, the following questions guide the analysis of each case:

• Was the onset of negotiations precipitated by a crisis?
• Was the crisis specific or general, disruptive or integrative, in terms of its impact on coalitions and bargaining behavior?
• Did consensual knowledge shape prenegotiations, leading to the formation of coalitions?
• Were the issues characterized by high or low levels of risk and uncertainty?
• Did public perceptions of a looming catastrophe (the "dread factor") pressure policy makers to enter into negotiations and encourage integrative bargaining?
• Did crosscutting and bridging coalitions reduce the confrontational elements of bargaining and promote the elements of an agreement?
• Was bargaining facilitated by the selection of representatives and the presence of leadership in the negotiations?
• Did the identification of simple solutions, or focal points, and clear-cut compliance mechanisms help to overcome strategic and positional impediments to cooperation?
• Did issue decomposition and sequencing and incremental negotiation tactics contribute to the realization of joint gains and attenuate or eliminate the influence of blocking coalitions?
• Where negotiations failed to achieve closure, can the outcome be explained by the absence of some or all of these conditions?

By addressing a common set of questions across different case studies, we can acquire a better understanding about potentially generalizable relations between a series of independent variables and outcomes. There is no guarantee that a focused comparison will lead to good results, but the methodology of a structured, focused comparison grounded in existing theoretical knowledge can, to quote George, "establish a sound empirical base on which to ground theory development."[101]

Chapters 3 to 5 address these questions in the context of multilateral arms control. The Limited Test Ban Treaty, as an early instance of multilateral diplomacy, is examined, followed by two later historical cases: the Stockholm Conference and negotiations leading to a Conventional Forces,

Europe Treaty. Each chapter provides a historical description of the negotiations, discussing the background to and subsequent development of the negotiations themselves. Conclusions pertaining to each set of negotiations are offered at the end of each chapter. Chapters 6 to 8 examine the origins of the GATT, the ITO, and the Uruguay Round of the GATT. These chapters follow the same sequence and address the same set of analytical questions, as do subsequent chapters on international environmental negotiations dealing with the ozone accords, the Basel Convention on hazardous wastes, and climate change. Given the highly empirical nature of this exercise, general analytic conclusions are left to the conclusion, as are comparisons of the three issue areas.

II Multilateral Arms Control Negotiations

3 The Limited Test Ban Treaty

The Limited Test Ban Treaty (LTBT) of 1963 was the first major arms control treaty in the nuclear age. It helped pave the way for a new era in arms control that saw the evolution of a more cooperative, less competitive, relationship between the two superpowers. Although the United States and the Soviet Union were the principal stakeholders in the test ban negotiations, these negotiations were in a genuine sense multilateral because they involved the direct participation of the United Kingdom as a negotiating partner and a number of non-nuclear powers who became involved in the negotiations when they shifted to the Eighteen-Nation Disarmament Committee (ENDC) conference in Geneva in 1962.

In discussing the origins of the Limited Test Ban Treaty, it should be noted, at the outset, that there was not really much of a negotiation on the limited test ban issue itself. Much of the negotiations in the late 1950s and early 1960s was focused on the issue of a comprehensive, as opposed to partial, test ban. Only when it became apparent that a comprehensive test ban treaty was not feasible did the parties settle on the more limited option. The case underscores the point that much of international negotiation is finding out what is not agreeable to the parties, rather than what is.

Although scientific knowledge shaped prenegotiations and the subsequent agenda for negotiations, it would be a mistake to characterize the nature of this involvement in terms of consensual knowledge, because there were significant differences of opinion within the scientific community about the feasibility of a comprehensive nuclear test ban. Instead, political judgments and value considerations proved to be crucial at key junctures in the decision-making process, ultimately bringing the negotiations to settle on the option of a limited, as opposed to comprehensive, test ban. In this respect, the case serves as a model for others discussed in this book. First, extranegotiatory factors—in particular, epistemic communities and growing public pressure—helped to bring the issue to the negotiating table but were not responsible for the ultimate outcome of these negotiations. Instead, exogenous shocks in the form of the Cuban missile crisis propelled negotiations forward as did mounting concerns about nuclear proliferation which redefined the attitudes and perceptions of key decision makers and changed the value they placed on a negotiated settlement. Second, mediation and political leadership were crucial to breaking bargaining impasses and resolving key differences among the players at critical turning points in the negotiation. The interplay between the external environment and the negotiating table are thus crucial to understanding why an agreement on a partial test ban was reached when it was. However, these pressures were not sufficient to overcome concerns about verification and compliance, which stood in the way of a comprehensive test ban treaty. Such a treaty, which would have banned nuclear testing in all four environments (air, water, space, and underground), continues to remain a goal.

Prenegotiation

Negotiations for a test ban were prompted by a growing sense of crisis in the scientific and international community about the harmful consequences for human health of atmospheric testing.[1] A series of dramatic events were to crystallize these concerns and make them the focus of public and international debate. On March 1, 1954, the United States detonated a hydrogen bomb in a nuclear test, code-named BRAVO, over the Bikini atoll in the heart of the Pacific Ocean. Unexpected wind conditions carried radioactive fallout from the blast over an unusually wide area, blanketing the Marshall Islands with radioactivity in the process. Japanese fishermen on a tuna trawler, the *Lucky Dragon,* were also showered by radioactive debris from the explosion; some of the fishermen became ill, and one died. The devastating effects of the explosion prompted the beginnings of what would become a worldwide outcry to end nuclear testing. The first call came from Prime Minister Jarwahl Nehru of India, who called for a "standstill agreement" on nuclear testing based on the health of present and future generations. Later, in 1957, he would again make the same appeal.[2]

Early international discussions about a test ban, however, were framed in terms of more sweeping initiatives for general disarmament measures. In June 1954, France and Britain unveiled a joint proposal for nuclear disarmament. The two countries called for cuts in conventional forces, to be followed by nuclear disarmament under international inspection and control. The Anglo-French initiative was followed on May 10, 1955, by a Soviet disarmament proposal that set levels for conventional force reductions and proposed the creation of an international agency to control nuclear disarmament.

President Eisenhower of the United States offered his own Open Skies proposal at the Geneva Summit conference of leaders of the world's four great powers (the United States, the United Kingdom, France, and the U.S.S.R.) in July 1955. Under the plan, the United States and the Soviet Union would allow reconnaissance flights over each other's territory to assure that no side was preparing to mount aggression. The Soviets, however, rejected the proposal on the grounds that it was simply an intelligence-gathering scheme intended to identify bombing targets for the United States Strategic Air Command (SAC).[3]

The first hint that the United States might be interested in negotiations came when President Eisenhower suggested to Marshal Bulganin, the Soviet Prime minister, that technical working groups be set up to study different disarmament proposals, including the idea of a ban on nuclear testing. In October 1956, the Soviet premier wrote back suggesting a test ban that would not rely on inspections of each side's national territory. It was readily apparent, even in preliminary discussions about a test ban, that onsite inspection would be a contentious issue for the Soviets.

Continuation of atmospheric testing by the United States, the Soviet Union, and now the United Kingdom, which had successfully tested its own first nuclear device, met with mounting national and international criticism. In 1957, Nobel Prize winner Linus Pauling collected signatures from 9,000 scientists in forty-three countries calling for a halt to testing. A nationwide Gallup Poll in the same year showed that 63 percent of Americans favored a test ban, compared to 20 percent in 1954. President Eisenhower responded by indicating that the United States would take appropriate measures to minimize the harmful effects of radioactive fallout. Public perceptions of the harmful consequences of nuclear testing were clearly beginning to exert a powerful influence on the administration's policies, even though no formal decision had been made to begin negotiations.

Although many scientists (along with public opinion) favored a test ban, scientific opinion was by no means unanimous, and it would be a mistake to conclude that prenegotiations were shaped by an emerging scientific consensus about the desirability and feasibility of a test ban. Among the opponents to a test ban were Edward Teller, director of the Atomic Energy Commission's weapons laboratory at Livermore, California, Ernest Lawrence, director of the University of California's Radiation Laboratory, and Mark Mills, head of Livermore's theoretical division. These scientists met with President Eisenhower to indicate their opposition to a test ban and the need, in their view, to continue with an active weapons-testing program in order to develop "clean" fallout weapons or "neutron bombs" that NATO could use on the battlefield. They argued that the Soviets would still be able to conduct secret tests under a test ban and that an active testing program would be required for peaceful nuclear explosions (Project Ploughshares).

On June 14, 1957, the Soviet Union proposed a two- or three-year moratorium on nuclear tests, to be supervised by an international commission that would use instrument detection stations on the territories of the nuclear powers. The Soviet proposal was made at the London session of the Subcommittee of the Disarmament Commission of the United Nations and was followed by an American offer of a limited disarmament package that included a test ban and a temporary cessation of testing for a period of up to two years. Although the American negotiator, Harold Stassen, who made the offer had gotten White House approval of some of the particulars, he had stretched them out a bit. President Eisenhower lost confidence in Stassen, particularly when it became clear that Stassen favored a test ban as a separate disarmament measure that would not be linked, for example, to a weapons-production cutoff and other measures.

A bureaucratic restructuring of the way scientific issues were handled by the White House was to have a major impact on the test ban issue and arms control priorities of the administration. On November 7, 1957, President Eisenhower created the new position of special assistant to the president for science and technology, appointing James R. Killian Jr., president of the Massachusetts Institute of Technology, to the post. He also established the President's Science Advisory Committee (PSAC). Before this post was created, most scientific advice had been filtered through the laboratories of the Atomic Energy Commission (AEC), scientists in the Defense Department, and the figure of Lewis Strauss, chairman of the AEC and special assistant to the president for atomic energy. The effect of the PSAC was to bring a greater diversity of scientific opinion into the policy councils of the administration. As Glenn Seaborg notes, the effect of these organizational reforms was to convey "a different flow of scientific information" and strengthen the bureaucratic position of the test ban's supporters: "To all the arguments about the difficulties of achieving and implementing a test ban agreement the Killian group responded with arguments about the *greater* difficulties that might ensue in the *absence* of an agreement."[4]

The State Department also began to voice its support for a more active U.S. role on the test ban issue, on the grounds that the United States was losing the propaganda war with the Soviets. These concerns were expressed to the president by none other than Secretary of State John Foster Dulles, who earlier had made no secret of his suspicions of entering into any arms agreement with the Soviets. However, Eisenhower's own leadership on the test ban question was weak; instead of offering proposals to counteract a new Soviet offer for a three-year moratorium on testing of nuclear weapons, which came late in 1957, the United States cast itself as naysayer by rejecting the Soviet proposal.

On March 27, 1958, Nikita Khrushchev became the new premier of the

Soviet Union. Acting on the new Soviet leader's directive, the Supreme Soviet issued a decree on March 31, 1958, prohibiting further nuclear testing by the Soviet Union on the condition that other nations would do the same. Premier Khrushchev sent special letters to British Prime Minister Harold Macmillan and President Eisenhower urging them to follow the Soviet lead.

While the United States was deciding how to respond to the Soviet offer, an interagency panel headed by Cornell physicist Hand Bethe delivered a report through PSAC chairman James Killian indicating that the United States could enter into a test ban without endangering its national security and that a test ban could be verified through a system of detection stations combined with on-site inspections of each side's territory. According to the panel, this system would be able to detect all but the smallest nuclear explosions. On April 8, 1958, Eisenhower wrote to Khrushchev proposing that the Soviet Union and Western nations examine the technical requirements for verification of a nuclear test ban. Khrushchev initially rejected the idea but then agreed to technical talks that would serve as a prelude to formal negotiations on a test ban. The prenegotiation phase was clearly moving beyond the problem identification stage, where negotiation is added to the array of options being considered by the parties, into the "search for options" phase (discussed in chapter 2), when the parties seriously begin to come to terms with the need to negotiate and decide upon the initial substance of negotiations.

These technical talks began on July 1, 1958, in Geneva, under the formal title of Conference of Experts to Study the Possibility of Detecting Violations of a Possible Agreement on Suspension of Nuclear Tests. The Western delegation included representatives from the United States, Canada, Britain, and France. The conference studied different methods of identifying nuclear explosions, including acoustic, seismic, and radio recording methods. While the Soviets took the view that a small number of recording stations would be required for an adequate verification system, Western experts argued for more extensive on-site verification systems. In its final communiqué delivered on August 21, 1958, the conference reported that it had "reached the conclusion that it is technically feasible to set up, with certain capabilities and limitations, a workable and effective control system for detection of violations of a possible agreement on the worldwide cessation of nuclear weapons tests."[5] This system would have involved somewhere between 160 and 170 land-based detection stations. Experts claimed that the Geneva System—as it later came to be known—could detect atmospheric tests as low as one kiloton and underground explosions as small as five kilotons. However, the conference did not address the problem of explosions at very high altitudes, and provisions for on-site inspections were purposely left vague because of differences of opinion between Soviet and Western delegates.

Negotiations

The onset of formal diplomatic negotiations can be said to have begun on August 23, 1958, when President Eisenhower suggested that the three nuclear powers, the United Kingdom, the Soviet Union, and the United States, meet to formally negotiate an end to nuclear testing. As a sign of the United States' good faith and commitment to the negotiation option, Eisenhower also announced that the United States would refrain from further testing for a year as soon as a date for negotiations was set. Seven days later, the Soviet Union said it would agree to a test ban conference in Geneva. On October 31, 1958, the Conference on Discontinuance of Nuclear Weapons Tests began.[6]

It is difficult to characterize these negotiations because they did not move forward and, in one sense, almost slid backward as a result of new scientific findings that cast serious doubt on the verifiability of a test ban at very low yields. The Soviet position also hardened on the matter of on-site inspections during the course of negotiations, and when the conference finally concluded, it was not clear whether there had been any real progress at all, since both superpowers announced that they would no longer abide by their moratorium on nuclear testing.

At the beginning of the conference, the Soviets tabled a draft treaty calling for the three negotiating nuclear powers to stop testing, a control and verification system for a test ban modeled along the lines of the Geneva System, and a series of initiatives to persuade other would-be nuclear powers to desist from testing.[7] The Western response was skeptical, and American officials openly voiced their reservations about the adequacy of the verification provisions in the Geneva System. In response, the Soviets agreed to a control system that would be part of a formal treaty. However, the basis for U.S. concerns was new scientific evidence that cast doubt on the ease of being able to distinguish underground nuclear explosions from earthquakes, especially at relatively low yields. Previous findings had been based on a single underground test. According to these new findings, the minimum detectable yield would be twenty, not five, kilotons, and this would require a much larger number of detection stations to be placed on Soviet soil. The Soviets were suspicious of U.S. motives, suspecting that these new claims were simply a smoke screen to increase the number of on-site inspections for intelligence-gathering purposes. They were also resistant to inspections because they regarded secrecy as a strategic asset and therefore did not want any third parties on their soil.

On April 13, 1959, Eisenhower suggested that because a comprehensive test ban would be extremely difficult to verify, a partial test ban covering atmospheric tests only up to an altitude of fifty kilometers should go into effect. Such a ban would not require on-site verification—an obvious point of contention with the Soviets—but the proposal was brushed off by Khrushchev. Instead, Khrushchev stated that he favored a British proposal to allow a fixed, limited number of on-site inspections each year on each side's territory. Eisenhower and Macmillan agreed to study the suggestion further.

The Geneva System came under serious challenge with the publication of two new scientific reports. The first of these was the Report of the U.S. Panel on Seismic Improvements, headed by Lloyd V. Berkner, which discussed ways to improve upon existing technologies to improve seismic detection abilities and also ways to conceal underground tests in order to avoid seismic detection. Analysis by Albert Latter of the RAND Corporation indicated that the explosion from underground tests could be "decoupled" if they were detonated at the center of a large underground cavity, thereby reducing the impact of the explosion on the surrounding earth. Thus, relatively large-yield explosions, on the order of 300 kilotons, might show up on seismographs as 1-kiloton explosions. In the spring of 1959, a second report, prepared by Robert F. Bacher of the California Institute of Technology, concluded that even on-site inspections would not necessarily detect a nuclear explosion if it was well concealed.

In the meantime, the Geneva conference agreed to form several working groups to assess the criteria for a verifiable test ban. Technical Working Group I convened on June 22, 1959, to consider the problem of detecting nuclear explosions at high altitudes. On July 10, scientists reported that high-altitude explosions could be detected by satellites but that it might nonetheless still be difficult to detect the originator of a high-altitude blast. On November 25, 1959, Technical Working Group II was established to work out the criteria for on-site inspection of underground tests. The Soviets rejected U.S. data attesting to the difficulties of distinguishing underground explosions from earthquakes in the Soviet Union. Technical Working Group II ended its deliberations on December 18, in an atmosphere poisoned by bitter recriminations from all sides. Obviously frustrated by the lack of progress in Geneva, Eisenhower announced that the United States would not be bound by its voluntary moratorium on nuclear tests, scheduled to expire on December 31, 1959.

The United States, however, was not about to give up on its efforts to negotiate a test ban. On February 11, 1960, Ambassador Wadsworth indicated that the United States was prepared to enter into an agreement that would prohibit only those nuclear tests that could be verified under the

Geneva System, thus allowing for expansion of an agreement later on as verification and detection capabilities improved. The proposal would limit atmospheric testing and underwater testing, as well as tests in space, where detection was feasible. Underground tests producing signals greater than 4.75 on the Richter scale would also be covered by the ban. The number of on-site inspections would amount to about twenty per year. The Soviets responded that they wished to prohibit all tests in space; they were willing to proceed with a moratorium on all smaller underground tests below 4.75 on the Richter scale, but they rejected any quota on the number of on-site inspections.

Some American politicians and scientists hailed the Soviet counterproposal, believing that an agreement was now within sight. Others argued that the Soviets could cheat under their counterproposal by conducting secret underground tests below the 4.75 seismic threshold. At their March 1960 meeting at Camp David, Macmillan and Eisenhower agreed to a moratorium on underground tests below the 4.75 threshold, but only after a treaty banning all verifiable tests had been signed and arrangements made for a joint seismic research program.

The Soviet Union agreed to a meeting of the Seismic Research Program Advisory Group to be held May 11. However, political relations between the United States and the Soviet Union were to suddenly take an abrupt downward turn. On May 7, 1960, Khrushchev announced that a U-2 reconnaissance aircraft piloted by Francis Gary Powers had been shot down over Soviet territory. The June Moscow summit between Eisenhower and Khrushchev was canceled. With the summit meeting off, on May 27 the Soviets announced that they were no longer interested in participating in a joint seismic research program, and the research group was disbanded. The precipitous decline in East-West relations was further exacerbated by the crisis in the Belgian Congo in Africa and Soviet attacks on U.N. Secretary-General Dag Hammarskjold. The Geneva conference adjourned on December 5, 1960, in an acrimonious mood, having done little to narrow differences between Western and Soviet positions on a test ban.

However, the election of President John F. Kennedy to the presidency in 1960 was to breathe new life into the test ban negotiations. Not only was Kennedy more strongly committed than his predecessor to achieving a test ban treaty, but he also was to display important qualities of political leadership in moving the negotiations forward when they showed signs of stalling. One of Kennedy's first acts as president was to initiate a comprehensive review of U.S. policies on a test ban.

Following the review and consultations with the British, on April 18, 1961, the United States and the United Kingdom tabled a new draft treaty for a test ban. The new proposal still envisaged a threshold treaty covering events larger than 4.75 on the Richter scale, but it now proposed that a moratorium on testing and a joint research program take place simultaneously. Furthermore, the United States also indicated that it would allow the Soviets to examine nuclear devices for research explosions without demanding reciprocal rights from the Soviets. The United States continued to stick with its demand for a quota of twenty on-site inspections in the Soviet Union but indicated that it was willing to allow the same quota to be assigned to both of the Western powers.

Whereas the previous Soviet position had showed some flexibility, the Soviets now proposed an international directorate for the control system that would involve a troika of three groups of states. They also linked the test ban to plans for general and complete disarmament. At the Vienna summit meeting between Khrushchev and Kennedy, Khrushchev insisted on no more than three on-site inspections per year. As U.S.-Soviet relations worsened over the ensuing Berlin crisis, pressure increased on the administration to break the moratorium on nuclear testing. On September 1, 1961, the Soviets resumed nuclear testing with a fifty-two-megaton explosion— the biggest ever. Khrushchev apparently had come under strong pressure from his own military to test a new weapon for the Soviet missile program, but there were dissident voices even in the Soviet Union. Academician Andrei Sakharov, one of the key scientists who had worked on the Soviet hydrogen bomb, unsuccessfully petitioned Khrushchev not to allow the military to conduct further tests, on the grounds that a test ban was crucial to stopping the arms race.[8] The White House was quick to condemn the Soviet action. Although the Western powers agreed not to conduct nuclear tests in the atmosphere that produced radioactive fallout, Kennedy announced on September 5, 1961, that the United States considered itself no longer bound by the moratorium.

As superpower negotiations bogged down, the U.N General Assembly passed a number of resolutions on the test ban issue. By a vote of seventy-one to eleven, the General Assembly approved a resolution, sponsored by the United States and the United Kingdom, entitled "The Urgent Need for a Treaty to Ban Nuclear Weapons Tests Under Effective International Control," which essentially endorsed the Western position in the test ban negotiations. The purpose of the resolution was to castigate the French, who had begun to test in North Africa. The African states pushed for a resolution urging respect for the continent of Africa as a denuclearized zone. India submitted its own resolution calling for a moratorium on nuclear testing until a test ban treaty was adopted, which was rejected by the Soviet bloc and the West even though seventy-one other countries voted for the resolution.

After the U.N. debate on the test ban, the United States proposed that the Geneva negotiations resume. The Soviets agreed, and the conference recommenced on November 28, 1961. Some thirteen meetings were held between that date and January 29, 1962, when the conference finally recessed.

During these negotiations, the Soviets argued for an agreement that would discontinue all nuclear tests but would be monitored by national detection systems only. They also favored a moratorium on underground tests, pending agreement on a system to control underground explosions, and indicated that France should join the negotiations. The Western powers rejected the Soviet proposal and indicated that they would negotiate only on the basis of the proposals previously tabled. The change in the Soviet position deadlocked the negotiations. The West suggested that the conference should adjourn and the issue be referred to the ENDC, which had been established by the United States and the Soviet Union and endorsed at the sixteenth session of the U.N. General Assembly.

Whereas negotiations on a test ban up to this point had been essentially trilateral in nature, involving the United States, the Soviet Union, and the United Kingdom, they now moved to a more genuine multilateral forum with the opening of the ENDC in Geneva, on March 11, 1962. The committee enjoyed a link with the United Nations, its composition having been endorsed by a resolution of the General Assembly. The committee's membership included Canada, France, Italy, the United Kingdom, the United States, Bulgaria, Czechoslovakia, Poland, Rumania, and the U.S.S.R. (the original members of the Ten-Nation Disarmament Committee) and eight additional members: Brazil, Burma, Ethiopia, India, Mexico, Nigeria, Sweden, and the United Arab Republic. The eight new members had all voted for previous U.N. resolutions urging a moratorium on all nuclear tests pending an international test ban treaty. Sweden was the only new state to have technical advisers formally attached to its delegation to Geneva. A special subcommittee, representing a continuation of the trilateral forum and consisting of the Soviet Union, the United States, and the United Kingdom, was also created. Both the Soviet and the American delegations tabled draft treaties linking a test ban to plans for general and complete disarmament.

From the outset of these talks, the Soviets indicated that national verification means were sufficient to detect tests in the atmosphere, in outer space, and underwater (their old position), but they now took the position that underground tests could be detected by national means as well. The United States and the United Kingdom asserted that the international control system called for in the Conference of Experts had demonstrated conclusively that on-site inspections would be necessary to assure adequate means of verification. This debate was carried into the ENDC, which had a full debate on these issues. The debate took place under the shadow of the looming possibility that both the United States and the Soviet Union would soon resume atmospheric testing. The eight new members of the committee threatened to break off the conference if the United States went ahead with its plans to resume testing. The delegations of the eight new member-nations then decided to join together to break the deadlock in negotiations. Sweden and India took the lead. Swedish scientists took the view that on-site inspections would not be terribly useful in detecting radioactive debris from underground explosions. Both Indian and Swedish representatives argued that if one side violated the ban then the only recourse for the other side would be to resume testing. The Swedes also advanced the novel suggestion that normal scientific channels, for example, the worldwide meteorological network, could be used to measure international radioactivity levels and thereby help to monitor a test ban.

These ideas found their way into the Eight-Nation Memorandum, which was presented to the plenary meeting on April 16, 1962. The memorandum urged the nuclear powers to renew their efforts to achieve a test ban treaty, arguing that an inspection system "might be based and built upon already existing networks of observation posts and institutions, or if more appropriate, on certain of the existing posts designated by agreement for the purpose together, if necessary, with new posts established by agreement." It also called for the establishment of an international commission staffed by scientists from neutral countries, which would be "entrusted with the tasks of processing all data received from the agreed system of observation posts and reporting on any nuclear explosion or suspicious event."[9]

The memorandum was greeted cautiously by the great powers. The Soviets informed the conference that they were prepared to accept the memorandum as a basis for continuing with negotiations, while the United States expressed reservations about ambiguities in the memorandum regarding the question of on-site inspection. Until the ENDC recessed on June 14, 1962, however, the memorandum became the basis for all further negotiations, even though both sides interpreted the memorandum on the basis of their own previous proposals. Although the eight-nation proposal did not break the negotiating deadlock, it nonetheless helped to sustain negotiations at a point when the two superpowers were deadlocked and there was some danger that they might just walk away from the table.[10]

On April 26, 1962, the United States resumed atmospheric testing. Some members of the ENDC expressed their dismay with the American action. The Soviets hinted that they too might resume atmospheric tests. Some members of the ENDC tried to intervene by suggesting that new discussions begin between scientists and technical experts on the question of on-site inspection. However, the Soviets rejected the idea.

At this point, the United States decided to reformulate policies toward a test ban. An ad hoc committee was created, chaired by Adrian Fisher, deputy-director of the Arms Control and Disarmament Agency (ACDA), and including representatives from the Department of Defense, the Joint Chiefs of Staff, the Central Intelligence Agency, and the Atomic Energy Commission. Several factors prompted the reassessment of U.S. policies. First, "perhaps what did most to trigger reexamination was the reaction in the Eighteen-Nation Committee, among world leaders, and within the United States to the resumption of atmospheric testing." During the spring of 1962, "as a consequence of the Soviet and American test series, the level of radioactivity resulting from fallout increased significantly. . . . Some scientists felt that concentration of certain elements [Cesium 137 and Strontium 90] . . . reached dangerous heights, and suggested that, if atmospheric testing continued at existing rates, some protective measures might have to be taken to guard against contaminated foodstuffs, particularly milk for children."[11] The United States was also in the process of changing its nuclear strategy to a "no cities" doctrine, which emphasized military installations in strategic targeting policy. This doctrine, combined with a shift to land-based missiles and reduced reliance on strategic bomber forces, demonstrated the United States' diminishing interest in high-yield weapons. Finally, new research as part of the Vela project suggested that the detection of underground tests was easier than previously thought. Estimates of the number of earthquakes in the Soviet Union was reduced on the basis of new scientific information. This would make it easier to detect nuclear explosions with seismic monitoring devices, which, if placed in deep holes rather than near the surface, could increase their sensitivity by several orders of magnitude. Explosions detonated in soft earth, as opposed to granite, though harder to detect with seismic equipment because they would be muffled by the surrounding medium, would be easier to detect by visual means because they would produce a cavity on the surface of the ground.

The ACDA's ad hoc group considered several options, including a partial test ban treaty that would ban testing in the atmosphere, in outer space, and underwater; a comprehensive test ban; a technical evaluation of the eight-nation proposal with no new treaty proposal; and a modified comprehensive treaty that would insist on some on-site inspections but would rely on a system of "internationally coordinated and standardized national control posts."[12] The United States and the United Kingdom decided to submit two new draft treaties to the ENDC, one calling for a comprehensive test ban, the other, for a partial test ban. At the same time, within the ENDC some countries felt that because there were so many obstacles to a comprehensive test ban between the nuclear powers, a partial test ban covering atmospheric, underwater, and outer-space testing might be more feasible. But there was no unanimity. The Soviets and their Eastern European allies rejected a partial test ban, and among the eight, views were divided. Sweden offered its own proposals to break the stalemate in the CTB context. On August 1, 1962, the Swedish delegate Alva Myrdal presented a detailed proposal that would use existing meteorological and seismological observation posts to help monitor nuclear testing, including some 7,800 land stations, 2 meteorological satellites, and some 3,000 ships.

On August 27, 1962, the United States and the United Kingdom tabled their draft treaties in ENDC. In Washington, the partial test ban idea had been under consideration for some time and had been approved as the fallback position. The draft of a partial test ban treaty received greater attention within the ENDC. Under the proposal, a partial test ban would cover testing "in the atmosphere, above the atmosphere, or in territorial or high seas; or in any other environment if such explosion causes radioactive debris to be present outside the territorial limits of the state."[13] The Soviets, however, rejected both Western proposals. They retorted that the comprehensive treaty proposal was simply a restatement of the previous Western position, even though under the new proposal inspections could be carried out by neutral and nonaligned third parties. They also opposed a partial test ban proposal because it would continue to allow underground tests. Although Soviet rejection of these proposals effectively dampened any hope that there would be an agreement, representatives of the eight nations continued their efforts to bring the two sides together, suggesting that a moratorium or "voluntary restraint" on underground testing along with a partial test ban might facilitate agreement on a comprehensive test ban. At a press conference on August 29, President Kennedy gave his approval to January 1, 1963, as a target date to cease weapons testing, and on September 7, 1962, the ENDC formally recessed.

On October 15, 1962, the Cuban missile crisis began, when U.S. intelligence discovered that the Soviet Union was constructing sites for medium-range missiles in western Cuba. The crisis brought the world closer than it had ever been to nuclear war, dramatizing the dangers of brinkmanship while illustrating the need for better communications and crisis control.[14] It also played a major role in resumption of negotiations for a limited test ban treaty by dramatizing the dangers of confrontation and the need for a more cooperative and conciliatory approach in superpower relations. As the crisis wound down, Nikita Khrushchev wrote to the president: "We would like to continue the exchange of views on the prohibition of atomic and thermonuclear weapons, on general disarmament and other problems relating to the relaxation of international tension." In his reply, Kennedy agreed that "perhaps now, as we step back from danger, we can make some real progress in this vital field. I think we should give priority to questions relating to the proliferation of nuclear weapons . . . and to the great effort for a nuclear test ban."[15] As Theodore Sorensen explains, "in response to Khrushchev's talk of new accords after the Cuban crisis, Kennedy put the test-ban treaty first. Indeed, since the day of his inauguration, a test ban had been his principal hope for a first step towards disarmament and other pacts. He had termed the collapse of the Geneva talks in 1961 'the most disappointing event' of his first year. He had hopes that a new treaty would be the most rewarding event of his third. The time was right."[16]

These communications raised new hopes that a test ban agreement could soon be reached. In the U.N. General Assembly a general debate began on the issue of nuclear tests.[17] During the course of the debate, representatives from Argentina, Brazil, Colombia, Peru, Australia, Canada, China, Denmark, Greece, Iran, Italy, Japan, New Zealand, Norway, the Philippines, the Federation of Malaya, Spain, Ireland, and Somalia spoke out in favor of a partial test ban as a first step that would lead the way to a comprehensive test ban. Thirty-seven non-nuclear states, including all eight nonaligned nations of the ENDC, introduced a resolution calling for the cessation of atmospheric tests by January 1, 1963, and a comprehensive or limited treaty accompanied by an interim suspension of underground testing. A second resolution, introduced by the United States and the United Kingdom, called for a comprehensive treaty with international verification or a limited treaty covering the atmosphere, the oceans, and space. Both resolutions were adopted with some modifications, although the Soviet Union and its allies voted against both proposals. During this period, both sides continued with nuclear testing, although on November 4, President Kennedy announced that the United States had concluded its atmospheric and high-altitude explosions testing program.

The third session of the ENDC, which ran from November 26 to December 20, 1962, was prompted by the U.N. resolution calling for a complete halt to all testing by January 1, 1963. Although the conference ultimately stalled on the question of on-site inspection and the difficulty of monitoring underground explosions, there were signs that the Soviet position was loosening. On December 3, the Soviets indicated that underground nuclear explosions could be monitored through the use of automatic, or "black box," seismic recorders stationed in the territory of nuclear powers and adjacent countries. The Soviets also signaled that they would allow foreign personnel onto their territory to deliver and replace these black boxes, an important concession over their previous position. Then, on December 19, 1962, Khrushchev sent Kennedy a letter in which he indicated that the Soviet Union was "prepared to agree to two to three inspections a year being carried out in the territory of each of the nuclear powers."

Khrushchev stated that "the time has come to put an end once and for all to nuclear tests, to draw a line through such tests."[18] The letter arrived at the same time Kennedy was holding meetings with British Prime Minister Harold Macmillan in Nassau, in the Bahamas, discussing the Skybolt crisis.[19] Khrushchev's letter took the Soviet position back to what it had been prior to November 28, 1961, opening the door to direct on-site inspections, even though the figure was lower than what the West was prepared to accept. Kennedy wrote back, welcoming the change in the Soviet position. Although he indicated that the Soviet's proposed two or three inspections were lower than the eight to ten figure the United States had mentioned in earlier negotiations, he suggested that the two sides could resolve their differences in direct discussions.

Informal talks between the United States and Soviet representatives began in Washington on January 14, 1963. They were later moved to New York, and British representatives were included. However, these discussions proved unproductive and stalled over the number of on-site inspections and the location of unmanned seismic stations to monitor underground testing. The United States wanted more inspections than the Soviet Union was prepared to accept, and once more negotiations were broken off.

The ENDC reconvened on February 12, 1963, a month later than planned. Both the United States and the Soviet Union lobbied hard in the ENDC to get the nonaligned members to support their respective positions regarding on-site inspections. Although some progress was made with regard to "challenge" inspections on each other's territory, the deadlock continued over the number of on-site inspections and how these would be carried out, even though the United States indicated that it was now prepared to lower the number of inspections to seven.

While negotiations continued in Geneva, the U.S. administration found itself facing mounting opposition to a comprehensive test ban from voices on Capitol Hill and in the Pentagon.[20] On February 21, 1963, Senator Thomas J. Dodd, a Democrat from Connecticut, argued on the Senate floor that the United States was making too many concessions in the Geneva negotiations and should return to its "original Geneva formula."[21] On February 28, Senators Richard B. Russell, Stuart Symington, and Henry Jackson, all influential Democrats, sent a letter to the president indicating that they could not support the most recent U.S. proposal for a comprehensive test ban. The Joint Committee on Atomic Energy attacked the verification aspects of the draft comprehensive test ban treaty while expressing support for a vigorous program of nuclear testing.

The president's own views about a test ban were linked to his fears about the growing dangers of nuclear proliferation. On February 8, President Kennedy stated at a press conference that the main reason to pursue a test ban was to arrest the spread of nuclear weapons: "I think people who attack the effort should bear in mind that the alternative is the spread of these weapons to a government which may be irresponsible, or which by accident may initiate a general nuclear war."[22] At a subsequent press conference on March 21, he declared that "the reason why he kept moving and working on this question [of a test ban], taking up a good deal of energy and effort, is because personally, I am haunted by the feeling that by 1970, unless we are successful, there may be 10 nuclear powers instead of 4, and by 1975, 15 or 20."[23]

Glenn Seaborg, chairman of the United States Atomic Energy Commission, recalls: "An important consideration in Kennedy's thinking was the power that the Chinese would have with nuclear weapons and how they would use that power. If a test ban treaty could lessen this prospect, the United States should take much forethought before turning it down. Kennedy suspected that the Soviets were thinking much the same way about it. He said that a test ban that affected only the Russians and the United States would have only limited value but, if there was a chance it could affect the Chinese, it could be worth very much indeed. In this sense it was more important to the world situation than it had been a year or two ago."[24] Kennedy was probably right about Soviet thinking. The Politburo had broken off relations with China, and the Soviets were fearful about having a battle with two major powers. In fact, Soviet foreign minister Andrei Gromyko was seeking a nonaggression pact with the United States at this time. Scientists were also having more input into policy in the Soviet Union after 1958, and there was growing East-West scientific contact. However, with the deadlock in Geneva and the impending threat of Chinese nuclear tests, hope for a test ban began to fade.

In retrospect, the intermediary role played by British Prime Minister Harold Macmillan may have been crucial to bridging the gulf between the United States and the Soviet Union and recovering some of the momentum that the negotiations had lost. On March 8, on receiving news of the stalemate in Geneva, Harold Macmillan called an "urgent lunch" to discuss strategy, at which Sir William Penney indicated that it was "quite clear that it's not science but politics which holds back the President." On March 16, Macmillan wrote to Kennedy to remind him that since the December 1961 conference, the Soviets had come to accept the principle of three annual inspections and the West had moved from twenty to seven: "So, from the man-in-the-street's point of view, the two sides have come a great deal nearer. Indeed, to the layman, we would seem so near that it would be almost inconceivable that the gulf could not be bridged." Macmillan told Kennedy that "the Test Ban is the most important step that we can take towards unravelling this frightful tangle of fear and suspicions in East-West relations." He also pointed out that the prospects of Germany acquiring nuclear weapons in the long run could only be averted by a test ban. Macmillan suggested several possibilities for resuming the initiative, including a possible summit meeting between Khrushchev and Kennedy in Geneva, and suggested that Kennedy might send his brother, Robert Kennedy, or Averell Harriman to discover what Soviet intentions might be.[25]

Kennedy welcomed Macmillan's suggestion that they should send a joint letter to Khrushchev that would include a new draft proposal. During the month of April, there were extensive consultations between the British and the Americans. The joint letter was delivered to Khrushchev on April 24.

Khrushchev's reply, which came on May 8, 1963, was rude and harsh. It indicated that there was now no need for inspections and no point going over old arguments. The letter charged that the demand for on-site inspections was nothing more that an effort by NATO to send spies into Soviet territory. Khrushchev suggested that if there was no hope for agreement, the Soviet Union would take whatever measures were necessary to strengthen its own security. Nonetheless, at the end of his letter Khrushchev indicated that he would be prepared to receive emissaries to discuss a test ban.[26]

The British ambassador to Washington, David Ormsby-Gore, advised the administration, over State Department objections, that Khrushchev's first conciliatory letter be answered and his second, more recent and abrasive letter, be ignored, along the lines of Robert Kennedy's advice regarding Khrushchev's two letters during the Cuban missile crisis.[27] President Kennedy agreed to this advice from the British. He also hoped that the Hotline Agreement, which had been signed earlier in the year, meant that one could do business with the Soviets. On May 30 a short letter was sent to Khrushchev supporting the idea of an exchange of emissaries at the end of June or in July.[28]

In a subsequent letter of June 8, Khrushchev agreed to set a formal date for the negotiation in Moscow and suggested July 15. In the meantime, congressional attitudes toward a test ban began to shift. Senator Dodd had an extensive exchange with Adrian Fisher of the ACDA. As Arthur Schlesinger Jr. explains: "The correspondence brought new points to Dodd's attention and the Connecticut Senator had the grace to change his mind. On May 27 he joined with Hubert Humphrey and thirty-two other senators in introducing a resolution declaring it "the sense of the Senate" that the United States should again offer the Soviet Union a limited test ban; if the Russians rejected the plan, the United States should nevertheless 'pursue it with vigor, seeking the widest possible public support.'"[29] At the same time, it was readily apparent that the Senate had serious reservations about the desirability of a comprehensive test ban. In a private survey of Senate opinion conducted by Senator Joseph S. Clark in May, it appeared that only fifty-seven senators, a number that fell short of the two-thirds majority required for Senate treaty approval, were prepared to offer their support for the American draft proposal for a comprehensive test ban involving seven on-site inspections annually.[30]

Public interest in the test ban, however, was growing. In May 1963, groups such as the Women's Strike for Peace and the Women's International League for Peace and Freedom lobbied members of Congress on behalf of the test ban. Numerous peace groups also made serious efforts to alert the public to the dangers of future testing, fallout, and the arms race. The Senate was showered with letters, phone calls, and petitions.[31] Public opinion had supported the moratorium on nuclear testing during the second Eisenhower administration. In a poll taken in November 1959, four out of five people supported an extension of the moratorium for another year. But the U-2 crisis, the Cuban revolution, and the cancellation of a U.S.-Soviet summit in Paris had helped bring about a change in public attitudes. By December 1960, half the American public believed it was impossible to reach a peaceful settlement with the Soviet Union. In June 1961, only 27 percent of the American public believed that the United States should not resume its nuclear testing program. In a March 1962 poll, 67 percent of Americans approved atmospheric testing and only 21 percent expressed concern about radioactive fallout in the atmosphere. But by July 1963, the aftermath of the Cuban missile crisis, 52 percent of the public expressed its unqualified support for a test ban; after the treaty was negotiated and signed, 81 percent would take this position.[32]

On June 10, President Kennedy gave the commencement address at the American University in Washington. He reaffirmed his desire for a test ban and announced that high-level discussions on a comprehensive test ban treaty would begin soon with the Soviet Union and the United Kingdom. He also stated that the United States would discontinue its atmospheric tests as long as the Soviet Union did likewise. One cannot underestimate the importance of Kennedy's speech and the message it sent the Soviets. It offered Khrushchev a clear way to an agreement with the United States, if he wanted one.

The undersecretary of state for political affairs, Averell Harriman, who had been ambassador to Moscow in 1943–46, was chosen to head the United States negotiating team. Lord Hailsham, minister of science and an ardent supporter of the test ban, was chosen to head the team from the United Kingdom.

In preparatory meetings for these negotiations, it became clear that bureaucratic and congressional support for a comprehensive test ban was lacking. The joint chiefs of staff opposed a comprehensive test ban because they thought the Soviet Union might cheat and could make important gains through clandestine testing. The air force was concerned about treaty restrictions that might prevent the study of missile-site vulnerability and the development of very high-yield weapons. The navy did not want to compromise its ability to test nuclear devices under water. The army was worried about prohibitions on the use of tactical nuclear weapons in the training and development of an antimissile system that was under army jurisdiction. The Atomic Energy Commission feared that a test ban would increase technical uncertainty and weaken the United States' nuclear stockpile.[33]

In a speech given in East Berlin on July 2, Khrushchev accepted Kennedy's idea of a partial test ban limited to the oceans and the atmosphere, dropping, for the first time, Soviet insistence on a policed moratorium on the underground testing as part of a partial test ban. At a White House meeting on July 9, just before Harriman was to leave for the Soviet Union, the joint chiefs expressed doubts about their ability to support even a limited test ban. Nevertheless, Kennedy instructed Harriman to try to achieve a comprehensive treaty, but, failing that, to seek a limited treaty banning nuclear testing in the oceans, the air, and space.[34] On July 15, the formal negotiation for a limited test ban began. It was concluded a mere twelve days later.[35]

Explaining Outcomes

The story of the negotiations that led to the Limited Test Ban Treaty of 1963 is a lengthy and complicated one. Having failed to reach an agreement on a comprehensive test ban, the parties settled on the limited test ban option. However, a number of important themes emerge from this tangled tale.

Crisis

Crisis is a crucial variable in the story of the test ban. Initially, negotiations were prompted by a growing sense of crisis in the scientific community (and the international community at large) about the adverse consequences for human health of radioactive fallout from nuclear testing in the atmosphere. The *Lucky Dragon* incident dramatized the urgency of this problem and the need for international cooperation to bring about a halt to testing, particularly in the atmosphere. In this respect, public perceptions of a looming catastrophe if unrestricted nuclear testing continued encouraged policy makers to consider the negotiation option and an integrative or cooperative solution to the problem. However, this was not the only crisis in the test ban story. The crisis in U.S.-Soviet relations brought on by the shooting down of an American U-2 spy plane and the advent of intercontinental ballistic missiles, where the Soviets believed they had the psychological advantage, helped seal the fate of the first round of formal negotiations on a test ban in Geneva. In this respect, these external events had a distributive impact on bargaining behavior by further encouraging the parties to see their interests in zero-sum terms.

In contrast, the Cuban missile crisis had the opposite, that is, an integrative, effect on the parties by forcing them to recognize their mutual interest in avoiding nuclear war and the need to find ways of moving their relationship to a more cooperative footing. Because the test ban issue was already on the agenda and had been the subject of lengthy negotiations, it was relatively easy for the leaders of the great powers to seize upon a test ban as an important symbol of a new era in great-power cooperation and arms control. Had the Cuban missile crisis not occurred when it did, evidence suggests that a treaty might not have been negotiated, because of the deep suspicions that marked East-West relations and obviously plagued the test ban negotiations.

However, the more important factor in getting an actual agreement through may have been China. President Kennedy himself worried openly about the dangers of a Chinese nuclear arsenal, and the growing rift in Soviet-Chinese relations was of major concern to the Soviets. The fact that both Kennedy and Khrushchev were concerned at the same time about China's potential to acquire nuclear weapons may have clinched the deal.

Consensual Knowledge and the Debate over Compliance

The question of what level of confidence to place in existing scientific techniques and methods for monitoring nuclear explosions was a key issue throughout the negotiations and obviously the most contentious because of the high levels of uncertainty involved. To whatever extent a scientific consensus on the verification requirements for a comprehensive test ban existed at the Conference of Experts in Geneva, it quickly unraveled as new scientific evidence cast doubt on earlier findings. Precisely because the experts could not easily resolve the question of the number of on-site inspections that would be required to effectively monitor underground explosions under a comprehensive test ban, the quota issue became a political football and the most contentious issue in the negotiations. However, the substance of this debate was not science but politics: the Soviets feared that the United States wanted high quotas in order to collect military secrets; the United States interpreted Soviet preference for small quotas as proof that the Soviets were untrustworthy and would try to circumvent a test ban treaty. Even though something of a scientific consensus did later emerge that underground explosions at very low yields could be monitored with a fairly high level of confidence, the political pressures on Kennedy were such that he could not agree to a comprehensive test ban— at least not on terms acceptable to the Soviets. And one can speculate that Khrushchev was probably under similar pressures from his own military.

What ultimately produced an agreement was not the emergence of consensual knowledge per se but the political realization that something had to be done to halt the fallout from nuclear weapons tests and slow the spread of nuclear technology and weaponry. To be sure, scientists were closely involved in defining the options and shaping the prenegotiation and negotiating agenda, but the critical choices lay with the politicians who, in making their choices, were responding to the pressures and interests of a wider audience worried about the effects of atmospheric testing on the health of children .

Bridging and Bargaining Strategies

The key actors in the negotiations leading to a test ban were the United States, the Soviet Union, and the United Kingdom. Harold Macmillan played a brokering role in the negotiations by coaxing Kennedy and Khrushchev not to break off negotiations and suggesting several alternative possibilities for Kennedy to resume the initiative. Various bridging proposals to address the issue of inspections were also offered by the group of Eight Nations in the ENDC. Although none of these proposals were acceptable to the great powers, they helped to maintain the negotiating momentum while creating external pressure for an agreement—along with the various resolutions of the U.N. General Assembly. In view of the countervailing pressures both in Congress and in the Pentagon, these external pressures also strengthened the president's hand in dealing with his own domestic critics.

Issue Decomposition and Sequencing

Issue decomposition and sequencing tactics eventually paved the way for a partial test ban agreement. Initial proposals for a test ban were couched in terms of a comprehensive agreement that would ban nuclear tests in all four environments and were also linked—whether for propaganda purposes or other reasons—to other disarmament measures. As negotiations evolved, however, the test ban was delinked from other disarmament measures, and discussions centered on two alternatives: a comprehensive ban and a partial ban that would allow for underground tests and might eventually pave the way to a comprehensive test ban. Because the compliance issue could not be resolved to the satisfaction of the parties, they eventually abandoned their search for a comprehensive ban and negotiated a partial agreement as the preferred alternative to no agreement at all. Prior to going into the final round of negotiations in Moscow, the U.S. administration had already settled on a partial test ban as its primary objective if Soviet objections to on-site inspection provisions for a comprehensive test ban proved insurmountable.

Although some—including Harold Macmillan himself—have argued with hindsight that the negotiations represented a missed opportunity and that had there been the requisite political will a comprehensive test ban could have been reached, it is difficult to see how Kennedy could have secured Senate approval of such a treaty, since suspicions about Soviet intentions in the aftermath of the Cuban missile crisis were still running high. And Kennedy was reluctant to press the issue, because he felt his political mandate—given his narrow margin of victory in the election—was weak.

Leadership

Finally, it is evident that entrepreneurial leadership was a crucial ingredient in the test ban negotiations. Negotiations had floundered under Eisenhower, partly because it was not a high priority and he was unwilling to devote the personal attention the issue required. Kennedy made the test ban a top priority for his administration and his own personal interest and direct intervention carried negotiations forward. In fact, the final round of negotiations in Moscow was run directly from the White House. The close bond forged between Kennedy and Macmillan also gave Macmillan access to the American president and helped nudge negotiations forward when they seemed in danger of stalling.

In short, a combination of factors—crisis, bridging, incremental bargaining strategies, and leadership—explain the eventual outcome of the test ban negotiations. At the same time, public and international pressure on the nuclear powers kept negotiations going, and eventually both external pressure and circumstance (the Cuban missile crisis) conspired to create the ripe moment for Kennedy, Macmillan, and Khrushchev together to exert the kind of decisive leadership that was required for a limited test ban agreement. These same elements accounted for the success of multilateral negotiations in arms control over two decades later, when issues of confidence building and conventional force reduction moved to the forefront of the arms control agenda.

4 The Stockholm Conference on Confidence- and Security-Building Measures and Disarmament in Europe

Confidence- and security-building measures were the focus of the first major success in conventional arms control as the Cold War began to wind down in the late 1980s. Although formal negotiations leading to the Stockholm Agreement lasted some two and a half years, they were the product of an extended set of prenegotiations dating back, by some accounts, to the early 1950s. The negotiations were in a genuine sense "multilateral" because they involved the NATO and Warsaw Pact countries and the neutral and nonaligned (NNA) nations of Europe. Unlike many of the other cases examined in this volume, consensual knowledge was not a factor in the prenegotiation and negotiation phases of this accord. As a result of an evolutionary process of incremental trial-and-error learning based on previous practices and encounters, the diplomats and military experts who conducted the negotiations had acquired a firm grasp of the issues and the risks and uncertainties associated with arms control confidence- and security-building measures; hence there was no need to rely on the advice of outside experts. However, like the other cases in this volume, extranegotiatory factors played a crucial role in propelling the negotiations forward from the prenegotiation to the negotiation stage and from the negotiation stage to the final agreement.

First, a key third party, France, was responsible for advancing the idea of a conference to address the issue of disarmament in Europe. (Earlier, the inclusion of confidence-building measures in the Helsinki Final Act had been the result of active diplomatic pressure by the neutral and non-aligned states.) Second, the growing crisis in East-West relations in the early 1980s and the resumption of the Cold War paradoxically strengthened interest in the Stockholm Conference and the delegates' desire to use it as a forum "for serious negotiations rather than fruitless propaganda encounters."[1] Third, mediation was crucial in moving prenegotiations and negotiation forward. Without the presence and active involvement of third-party intermediaries, like the NNA countries, it is unlikely that an agreement would have been achieved. Fourth, domestic developments, in particular the emergence of a new political leadership in the Soviet Union and a president in the United States who was keen to see the negotiations succeed, proved crucial at various junctures in the negotiation and to the final outcome. Finally, much of the hard bargaining concerned questions of verification and compliance and how to address the legitimate national security interests of the principal parties to the negotiation, namely, the United States and the Soviet Union. Ultimately, the willingness of the Soviet Union to overcome its longstanding opposition to on-site inspection paved the way for a final agreement. In this regard, the recognition of a new set of security interests based on a conception of "common," as opposed to "national," security led to a new conventional arms agreement for Europe at Stockholm.

Prenegotiation

The prenegotiation phase of the Stockholm Conference on Confidence- and Security-Building Measures and Disarmament in Europe (CCSBMDE) in one sense can be said to have begun in February 1954, when Soviet Foreign Minister Vyacheslav Molotov proposed a draft treaty on collective security and nonaggression at the four-power ministerial conference in Berlin. At the same time, he also proposed a conference that would lead to German disarmament and neutralization as a prelude to German reunification. The timing of the proposal was clearly an attempt to prevent the Federal Republic of Germany's rearmament and membership in NATO, which occurred in the spring of the following year. Following the FRG's entrance into NATO and the creation of the Warsaw Pact in response, the Soviets again proposed a security zone covering the two Germanys and neighboring states, which would limit armaments and be subject to inspection. The Western response, in what came to be known as the second Eden plan (named after British Prime Minister Anthony Eden) proposed arms limitations in a zone between a reunified Germany and Eastern Europe, along with special measures for inspection and control of forces that would warn against surprise attack. This proposal was delivered at the Geneva meeting of foreign ministers on October 27, 1955. On October 29, the Soviets responded with an offer similar to their earlier proposal for a demilitarized and reunified Germany.

Various proposals for related and additional confidence- and security-building measures were offered at the 1958 Geneva Surprise Attack Conference and the Eighteen-Nation Disarmament Committee (ENDC) conference. At the Surprise Attack Conference, for example, the Soviets suggested that weapons of mass destruction be eliminated from the two Germanys, armed forces be reduced in tandem, and control posts be set up in predesignated areas to reduce the risks of attack. U.S. proposals at the ENDC were for troop notification measures, direct contact between military observations, direct communication facilities, and aerial and ground-based observations facilities. However, none of these initiatives bore any fruit because of continuing Cold War tensions, successive crises over Berlin (in 1958 and 1961), and an inability of two confrontational alliance systems to agree on the future of German reunification.

On December 14, 1964, Polish Foreign Minister Adam Rapacki suggested the convening of a European security conference, which was endorsed by the Warsaw Pact. The West viewed this as a ploy to derail the proposed NATO Multilateral Nuclear Force (MLF). Following France's withdrawal from NATO's integrated nuclear command structure in 1966, the Soviets reintroduced their earlier proposals for a pan-European security conference that would lead to the liquidation of NATO and the Warsaw Pact and the removal of all foreign forces from Europe. The plan also called for a denuclearized Germany and a peace settlement that would pave the way for eventual German reunification. The idea of a security conference was resurrected again after the Warsaw Pact invasion of Czechoslovakia in 1968, and on May 6, 1969, Finland formally offered to host a conference on European security. NATO remained skeptical of these offers but announced in May 1970 that it would be willing to begin discussions leading toward a Conference on Security and Cooperation in Europe, provided that it would also include cultural matters and freer movement of peoples and ideas.

At its own meeting in June 1970, the Warsaw Pact offered a similar agenda minus cultural and human rights considerations. In late 1970, the Federal Republic of Germany signed treaties with Poland and the Soviet Union guaranteeing the inviolability of frontiers. In September 1970, the quadripartite agreement on Berlin was concluded, shortly followed, in December 1971, by a treaty between the two Germanys guaranteeing their own frontiers. At the May 1972 meeting between President Richard Nixon and Soviet leader Leonid Brezhnev to sign the SALT (Strategic Arms Limitation Talks) agreements, the Soviets agreed to begin talks on conventional force reductions (MBFR) in exchange for a U.S. commitment to negotiations on the CSCE (Conference on Security and Cooperation in Europe). The ground was thus paved for the CSCE preparatory negotiations, which formally began in Helsinki in December 1972.[2]

Helsinki Conference

The Helsinki preparatory talks agreed to the formation of a subcommittee that would submit "appropriate proposals on confidence-building measures such as the prior notification of major military maneuvers on a basis to be specified by the Conference, and the exchange of observers by invitation at military maneuvers under mutually acceptable conditions."[3] According to John Borawski, "the NATO states sought to inject some military content into the conference on 'security and cooperation' but were opposed to discussing arms reductions or other far-reaching measures that would intrude on MBFR." Nonetheless, the United States was unenthusiastic about CBMs, "viewing them as possessing only marginal military significance and as possibly counterproductive in a crisis by potentially impeding a prompt defensive response." The same was true of France. But other NATO European countries such as Norway, Denmark, and the Netherlands adopted a more serious approach to CBMs and favored notification of major troop movements as well—"a better indicator of potentially hostile activity underfoot or at least a necessary accompaniment to maneuver notification." The countries of the Warsaw Pact were openly hostile to CBMs. "Despite references to 'military detente,' the Soviets desired a relatively brief, pro forma CSCE meeting that would serve first and foremost to codify the post–World War II geopolitical equation and 'create an atmosphere of detente in Europe' and not lengthy negotiations aimed at achieving detailed, substantive accords."[4]

The third group of states involved in the negotiations were the neutral and nonaligned European states (NNA) (Austria, Cyprus, Finland, Liechtenstein, Malta, San Marino, Sweden, Switzerland, and Yugoslavia), which were not parties to the MBFR talks and therefore were keen to develop a military focus to the CSCE that would go beyond moderate CBMs to measures that would restrict military activities and constrain movement of forces.[5]

Whereas the Soviet draft proposal simply called on participating states to "notify each other in advance, on the basis of agreed procedures, of major military maneuvers in specified areas," the NATO position was much more detailed, calling for notification sixty days in advance to all CSCE states of maneuvers at the division level (10,000 or more troops) to "all of Europe" as far east as the Ural mountains.[6] The NNA proposal called for notification thirty days in advance of maneuvers involving 18,000 or more troops. After two years of negotiations, agreement was finally reached on a rudimentary set of CBMs in the Helsinki Final Act. Agreement was reached partly on the basis of a series of modified proposals offered by the NNA states. Under the terms of the agreement, CSCE participants committed themselves to notifying each other of major maneuvers involving more than 25,000 troops and to a voluntary exchange of observers. Voluntary notification of small-scale exercises involving fewer than 25,000 troops was also provided in the agreement. The zone of application covered all of Europe and a 250-kilometer strip of the Soviet Union.

Belgrade

The first review conference of the Helsinki Final Act was held in Belgrade from the fall of 1977 to the spring of 1978. Several new CBM proposals were put on the table by NATO, the NNA nations, and the Warsaw Pact states. NATO proposals sought to raise the number of notifications in order to increase transparency and allow for a better exchange of information. The NNA nations pursued similar objectives with their proposals and also sought promotion of greater openness regarding military budgets. The Warsaw Pact called for a ban on neutron warheads, no-first-use declarations, notification of major military maneuvers, including air and naval maneuvers, and a ban on multinational maneuvers near frontiers. However, there was no agreement on a new set of CBMs at Belgrade because of disputes over Eastern-bloc countries' implementation of human-rights and humanitarian provisions in the Helsinki accords.

The French Proposal, Madrid, and Beyond

On May 25, 1978, French President Valery Giscard D'Estaing proposed the concept of a conference "to discuss disarmament in Europe." The conference "would aim in the first stage at building trust among all the countries of Europe by instituting measures to provide appropriate information and notification and in the second stage at achieving a genuine reduction in weapons within the geostrategic complex of Europe from the Atlantic to the Urals."[7]

The French proposal was motivated by several considerations: a desire to provide an alternative forum to the NATO–Warsaw Pact MBFR talks, which had been underway since 1973; a desire to address the threat of a surprise attack from the Warsaw Pact, which was widely perceived as enjoying conventional military superiority; and a desire to provide a "constructive response" to Soviet proposals for a European security conference, which had emphasized declarations of good will, nonuse of force, and nuclear no-first-use.[8] At the same time, the initiative marked an important change in French policy, since France up to that point had excluded itself from arms control discussions. The French proposal for a Conference on Disarmament in Europe (CDE) contained several elements: data exchanges on force deployments and command structures; measures to reduce the risks of surprise attack, including prenotification of troop and air movements; and stabilization measures that would restrict the size of air and land force maneuvers. Details of the French proposal were formally provided on May 19, 1978.

The European Community and the North Atlantic Council gave their endorsement to the French idea in December 1979, as did the NNA governments. However the United States wanted to link the French proposal to the CSCE, as did a number of other countries. The United States was also concerned that negotiations in the CDE not derail or interfere with negotiations in the MBFR talks. The French CDE proposal was tabled at the second CSCE review conference in Madrid in December 1980.[9] A number of other countries (Sweden, Yugoslavia, and Romania) also offered their own suggestions for confidence- and security-building measures (CSBMs), as they now came to be known, that would eventually pave the way to arms reductions.

Although initially lukewarm to the idea, the Carter administration gave its informal support to the CDE in November 1980 but left the formal decision to the incoming administration of Ronald Reagan. In February 1981, President Reagan announced his formal endorsement of a CDE on the condition that it be linked to the CSCE process, deal only with CSBMs, and not interfere with conventional arms control negotiations occurring in the MBFR talks.

The Soviets, however, took somewhat longer to accept the idea. At the Madrid conference, they made it quite clear they were not happy about confidence-building measures that would extend to the Urals but not include Canada and the United States. If a pan-European confidence-building regime did cover Soviet territory, it would also have to include North America. Nonetheless, by the fall of 1981, they appeared to retract this demand, although they were insistent on the inclusion of adjacent sea, ocean, and air space in insular territories adjacent to Europe. This latter suggestion of a geographic approach to air and naval CSBMs was anathema to NATO because it might limit NATO activities in areas (e.g., the Mediterranean) that were unrelated to European security. The impasse was eventually resolved by a French suggestion that air and sea activities in adjoining areas that were functionally related to notifiable ground force activities would be covered and subject to notification, whereas activities that concerned out-of-area contingencies would not. This proposal proved acceptable to the East, as long as adjoining areas that could support geographic air and naval activities were included as well.

On July 15, 1982, the mandate for the CDE as a substantial and integral part of the CSCE was agreed upon, and January 17, 1984, was the date set for the CDE to begin in Stockholm.

Negotiations

Formal negotiations for the CDE began on the designated date against a backdrop of worsening U.S.-Soviet relations and heightened tensions. The KAL incident had occurred a mere four months earlier, when the Soviets shot down a civilian South Korean airliner, killing everybody on board. Negotiations on an INF (intermediate-range nuclear forces) treaty had been put on hold because of Soviet unhappiness about U.S. deployment of Pershing II and ground-launched cruise missiles in Europe. Strategic arms talks had also reached a hiatus, and the United States was in full swing in pursuing the biggest buildup of its defense establishment since the Korean War.

During the first weeks of the conference, the different negotiation positions became clear as each side tabled its own proposals.[10] Various CSBM proposals were tabled by the different delegation groups:[11]

NATO

Exchange of military information at the beginning of each calendar year; annual forecasts of notifiable military activities (out-of-garrison land activities, mobilization activities involving three or more divisions or 6,000 or more ground troops, and amphibious activities involving three or more battalions or 3,000 troops) and prenotification of such activities forty-five days in advance; observation and verification measures under which observers would be invited from participating states to all notifiable activities, including alerts, and agreement not to interfere with national technical means of verification; and provisions allowing for enhanced communication between participating states.

Romania

Notification thirty days beforehand of military activities involving land or combined forces in excess of 20,000 troops, special forces exceeding 5,000 troops, surface capital ships totaling more than 12 ships, and air forces exceeding 50 aircraft; prenotification of military movements of two or more divisions; prenotification of emergency placing of forces on alert; and a variety of measures to prevent nuclear conflict by error or accident (e.g., nuclear-weapon-free border zones, bans on nuclear-capable ships and aircraft along land and coastal borders).

Neutral and Nonaligned Nations

Prenotification of military maneuvers that would strengthen CBMs in the Helsinki Final Act; prenotification of small-scale maneuvers in adjacent territories; prenotification of amphibious, sea-transported, airborne, and airmobile maneuvers; notification of major military movements; provision for observers of maneuvers and movements; notification of major military redeployments; notification of other major military activities (e.g., alerts); prescribed ceilings on military maneuvers; and geographic restrictions on certain kinds of force deployments.

Soviets

No-first-use of nuclear weapons; treaty on nonuse of military force and maintenance of peaceful relations; chemical weapons ban in Europe; zero increases in military spending to be followed by spending reductions; support for nuclear-weapon-free zones in various parts of Europe; CSBMs covering numerical ceilings on ground force exercises; advance notification of major ground, naval, and air exercises conducted independently or jointly in Europe; advance notification of major force movements and redeployments; and observation of major military exercises.[12]

Malta

Exchange of information on armed forces stationed in the Mediterranean; prenotification of naval maneuvers; restrictions on naval deployments; observation and verification of notified activities; and security measures obliging signatories to refrain from use of force against riparian states.

The Soviet proposal was essentially a restatement of previous Warsaw Pact positions. NATO's preference was for "militarily meaningful" CSBMs. The NNA countries, which were an important swing vote in the conference, offered a set of proposals that were similar to those of NATO but went further in setting limits on the way forces could be deployed.[13]

The pace of negotiations was forced when, on June 4, 1984, American President Ronald Reagan responded positively to the Warsaw Pact request for confidence-building measures that would subscribe to the principle of the nonuse of force. In a speech before the Irish Parliament, he indicated that the United States would reaffirm "the principle not to use force" if doing so would bring the Soviets into negotiating agreements on CSBMs. Although the Soviets continued to press the conference to address "large-scale political measures," they were unsuccessful in getting the other participants to broaden the mandate that had been agreed to at Madrid. Moreover, given the high state of tensions in East-West relations, most delegates realized that Stockholm was "the only game in town" and that turning it into a propaganda circus might jeopardize East-West relations even further.[14]

In the early rounds of negotiation in the spring and summer of 1985, each side tabled detailed proposals outlining its suggestions for notification and observation of military activities. The NATO allies introduced their proposal in the spring. The Warsaw Pact responded with a series of working papers detailing the pact's views on notification and observation measures in the early summer. The neutral and nonaligned countries worked hard on their own comprehensive proposal, which was formally tabled in November. The fact that the conference was operating under a deadline, namely, the next review meeting of the CSCE in Vienna in November 1986, forced the pace of negotiations.

As negotiations moved forward, the key differences between the NATO and Warsaw Pact positions were sharpened. They centered on a Western preference for military-technical proposals versus a Soviet preference for political-legal ones. Other differences surfaced over the kinds of notifiable military activities, operational constraints, and verification measures to be covered by the agreement. According to the U.S. ambassador to the talks, James Goodby, the main problems to be overcome before an agreement could be reached were the size of land force operations to be covered by the agreement, with the Soviets favoring large-scale military activities and NATO operations at a lower level; out-of-garrison activities, with NATO favoring a more restrictive definition than that of the Soviets; the inclusion of air and naval operations, with NATO maintaining that only combined operations related to land force operations be included in the agreement and the Soviets favoring inclusion of all independent air and naval operations; NATO's preference for on-site inspections and the Soviets' for inspection by "national technical means"; the NATO proposal for annual information exchanges covering the structure and location of land and land-based air forces; and a Soviet preference for a mandatory ceiling on land force exercises (40,000 men) versus NATO's preference for constraints on military operations and annual forecasts of military activities.[15]

The Soviet penchant for secrecy lay behind their rejection of the NATO proposal for information exchanges and on-site inspection. As Goodby writes, "all of these proposals obviously had at their root a traditional Soviet belief that security can be found in secrecy rather than in openness. . . . In fact, Warsaw Pact countries sometimes spoke of NATO proposals as likely to create the opposite of confidence—suspicion. Thus the contrast between the relatively open West and the relatively closed East became a major obstacle to negotiation of a successful agreement."[16]

The Soviets also wanted to sign a nonaggression pact between themselves and the United States. This had been a long-standing objective in their approach to arms control, conventional arms control in particular. At the same time, they were upset that U.S. territory was not covered by the negotiations, whereas Soviet territory was. Part of the problem was that geography introduced asymmetry into the negotiations, and the Soviets tried to compensate for this by proposing a notification ceiling of 40,000 men, sufficiently high to only occasionally affect Soviet territory. Their emphasis on independent air and naval activities also aimed at covering U.S. activities in these areas by broadening the scope of the agreement.

With the November 19–22, 1985, summit meeting in Geneva between President Reagan and Soviet leader Mikhail Gorbachev (who had become General Secretary in March), the negotiations gained new impetus. The two leaders announced their desire "to facilitate . . . an early and successful completion of the work of the [CDE] conference."[17] However, in the next round of negotiations in Geneva in January 1986, the Soviets continued to flog their proposals for a treaty on the "mutual . . . non-use of military force," although there was modest progress on CSBM negotiations. At the same time, Gorbachev suggested that the question of notification of naval activities on the high seas might be deferred to a later stage of the conference, thus effectively removing one of the key stumbling blocks in the negotiations, although the Soviets continued to press for notification of air activities not tied to ground force maneuvers.

The threshold for notification of land force maneuvers was lowered from 20,000 troops to 18,000 (a figure still well above the NATO position of 6,000) in the next round of negotiations in April and May 1986. The Soviets and their Warsaw Pact allies also made new proposals on notification of air activities, moving in the direction of NATO's own functional approach. In a speech delivered in East Berlin on April 18, Gorbachev called for nuclear weapons reductions in Europe and for an agreement to be reached on "substantial reductions in all the components of the land forces and tactical air forces of the European states and the relevant forces of the USA and Canada deployed in Europe."[18] Gorbachev also spoke about the need for on-site inspection involving "international" forms of verification. His speech was followed on June 11 by a Warsaw Pact communiqué (known as the second Budapest Appeal) calling for pan-European conventional and nuclear arms control talks that could be held either in the second phase of the CDE or in an expanded MBFR forum or some new forum that would include Canada and the United States.

The Budapest Appeal underlined the importance of completing the first stage of negotiations in the CDE before moving on to new negotiations on arms reductions. Although the declaration did not offer any new proposals, it gave renewed hope that an agreement would be reached before the Vienna conference. But by the early summer of 1986, the conference seemed to be stalled again. On June 30, 1986, the Canadian ambassador to the CDE, Tom Delworth, stated that "this negotiation is still spinning its wheels in the sands of political indecision and time is passing quickly."[19] However, a short time later some important breakthroughs were achieved, largely as a result of Soviet concessions on a number of key issues.

At a meeting in Moscow between Gorbachev and French President François Mitterand in July, the French delegation was informed that the Soviets were prepared to drop their insistence that notification of independent air activities be included in the agreement. The Soviets also dropped their requirement to define the agenda for a second stage of the conference. The head of the Soviet delegation also made a very important concession, in his closing plenary statement, on the issue of on-site inspection. He noted that the Warsaw Pact countries "are ready to consider the issue of inspection and believe that it is also possible to move forward in this area. In particular, the socialist countries are ready to record agreement that the participating states will conduct on-site inspection of confidence-building measures in the process of verification of reductions and armed forces and conventional armaments."[20]

The final round of negotiations began on August 19. At the opening plenary session, the Soviet ambassador to the talks, Oleg Grinevsky, announced that his country was prepared to agree to on-site inspections on a quota basis. This announcement broke the logjam on verification and was followed by further concessions by the Soviets to previous Western demands. The accord reached in September represented the first major security accord since the Strategic Arms Limitation Talks agreement signed by the United States and the Soviet Union in 1979. It covered all of Europe, from the Atlantic to the Urals, and provided for new rules for the notification, inspection, and observation of military exercises, requiring all countries to give advance notice of all maneuvers above the level of an army division, thereby making the military situation in Europe more predictable.[21] The agreement stipulated that the members of NATO and the Warsaw Pact must notify the other bloc at least forty-two days in advance when planning military activities involving 13,000 or more soldiers, 300 or more tanks, 200 fixed-wing sorties, or transfers of a division equivalent. A country conducting military maneuvers involving 17,000 or more soldiers must invite observers from other participants in the Stockholm Conference. When maneuvers involve amphibious landings or paratroopers, countries must notify the other side if 3,000 or more soldiers take part and invite observers if the number of troops is 5,000 or more.

If one country suspects another is conducting sizable military maneuvers without notifying the other side, it can demand on-site inspection using aircraft or land vehicles. The request can be made within twenty-four hours of the reported violations. The two sides compromised on the number of on-site inspections a country would have to allow, agreeing on at least three annually. However, each country would be allowed to request only one inspection of another country's forces each year. Furthermore, each November 15, participating states must provide the others with a schedule of all planned military activities involving 40,000 or more troops over the next two-year period (no activities involving more than 75,000 troops were permitted without a one-year calendar forecast). On Western insistence, the accord contained detailed rules on how the inspection teams may travel and communicate. The accords required NATO and the Warsaw Pact to notify each other of roughly twenty exercises a year and to invite foreign military observers to about ten military exercises. The U.S. delegation head, Robert Barry, said that the Stockholm Agreement had "a very positive effect on the security situation in Europe"; he was, nevertheless, not totally happy, since the West had been forced to give up its demands for much more detailed exchanges of information, which would have allowed both sides to create a complete database on the military forces in Europe.[22]

Explaining Outcomes

Crisis

The formal negotiations began against a backdrop of heightened tensions in U.S.-Soviet relations, which had deteriorated to their lowest point in many years. This crisis atmosphere dramatized the need for dialogue and a more cooperative relationship between East and West. The Stockholm Conference, ironically, was the immediate beneficiary of this strained relationship. As Goodby notes, "The Soviet invasion of Afghanistan, Soviet pressure on Poland, the imposition of martial law in that country, the Soviet bitter reaction to the INF [Intermediate-Range Nuclear Forces] deployment—all contributed to a mood of tension in Western Europe and naturally affected everything connected with the Helsinki process. Just as the Soviet negotiators had finished their work, Soviet air defense units downed a South Korean civilian airliner, triggering a burst of outrage through the Western world and bringing U.S.-Soviet relations to their lowest point in years."[23]

At the same time, ironically, the collapse of detente caused the United States to take the whole CSCE process more seriously. James Macintosh argues that initially the United States neither took the CSCE process very seriously nor wanted "to allow it to impair the operation of what was, from the U.S. perspective, the more important bilateral U.S./Soviet Union relationship. Only as detente collapsed did the United States treat the CSCE as a useful forum."[24] The Stockholm Conference was the only game in town, given the Soviet walkout from the INF talks, the suspension of the Strategic Arms Reduction Talks (START) following NATO deployment of Pershing II and ground-launched cruise missiles (1983), and the failure to agree to a date for the next session of the MBFR talks. By the end of 1983, almost all formal arms control contacts between East and West had been severed, and only one contact survived: the consensus of thirty-five CSCE states reached at Madrid in 1983 to open the Stockholm Conference on January 17, 1983. The fact that it was the only forum made Stockholm an important venue for a much wider range of East-West political issues than just the negotiation of CSBMs. This was both an advantage and a disadvantage for the Stockholm negotiations, because progress became linked to external events and developments beyond the immediate negotiations.

Consensual Knowledge

The development of consensual knowledge was not a factor in the negotiations on CSBMs. Nor were there epistemic communities involved in efforts to shape and manipulate the negotiating agenda. However, the negotiations themselves took place between military and arms control experts well versed in the exacting details of arms control and confidence-building measures. Goodby observes that even though the multilateral negotiating machinery was cumbersome, "one should never underestimate the creativity of an assemblage of highly qualified professional diplomats and military officers from some of the world's most sophisticated government establishments. They are not only the heirs of a long diplomatic and military tradition, but also the possessors of a new kind of international lore that was developed with the evolution of the Helsinki process."[25]

Coalitions and Representation

Negotiations in the CDE took place between the two blocs, with the United States acting as leader and key negotiating partner of the Western group of NATO countries and the Soviet Union as leader of the Warsaw Pact nations. The NNA countries had no single spokesperson or country representing their interests, although the members of the group tended to act together as a coalition. The final stages of the negotiation have been described as "a deal among the superpowers," because "this was the only way the Soviet Union could make sure it would 'get something in return' for all the concessions that had been made thus far. This way, the USSR could make sure that the transfers of large military units across the Atlantic Ocean would be included among the activities to be notified. Only the Americans could make this concession."[26] However, there was extensive consultation on most issues between the Western allies, with certain allies, like France, playing a crucial role in setting the agenda in the early stages of the negotiation.

Bridging and Bargaining Strategies

During the prenegotiation and negotiation phases of the Stockholm Conference, the NNA countries played an important bridging and intermediary role in the bargaining process, as did France, the first country to call for a pan-European conference to discuss disarmament issues.

According to Karl Birnbaum, the NNA states had two overriding goals: "1) to safeguard and promote the CSCE as *a vehicle of pan-European politics and diplomacy,* serving a long-term process of mutual accommodation and cooperation across political and ideological barriers and 2) to emphasize and enhance the significance of the *military aspects of European security* on the agenda of the CSCE."[27] The NNA states played a critical role in ensuring that confidence-building measures were included in the Helsinki Final Act and secured the support of several key Western European countries (Britain, Germany, and Norway). At the CSCE follow-on meetings in Belgrade, Madrid, and Stockholm, they worked hard to extend the scope of the nascent CBM regime. They played a particularly important role at the Madrid meeting, where the worsening of East-West relations threatened the entire CSCE process:

> The very start of the Madrid meeting was marred by severe tension between the superpowers and the general acrimony of the East-West dialogue. An initial deadlock on procedural issues could be overcome by a provisional solution brought about through the joint action of the NN-group. . . . The next important initiative by the NN-states followed in March 1981. By then, a considerable number of proposals had been tabled by the participating states. Neither the East nor the West showed any inclination to enter into serious bargaining on substantive issues. At that juncture, the NN-states managed to initiate the process by submitting the first complete draft for a concluding document. This was subsequently accepted by all participating states as a basis for concrete negotiations.[28]

Also, when the Madrid meeting appeared doomed to failure, the NNA states asked for and got a recess. Their final mediating initiative occurred in the summer session at Madrid in 1983, where they helped to negotiate a compromise to continue talks, which was acceptable to all of the participating states.

At the Stockholm Conference, the NNA countries played an important mediating role in the first year of the conference, when procedural matters were being decided.[29] But when the conference moved to more substantive matters, the positions of the West and the NNA countries were pretty much in alignment, so the NNA group was not able to play the kind of intermediary role it had previously. Both the West and the NNA group emphasized the adoption of militarily effective measures that would help to make military activity more transparent and predictable. However, "the NNA proposals were politically important because they largely conformed to the mandate and helped to define the 'center of gravity' of the conference."[30]

Because NNA representatives served as coordinators of the informal working groups that helped to prepare compromise solutions, they continued to play an important role in behind-the-scenes negotiations and discussions. One observer writes that although "the neutral and non-aligned countries were also active as far as coordinating negotiations and serving as an intermediary between the rival sides," they "were not able to influence, in any substantial manner, the pace and range of the process of reaching an agreement."[31] However, according to James Goodby, U.S. ambassador to the talks, "the role of the neutral and non-aligned countries was of decisive importance throughout the conference. . . . Although their coordinating and brokering roles were important, an even more important contribution was their commitment to achieving a solid outcome."[32] In particular, Goodby makes special mention of the fact that during the first two years of the conference, when U.S.-Soviet relations were at a particularly low ebb, the Soviets were able "to shift their positions as responses to neutral initiatives, even when bilateral U.S.-Soviet negotiations had paved the way for such shifts. This enabled them to avoid crediting the United States with any positive attitudes while keeping in good standing with the neutral countries."[33]

Issue Decomposition and Sequencing

The process of negotiation at the Stockholm Conference was also characterized by issue decomposition and sequencing and, to a lesser extent, by incremental bargaining strategies. In the first year of the talks, five separate CSBM proposals were tabled at Stockholm: by NATO, Romania, the NNA nations, the Soviet Union, and Malta. The proposals were expected to meet the criteria for the conference that had been agreed on previously at Madrid, that is, CSBMs would apply to "the whole of Europe as well as the adjoining sea area and air space." As well, they were to "be of military significance and politically binding and . . . provided with adequate forms of verification."[34] The principal difference was between East and West negotiating positions. The West, supported by some NNA countries, adopted a functional approach providing for notification of military activities in the adjoining sea area and air space that were linked to notifiable activities on land. The East, however, argued for a geographical approach that would have extended the zone of application beyond Europe. The East also called for measures concerning the no-first-use of nuclear weapons, a treaty on the nonuse of force and maintenance of peaceful relations, the elimination of chemical weapons, nuclear-free zones, and curtailment of military budgets and expenditures. The conditions of many of these proposals were not verifiable. During the first year of negotiations, the only common ground was the willingness of participants to elaborate further the Helsinki CBMs concerning prior notification of military maneuvers, movements, transfers, and observations.

External political developments, namely, the accession of Gorbachev to the Soviet leadership in 1985 and the superpower summit in Geneva, helped narrow the gap in earlier positions; the Warsaw Pact dropped its earlier insistence upon broad declaratory measures (e.g., nuclear no-first-use). (Later on, General Secretary Gorbachev offered to postpone the question of naval activities to the next stage of the conference.) By the end of 1985, the conference had established five separate informal working groups chaired by a representative of the NNA countries. The groups covered notification of military activities; observation of certain military activities; exchanges of military information and the issue of compliance and verification; constraining measures; and the nonuse of force.[35] These groups were responsible for discussing and drafting proposals covering the area of application of CSBMs.

Compliance and Verification

Outstanding issues concerning the threshold of notifiable military activities and compliance and verification were only resolved in the final round of negotiations, in August 1986. As one participant notes, once these issues were resolved "other outstanding problems sequentially fell into place."[36] The West agreed to a numerical threshold, rather than a preferred structural threshold, based on ground force divisions at a figure that was higher than it wanted (13,000 versus 6,000 troops). The East relinquished its demand for notification of independent naval and air activities except in instances where such activities were part of a notifiable activity on land. Finally, both sides agreed to a verification and compliance regime based on the concept of on-site inspection on demand. Previously, the East had rejected the idea of independent verification on the grounds that such activity was tantamount to spying. The West preferred its inspectors to use their own transportation vehicles; the East called for the inspected states to provide vehicles; the NNA group suggested, as a compromise, that aircraft be supplied by countries that were not members of either alliance. The Soviets rejected the NNA idea. It was finally decided that aircraft for inspection would be chosen by mutual agreement between the inspecting and inspected states and in certain circumstances the inspecting state would be allowed to use its own vehicles. Both sides also agreed to the notion of challenge on-site inspections with no right of refusal. In the end, the East secured only one of their declaratory proposals, the nonuse of force. The West, for its part, failed to get its measures regarding the exchange of information on force locations, notification of mobilization, out-of-garrison activities, and a lower notification threshold.

Leadership

Political leadership was crucial to the negotiations and to a successful outcome of the Stockholm Conference, and it tended to come in the form of what Goodby calls positive "signals from the top."[37] Most observers credit President Reagan's speech to the Irish Parliament in Dublin, in June 1984, as playing a crucial role in paving the way for an agreement on working structures that enabled a more detailed exchange of views. At the same time, Reagan's own support for the general idea of confidence-building measures helped to convince a somewhat skeptical domestic bureaucratic and political audience about the value of the CDE and confidence-building measures in arms control.

On the Soviet side, the leadership succession crisis following the death of Leonid Brezhnev was an important factor in Soviet disinterest in negotiations on CBMs, which contributed to a lack of progress in the first year of the talks at Stockholm. The accession of Mikhail Gorbachev to the leadership of the Soviet Union in 1985 marked an important change and freshness in Soviet policies and in attitudes toward the talks. Observance of the tenth anniversary of the Helsinki Final Act and the U.S.-Soviet Geneva Summit statement, which committed both countries to seek a successful conclusion to Stockholm, positively affected the dynamics of the talks. Soviet concessions on the important issues of on-site inspection and notification thresholds were undoubtedly facilitated by direct intervention from above and Gorbachev's own personal commitment to an agreement at Stockholm.

In sum, the Stockholm accords represented the culmination of a lengthy and protracted set of negotiations. Although formal negotiations only lasted some two and a half years (a period that was short in comparison to arms control negotiations between the superpowers on nuclear issues), the prenegotiation phase was a lengthy one but, importantly, contributed to the development of convergent expectations by narrowing the negotiating agenda and identifying salient points of agreement and disagreement between the parties, which facilitated negotiations later on. Like the other cases in this volume, the negotiations took place against a backdrop of crisis (brought about by a dramatic downturn in East-West relations), which had a critical, integrative impact on negotiations. Similarly, intermediaries, in particular the NNA countries, played a critical role in the prenegotiation and negotiation phase: defining the agenda, packaging issues, keeping negotiations on an even keel and sustaining them when the superpowers lost interest or threatened to disrupt them, and acting as intermediaries or go-betweens for proposals that East or West could not accept directly from each other. Political leadership was also crucial to sustaining the negotiations; observers have noted the important roles played by President Reagan and Soviet General Secretary Gorbachev at key points in the negotiation. Finally, the success of the negotiations depended importantly on the extranegotiatory context. What happened outside the conference halls—be it a diplomatic crisis, a change in leadership, or a key intervention by a political leader—was just as important as the discussions that took place at the conference table.

5 Conventional Arms Control: Failure and Success

Conventional arms control had floundered since the onset of talks between NATO and the Warsaw Pact in 1973. However, in 1986 they received a new lease on life, and barely two years after the commencement of formal negotiations in 1988 a new agreement, the CFE (Conventional Forces in Europe) Treaty, was signed. It provided for reductions in conventional forces and symbolically marked the end of almost forty-five years of fear and mistrust between East and West. This chapter traces the evolution of the CFE Treaty in an attempt to explain why an agreement was reached when it was. The incremental process of trial and learning in the mutual and balanced force reductions negotiations, which occurred during the 1970s and 1980s, helped set the stage for subsequent negotiations in the CFE talks. However, the emergence of a new leadership in the Soviet Union committed to achieving reductions in conventional forces to alleviate economic hardship at home and to reducing the drain of resources that went into the defense budget was crucial to the outcome of these negotiations. So, too, was the high level of U.S. presidential involvement and George Bush's personal commitment to achieving an agreement—leadership factors that had not been evident in earlier talks.

In addition to political leadership, extranegotiatory factors were crucial to the substance and pace of negotiations. Among these were the collapse of the Soviet empire in Eastern Europe, German reunification, and the impending collapse of the Soviet Union itself, which propelled negotiations forward at a much faster pace than any of the participants could have anticipated at the outset. Ironically, though, the collapse of the Warsaw Pact created its own unique set of problems of coordination and consultation for the negotiators. The new spirit of cooperation that marked political relations between East and West during and following the demise of the Cold War also engendered feelings of trust that enabled the negotiators to overcome some of the major problems of verification and compliance that had plagued previous negotiations in conventional arms control.

Intermediaries were less crucial to negotiations than they were in the other cases of arms control examined in this volume. But it would be a mistake to characterize the CFE negotiations as merely a bilateral affair between the United States and the Soviet Union, with their allies cast in a secondary supporting role. The Federal Republic of Germany's own diplomatic efforts to assuage Soviet fears about German reunification removed a key roadblock in the negotiations. Various bridging proposals offered by Soviet and U.S. allies at key junctures in the negotiation also helped to remove other obstacles. Although the rapidness of political change in the East overtook the CFE negotiations as the old security system of the Cold War was dismantled, the conclusion of one commentator that "the CFE Agreement was marginal to the European security debate" is an overstatement.[1] To be sure, arms control was second-stage to the political drama that unfolded in Europe at the end of the 1980s, but it also lent an element of predictability in a world where uncertainty was very much the hallmark of the new world order. In this respect, the outcome of the negotiations was less important to the new security environment than the negotiation process itself, which allowed for orderly change in an otherwise unpredictable world.

Background

Conventional arms control negotiations began in 1973 in the talks on mutual and balanced force reductions (MBFR) in Vienna.[2] The aim of these talks was to reduce the level of conventional forces in a Central European zone covering the territories of the Federal Republic of Germany (FRG), Belgium, Luxembourg, the Netherlands, the German Democratic Republic (GDR), Czechoslovakia, and Poland. The direct participants in these negotiations were the eleven NATO and Warsaw Pact nations with troops stationed in these countries—the above seven, plus the United States, Canada, the United Kingdom, and the Soviet Union. The eight "flank" nations (Denmark, Greece, Norway, Italy, and Turkey, from NATO; and Bulgaria, Hungary, and Rumania, from the Warsaw Pact) were indirect participants in these talks. Although the MBFR talks showed some progress through the 1970s, including an agreement in principle in 1977 to reduce each side's forces in the region to 900,000 air and ground personnel with a 700,000 subceiling for ground forces alone, in the 1980s the talks came to a stalemate, largely over the issues of the number of troops each side had stationed in the area and the methods that would be used for verifying any troop reductions. During the course of these negotiations, NATO's positions centered on achieving parity with the Warsaw Pact in military manpower; agreeing on effective verification measures to ensure treaty compliance; allowing for geographical asymmetries, given the greater distance to the central front from North America and the United Kingdom; and requiring collectivity in force reductions, enabling deployments of troops from one nation to substitute for those of another while remaining under the overall manpower ceiling. The Warsaw Pact, on the other hand, opposed collectivity and pushed to have national subceilings on force levels in any agreement; desired the inclusion of equipment reductions in addition to manpower reductions; and wanted verification measures to be less intrusive than those proposed by the West.[3]

A long-standing dispute in the negotiations was the size of current force levels, with the West counting 230,000 more Warsaw Pact troops than officially declared by the Eastern bloc.[4] In December 1985, the West called for the immediate withdrawal of 5,000 U.S. and 11,500 Soviet troops from Central Europe without prior agreement on force levels. The proposal also included provisions for exchanging force data following the reduction; freezing force levels in Central Europe for three years; and a verification regime allowing for up to thirty on-site challenge inspections annually, as well as permanent entry/exit points for troops moving in and out of the zone. The Warsaw Pact responded by suggesting force reductions of 6,500 American and 11,500 Soviet personnel. According to Eastern figures, this would leave overall postreduction force ratios unchanged and, as a result, would set a precedent for further force reductions. The Eastern bloc agreed to on-site inspection if the basis for the request to inspect was well founded. But there was failure to secure agreement on even these modest proposals.

Underlying the failure of the MBFR talks to achieve significant progress were deeper reasons for disagreement. As Coit Blacker explains,

> The central Western objective in MBFR from 1968 to 1973 was to negotiate a mutual reduction of U.S. and Soviet forces from Europe to relieve pressures generated by the American Congress for U.S. troop reductions. All other Western goals were secondary to this consideration, whatever the objective appeal to NATO of devising a mechanism to trim Soviet and Warsaw Pact military power in Europe. The major Soviet objective during those years was to underwrite the emerging political detente in Europe by undertaking relatively modest reductions in NATO and Warsaw Pact manpower and military equipment while leaving more or less undisturbed the prevailing balance of forces on the continent. In other words, both sides had a strong interest in seeing the negotiations succeed, although for very different reasons.
>
> Once the negotiations were underway, however, Western, and particularly U.S., purposes began to change. With the formal convocation of the talks, Congressional support for the redeployment of at least some American forces in Germany to the continental United States all but evaporated. Few lawmakers were prepared to endorse a course of action that would undermine, according to the Nixon administration, American bargaining leverage.

As a consequence, U.S. policymakers, in consultation with the NATO allies, were able to formulate a much "tougher" negotiating position than if the pressures for a unilateral American withdrawal had been maintained.[5]

Thus, the decline in U.S interest in the negotiations as a result of easing domestic pressures to withdraw American forces from Europe weakened the prospects of an accord by toughening the Western stance. The worsening tenor of East-West relations in the late 1970s and early 1980s, particularly following the Soviet invasion of Afghanistan, further diminished interest in conventional arms control.[6]

Prenegotiation

With Mikhail Gorbachev's rise to power in the Soviet Union, however, the Warsaw Pact began to advance new proposals on conventional arms reductions in Europe. First, in April 1986, General Secretary Gorbachev proposed to expand the "zone of reductions" to the "entire territory of Europe, from the Atlantic to the Urals."[7] Subsequently, on June 11, 1986, in Budapest, the Soviet Union and its Warsaw Pact allies proposed major new reductions in land and tactical air forces as well as theater nuclear weapons, in an area covering Europe from the Atlantic to the Urals. They also proposed troop cuts of 100,000 to 150,000 over the next two years and cuts of up to 500,000 for each side by 1990. The Soviets suggested that negotiations on these proposals could take place in an expanded MBFR forum (including countries not already involved), in a forum related to the Conference on Confidence- and Security-Building Measures and Disarmament in Europe (CCSBMDE), or in a new forum altogether.

The Budapest Appeal was noteworthy, as one observer explains, because it represented "an Eastern initiative in a field where up to now the West was *demandeur*." The general feeling at the time was that the initiative was more than just propaganda, reflecting the Soviet need for "significant savings in defense expenditures" and the recognition that these savings could "be best made in conventional forces." Related to this argument was the view "that the restructuring of the Soviet economic system [required] another phase of *detente*, promising some advantages in the trade relations with the West." Still, there were those who attributed a more sinister motive, namely, that the Soviets were keen to advance proposals that would denuclearize the West "by persuading Western publics that a balance in the conventional force level eliminates the need for nuclear weapons as a deterrent."[8]

In May 1986, NATO formed a new high-level task force as a steering body for the review and development of the Western position on conventional arms control. Then in September 1986, the first stage of the CCSBMDE concluded with an agreement signed in Stockholm (see chapter 4). There was growing hope that the success of these talks in creating a more open and predictable security regime in Europe would carry over to the MBFR negotiations.

But there were also encouraging signs that the general climate of East-West relations was improving. The October 11–12, 1986, summit meeting between General Secretary Gorbachev and President Ronald Reagan, which took place in Reykjavik, Iceland, set in motion dramatic new efforts to promote far-reaching measures of arms control and disarmament. The first two objectives emerging from the summit were treaties on strategic nuclear weapons and intermediate-range nuclear forces, but it soon became clear that conventional arms control was also a priority item. America's allies had expressed grave concern that unless cuts in nuclear forces were matched by reductions in conventional forces, Western Europe would find itself at the mercy of the perceived superiority of the Warsaw Pact.

NATO was interested in conventional arms stability, whether it came about through asymmetric reductions to achieve parity or by an increase in its own forces. This issue had been at the forefront of internal NATO discussions in 1986, and in December 1986, the North Atlantic Council issued the Brussels Declaration on Conventional Arms Control. It recommended that two distinct negotiations take place: one to expand upon the results of the Stockholm Conference on Confidence- and Security-Building Measures; and the second to establish conventional stability at lower levels from the Atlantic to the Urals. The former would be for all CSCE participants, while the latter would be restricted to the nations of NATO and of the Warsaw Pact. The declaration sought to establish a new mandate for East-West negotiations on conventional arms control while also listing a new set of objectives and criteria for an agreement. Another important aspect of this meeting was that France and Spain for the first time participated fully in working out major NATO policies on conventional arms control.

In February, 1987, the Conventional Mandate Talks between the Warsaw Pact and NATO began, with the aim of drafting a mandate for the anticipated negotiations on conventional stability in Europe.[9] At the time, these negotiations were referred to as the Conventional Stability Talks.[10] On January 10, 1989, agreement was reached on the mandate for the new talks, at which point their formal title became Negotiations on Conventional Armed Forces in Europe (CFE). These talks would take place within the framework of the Conference for Security and Cooperation in Europe (CSCE) and include the twenty-three members of NATO and the Warsaw Pact. The mandate stated that the objectives of the talks were "to strengthen the stability and security in Europe through the establishment of a stable and security balance of conventional armed forces, which include conventional armaments and equipment at lower levels; the elimination, as a matter of priority, of the capability for launching surprise attack and for initiating large-scale offensive action."[11] It was stated that these objectives would be achieved through such militarily significant measures as reductions, limitations, redeployment provisions, and equal ceilings. Measures would be pursued step by step and for the whole area of application, from the Atlantic to the Urals (ATTU), allowing for regional differentiation to redress disparities, if necessary.

The mandate talks had run parallel to the MBFR negotiations with the expectation that once a mandate was reached, the MBFR talks would be suspended. Following the decision to open the first round of new negotiations in March 1989, the participants decided to conclude the MBFR talks. On February 2, 1989, the forty-seventh and final round of MBFR ended without agreement.

Prior to the agreement on the CFE mandate, a series of major events established the groundwork on which the talks began. The first major event was the signing of the intermediate-range nuclear forces (INF) agreement in December 1987 by the United States and the Soviet Union.[12] This agreement not only signaled a new sense of optimism about arms control in general but gave impetus to conventional arms negotiations in Europe because of concerns about the impact of nuclear arms reductions on the conventional military balance.

The second major development was Gorbachev's U.N. announcement on December 8, 1988, of unilateral cuts in the Soviet armed forces of 500,000 troops, 8,500 artillery pieces, 800 aircraft, and 10,000 tanks within two years. Of these, 50,000 troops and 5,000 tanks would come out of Czechoslovakia, Hungary, and the GDR by 1991. Six tank divisions in these countries would also be disbanded. Gorbachev also stated that the remaining forces in Eastern Europe and the Western portion of the Soviet Union would be reorganized into defensive formations.[13]

Not to be upstaged, the following day NATO issued its own proposal for arms reductions. The tank holdings of each alliance would be limited to 20,000, with no one nation allowed more than 12,000. Equal limits were proposed on all other weapons categories, at levels slightly below those assessed for Western forces in NATO's 1988 report on the conventional balance. As with tanks, no single country would be permitted more than 30 percent of the total holdings of both alliances in any category of weapons systems. Other elements of the proposal included specific limits on stationed forces and sublimits within particular zones to avoid a concentration of forces.

In the two months following Gorbachev's announcement of unilateral reductions, a number of other Warsaw Pact countries made similar moves. The GDR announced cuts of 10,000 troops, including 6 armored regiments, 600 tanks, and 50 fighter aircraft, to take place by the end of 1990. Czechoslovakia stated that over the next two years it would reduce army combat units by 12,000 troops, while phasing out 850 tanks, 165 armored vehicles, and 51 combat aircraft. Poland, which stated it had cut two motorized rifle divisions totaling 15,000 troops in the past two years, announced it would further reduce its forces by 40,000 troops, 850 tanks, 900 artillery pieces, 700 armored vehicles, and 80 combat aircraft. Hungary announced plans to cut its armed forces by 9,300 troops, 251 tanks, 30 armored personnel carriers (APCs), 420 artillery pieces, 6 missile-launching pads, and 9 interceptor aircraft. Finally, Bulgaria announced that by the end of 1990 it would reduce its forces by 10,000 troops, 200 tanks, 200 artillery pieces, 20 airplanes, and 5 ships.

On January 30, 1989, the Warsaw Pact, for the very first time, released its own assessment of the European military balance. In general, it judged that much more parity existed between the two alliances than was indicated in NATO figures. NATO was estimated to have a higher troop strength than the Warsaw Pact and more combat helicopters, antitank missile launchers, and large surface ships. The Warsaw Pact was credited with more tactical combat aircraft, tactical missile-launch systems, tanks, infantry-fighting vehicles, artillery pieces, and submarines. Different counting rules and definitions were responsible for most of the discrepancies between the two alliance's assessments. For example, NATO figures did not include shipborne naval aircraft, ships, naval personnel, or stored material.

In spite of the problems, however, a sense of optimism surrounded the talks as their opening drew near. On March 6, the two sides met to outline and add more detail to their initial negotiating positions. Soviet Foreign Minister Eduard Shevardnadze set out the Warsaw Pact's proposal, consisting of three stages. In the first stage, lasting two to three years, each alliance would reduce its personnel and conventional arms (including tactical fighter aircraft, tanks, armored personnel carriers, artillery, combat helicopters, multiple rocket launchers, and mortars) by 10 to 15 percent below the lowest levels currently held by either side. The second stage, lasting another two to three years, would involve further reductions of 25 percent in these categories as well as cuts in battlefield nuclear arms. In the final stage, each side's forces would be given a strictly defensive character, and agreements would be reached limiting all other categories of arms.[14]

British Foreign Minister Geoffrey Howe presented the West's proposal, adding detail to the plan outlined in December. Under the Western proposal, each side would be allowed 20,000 tanks, with no single nation having more than 12,000. Ceilings of 16,500 artillery pieces and 28,000 armored personnel carriers were proposed. Each side could station no more than 3,200 tanks, 1,700 artillery pieces, and 6,000 armored personnel carriers outside national territory in active units. For example, tank deployments in Belgium, the FRG, Luxembourg, the Netherlands, Czechoslovakia, the GDR, and Poland would be restricted to 8,000 by regional sublimits.

In sum, key areas of agreement between the two sides included the setting of equal limits on critical weapons (tanks, armored personnel carriers, and artillery), the general size of reductions envisaged, and the need for stringent verification measures. Important differences existed, however. These included Soviet proposals for partially demilitarized zones along the East-West border and limits on aircraft; their specification of follow-up reductions in arms and troops; and their view of the relationship of naval forces to negotiations.[15]

Negotiation

Round I

Both alliances tabled their formal proposals on March 9, 1989, the opening day of negotiations. The West's proposals were tabled by David Peel, Canada's representative, and were in line with earlier NATO thinking. The first round of talks ended just two weeks later, on March 23.[16]

With the onset of formal negotiations in the CFE, world attention shifted to the question of short-range nuclear weapons, which presented particular difficulties for the West. The FRG's government was keen for NATO to delay modernization of existing systems while engaging immediately in negotiations, whereas the United States and Britain felt that modernization should go ahead and that negotiations should be postponed to an indefinite future. The other allies were divided; there was considerable press comment about a perceived failure of American leadership and about the risk that the dissension might bring about the collapse of NATO as the alliance approached a new Western summit meeting, scheduled for the end of May.

Round II

The second round of the CFE talks began May 5 and ended July 13. On May 25, the Warsaw Pact, in a major shift, accepted the NATO principles of ceilings on any one country's forces, on foreign deployments, and within three subzones. Specifically, the pact proposed reductions in each alliance to 20,000 tanks, 28,000 APCs, 24,000 artillery pieces, and 1.35 million troops. Strike aircraft would be limited to 1,500, and helicopters to 1,700. Reductions to these levels would occur over six years, from 1991 to

1997, after which the alliances would begin a 25 percent reduction in remaining forces. These proposals narrowed the gap between East and West on the CFE question. Although the pact accepted the Western approach to reductions in tanks, artillery, and armored troop carriers, outstanding differences remained over the East's call for the establishment of limits on troop levels and aircraft.

As Western leaders prepared to gather for the NATO summit meeting in Brussels, new thinking was reported in Washington about the short-range nuclear issue and conventional arms control. These proposals were unveiled at the May 29–30 summit meeting, producing a diplomatic triumph for President George Bush and contributing to a sense of achievement among the other Western leaders. The problem of short-range nuclear weapons was resolved by an agreement authorizing U.S.-Soviet talks on partial reductions once CFE cuts had begun. The conventional forces issue was covered in the main declaration of the conference and in a major statement.[17] NATO leaders agreed to U.S. proposals to include the pursuit of new ceilings on helicopters and land-based combat aircraft in the negotiations. They also proposed "a 20 percent cut in combat manpower in U.S. stationed forces, and a resulting ceiling on U.S. and Soviet ground and air force personnel stationed outside of national territory in the Atlantic-to-the-Urals zone at approximately 275,000." This would require the Soviet Union "to reduce its forces in Eastern Europe by some 325,000."[18] To maintain momentum, the NATO allies also stated that an initial CFE agreement should be sought within a period of six months to a year and that the reductions it would stipulate should be carried out by 1992 or 1993. Accordingly, they directed that work on their new proposals should be given high priority and completed in time for the third round of CFE negotiation, due to open on September 7. The Warsaw Pact characterized the Bush proposal as positive and agreed that a treaty was possible as early as 1990.

On July 12, ahead of schedule, NATO announced further details of the Bush proposals dealing with aircraft. These included limiting each side to 5,700 combat aircraft and 1,900 combat helicopters.[19] The former category would include those designed primarily for air-to-ground bombing and air-to-air fighting operations. NATO indicated that it had about 6,700 such aircraft, while the Warsaw Pact possessed approximately 9,600. Major differences between the two sides remained on how to define the types of aircraft to be included in any agreement, however.

In August 1989, the U.S. House Armed Services Committee visited Soviet military headquarters in the German Democratic Republic. During a meeting with Lieutenant-General Valery I. Fursin, the chief of staff for Soviet forces in the GDR, committee members learned that not all the elements of six tank divisions would be withdrawn from Eastern Europe under the plan announced by Gorbachev at the United Nations in December 1988. Instead, Fursin explained, weapons used for air defense and artillery would remain, to be added to new nonoffensive motorized rifle divisions in the GDR. Still, the American visitors concluded that the unilateral reductions in tanks alone would effectively and measurably reduce the Soviet military threat to NATO.

Round III

The opening session of the third round of CFE talks began as scheduled on September 7, 1989. At that session, the Soviet Union declared that it accepted the Western challenge to sign a treaty in 1990 reducing conventional arms. Two weeks later, NATO tabled proposals on information exchange, stabilization measures, and verification provisions. The proposed information exchange measure stipulated that each alliance would provide information on the structure of its land, air, and air-defense forces down to the level of battalion (land forces) and squadron (air forces). This would include detailed information exchanges on the organization and location of these units and itemization of their holdings of treaty-limited equipment and non-treaty-limited equipment, such as main battle tanks, that could have a potential for treaty circumvention. The verification proposal included measures pertaining to the validation of baseline data, monitoring of reductions, and confirmation of compliance with force limits. It included stipulations for short notice inspections of declared sites and the right to request inspection of undeclared sites. It also contained provisions for the monitoring of stabilization measures and for aerial inspections.

NATO also tabled proposals on stabilization measures that included at least forty-two days' notice of troop movements or the call-up of 40,000 or more reservists; monitored storage sites and monitored low-strength units; and restrictions on the size of military activities to 40,000 troops and 800 main battle tanks, this level to be exceeded only once every two years, with at least twelve months' notice.

On September 1989, the Soviets presented their own revised position on aircraft limitations, proposing an overall limit of 4,700 on each side. Included in the limit would be some types of interceptors, reconnaissance planes, and electronic warfare aircraft. However, training aircraft were excluded from the Soviet proposal, as were the Backfire bomber and approximately 1,800 fighters, which the Soviets claimed were designated for defense against strategic air attack. The Soviets proposed that limits on the numbers of helicopters possessed by each side be set at 1,900 (the same number proposed by NATO).

Round III of the CFE talks concluded on October 19 with the tabling by the Warsaw Pact of counterproposals to NATO's proposals on stabilization measures, information exchange, and verification. The East proposed the establishment of entry/exit points in the area of application at railway junctions, ports, air bases, and airfields. In its information exchange package, the pact asked for data down to the level of regiment, rather than battalion or squadron. The stabilization measures proposed by the pact included limiting exercises of more than 40,000 troops to one every three years and exercises of more than 25,000 troops to only twice a year.

In the fall of 1989, some Warsaw Pact countries began to reduce their conventional defense forces. At the end of November 1989, Czechoslovakia announced that it would begin immediately to eliminate the fortifications along its 240-mile border with Austria. The following month Prague told of a similar intention to dismantle defenses along its 150-mile border with the FRG. The government of Czechoslovakia also stated its intention to shorten compulsory military service from two years to eighteen months and to reduce the number of active reserves from 290,000 to about 200,000. The Czechoslovak initiative followed a similar one made by Hungary, in September 1989, to pull back and reduce the defenses along its borders with Austria and Yugoslavia.

Prior to the December 2–3 summit meeting between President Bush and General Secretary Gorbachev at Malta, America's European allies voiced their concern about the possibility of unilateral troop cuts by the United States that would be greater than those proposed by President Bush in May 1989. On December 4, President Bush met with his NATO counterparts and reassured them that he and Gorbachev had discussed only their broad aspirations for arms control and had not gotten into specifics. The President also emphasized in his press conference following the NATO meeting that he was interested in getting a CFE treaty and was not thinking about any follow-on conventional arms reductions or CFE II.

Round IV

NATO and the Warsaw Pact exchanged draft treaty texts on December 14, 1989. The two sides appeared closer to agreement on reductions in three types of armament: main battle tanks, armored troop carriers, and helicopters. East and West agreed that limits should be placed on these types of equipment at 20,000, 28,000, and 1,900 respectively. As for limits on other types of equipment, the two texts did not differ all that much. The biggest difference in numbers was in the proposed limits on artillery, with NATO's suggested ceiling of 16,500 versus the pact's suggested ceiling of 24,000. However, the two sides had agreed upon a definition in this category. In addition, NATO continued to propose a limit of 5,700 aircraft compared to the pact's suggested limit of 4,700. NATO's draft also embodied a ceiling of 270,000 on U.S. and Soviet stationed manpower, whereas the Warsaw Pact draft restricted each alliance to a total of 1.35 million troops, with a sublimit of 350,000 stationed forces for each country.

Both proposals also included "sufficiency" limits (the maximum percentage of manpower and equipment that could be held by any one country) as well as verification and stabilization measures. Differences in definition of equipment remained. The East continued to insist that certain types of aircraft (air-defense interceptors, land-based naval aviation, and trainers) be excluded. NATO insisted on including all combat-capable aircraft. NATO defined a main battle tank as a tracked vehicle weighing twenty tons or more with a 75 mm barrel. The pact set the weight limit at 10 tonnes.

The CFE process was influenced by the dramatic changes that took place in Europe in 1990. Most significant were the demands by several Eastern European countries for the negotiated withdrawal of Soviet forces stationed on their territory. The Soviets agreed on March 10, 1990, to remove their contingent of 50,000 to 60,000 troops from Hungary by June 30, 1991. In Czechoslovakia, withdrawal of approximately 75,000 Soviet troops began on February 26, 1990, with completion scheduled for July 1, 1991. The Kremlin also expressed its willingness to remove its 40,000 troops from Poland.

There were also rumblings of more far-reaching troop cuts in Washington and Moscow. On January 1, Sam Nunn, the chairman of the U.S. Senate Armed Services Committee, suggested that the United States reduce its troop presence in Europe from 305,000 army and air force personnel to as low as 200,000, on the grounds that the NATO manpower proposal tabled at the CFE talks in December had been overtaken by events.

On January 5, 1990, it was reported that chief Soviet negotiator Oleg Grinevsky had informally submitted a plan during the fourth round of talks calling for an overall limit of 600,000 troops for each side in Central Europe. The sublimit for Soviet and American forces under this proposal was set at 275,000, which corresponded to NATO's proposal.

Round V

At the talks on January 26, the FRG, France, and Italy called for an acceleration of the pace of negotiations in order to address the rapid political changes that were taking place in Europe. With an eye to these changes, the Soviet Union announced on February 11, 1990, that it was ready to reduce its troop strength in Europe prior to the signing of a CFE agreement. The Soviets maintained that their forces stationed in the GDR would have to be dealt with separately, however.

In his January 31, 1990, State of the Union message, George Bush proposed reductions in Soviet and American forces stationed in Central Europe to 195,000, with a provision for 30,000 American forces stationed in the central zone.[20] The Soviets initially balked at this proposal, primarily because of the latter provision, which would have given the United States superiority in stationed troops in Europe as a whole. At the Open Skies conference in Ottawa on February 14, however, the Soviets relented and agreed to the proposal on condition that the separate troop levels for the Americans constitute individual ceilings; U.S. troop levels could not be increased beyond the ceiling in either zone, nor could troops be transferred from one zone to the other.

The following month, NATO agreed to allow each side to keep up to 500 air-defense interceptors over and above the ceiling on combat aircraft. NATO also agreed to exclude approximately 2,000 "primary" trainer aircraft (those without weapons) from that ceiling, which it lowered to 4,700. The revised NATO position on aircraft was prompted by a pact promise to allow on-site inspection and its willingness to limit air-defense interceptors under a separate ceiling. At the same time, NATO lowered to thirteen tons its previous weight stipulation in defining a main battle tank.

NATO was surprised when, on February 23, 1990, Moscow and the GDR proposed limits on alliance-wide troop holdings of East and West between 700,000 and 750,000 troops each. NATO had assumed that Soviet agreement to the Bush proposal meant that the East had yielded in its attempt to impose troop limitations on overall holdings. Because of Hungarian opposition to the Soviet-GDR proposal, however, it was not formally tabled.

Round VI

Prior to the sixth round of talks, NATO agreed on verification proposals that were less strict than those tabled previously. At U.S. insistence, NATO verification plans would have required monitoring of key weapons production plants and shipments of restricted equipment into or out of the region covered by an agreement. Now, the allies agreed to forego strict monitoring of some shipments and production, relying in some instances on private notification. Parties to an agreement would still be required to allow on-site inspection of key storage sites and weapons destruction.[21]

On March 15, 1990, when the sixth round of talks began, NATO tabled protocols stipulating that all equipment in excess of the residual levels would have to be destroyed, with destruction taking place over a period of three years. With the tabling of these protocols, NATO had virtually completed its draft treaty.

The promise of a quick and easy CFE agreement ready to be signed at the June 1990 Bush-Gorbachev summit or even by the end of the year began to fade during the sixth round, as the Soviets became preoccupied with events at home and the future status of a united Germany.[22] On the opening day of the round, Grinevsky, the Soviet negotiator, called for cuts in the armed forces of a united Germany as part of any agreement on German reunification. He indicated that such cuts should be related in some way to the CFE talks, reflecting Soviet concerns about the need to impose some upper limit on the manpower of a united Germany. However, the NATO allies were resistant to such a proposal. France and the United Kingdom did not want negotiated reductions of their own personnel, and the FRG was loathe to be singled out for special cuts. As a result of these disagreements, the talks bogged down over such issues as the height requirements for fences at depot facilities and whether a tank's weight should include fuel and other items.

Still, the major hurdle to overcome, about which there was little or no movement in Round VI, involved aircraft. At the April 5–6 Washington meeting between U.S. Secretary of State James Baker and Soviet Foreign Minister Eduard Shevardnadze, the Soviets presented a proposal limiting the number of American and Soviet aircraft stationed in Central Europe to 500 each. Baker immediately rejected the offer, primarily because it did not include aircraft stationed in the Soviet Union that were within easy reach of Central Europe. On April 26, Hungary tabled a compromise aircraft proposal limiting air-defense interceptors to 800 and combat aircraft and trainers to 5,600, for a combined aircraft ceiling of 6,400. A no-increase limit would be placed on land-based naval aviation. The aircraft issue was proving so intractable that, on a number of occasions, U.S. and Soviet officials had suggested deferring it to future negotiations.

There were also other areas of disagreement, including sufficiency rules, with NATO proposing that no country should have more than 30 percent of total equipment in each category (60 percent of each alliance total) and the Warsaw Pact suggesting 35 to 40 percent (70 percent of each alliance total); and verification, with the main issue in dispute being how to calculate the number of inspections each country would have to host. NATO favored a formula based on the number of treaty-limited items in each country and its geographic size. The East objected that such a formula would subject them to 900 inspections, compared to just 400 for NATO. The pact wanted to determine quotas based on the number of each country's military units, storage sites, and training camps.

At the ministerial meeting in Moscow between Baker and Shevardnadze on May 16–19, the United States presented new ideas to break the CFE logjam, including higher limits on tactical aircraft and a willingness to explore a compromise over sufficiency rules. The American aircraft proposal, revealed in a letter to NATO foreign ministers the day Baker arrived in Moscow, suggested that the United States was prepared to discuss a limit in the 6,000 range.[23] It also included greater flexibility on the mix of combat aircraft, trainers, and air-defense interceptors. However, there was no compromise on these issues at the meeting.

Bush and Shevardnadze's failure to reach a compromise dimmed the prospects of any major announcement on CFE results at the June Washington summit meeting between Presidents Bush and Gorbachev. The Soviets were cautious about moving ahead in the CFE negotiations until they had been assured at the "two-plus-four" negotiations on German unification (talks between the two Germanys and the four powers with postwar rights in Germany: the United States, the Soviet Union, the United Kingdom, and France) that the size of a united German army would be limited. NATO argued that the subject of German troop levels should be discussed exclusively at the CFE conference, that this should take place only after an initial conventional forces treaty had been signed, and that it should avoid singling out Germany for reductions.

At the May 30–June 3 summit in Washington, Bush and Gorbachev reaffirmed their commitment to conclude a CFE agreement by the end of 1990. A week later, the NATO foreign ministers meeting in Turnberry, Scotland, instructed their negotiators in Vienna "to pursue new approaches to a mutually acceptable solution, in particular on aircraft, armor and verification."[24] These new approaches were to be based on the proposals made by Baker to Shevardnadze in May.[25]

Round VII

In late June, in an effort to move talks forward, NATO began to consider offering Moscow a commitment to limit the size of the future German army in connection with a CFE treaty. Specific numbers would be left to a CFE II negotiation. On June 23, Shevardnadze proposed at the two-plus-four talks that "an international endorsement of German unity include provision for a staged withdrawal of foreign troops from a united Germany and strict limits on its military."[26] The proposal was immediately rejected by the other participants as an unwarranted restriction on the sovereignty of a future Germany.

On June 27, 1990, however, the two sides agreed to definitions for and reductions of tanks and armored combat vehicles. According to this compromise, first tabled on June 14 by France and Poland, tanks would be defined as tracked or wheeled armored vehicles weighing 16.5 tonnes or greater (unladen) and with a main gun of 75 mm or larger. There would be three categories of armored combat vehicles: armored personnel carriers, armored infantry-fighting vehicles with a gun of 20 mm or larger, and heavy armament combat vehicles with a gun 75 mm or larger. The agreed limits on tanks would be 20,000 for each alliance. The limit on armored combat vehicles was set at 30,000 with a combined sublimit of armored infantry-fighting vehicles and heavy armament combat vehicles of 18,000, of which no more than 1,500 could be heavy armament combat vehicles. Under this plan the Warsaw Pact would be forced to reduce its inventory of tanks by 35,000, compared to a reduction of 4,000 by NATO.

As talks progressed, NATO also began to adapt itself to the realities of the quickly evolving post–Cold War situation by changing alliance strategy while also undertaking a series of political initiatives intended to reassure the Soviet Union that they saw their relationship in terms of partnership rather than confrontation. These initiatives, which had an important impact on the momentum of the CFE talks themselves, came at the foreign ministers' Turnberry meeting in June and the heads of government meeting in London in July. The intention was, as the London Declaration said, to "profoundly alter the way we think about defense," in accordance with the principle that "in the new Europe, the security of every state is inseparably linked to the security of its neighbors."[27]

Recognizing that the military risks facing its alliance had already decreased substantially and that implementation of a successful CFE treaty would result in further improvements, the NATO allies agreed in principle on a number of fundamental changes to NATO integrated force structure and strategy. Active forces were to be made smaller and more mobile, and they were, to an increasing extent, to be organized as multinational corps. The readiness of the active units was to be scaled back, training requirements reduced, and exercises cut. NATO would rely more on the ability to mobilize larger forces in case of emergency. The role of substrategic nuclear systems of shortest range would be reduced. The reciprocal elimination of all nuclear artillery shells would be proposed. Nuclear weapons would henceforth truly be regarded as weapons of last resort, though they would continue to ensure "that there are no circumstances in which nuclear retaliation in response to military action might be discounted." The concept of forward defense would be replaced by a new concept of mobile defense, the concept of follow-on forces attack would be replaced by a new concept of defensive defense, and the flexible response strategy would be modified to reflect a reduced reliance on nuclear weapons and a de facto no-first-use nuclear regime.

On the political side, the allies decided that NATO, while continuing to provide for their common defense, must also become "an agent of change," by helping to "build structures of a more united continent," by "supporting security and stability," and by enhancing "the political component of our Alliance as provided for by Article 2 of our treaty."[28] In the spirit of extending the "hand of friendship" to its former adversaries, the NATO allies invited President Gorbachev and representatives of the other

Warsaw Pact members to address the North Atlantic Council and to establish diplomatic liaison with NATO. They also accepted the Soviet invitation to NATO Secretary General Manfred Woerner to visit Moscow. The allies thus confirmed their belief that NATO remained a crucial instrument for European security but that it would also have to adapt to changing political realities.

The London Declaration was a crucial turning point in the negotiations concerning membership of a unified Germany in NATO. Another key development was the bilateral meeting between Chancellor Helmut Kohl and President Gorbachev that took place shortly afterward, on July 16, in Zheleznovodsk, U.S.S.R. There the Germans gave the following assurances: they would deny themselves weapons of mass destruction; they would accept a ceiling of 370,000 on the size of the Bundeswehr; there would be no extension of NATO military structures in the GDR until 1994; and a Soviet-German treaty of cooperation and nonuse of force would be negotiated. The Soviet Union also received a promise of substantial economic aid and assistance with Soviet troops when they were brought home. Another key element was the assurance the Germans gave the Poles that they would confirm by treaty their recognition of the Oder-Neisse frontier and their renunciation of all claims to former German territories east of that line.

At the two-plus-four meeting in Paris that followed, Soviet Foreign Minister Shevardnadze spoke of a "qualitatively new political-military situation evolving in Europe today" as a result of the move from military confrontation to defensive military doctrines, the creation of "European structures of security and political cooperation," and the establishment of "relationships of partnerships between members of the two alliances."[29] In these circumstances, he said, the Soviet Union was prepared, for its part, to grant full sovereignty to a unified Germany and to allow Germany, as a sovereign state, to decide which alliance it would belong to. At the last two-plus-four meeting in Moscow in September, the four signed a treaty suspending their wartime rights in Germany, effective on the day of reunification. It was, therefore, a fully sovereign and united Germany that was welcomed by the Secretary General of NATO on October 3 and signed the promised treaties with the Soviet Union and Poland in the following weeks.

Endgame

The signing of these treaties effectively removed a major barrier to a CFE agreement, namely, the size of the Bundeswehr in a united Germany. But a number of other outstanding issues remained to be resolved, concerning the counting rules for stored versus active units, single-country sufficiency rules, aircraft limits, subzonal limits, and verification provisions. Ironically, the imminent breakup of the Warsaw Pact, as those states in Eastern

Europe that had negotiated the withdrawal of Soviet forces from their territory began to show their independence, proved a complicating factor in the negotiations.[30]

Stored versus Active Units. NATO's initial proposals of treaty-limited equipment had excluded prepositioned organizational material configured to unit sets (POMCUS) to be used as U.S. reinforcements in a crisis. In contrast, the Warsaw Pact proposal set limits on active and stored treaty-limited equipment in order to limit U.S. POMCUS. A compromise, setting limits on both categories, was reached in October as a result of pressure from Turkey and Norway, which sought limits on stored equipment in order to prevent the Soviets from doing the same along their borders, and Poland, which sought to avoid giving the Soviets an excuse to do the same in their territory (although separate Hungarian- and Czechoslovak-negotiated withdrawals of Soviet forces from their territories in 1990 somewhat reduced this fear).

Single-Country Sufficiency Rules. With the agreements to withdraw Soviet forces from Hungary and Czechoslovakia and Soviet agreement to a unified Germany, the Soviets sought a higher sufficiency count (40 percent) than the earlier 30 percent to compensate for their lost allies. However, this new figure was deemed to be too high by their Warsaw Pact allies. As a result, a new set of more flexible sufficiency rules were negotiated between U.S. Secretary of State James Baker and Soviet Foreign Minister Shevardnadze on October 3 in New York. These figures were still too high, especially for Poland, and a new set of more flexible rules, ranging from 33 to 38 percent for different weapons categories, was negotiated. Even then, as a result of pressure from Poland, Rumania, and Bulgaria, some national allocations were actually increased from those that had been initially assigned, reflecting the new assertiveness of Moscow's "allies."

Aircraft and Helicopter Limits. Aircraft limits had proved to be one of the most intractable issues in the summer, and there was a growing desire to defer the issue to the next stage of CFE negotiations. However, in early October Shevardnadze informed Baker that the Soviets would accept minimum limits of Soviet combat aircraft of 5,150, including the Backfire bomber. Agreement then set alliance ceilings at 6,800 and on land-based naval aircraft at 430, with single-country limits of 400. Definitional agreements were also reached in October on combat helicopters, with limits raised to 2,000 for each alliance and single-country limits of 1,500.

Subzonal Limits. Subzonal limits were of special concern to Turkey and Norway, which were concerned that the Soviets might move their treaty-limited equipment from Central Europe to areas near their borders, given the initial lack of limits for so-called flank zones. There was already evidence that Soviet combat aircraft that had been withdrawn from Central Europe had been redeployed in the northern U.S.S.R. near Norway and that the same thing was happening with troops near Turkey. Norway and Turkey successfully pressed for treaty-limited equipment ceilings in flank zones, although this caused difficulties for the Soviet Union because returning troops from Afghanistan were being stationed in the Kiev military district, necessitating the transfer of Kiev to another subzone. Hungary also sought changes in subzonal limits, insisting on being moved from one subzone to another so that it could be considered a Central European, as opposed to Balkan, power. This was partly because Hungary had been left out of the MBFR talks and because Hungary wanted to avoid unfavorable manpower ratios with Rumania.

Verification. The verification issue had been one of the principal stumbling blocks in the MBFR talks. Although Gorbachev agreed to inspection of Soviet territory and data exchanges, thus removing one of the principal obstacles to conventional arms agreement, there still remained the question about the actual number of inspections that would be permitted. NATO wanted a higher number of annual inspections than the Soviets preferred. However, in the final weeks of negotiations in New York, the United States agreed to a lower number, prompting criticism from its European allies and the non-Soviet Warsaw Pact states, which favored a more stringent inspection regime. These negotiations were also complicated by Hungary's insistence on the right to inspect Soviet territory and its threat not to ratify a CFE agreement unless its demands were met. This demand created a new set of dilemmas for the West: on the one hand, Hungary's newfound independence from Moscow and assertiveness was to be welcomed; on the other, Hungarian inspections of Soviet territory (as well as those by other non-Soviet Warsaw Pact states) would be at the expense of NATO, especially under the reduced number of inspections that had been agreed on by the United States. This would require sharing of information by different national inspection teams in order to ensure confidence in the new verification regime.

Agreement

The CFE treaty was ready for signing at the Paris summit meeting of the Conference on Security and Cooperation in Europe on November 19,

1990. The treaty called for major reductions in five categories of equipment of NATO and Warsaw Pact forces, covering an area stretching from the Atlantic to the Urals. The treaty stipulated reductions in battle tanks, artillery, armored combat vehicles, armored infantry-fighting vehicles, heavy armament combat vehicles, and attack helicopters. Ceilings for specific categories of equipment were established for several geographical subzones within each alliance group. Definitions, counting rules, and zonal limits were set out in Articles II, IV, V, VI, and XII in the treaty. Special provisions in the treaty stipulated how equipment was to be destroyed, inactivated, or converted (Art. VIII of the treaty). Altogether the treaty contained twenty-three articles and eight protocols.[31] The treaty was of historic importance not only because it provided the first limits on the large number of weapons deployed by NATO and the Warsaw Pact but also because it marked the symbolic end to a long period of fear and mistrust between the two alliances. Moreover, the treaty not only established limits on certain categories of equipment and arms but also reduced the capability for surprise attacks or offensive military action.[32]

Under Article IV of the treaty, each side is bound to an upper limit of armaments as follows:

Tanks	20,000
Artillery	20,000
Armored combat vehicles	30,000
Aircraft	6,800
Helicopters	2,000

These limits refer to the entire area of application of the treaty, which includes all of the European territory of states party to the treaty, stretching from the Atlantic to the Ural mountains in Russia. U.S. and Canadian territory is not affected by the treaty. Separate regional sublimits are established for specific zones within the area of application. In order to guard against any one state having a preponderance of the arms limited by the treaty, no one state may possess more than approximately one third of the total arms permitted in a given category. Specific maximum levels are outlined for each category. These limits require only modest cuts in NATO tanks and helicopters and no NATO cuts at all in the other categories. The Warsaw Pact, however, was required to make significant cuts in its forces across the board. Reductions are to be completed forty months after the treaty comes into force and are to occur in three phases. After sixteen months, 25 percent of the reductions must be completed. After another twelve months, 60 percent of the reductions must be completed. Forty months after the treaty comes into force, all reductions must be completed

(Art. VIII, Sec. 4). The treaty comes into force ten days after all signatories to the treaty have deposited instruments of ratification in the Netherlands.

Detailed exchanges of information and notifications are required under the treaty. These include the structure and peacetime location of the command organization of land, air, and air-defense forces, designation and location of units holding specified conventional armaments and equipment, and location of designated permanent storage sites and reduction sites, all within the zone affected by the treaty. The treaty also outlines specific measures for the destruction of each category of weapon. For aircraft and helicopters, states have the option of disarming and reconfiguring the equipment for training purposes, rather than simply destroying it. Methods outlined in the treaty must be followed, and the process is monitored by inspectors.

Different types of inspection are available as verification measures. Inspections are to be used to verify information exchanges and compliance with the limits established in the treaty. Inspections are also used to monitor the destruction of equipment and arms and the processes used to convert aircraft and helicopters. A state cannot refuse an inspection of a declared site, but a system of quotas is established in the protocol on inspection to ensure that no one state will be subject to an excessive number of inspections. Challenge inspections of specified areas (nondeclared sites) are permitted, but the state to be inspected has the right to refuse inspection. A joint consultative group is also established by the treaty, to provide a framework for all the states party to the treaty to discuss ambiguous issues, questions of compliance, and other questions relating to the treaty. The consultative group meets twice a year, and extra sessions can be held at the request of individual states.

The treaty does not place limits on personnel levels or on the number of troops deployed in the European area. In February 1989, the United States and the Soviet Union agreed to limit personnel to 195,000 troops each. However, this commitment was overtaken by planned Soviet withdrawals from Eastern Europe, the reunification of Germany, and proposed U.S. budget cuts calling for far fewer than 195,000 U.S. troops in Europe. Rather than begin negotiations on new levels, in September 1990 the negotiators agreed to postpone this question in order to complete the treaty by the November deadline. A commitment to proceed with negotiations on personnel levels and aerial inspection methods as the next stage in the CFE negotiations (known as CFE 1A) is part of the CFE treaty. Aerial inspection is important to the verification procedures of the treaty. However, as with troop limitations, the effort to complete the treaty by November led negotiators to postpone the issue. The first round of the CFE 1A negotiations began on November 29, 1990, ten days after the treaty was signed.

In a declaration on the same day the treaty was signed, Germany reaffirmed its commitment to reduce its armed force levels to 370,000. These reductions were to begin once the treaty entered into force. In separate declarations, all signatories to the treaty agreed that they would not increase their peacetime authorized conventional personnel strength until the CFE 1A negotiations on the issue were completed. One day prior to the signing of the treaty, the Soviet Union announced a ten-year draft plan for reductions and restructuring in Soviet armed forces, the first stage of which involved a complete withdrawal of all Soviet troops from Czechoslovakia, Hungary, Mongolia, and Germany by 1994.

Prologue

Soon after the signing of the CFE treaty, NATO countries expressed concern about Soviet movements of large number of tanks and artillery out of the European zone, and therefore outside the limits of the treaty, prior to its signing.[33] Questions were also raised about the validity of the data supplied by the Soviet Union in the first information exchange. In response, the Soviet Union explained that in a number of cases, the movement of equipment beyond the Ural mountains was related to unilateral Soviet reductions announced in December 1988 and still being implemented. Some of the equipment that had been moved had already been destroyed. The Soviets invited U.S. experts to come to the Soviet Union to discuss the matter.

In March, a second issue surfaced. The Soviet Union recategorized three motor rifle divisions, previously under the jurisdiction of the army, as naval "coastal defense" units, claiming that the equipment associated with these units was not limited by the treaty. The Soviet Union also claimed that equipment held by the Strategic Rocket Forces was not subject to the terms of the treaty. This indicated fundamental differences of interpretation in the treaty's provisions between the Soviet Union and other signatories. President Bush wrote to Gorbachev in an effort to find a compromise that would maintain the terms of the treaty. The issue was of such concern that it put all other arms control negotiations, including the U.S.-Soviet bilateral START (Strategic Arms Reduction Talks), on hold until the matter could be resolved.

After considerable high-level diplomacy throughout the month of May, U.S. Secretary of State Baker and Soviet Foreign Minister Eduard Shevardnadze reached a compromise agreement, on June 1, 1991. And on June 14, in an extraordinary meeting of the treaty signatories in Vienna, the compromise was made formal and official. In a binding statement in which the Soviet Union pledged its full compliance with the treaty's terms, the Soviet Union also agreed to destroy or convert 14,500 of the 57,000 weapon systems it had moved out of the treaty zone prior to November 1990. It was agreed that the Soviet Union could maintain its disputed coastal defense and naval infantry units on the condition that these units not be expanded. It was also agreed that the equipment of the Strategic Rocket Forces would be exempt from treaty limits by considering them internal security forces. The other signatories gave binding declarations accepting the Soviet pledges.

The collapse of the Warsaw Pact rendered irrelevant some of the arithmetical details of the CFE treaty. However, the collapse of the Soviet Union in late 1991 created new complications for implementation and ratification as Moscow and the newly created states, the former republics of the Soviet Union, argued over their force structure allocations under a CFE regime.[34] The Baltic states (Lithuania, Latvia, and Estonia) did not want to be part of the ATTU zone, because they did not want their ability to create their own national forces to be compromised by CFE treaty limits. It was eventually agreed that Russian forces stationed in the Baltic states would remain subject to CFE limits, whereas Baltic national forces would not.

However, this created an unfortunate precedent for other Soviet successor states such as the Ukraine, which was in the process of creating its own national army. As one observer writes, "the military ambitions of new political elites in Moscow, Kiev and other CIS [Commonwealth of Independent States] became the new dominant factor. In emotional clashes, the question of the distribution of CFE ceilings was linked to such controversial issues as control of the Black Sea Fleet, Russia's nuclear monopoly, the financing of strategic forces and so on."[35] These issues were resolved only after considerable negotiation and the growing realization that worsening economic conditions would make it all but impossible for Russia and the former Soviet republics to support the army and air force at CFE treaty ceiling levels anyway. Russia and the republics agreed to new, individual force ceilings at Tashkent in May 1992, which were endorsed by the North Atlantic Cooperation Council in Oslo in early June.

On July 10, 1992, the members of NATO, along with six non-Soviet former Warsaw Pact countries and seven former Soviet republics, signed two new accords: the Provisional Application of the CFE 1 treaty, which brought it into force even though Armenia, Belarus, Portugal, and Russia had not yet deposited instruments of ratification; and the Concluding Act of the Negotiation on Personnel Strength of Conventional Armed Forces, Europe (CFE 1A), which set limits to the numbers of military personnel in the territory of the twenty-nine states party to the treaty.[36] However, four former Soviet republics (Armenia, Azerbaijan, Georgia, and Moldova) did not agree to set limits, because they were engaged in armed hostilities against one other.[37]

Explaining Outcomes

Crisis

In one sense, the catalyst for the MBFR talks was the political crisis brought on by Senator Mike Mansfield's attempts in 1966 to organize a unilateral withdrawal of U.S. forces from Europe. The administrations of Presidents Johnson and Nixon sought to stave off congressional pressure by proposing a mutual reduction of forces in Europe. In 1971, when Senate pressure peaked for a second time, the United States and its allies were successful in getting Moscow to agree to negotiations. However, as noted above, domestic pressure quickly dissipated once formal negotiations began, thus removing much of the original incentive to reach an agreement on force reductions. The corresponding lack of high-level political interest in these negotiations insured that they languished in relative obscurity for well over a decade.

In the mid-1980s, conventional arms control received a much-needed infusion of political capital with Gorbachev's rise to leadership in the Soviet Union. This time, however, it was domestic pressures on the Soviet side that brought the two sides to the negotiating table. The growing economic crisis in the Soviet Union prompted the country's new political elites to seek ways to reduce defense spending and alleviate the burdens that foreign military commitments were imposing on the Soviet economy. The West soon came to realize that the Soviet Union's newfound interest in conventional arms control was genuine and motivated by a sincere desire to reduce the size of its military presence abroad. Thus, the economic crisis in the Soviet Union had an important impact on the onset of a new round of conventional arms control talks. And as the domestic crisis continued and the pace of political change in Eastern Europe accelerated, the incentive to reach an agreement on conventional arms reductions also grew.

Consensual Knowledge

Consensual knowledge in the form of ideas emanating from groups of experts outside government and policy circles was not crucial to progress in conventional arms control per se. The process was managed largely by a closed community of diplomats, military officials, and policy experts in the governments of the countries participating in the formal negotiations. Nonetheless, the process of incremental trial-and-error learning that resulted from almost decades of MBFR talks was important to the CFE negotiations that followed. The technical difficulties and pitfalls of conventional arms control were well understood by the participants, and CFE negotiators could draw upon a wealth of experience. Thus, the CFE negotiations were able to build on the foundations that had been laid in the

MBFR talks, and this is one reason the negotiations moved ahead as quickly as they did once the political will and commitment were there. Both sides had developed a good appreciation of the composition and structure of each other's forces and what sorts of integrative bargains and trade-offs might be struck to achieve reductions that would be mutually acceptable. Without the record of experience and knowledge that was acquired in MBFR negotiations, it is quite likely that an initiative to initiate conventional arms reductions de novo would have taken longer and not proceeded quite as smoothly as the CFE negotiations did.

Coalitions and Representation

The key parties in the CFE negotiations were the United States and the Soviet Union, which formally stood at the head of their respective alliance structures. Many of the logjams that surfaced in the negotiations were resolved in bilateral discussions between the heads of state or foreign ministers of the two superpowers. However, NATO positions were typically worked out beforehand and only after considerable consultation among the allies. The allies were quick to express their concerns if they felt the United States was moving too quickly or not taking sufficient account of their interests. Thus, with the onset of formal CFE negotiations, the Federal Republic of Germany made clear its own desire to delay NATO's modernization of short-range tactical nuclear weapons, whereas the United States and Britain were keen to press ahead. After extensive consultations, Bush unveiled a new compromise at the NATO summit meeting in Brussels, which authorized U.S.-Soviet talks on partial reductions once negotiated CFE cuts were underway. Similarly, after the Malta summit between Bush and Gorbachev, Bush was quick to reassure his allies that the United States would not undertake unilateral troop cuts above and beyond those levels that had previously been stated. West Germany, France, and Italy also forced the pace of negotiations, once it became clear that Soviet forces were going to be withdrawn from the territories of the newly emerging democratic states of Eastern Europe.

In the case of the Soviet Union and its Warsaw Pact allies, there was obviously a shift in the pattern of intra-alliance politics from the days of MBFR talks. As the Soviet empire in Eastern Europe crumbled, Moscow found it could no longer call the shots and expect its Warsaw Pact allies to fall in line. The demands by several Eastern European countries (notably, Czechoslovakia, Hungary, and Poland) for the withdrawal of Soviet troops from their territory was symptomatic of this trend. Confusion in the Eastern bloc mounted with the impending collapse of the Soviet Union itself. The ability of Russia and the former republics of the Soviet Union to implement key provisions in the CFE proposals was thrown into question by mounting conflict over who would control the tattered remains of the Red Army and the formidable arsenal that had once been under Moscow's sole control. The dissolution of the Soviet empire and of the Soviet Union itself thus created formidable problems not only of negotiation but of treaty implementation as well—problems that have not yet been fully resolved.

Bridging and Bargaining Strategies

It is almost certainly accurate to portray the CFE treaty-making process as essentially a bilateral bargaining process between the two key veto powers, the United States and the Soviet Union, although this process was complicated by the collapse of the Soviet Union's Eastern European empire and the evolution of the Soviet Union into the Commonwealth of Independent States—a group of states which did not necessarily see eye to eye on their fundamental security interests. On a number of occasions, key third powers made important contributions to the negotiation process itself by advancing bridging proposals (e.g., Hungary's compromise proposal on combat aircraft and interceptors) or by taking independent initiatives (as in the case of the Federal Republic of Germany's offer of security guarantees to the Soviet Union, restricting the size of the Bundeswehr in a United Germany) that were crucial to the success of the negotiations. However, it is fair to say that bridging contributions were probably less crucial to advancement of these negotiations and to closure than the Soviet Union's decision unilaterally to cut the size of its forces, followed by pressure from some Eastern European states for the Soviet Union to withdraw its forces completely from their territory. These developments, along with German reunification, put pressure on negotiators to reach an agreement that would not be completely overtaken by political events and developments.

Issue Decomposition and Sequencing

Issue sequencing and staging strategies facilitated the negotiating process. Partly as a result of the MBFR experience, which had shown how difficult it was to negotiate parity in military manpower because of the inability of NATO and the Warsaw Pact to agree on the size of pact forces, a conscious decision was made in the CFE negotiations to focus on equipment, as opposed to manpower, reductions. This was also based on the realization that manpower reductions would likely follow from force reductions. Similarly, the decision to defer talks on short-range nuclear weapons until after CFE-mandated cuts had begun removed another potential barrier to negotiations by disentangling the complex linkage between conventional and nuclear forces in both NATO and Warsaw Pact strategy. Reductions in different equipment categories were also dealt with separately in the talks, as were issues of verification, compliance, and subzonal limits. This further

demonstrates the importance of issue sequencing and staging to the negotiation process.

Leadership

Much like the Stockholm Conference and agreement on confidence- and
security-building measures, political leadership was crucial not only to the
onset of new negotiations aimed at limiting conventional arms in Europe
but also to forcing the pace of negotiations. In the prenegotiation phase,
two events were crucial to the onset of new negotiations: the first was the
Budapest Appeal following Gorbachev's call for an expanded zone of arms
reductions from the Atlantic to the Urals; the second was Gorbachev's December 1988 U.N. announcement of unilateral cuts in the size of Soviet
armed forces. Gorbachev was clearly the chief architect of these proposals,
and his announcements dramatically changed the context of conventional arms control, providing the much-needed impetus to launch a new
round of talks. George Bush and his NATO allies were quick to respond to
these initiatives, offering NATO's own proposals for new negotiations.
Once negotiations were underway, leadership was crucial to keeping the
negotiations on track and ensuring that they were responsive to the rapid
social and political changes that were changing the face of Europe. Such
leadership was also crucial to forging compromises on some of the most
intractable issues in the negotiation, such as Bush's proposal to defer modernization of short-range nuclear weapons until CFE negotiations were
concluded, the Baker-Shevardnadze agreement on tactical aircraft, the
Kohl-Gorbachev summit on the future of Germany, or U.S. proposals on
verification and inspection arrangements in the CFE treaty.

Compliance

Verification and compliance issues had been one of the principal stumbling blocks in the MBFR negotiations. Not only were there major and un-
resolvable differences over data and interpretation, but the long-standing
Soviet resistance to on-site inspection created its own barriers to agreement on conventional force reductions. In 1985, however, the Soviets
agreed in principle to on-site challenge inspections under the MBFR agreements. Gorbachev's subsequent offer allowing inspections of Soviet territory and data exchanges was crucial to the success of the CFE talks. To be
sure, NATO and the pact continued to quibble over the number of inspections that would be allowed under a CFE regime, with the West favoring a
higher number than the Soviets were prepared to accept. But, importantly,
the principle of on-site inspection was not an issue. The United States also
agreed to a lower number of inspections than its allies wanted. Further, although charges of Soviet noncompliance surfaced almost immediately as

soon as the treaty was signed, these issues were resolved to the apparent satisfaction of the parties concerned. However, the breakup of the Soviet Union itself has created its own special problem of treaty compliance, and such problems could conceivably worsen if conflicts among some of the former republics of the Soviet Union continue.

The story of conventional arms control is thus one of failure followed by success. Although the beginnings of the MBFR negotiations were auspicious, they floundered on the shoals of the Cold War and the fact that neither side was seriously committed to achieving conventional arms reductions. The initial domestic crisis—the threat that the U.S. Congress would mandate troop cuts against the wishes of the president—that had brought the United States to the negotiating table quickly dissipated once formal negotiations began. There was neither sufficient outside political pressure nor the will to propel negotiations forward. Once Gorbachev, who confronted a growing domestic economic crisis, arrived on the scene, the context of negotiations on conventional arms changed dramatically. For the first time, the East was serious about achieving reductions, and it had a leader who was willing to make the necessary concessions and compromises to make negotiations succeed. Western leaders sought reductions as well and were willing to compromise and provide the necessary reassurances to the Soviet Union at a time of extraordinary political change and internal transformation. In this case, bridging and bargaining strategies by lesser powers were less crucial to the outcome of these negotiations than the end of the Cold War itself, marked by the collapse of the Soviet empire in Eastern Europe soon followed by the demise of the Soviet Union itself. The CFE experience thus dramatically underscores the singular importance of the external political context to arms control and behavior at the bargaining table.

III Multilateral Trade Negotiations

6 The 1947–1948 United Nations Conference on Trade and Employment

The signing of the Final Act of the United Nations Conference on Trade and Employment at Havana, Cuba on March 24, 1948, was supposed to mark the culmination of an ambitious plan to establish an international trade organization (ITO). In fact, it was the signing of a Final Act on October 30, 1947, at Geneva, Switzerland, that proved to be of lasting significance. It brought to a close the interim tariff-negotiating conference held in conjunction with the second session of the preparatory committee for the United Nations conference. When, in 1950, the Truman administration quietly withdrew the Havana Charter from consideration by the U.S. Senate, it acknowledged that the ITO was not to be. As a result, the General Agreement on Tariffs and Trade (GATT), adopted at Geneva in 1947 as an interim agreement to cover the agreed tariff concessions, has functioned ever since as the proxy for an international trade organization.

The more limited objectives and careful preparation that eventually led to a successful multilateral tariff conference among twenty-three countries in Geneva and the "interim" GATT stand in sharp contrast to the much more ambitious, less well-prepared, and less widely shared objectives for the ITO. Even the United States, the principal mover in these two parallel negotiations, could in the end accept only the lesser instrument. At the same time, because the negotiations took place in parallel and were so intimately intertwined, the success of the GATT negotiations in part spelled doom for the ITO and made the failure of the Havana Conference more acceptable. The prenegotiations and preparatory meetings held in Washington, London, Lake Success (New York), and Geneva, as well as the Havana Conference, thus offer a rich series of examples of the factors in multilateral commercial diplomacy that lead to success or failure.[1]

The Setting

Issues and Players

Preparations for the negotiations began in the very early stages of the Second World War and were carried to a conclusion at a full-scale conference sponsored by the fledgling United Nations three years after the war's end.

In both London and Washington, groups of officials—many of them on temporary leave from their regular careers as academic economists, lawyers, or business executives—were assigned the task of postwar economic planning. In other capitals around the world, officials responsible for trade and economic policy were aware of this planning and prepared for the moment when their ideas would be sought.

For many of these officials, the dominating events in their lives had been depression and war. Many of them were old enough to have vivid memories of the 1914–18 war, and all of them had lived through the dislocation and anxieties spawned by the depression. As either academics or government officials, they had analyzed the policy responses to these defining events and concluded that the beggar-thy-neighbor policies adopted almost universally had deepened the depression and paved the road to a second world war. They knew that while world production had gradually recovered starting in 1932, reaching predepression levels again in 1937, world trade had not recovered, because many of the barriers and currency problems remained, complicated by the deteriorating political situation. Many of them knew that the extreme bilateralism pursued by Germany in the 1930s, which had influenced its increasing sense of isolation, had been made too easy by their own governments' policies. As a result, therefore, they were determined not to repeat the mistakes made at the end of the First World War. They were determined to be better prepared to deal with peace once the war was over. They would help their governments adopt policies that would promote cooperation, leading to prosperity and a lasting peace, within a framework of international rules designed to ease governments' task in implementing appropriate policies.

However, officials in the United States, Britain, and elsewhere thought primarily in terms of their own recent experiences, which differed greatly. Thus, while it was not difficult to find commonly held objectives based on their common exposure to depression and war, their different national experiences strongly colored their perceptions of how these objectives could best be met. As negotiations progressed, these differing perceptions, coupled with differing national values and priorities, would lead to the conflict and compromises that eventually overwhelmed the ITO but left enough room for its more truncated version, the GATT. In effect, the negotiations provided a curious mixture of internationalist idealism and nationalist realism. In the end, it was the latter that triumphed.

In the United States, the defining experience was the adoption in 1934 of Secretary of State Cordell Hull's Reciprocal Trade Agreements program. Hull's program took account of the limits placed on the president by the constitution and the reality of congressional politics but allowed the United States to adopt a reciprocal, nondiscriminatory bargaining tariff.

For the first time in U.S. history, Congress gave the president the authority to negotiate agreements that reduced tariffs and to establish the machinery and resources to carry out the necessary analysis, consultations, and negotiations. The Reciprocal Trade Agreements (RTA) Act proved a powerful tool for reversing nearly a century of increasing U.S. protectionism and for allowing the United States to play a leadership role for the first time in international economic affairs.

Hull's original desire had been for a broad, horizontal, multilateral cut in tariff protection, but he and his advisors had wisely judged that neither Congress nor other governments were ready for such a bold move. Instead, they opted for a less ambitious approach and used their authority prudently to conserve what they had gained. By 1947, on the eve of the GATT negotiations, twenty-nine countries had taken advantage of the program and improved and secured access to what was by then the largest and most dynamic economy in the world. The average level of U.S. tariffs at the beginning of the program approached 60 percent; by 1947, it had been reduced to under 30 percent for participants in the program. By mutual agreement, the U.S. and twenty-nine of its trading partners had reduced tariffs, enlarged or eliminated quotas, liberalized exchange controls, bound thousands of tariff levels, and entered into a long-term commitment to end discrimination and develop a body of international trade rules.[2]

Admittedly, most of the participants in the program were relatively small Western Hemisphere countries, and the overall trend of increasing protection in Europe had continued. Additionally, the American tariff remained high, and the United States remained unwilling to take a broader, multilateral approach. Nevertheless, Hull's team had learned to negotiate international trade agreements based on a technique tailor-made for the peculiarities of the U.S. constitution and congressional politics. As negotiations progressed, they steadily learned how best to address the issues and provided as complete a code of conduct as current commercial policy practice allowed.[3]

Adoption of the Reciprocal Trade Agreements program marked a revolution in U.S. trade policy. It radically altered not only the basic orientation of U.S. trade policy (from a built-in bias favoring protection to one favoring liberalism) but also the process by which it was formulated and delivered. Congress thus blessed the adoption of a "bargaining" tariff and, through delegation of its power over the details of tariff making, married trade policy making and foreign policy making. The details of both would now be the responsibility of State Department professionals, pursuing their work within guidelines established in consultation between the president and the Congress. The experience in designing and managing this innovative and revolutionary program would greatly color the U.S. approach to the postwar trade negotiations, not only in terms of what should or should not be addressed in trade agreements but also in terms of how to steer a course consonant with the peculiar demands of the U.S. constitution and U.S. congressional politics.

While developments in U.S. trade policy conditioned the United States to take a leading role in the postwar trade and economic discussions, equally momentous developments in Britain disposed it to play a very different role from what its earlier history would have suggested. During the 1930s, the United Kingdom gradually abandoned its long-standing free-trade principles and steadily turned inward. This historic reversal in U.S. and British trade policy symbolized a slow shift in leadership. From the late eighteenth century until the beginning of the twentieth century, the United Kingdom had been the world's premier economy, confident, outward-looking, and rich. Since 1846, it had practiced and preached free trade and kept its markets open to the products of the world. But except for the brief interlude ushered in by the Cobden-Chevalier treaty of 1860, Britain had stood alone. With the collapse of the world economy in 1929, British resolve crumbled, and Britain adopted not only tariffs but the discrimination advocated by its former colonial possessions and long the mainstay of European trade policy.

Nevertheless, postwar British governments sought to maintain international leadership, through both the League of Nations and the Commonwealth. Neither effort, however, led to liberalism and order. Efforts in the League in the absence of the United States and Germany proved feeble and became more so over time. Much was discussed and studied, but little was agreed and implemented. This failure further accentuated an air of pessimism in Britain about the benefits of free trade and freely convertible currencies. Even John Maynard Keynes, who later played such an influential role in establishing the postwar system of nondiscriminatory multilateral agreements, despaired about the benefits of an open and nondiscriminatory exchange of goods: "I sympathize, therefore, with those who would minimize, rather than those who would maximize, economic entanglements among nations. Ideas, knowledge, science, hospitality, travel—these are the things which should of their nature be international. But let goods be homespun whenever it is reasonably and conveniently possible, and, above all, let finance be primarily national."[4]

Britain's most immediate trade policy experience as it began planning for a postwar international trade regime, therefore, had been based on its acceptance of a protective tariff married to a system of bound preferences among its Commonwealth trading partners. That experience had proved popular among business and labor interests alike and had been given an intellectual underpinning by economists like Keynes, who believed that one of the most important challenges facing government during a depression was to increase total demand and thus boost domestic production and employment. In such circumstances, it might be necessary to adopt discriminatory trade actions and exchange controls in order temporarily to shelter a depressed economy from foreign competition. Practical British trade policy thinking, therefore, was increasingly based on the principles of protection, preference, and discrimination.[5]

Britain was not alone; Europe had similarly embraced protectionism as a principle in the period leading up to the First World War and gradually abandoned the treaty system that had imposed order and kept protection within reasonable bounds for much of the second half of the nineteenth century. By the end of the war, trade barriers were considerably higher all around as various governments moved to protect new industries established by war, safeguard their balance-of-payments positions, and promote employment. Initially guarded by various quantitative restrictions and similar nontariff barriers, these were gradually replaced by more neutral tariffs after the war; but these in turn gradually began to march ever higher in the absence of any treaty obligations to impose restraint. Where tariffs proved insufficient, quantitative restrictions were again introduced, as were exchange controls. Few treaties were concluded aimed at reducing tariffs or even stabilizing them; nor was the principle of unconditional most-favored-nation treatment rehabilitated. France's decision to go it alone, on a basis other than an unconditional most-favored-nation treaty system, doomed any efforts to reintroduce such a system. The popular appeal of protectionism and its link to nationalism gave the fragile French governments of the interwar years little room to maneuver.

Throughout the 1920s, various conferences sponsored by the League of Nations tried to stem the tide, but each had at best a temporary effect. Thus when recession struck agricultural production in 1928 and gradually spread, hastened by the Wall Street crash of 1929, there were no restraints in place in Europe or elsewhere to prevent countries from adopting policies aimed at exporting their problems. As the recession turned to depression, countries further aggravated the fall in demand by creating ever higher barriers to protect their own industries; the 1930 Smoot-Hawley Tariff in the United States was the most flagrant example. By 1931, these competitive tariff increases culminated in the introduction by the United Kingdom of a major protective tariff, succeeded the following year by the Import Duties Act. To further unsettle matters, Britain abandoned the gold standard the following year, followed by many of its trading partners, while the United States devalued the dollar. Currency instability and inconvertibility now added another dimension of fragility to international commerce and further deepened the depression.

Thus, while European countries had enjoyed a long period of stability and prosperity underwritten by an effective system of trade treaties during the 19th century, their more recent experience fairly bristled with discrimination, preferences, autonomous trade policies, and failed negotiations. Without a strong leader to forge a new treaty system, there was little prospect that the growing attachment to autarkic full employment policies could be easily overcome. Certainly the experience of the League of Nations confirmed this pessimistic assessment.

While it would be premature to speak of developing countries or the third world—terms that did not come into vogue until later—the Havana Conference also included a large contingent of countries referred to as the poor or underdeveloped countries. Most of these were in Latin America and Asia and included India, Lebanon, Argentina, Brazil, and Mexico. The decolonization of Africa and the Caribbean still lay in the future, and the interests of these territories were covered by the metropolitan powers.

The attitudes and experiences of these poorer countries differed vastly from those of the United States, the United Kingdom, Canada, France, and the other major players but were shared somewhat by Australia, New Zealand, and South Africa. Many participated in the negotiations firmly convinced that their economic development needs required agreements that would allow them to continue to protect infant industries and their fragile balance of payments. They were prepared neither to make significant concessions to the major powers nor to enter into commitments that would seriously compromise their ability to pursue autarkic economic development policies. The experience of some in negotiating reciprocal trade agreements with the United States—particularly in Latin America, where sixteen countries had taken up the call—had in no way diminished their views that protectionism was a desirable principle. They had been unable to convince the United States to make any meaningful concessions to their export interests, either because they failed the principal supplier rule or because their interests lay in politically sensitive sectors, such as agriculture. They were unprepared, therefore, to have the United States lecture them about the merits of nondiscrimination, reciprocity, tariff concessions, and serious discipline on nontariff measures. As early as 1945, for example, at the Chapultepec Conference in Mexico, underdeveloped countries had insisted that trade obligations should not undermine their development aspirations.[6]

Ideas and Objectives

While the policies and objectives of the various participating governments ultimately came from practical men steeped in the political and bureaucratic experiences of the recent past, the negotiations that led to the Havana Charter and the GATT were more than casually influenced by men of ideas, particularly in the early stages. The unusual circumstances of first depression and then war had provided unprecedented opportunities for professional economists, lawyers, and business executives to take temporary leaves of absence from their regular careers and serve governments not only as planners and policy advisors but also as negotiators and administrators. Economic thinking, therefore, played a critical role in setting objectives, as well as in determining the success and failure of the negotiations.

As negotiations progressed, two sets of ideas provided the main ingredients for conflict and controversy. They can be described in a variety of ways: mercantilism versus free trade, free-enterprise versus state control, or discrimination versus nondiscrimination. What they had in common was the conflict between mainstream economic thinking attuned to letting markets work and what Deepak Lal calls "the dirigiste dogma."[7] While today these conflicting views are frequently encountered in debates about development economics, managed trade, or industrial policy, many of these ideas had their origin in the debates that took place in the 1930s and 1940s. Those unhappy with the operation of the market and private enterprise, particularly during the depression, were convinced that the market should be supplanted by strategic planning and that they should devote their energy to devising appropriate plans and policies.

The most comprehensive theoretical approach to these new policies was provided by John Maynard Keynes. His *General Theory of Employment, Interest, and Money* provided the intellectual rationale for policies aimed at using government measures to stimulate demand until employment was restored. For maximum effect, it required national self-sufficiency, in the form of tariffs and quantitative restrictions to safeguard the balance of payments. Gerard Curzon concludes that "the predominance of national economic policies over international policies thus followed logically from Keynes's approach to income determination."[8] It also led naturally to skepticism about the benefits of multilateralism and nondiscrimination in all but ideal circumstances and an inclination to pursue bilateralism and preferences. These ideas traveled well and were soon the main topic of discussion across the Atlantic, particularly among young New Deal economists.[9]

While these ideas fit in well with evolving British tariff policy, they were at odds with evolving U.S. trade policy. Cordell Hull had built his position on the classical doctrine of free trade as developed by more traditional economists, such as Frank Taussig at Harvard and Jacob Viner at Princeton University. Both had been on the staff of the U.S. Tariff Commission and had provided the economic rationale for much of the new trade policy. The economists and lawyers Hull attracted to his staff all shared his views.[10] Hull's Wilsonian internationalism was also part of an older intellectual tradition, although, again, widely shared among his advisors. His view that open, nondiscriminatory markets nurtured peace and good international relations permeated the statements of other senior officials, ran through congressional hearings, and formed a major theme in the occasional literature.[11]

Of course, in neither Washington, London, nor elsewhere was there a monolithic view of these problems. The theories and ideas that appealed to the planners and decision makers were those that seemed most suited to the political and economic circumstances of the moment, as well as to the dynamics of the negotiating process. British planners, for example, were not all Keynesians, nor was every member of the U.S. team a fully paid-up member of the neoclassical school. In London, for example, one of Keynes's closest collaborators in postwar planning was Lionel Robbins, whose writings during the 1930s had been critical of Keynes, particularly their implications for international policy.[12] In Washington, the U.S. dislike of quantitative restrictions did not include those established under the Agricultural Adjustment Act of 1933, nor did Hull's free-trade principles extend to a willingness to countenance an across-the-board cut in tariffs. Good economics was one thing; the reality of congressional politics was quite another. As the negotiations progressed, however, U.S. thinking coalesced strongly around that of Hull and his closest advisors in their strong attachment to free enterprise and nondiscrimination, while British thinking was much more sympathetic to maintaining room for a higher level of state control of the economy. Such thinking became even stronger when Labour formed the government after 1945.

In thinking through the kinds of policies and forms of international cooperation that would be required, U.S. planners thus sought to establish free, nondiscriminatory trade, unhampered by arbitrary or discretionary government measures within a framework that would allow for the gradual reduction in tariffs. The method they eventually chose to achieve this goal was a comprehensive code governing world trade, interpreted and enforced by a strong institution within the framework of the United Nations and complementary to the Bretton Woods financial institutions. "The code would lay down the law, and the members would be law-abiding."[13] At a general level, this was a goal others could share, but not immediately, and not at the level of detail prescribed by the United States. In the context of their need to reconstruct war-torn economies or promote economic development in a world that now accepted a much larger role for government, other countries saw the U.S. approach as too confining and too interfering. The details of what they preferred or disliked might differ, but virtually all other participants in either the preparatory meetings or the conference itself—with the notable exception of Canada—preferred a less confining set of obligations. In pursuing their goals, they were able to draw on the more fashionable ideas of Keynes, Gunnar Myrdal, and other economists developing theories more appropriate to the new planning ideology. Finding an acceptable compromise between these two conflicting sets of views, therefore, would become the principal challenge facing the negotiators.

Prenegotiation

As they prepared for the victory they felt confidently would be theirs, postwar planners in the United States were guided by several lessons they had learned from the recent past. In their view, the rise in protectionism in the 1930s was a failure not of theory, knowledge, or effort but of policy, including U.S. policy. They were convinced that the United States had not sufficiently focused on the economic dimensions of postwar planning. By carefully preparing the ground, in terms of both detailed staff work and informal discussions with other governments, U.S. officials believed that they would be able to avoid the mistakes of the past.[14] As a result, they were optimistic about their ability to resolve the problems of the 1930s by planning for more appropriate policies built upon both a much higher level of U.S. involvement and a much more intensive level of international cooperation.[15]

With these lessons firmly in mind, American officials in Cordell Hull's office began as early as 1939 to draw up plans for a postwar world, plans that took on greater urgency when the United States entered the war and soon began to involve officials of allied governments.[16] Joint planning on postwar economic policy was not an isolated incident. Throughout the war, American, British, and Canadian officials devoted considerable energy to joint planning of production, allocation, trade, and monetary affairs. The successful prosecution of the war by the allies was as much the result of economic planning and cooperation as of military strategy and superiority. The high level of joint planning activity had two direct influences on the preparation for and negotiation of the postwar commercial policy regime: it deeply ingrained the habit of working things out together among a select group of countries with the general support of others, and it boosted confidence in the capacity of governments and their officials to solve problems.[17]

Insofar as trade was concerned, U.S. planners sought initially to build on and extend their experience in negotiating reciprocal trade agreements. This somewhat cautious approach was taken not because they lacked ideas but because they had no illusions about the extent to which Congress would support grander ideas. As planning progressed, however, they listened to British officials armed with much more ambitious schemes, including plans for an international trade organization. British officials had not been alone in their bolder thinking. Canadians had also fed such ideas to their American colleagues.[18] Thus, while American officials are usually held responsible for the more ambitious proposals that became the ITO, they had been encouraged to take this direction as much by their British and Canadian colleagues as by their own idealism and that of American think-tank advisors, such as those in the Council on Foreign Relations.

Nevertheless, American officials kept one foot firmly planted on the ground of congressional reality. The RTA program, while it might have been a cumbersome and slow instrument for reducing tariffs, had the merit of bypassing Congress on the detail of negotiations and thus made it possible for U.S. negotiators to conduct serious negotiations. Hull's program had successfully demonstrated how the United States could solve the negotiating dilemma posed by the constitutional assignment of trade policy to the Congress. It had proven a powerful tool in overcoming the U.S. penchant for economic isolationism. American officials, therefore, stubbornly insisted throughout the preparation for and conduct of the negotiations that at least part of the final result had to build on their successful RTA experience.

While British and Canadian officials were well aware of these considerations, they were equally concerned to find the necessary means to ensure that the United States would remain fully engaged in postwar economic agreements and organizations. Additionally, they were not confident that the RTA approach would lead to a substantial enough reduction in U.S. tariffs. U.S. tariffs may have been cut in half for countries participating in the RTA program, but they remained high by their own and historical standards. From the British perspective, therefore, a multilateral approach backed up by an international organization would more effectively forestall any return to either bilateralism or isolationism, or both, by the United States than would a mere continuation of the RTA program.[19]

The more ambitious approach that eventually emerged was also an offshoot of the broader schemes being hatched for postwar cooperation. More than trade was at stake. Monetary matters and political issues were also included, and all these elements evolved into the grand design of a U.N. organization under whose umbrella various institutions would be established to address monetary and trade issues as well as more specialized programs dealing with labor, food and agriculture production, aviation, shipping, health, telecommunications, and more. The planners thus began to develop the view that postwar arrangements should lead to an integrated set of agreements addressing trade and payments as well as more technical issues.[20] The idea that international monetary and commercial policies could be coordinated and managed through international organizations was a novel idea and materially differentiated this period from the earlier *système de traités,* which had involved no more than an interlocking set of bilateral agreements. It was an idea, however, that seemed a natural extension of the planning ideology that had matured over the previous twenty years.

As the planning proceeded in Washington, London, Ottawa, and elsewhere, the normal division of labor within governments ensured that trade officials dealt with trade issues, treasury officials with monetary matters, and political specialists with political issues. In Washington, Cordell Hull's trade policy staff in the State Department concentrated on trade issues, while Harry Dexter White and his staff at the Treasury Department zeroed in on monetary matters. There was a similar division of labor in the United Kingdom. Keynes, loosely attached to the Treasury Office, was the principal strategist on postwar economic matters, but he was assisted, for example, by Lionel Robbins in the Cabinet War Office and by James Meade, assigned by the Cabinet Office to work under Hugh Dalton at the Board of Trade. Thus, while there was broad agreement on the need for an integrated approach, there was also acceptance that each component would be pursued separately by officials trained in the detail of that component, which in turn ensured that each element would be cast in the bureaucratic mold favored by that group of specialists.[21]

The first public fruits of this planning became evident in the Atlantic Charter. In August 1941, before the United States had entered the war and while President Roosevelt steered a delicate course between official neutrality and helping Britain as much as possible, Churchill and Roosevelt met off the coast of Newfoundland to cement their commitment to work toward a just peace. At the end of the meeting, they issued a statement setting out their vision of a postwar world. The document was the result of careful preparation and, while penned in immortal words, reflected carefully negotiated language. It read, in part: "The President . . . and the Prime Minister . . . deem it right to make known certain common principles on which they base their hopes for a better future for the world. . . . *Fourth,* they will endeavour, with due respect for their existing obligations, to further the enjoyment by all States, great or small, victor or vanquished, of access on equal terms, to the trade and to raw materials of the world which are needed for their economic prosperity. *Fifth,* they desire to bring about the fullest collaboration between all nations in the economic field with the object of securing, for all, improved labour standards, economic advancement and social security."[22]

State Department officials had insisted on adding a reference to nondiscrimination ("on equal terms"). British officials had demurred, and Roosevelt found it difficult to understand why the State Department needed to insist. Churchill was similarly mystified. U.S. dislike of preferences was not news to the United Kingdom. Churchill, who was not greatly attached to preferences as an economic policy, found U.S. insistence on attacking them in the context of a broad statement of principles distasteful and unnecessary. In response, therefore, the United Kingdom insisted on the additional phrase "with due respect for their existing obligations."[23] As a result, Churchill was able to assure the House of Commons three years later that the Atlantic Charter no more committed the United Kingdom to the abolition of imperial preferences than it committed the United States to the abolition of its high protective tariffs.[24] The United States, by overplaying its hand, had forced the United Kingdom to dig in on a critical issue at an early stage of the preparatory discussions, thus limiting the United Kingdom's ability to address the issue creatively at a later stage.

British opposition to any erosion in imperial preferences was more the result of political and sentimental considerations than of any economic arguments. Imperialists were offended that the United States, not a combatant until forced by the Japanese bombing of Pearl Harbor later that year, should tell Britain to kick its Commonwealth allies in the teeth for a point of economic principle. Churchill found these political arguments persuasive. To Churchill, alienating his Commonwealth allies and cabinet colleagues on a point that would only become important after the war was a stupid way to prosecute the war effort.[25]

This initial mistake was compounded in the next stage of the discussions when, in the context of negotiating the text of the Mutual Aid Agreement, which would provide the United Kingdom with lend-lease aid, American negotiators, at the insistence of Secretary Hull, sought a much stronger British commitment to nondiscrimination—the so-called Consideration. They contended that only if the United Kingdom made a strong commitment to the U.S. vision of a postwar world would it be possible for the U.S. government to extend lend-lease assistance. The United Kingdom, on the other hand, took the view that the United States, a combatant after December 7, 1941, should now take a different view of the Consideration. It found U.S. insistence on it increasingly offensive.[26] Various formulations and reformulations of the language of Article VII were tried out over the course of the six months that it took to conclude a satisfactory agreement.[27] During these discussions, the Dominions Secretary in London kept the Commonwealth governments informed and sought their agreement that the British government could proceed with a commitment in principle that would have grave implications for the continuation of the Ottawa system of preferences. Both Canada and Australia agreed that they would not stand in the way, but both noted that the elimination of imperial preferences would only make sense in the context of a major reduction in U.S. tariff protection, a view that dovetailed with that held in London.[28]

Against that background, the government of the United Kingdom reluctantly agreed to the provisions of Article VII. Negotiations had given the offensive language ("the elimination of all forms of discriminatory treatment in international commerce") a context that made clear that discrimination would be tackled, along with the reduction of tariff and other trade barriers, with a view to "the expansion, by appropriate international and domestic measures, of production, employment, and the exchange and consumption of goods."[29] The United Kingdom had bowed but not caved in to the U.S. vision, keeping its own counsel for a later day.

More positively, Article VII of the Mutual Aid, or Lend-Lease, Agreement committed the two governments to a process of joint planning on the basis of an agreed set of principles aimed at working out how best to set up an effectively functioning trade and payments system at the conclusion of the war. Over the course of the next few months, the United States negotiated more lend-lease agreements with other allied governments, each of which contained the language of Article VII involving commitment to the establishment of a nondiscriminatory postwar trade and payments system. Canada had agreed to similar conditions, but not in the context of a lend-lease agreement.

The success of American officials in getting various allied governments to commit to its vision of a postwar trade and payments system seemed, for a while, to have been its own reward. No urgency appeared to be attached to pursuing the conversations that the agreements with both the United Kingdom and Canada called for, nor is there much evidence that American officials had any clear ideas of how to take these commitments and flesh them out into concrete plans and proposals beyond the development of a more robust version of the RTA program. Having gotten commitments, American officials apparently feared that Congress would not approve any further aggressive postwar planning and resisted all efforts by both the United Kingdom and Canada, as well as by the American Embassy in London, to move to the next stage.[30]

More than a year would go by before the promised bilateral discussions on commercial policy were taken up, in August 1943. The intervening period, however, was not wasted, as officials—particularly in the United Kingdom—used it to develop ideas and test them in various arenas.[31] More progress was made in the United Kingdom than in the United States, in part because the parliamentary system provided more room for flexibility and pragmatism. Much of the thinking, of course, took place in an atmosphere of constant war-induced crisis that made political consideration of longer term issues difficult. The expedient adopted in the United Kingdom was to give the planners broad, general mandates within which to operate and which did not commit the British government until such time as specific ideas were brought forward in a negotiating context. On the whole, this gave the planners the room they needed. In Washington, on the other hand, congressional attitudes tended to be hostile to postwar planning, fearful that the administration would create a basis for future foreign entanglements at odds with the isolationist tendency still prevalent among many members of Congress. As a result, the next stage in the planning tended to be dominated by British thinking.[32]

In the United Kingdom, from the beginning, Keynes dominated the discussions with his usual compelling and penetrating analysis. Within his mind, however, there was constant struggle between two sets of incompatible ideas: restrictionism and expansionism. He favored trade as well as planning; he wanted to reap the advantage of trade and at the same time avoid its inconveniences. These conflicting views were evident in the two main themes that preoccupied British postwar economic planning: employment policy and monetary and commercial policy in relation to the rest of the world, which, given the interwar experience, the planners saw as closely tied together. The United Kingdom's precarious position both before and during the war had made support for expansionist liberal policies tenuous. British thinking concentrated on how to find a formula that could be expansionist in the long run but not until such time as the United Kingdom was in better shape economically.[33]

In his initial conversations with American officials, Keynes emphasized the restrictionist side of his approach to postwar commercial policy, ideas which did not please the Americans. At the same time, he recognized that the United Kingdom had little choice but to explore with the United States the most effective way of organizing a liberal approach to postwar trade; anything else would jeopardize critical matters such as the continuation of financial assistance. After hearing from all sides and weighing matters carefully, Keynes's considered view was that officials should concentrate first on monetary matters, reflecting not only his own intellectual strong suit but also the conviction that an effective payments system would facilitate establishment of a more expansionist trade regime. The result was his plan for a Clearing Union, which, when combined with ideas formulated by Harry Dexter White in the United States for a stabilization fund, led eventually to the International Monetary Fund (IMF).[34]

Planning developed more slowly but no less rigorously on commercial policy issues at the Board of Trade under the general direction of its president, Hugh Dalton, and Sir Percivale Liesching, its permanent secretary. During the course of 1942, James Meade, an Oxford economist, developed plans for a Commercial Union within which it would be possible to meet the American objective of eliminating discrimination and Britain's desire for a deep cut in tariff protection on an across-the-board, multilateral basis and to secure both by means of a clear code of conduct administered by an international organization.[35] Meade had had experience as a League of Nations official, and it is not surprising that he thought in terms of an international institution.[36]

Meade's plan quickly gained support among other officials and in the cabinet, and it became the agreed basis for the anticipated discussions with American officials. Gaining approval involved vigorous debates as to whether bilateral or multilateral negotiations and agreements were most likely to address access to markets and balance-of-payments requirements, ultimately won by the multilateralists and expansionists.[37]

Having agreed among themselves that Meade's plan made sense, British officials next moved to discuss their plans and ideas with the Dominions in the summer of 1943. Already the previous fall (October 23–November 9), they had had a full exchange of views with the Dominions reflecting the Keynesian consensus that the original focus should be on monetary matters and on the Clearing Union. At that meeting, however, they had had a preliminary exchange of views on commercial policy issues.[38] These and other discussions on the margin of ongoing consideration of monetary arrangements had suggested that some of the Dominions were more interested in building on new bilateral arrangements with the United States than in strengthening ties with the United Kingdom. Diplomatic exchanges of views also indicated that not all fully shared the British desire for a bold multilateral approach.[39]

From June 15 to 30, officials of the United Kingdom were able to conduct a thorough discussion of their commercial policy ideas with the representatives of Canada, Australia, New Zealand, India, and South Africa. In Canada, they found a staunch and well-prepared ally. Detailed instructions from the Canadian cabinet had prepared Canadian officials to provide strong support as well as suggestions for improving the proposal. New Zealand was also supportive, but both Australia and South Africa had many problems. Australia found the whole tone and direction wrong and not attuned to its view that economic development and full employment policies would be the focus of its requirements after the war. South Africa did not like the discipline on quantitative restrictions. In addition, neither was convinced that a strong multilateral approach was necessarily the best or only way forward. To keep the Dominions on side, British officials agreed to make some changes in their proposal to reflect both Australian and South African preoccupations without changing its basic thrust. Cabinet approval to proceed had been narrowly achieved and had been contingent on Commonwealth support; British officials thus did not want cabinet support to unravel at this early stage.[40]

During the course of these consultations, American officials nervously called on officials in Ottawa and London to seek observer status. The United States feared that the United Kingdom might take this opportunity to discuss how to defend and strengthen preferences or otherwise consolidate Commonwealth views on the issues at the expense of U.S. interests. While some in Ottawa were not averse to briefing American officials or even inviting them to sit in, the final decision was that these were discussions among the British family, at which the presence of American observers would be inappropriate.[41] In reality, however, the time had come for the United States to overcome its congressional sensitivity and pursue with the United Kingdom and others the talks called for by Article VII of the Mutual Aid Agreement.

The conversations were finally scheduled to take place at the end of August in Washington. They concentrated initially on monetary matters, where some progress had already been made. For a variety of reasons, including that they did not tread as heavily on congressional sensitivities, American officials had been much more prepared to pursue this dimension of the Article VII commitment.[42] Starting in the middle of September, however, and lasting into October, British and American officials collectively considered, in an informal series of meetings, their approach to the full range of commercial policy issues. These discussions conveyed no government commitments. Rather, they were conducted, in Richard Gardner's phrase, as a kind of seminar.[43]

The nonfinancial side of postwar economic planning in fact involved four distinct if related sets of issues: trade in raw materials or commodities, where the goal was to find means to stabilize that trade by putting in place agreements addressing both prices and production; restrictive business practices, where the goal was to find ways to control the activities of international cartels; employment, where the goal was to agree on which kinds of policies—both trade and investment—should be adopted to promote full employment; and trade, where the goal was to reduce and eliminate tariff and nontariff barriers and discipline a range of practices in a broadly agreed code of behavior. These four sets of issues, which would come together toward the end of the planning period into an integrated plan for an international trade organization, were initially discussed separately, to the same extent that financial and commercial policy issues were being considered separately. Indeed, wartime experience in coordinating trade in raw materials had made the discussion on a postwar approach to commodity agreements move more quickly and more smoothly than discussion on the other issues.[44]

As far as the core commercial policy issues were concerned, U.S. thinking again focused on an expanded version of the RTA program. British officials, however, were now armed with their own plan for a more ambitious "multilateral convention laying down a code of behavior, and a new international organization to implement that code."[45] The idea intrigued American officials, and it did not take long for the two sides to reach broad agreement that such an organization made sense. From then on, the idea of an international organization became an integral part of their common thinking about the best way to proceed.

At this stage, there was also broad agreement on the approach to many of the issues that would need to be covered. As professional economists and experienced trade negotiators, they agreed that the ultimate aim of a multilateral commercial policy agreement was to eliminate discrimination, reduce tariffs, and eliminate or discipline quantitative restrictions, balance-of-payments measures, export taxes and subsidies, and state trading. In effect, they pooled common American and British experience to come up with broadly agreed objectives and approaches. This degree of consensus at the professional level, of course, did not necessarily reflect political or national consensus, and therein lay the problem.[46]

At the political level, there was very broad disagreement, both philosophical and practical. In the United Kingdom, a consensus had emerged around the precept that full employment policies would pave the way for liberal policies, while Cordell Hull and his team strongly believed that liberal policies would lead to the growth that would increase employment. This philosophical difference showed up most clearly in the approach to the balance-of-payments issue, because the pursuit of full employment policies would lead to balance-of-payments problems, necessitating discriminatory quantitative restrictions at a time of fixed exchange rates. The crunch would come in setting out the criteria—tight or permissive—that would have to be met. The practical question would be whether the Commercial Union would promote private enterprise by allowing the market to determine who would sell what to whom or sanction state-controlled trade through the mechanism of balance-of-payments-inspired quantitative restrictions. It would become the central issue. The only way through it was by compromises that would satisfy neither side and would create bitter divisions.

A further fundamental difference between British and American thinking was apparent in their respective views of how to negotiate. British officials wanted to start by establishing broad principles and objectives and consider how best to achieve them in a grand design. American officials, mindful of their recent experience under the RTA, looked at how to solve immediate problems and in that way build confidence step by step for a more complete regime.[47]

More practically, discussion on discrimination indicated the deep division regarding imperial preferences. American officials probably were personally more flexible, but public debate and congressional and business expectations raised by Article VII made them politically inflexible. British officials, while they might have been personally inclined to see such preferences eliminated, were pushed into more rigid positions by the doctrinaire U.S. approach, particularly in the face of the United States's defense of their high tariffs and insistence on reciprocity. British officials were prepared to address preferences, but only if American officials were prepared to make some meaningful concessions on issues of importance to the United Kingdom and the Dominions, particularly the high U.S. tariff. The British plan, for example, had not dismissed the eventual elimination of preferences—including U.S. preferences to Cuba—but only in the context of a multilateral approach to tariffs that included a ceiling significantly lower than many existing U.S. tariffs. In their view, American economic strength should translate into a leadership that would allow the United States to make the kinds of short-term concessions that would allow the United Kingdom to make the necessary long-term commitments. In order to avoid chronic payments difficulties, the United States would have to increase imports from the sterling area, while the United Kingdom would need to increase exports to the dollar area; appropriate changes in tariff barriers would therefore be required, in a manner at odds with American principles of reciprocity and equivalence. American officials were well aware of this but were equally aware of congressional complications that would arise from anything other than reciprocity. Time would show that the U.S. political system was not geared to the magnanimity necessary in trade matters. For American officials, it was a lot easier to insist on the need to deal with discrimination as the main evil.[48]

The professional consensus of the 1943 seminar, therefore, was that there needed to be rigorous discipline on all trade restricting practices, the institutional capacity to enforce these disciplines, and a substantial, across-the-board reduction in tariffs leading to the erosion and even disappearance of preferences. Both sides accepted that political considerations would modify these principles. U.S. tariff negotiating authority, for example, could only be deployed in bilateral, item-by-item reciprocal negotiations subject to an escape clause. American agriculture support programs needed to be protected by means of quantitative restrictions shielding agricultural production from the vagaries of world prices, and consequent surpluses needed to be disposed of with export subsidies. British officials had a similar farm problem. They could only tackle preferences in very limited circumstances. Despite these known difficulties, much had been accomplished. British and American officials had fully explored the issues on which they could agree and on which they needed to disagree. As a result, they had laid a much more informed foundation for proceeding to more detailed planning.[49] But they may also have laid the foundation for future problems. The degree of intellectual consensus evident at the seminar appears to have given each side a false impression of its ability to meet the political sensitivities of the other side. Ironically, the openness of the communications among them about what was desirable probably led to false conclusions about what was possible.

It did not prove possible to translate the positive feelings generated during the seminar into a commitment to proceed to a further stage. Two factors appeared to have led to the rapid evaporation of the momentum attained in Washington. Within the British cabinet, the imperialists, led by Lord Beaverbrook, took exception to the threat to imperial preferences inherent in the discussions and wanted the United Kingdom to take a firmer stand on the issue. Churchill recognized that such a stand would create deep rancor in relations with the United States and undermine necessary financial support and military cooperation. Instead, he ordered a standstill in the commercial discussions so that disagreement over the future would not sour the need for cooperation in the present.[50]

More fundamentally, however, both sides recognized that it was more important to devote the available energy and negotiating coin to the monetary discussions. These were substantially further along than those on commercial policy. Additionally, more progress on commercial policy was likely to be made, once it was clear what kind of payments system would underpin it. The monetary discussions, therefore, continued through 1943 and into 1944 and concluded successfully in July 1944 at Bretton Woods, New Hampshire. While the end result was satisfactory to both sides, it involved much recrimination and suspicion, particularly since the devious tactics adopted by Harry Dexter White on the American side to steer consensus toward his stabilization scheme at the expense of Keynes's Clearing Union did not increase British confidence in American negotiators and motives. In the end, Canadian officials proved critical in bridging the gap and ensuring that a satisfactory outcome was worked out for the future of monetary cooperation.[51] The results, however, were not ratified or made operational, pending the return to more normal conditions after the war.

Despite the focus on the monetary side, State Department trade officials, who were not deeply engaged in this dimension, now regained the initiative. Within days of the conclusion of the seminar, they had armed Secretary Hull with a paper providing a detailed summary of what they saw as the emerging consensus on postwar economic issues for his use at a conference of the United and Allied Nations in Moscow.[52] Little concrete came of these discussions, except to give the allies insight into the direction of U.S. planning and apparent British concurrence with the broad outline of these ideas. Nevertheless, it was clear that American officials no longer felt hemmed in by their concern about congressional criticism.

Two months later, the conclusions had been fleshed out into an Interim Report of the Special Committee on the Relaxation of Trade Barriers and circulated among involved officials in Washington.[53] This report provided a fairly complete picture of what was now the U.S. position. It had moved considerably beyond a more ambitious version of the RTA program. The United States was now committed to the negotiation of a multilateral convention on commercial policy, which would provide for a substantial reduction in tariff and other barriers to trade and the elimination of all forms of discrimination, particularly imperial preferences. American officials had further concluded that eliminating preferences would require a substantial reduction in U.S. tariffs. An international commercial policy organization was now considered essential to making the multilateral convention function effectively. Additional organizations might also be required to deal with commodity and cartel policies. Finally, the report suggested that it might be desirable to negotiate bilateral tariff agreements as a supplement to or substitute for a multilateral tariff agreement.

U.S. thinking had moved significantly beyond Cordell Hull's original ideas and would require that the United States move well beyond the congressional delegation of authority inherent in the RTA program. Nevertheless, the report retained as a supplement or alternative a less ambitious plan involving bilateral tariff agreements fully consistent with the RTA program. Already at this early stage, therefore, we see hints of a possible double-track approach. While not impossible, the more ambitious plan would require congressional ratification and involve a major commitment by the United States to postwar trade and economic cooperation. The alternative approach would not require ratification, nor would it commit the United States to postwar commercial policy institutions. There was little evidence at this stage that the planners were engaged in the kind of coalition building in Congress and elsewhere that would ensure that the more ambitious plan would stand a chance of success. Unlike the United Nations and the IMF, whose fields of activity fell within the president's authority, the proposed trade organization clearly engaged congressional prerogatives and would not survive without its support. However, wartime secrecy prevented any of the public diplomacy necessary to build such support.

The consultations that did take place were not with Congress or the United Kingdom but with the Canadians, and discussions with the Chinese, Russians, and others were also planned, although in the end they did not materialize.[54] Diplomatic exchanges throughout 1943 on commercial policy planning had clearly suggested that Canada was a potential ally as well as a source of good ideas. Indeed, in December, Canadian officials had gone so far as to suggest to their prime minister that Canada could help to get the ball rolling by negotiating a far-reaching bilateral accord with the United States that would help to set the stage for the multilateral accords to follow.[55] With that in mind, discussions between Canadian and American trade officials took place January 3–7, 1944, in Washington, and February 12–13, in New York. Little came of the bilateral accord, but the United States could from then on count on Canada as a staunch ally in pursuing its bold approach.[56]

By this time, Canada-U.K. trade and economic relations had become strained, with Canada increasingly feeling it was being used and not too happy with British blackmail and imperial hauteur. To senior officials, the United Kingdom appeared profuse in its requests for assistance but not so in its appreciation of Canadian help. Additionally, Canadian officials were extremely worried that Britain would solve its chronic payments problem by creating a *cordon sanitaire* around the sterling area at the expense of the rest of the world. At all costs, Canada did not want to see the establishment of two opposing trade blocs. Britain's attitudes, of course, were colored by the much bigger problem they had with the United States and its demands for a multilateral and nondiscriminatory postwar trade regime in return for financial and other aid. Canadians understood these anxieties but still feared that Britain would isolate itself from the dollar trading area. Canada needed a world economic order that did not need such drastic measures, and on that they found more assurance in U.S. than in U.K. thinking.[57]

With the successful conclusion of discussions on financial matters at Bretton Woods in July 1944, the embargo on U.S.-U.K. commercial policy discussions was lifted, and rapid progress was made on some of the less contentious issues, such as commodity agreements.[58] Further discussion among American, British, and Canadian officials later that year and again the following year gave further shape and substance to U.S. thinking.[59] These conversations were complemented and aided by the ongoing work to establish the Food and Agriculture Organization (FAO) and the United Nations Relief and Rehabilitation Administration (UNRRA), to strengthen the International Labour Organization (ILO), and to put together the political framework of the United Nations to hold everything together.[60]

The idealism of a better functioning multilateral trade and payments system excited all of the planners, but they could only get there if they had a package of proposals that would appeal to political and business export interests and that did not expose import-competing interests to more pressure than the political system could bear. Wartime had made these concerns somewhat more remote, but the end of the war in 1945 brought these more traditional concerns back into the fore and dominated the remaining preparations and negotiations.

When peace finally came in the summer of 1945, the allies were ready with a payments regime, but they had not yet agreed on a trade regime. Plans had been developed and discussed over the previous four years, but as yet no concrete negotiating proposals had emerged. The momentum that had developed on the monetary side and had carried those negotiations to a successful conclusion appeared to be absent on the commercial policy side. Indeed, the differing philosophies and priorities evident during the 1943 U.S.-U.K. "seminar" appeared to be evolving into positions that were even wider apart.

In the United States, the death of President Roosevelt in April 1945 led to a new administration under Harry Truman. Cordell Hull had already resigned as Secretary of State a year earlier, pleading ill health, and some of his closest economic advisors had followed him into retirement. More of these officials left with the end of the war and further changes resulting from Truman appointments. In June, Congress gave Truman a new three-year tariff-negotiating authority allowing him to negotiate agreements that would cut tariffs by up to 50 percent, which, in many cases, reduced them to 25 percent of their 1930 levels. The new authority, however, did not extend to the negotiation of a multilateral tariff-cutting convention or an international trade organization; nor is there any evidence that the administration even sought such a mandate.

On the other side of the Atlantic, a fickle British electorate, concluding that Churchill might have been well suited to prosecuting the war but not to solving postwar economic problems, had elected a Labour government led by Clement Attlee. The Attlee government was even more committed to full employment policies and their consequent protectionist trade implications than the wartime planners had been. Britain's economic problems were substantial, and the British electorate was in no mood to open its markets for the benefit of American producers. What Britain needed was financial help from the United States, not sermons on the evils of discrimination and protection.

Against this background, the United States's abrupt ending of its lend-lease program at the end of the war came as a shock to the United Kingdom and created a crisis for the new Labour government. In response, Keynes went to Washington with a view to reversing this error, obtaining financial aid, and settling any remaining differences about the commitments arising out of Article VII of the Mutual Aid Agreement. Keynes forcefully put the British case and was as forcefully rebuffed by the Americans. They were even more hard-nosed and doctrinaire now than during the war and in no mood to accommodate British demands and expectations arising out of both its desperate economic straits and the feeling that its sacrifices during the war should be rewarded.[61] More formal negotiations ironed out the differences, and the United Kingdom got a new loan agreement, but more out of fear of the rapidly emerging Soviet menace than because of the merits of British arguments. The new agreement provided for the forgiveness of all lend-lease indebtedness, delayed payments on new loans, and a low interest rate. Part of the deal, however, was British acquiescence in a fully fleshed-out set of proposals reflecting the U.S. vision of postwar commercial policy.[62]

While the United Kingdom had agreed to the proposals as a basis for future negotiations, it was not prepared for the way they were released, jointly with the terms of the new loan agreement, clearly establishing a quid pro quo relationship that did not help in the fragile political climate in Britain. Conversations earlier in 1945 had indicated a broad level of agreement, but the United Kingdom would clearly have preferred that the product of those conversations stand on its own merits rather than as a forced concession flowing from their financial requirements.[63] The proposals were made public on December 6, 1945, and copies were sent to every government around the world.[64] The British government published its own version and felt constrained to put its own spin on the document, clearly identifying it as a U.S. set of proposals with which the United Kingdom broadly agreed.[65] Nevertheless, the deal received a hostile reception in the United Kingdom, as much because of the crude way in which American negotiators had gained British agreement as because of British ambivalence about some of the contents. U.S. negotiating tactics had ensured an inauspicious beginning to the next stage of the negotiations.

In Washington, of course, it was considered perfectly legitimate to use the advantages it now possessed to impose a hard bargain on the United Kingdom that would undo once and for all the evil of imperial preferences and create a package that would sell in Congress. But the United Kingdom was neither politically nor psychologically prepared in 1945–47 to accept a major attack on its tariff policies and Commonwealth ties; the Dominions agreed. Only a massive reduction in U.S. tariffs would have made this possible, and American officials remained unprepared to consider this, even though they were well aware of the problems that their approach created for the United Kingdom.[66] To complicate matters further, Keynes died on April 21, 1946. His towering insight and powers of persuasion had been critical elements in ensuring the success of the monetary discussions; Britain could not now count on them for the commercial policy discussions.

Hardening attitudes to commercial policy issues were evident on both sides of the Atlantic. The United Kingdom and the continent faced not only immediate problems of food and cash shortages but also very major problems of economic and political restructuring. Both required massive assistance from the only country capable of providing it, the United States. The American public, however, believed that the United States had already made sufficient sacrifices to address Europe's problems, and political leaders in Washington agreed. In these circumstances, therefore, only the United States was in a position to make detailed proposals on a multilateral approach, and its proposals would from that point on be the focus of discussion and negotiations.[67]

The assumptions and objectives that underpinned the U.S. approach as embodied in the December 1945, proposals included the following:

- trade would expand—both exports and imports—through the reduction and even elimination of barriers;
- trade should be a private sector activity;
- trade should be multilateral rather than bilateral;
- trade policy should be nondiscriminatory;
- trade policy and economic stabilization policy should go hand in hand; and
- consultation and cooperation should be the basis for progress and for resolving conflict.[68]

These objectives led to four sets of interrelated concerns focused on:

- restrictions imposed by governments;
- restrictions imposed by private combines and cartels;
- disorder in the markets of certain primary commodities; and
- fear of disruption or irregularity in production and employment.

The 1945 proposals now integrated these four sets of issues into a single code of conduct to be implemented and administered by a single international trade organization (ITO). They also clearly spelled out that an ITO would complement and complete what had already been achieved on monetary and financial cooperation—the IMF and World Bank—and in such specialized areas as food and agriculture—the FAO.

While the proposals clearly reflected U.S. preoccupations and assumptions, they were not indifferent to the discussions of the previous four years and incorporated ideas and suggestions that had flowed from those discussions as well as from American scholars and various business and academic groups that had advised the U.S. planners or had written on the subject.[69] The inclusion of provisions concerning employment, for example, reflected British and Australian concerns, but the fact that they were set out as preambular rather than contractual provisions underlined the U.S. view of these matters. In an effort to broaden support, the State Department quickly held discussions with Belgium, Greece, Poland, France, Turkey, Czechoslovakia, and the Netherlands and gained their general endorsement, thus setting the stage for fruitful negotiations.[70]

While the State Department was firmly wedded to the proposals, it had not lost sight of potential congressional difficulties. It thus also proposed, concurrent to the consideration of an ITO and in order to take advantage of the negotiating authority contained in the 1945 renewal of the RTA, that the United States and fifteen other countries enter tariff negotiations. Such negotiations, as had been suggested by Canada the previous year in the context of proposed bilateral Canada-U.S. negotiations, would help to get the ball rolling. To that end, therefore, the administration gave Congress notice early in 1946 of its intent to enter into tariff negotiations.

After four years of on-and-off discussions, the United States, with the concurrence of the United Kingdom and the support of a number of second-level countries, had reached the stage where the product of their discussions could be exposed to a more formal and more broadly based negotiating process. The issues had by now been clearly developed, and concrete proposals circulated to provide an informed and focused basis for the next stage. The prenegotiations stage was finished. The issues had been defined, the agenda set, and the players identified. The time had come to negotiate.

Negotiations

Early in 1946, the newly formed Economic and Social Council of the United Nations (ECOSOC), at a meeting in London, passed a U.S.-introduced resolution calling for an international conference on trade and employment. The resolution appointed the United States and the same fifteen countries it had already invited to its multilateral tariff conference, with the addition of Norway, Chile, and Lebanon, to form a preparatory committee for the conference. The United States promptly invited these three also to participate in its tariff conference.[71]

To get ready for the first session of the preparatory committee, scheduled to open in London in mid-October, American officials took the 1945 proposals and elaborated them into a draft charter. Discussions with the United Kingdom and others, either through diplomatic channels or directly, kept the officials in charge of the drafting informed of the preoccupations of others.[72] In order to promote discussion, the draft charter was made public a few weeks before the opening meeting of the preparatory committee, despite misgivings in the United Kingdom that the publication would make negotiations more difficult.[73] The committee met from October 15 until November 26 with all but the Soviet Union participating. Despite initial reluctance on the part of Australia, the United Kingdom, and France, the committee agreed to work on the basis of the U.S. draft.[74]

The draft charter was an amalgam of the previous discussions and American experience in negotiating reciprocal trade agreements, especially the most recent agreement, that with Mexico in 1942.[75] In preparing the draft, however, American officials reflected what they had learned over the course of the previous five years from others. The need to make some compromises was evident in the unique ITO-GATT drafting style that now began to emerge: a clear statement of principle followed by various provisions allowing for specific exceptions or exemptions. This allowed practices not identified as exceptions to be subject to the basic principle. The U.S. origin of this first draft, however, was evident in the fact that the firmest rules covered areas where the United States had little to worry about, such as discipline on balance-of-payments measures; more flexible rules covered areas where U.S. practice could not meet a more rigorous test, such as export subsidies and escape clause action.[76] As discussions progressed, of course, other governments saw the need for greater or lesser disciplines to differing degrees and thus indicated where negotiations would be tough.

The balance-of-payments issue was probably the most difficult, because most governments other than the United States had balance-of-payments problems. From the perspective of 1994, when most major currencies float relatively freely and exchange rate adjustments and the need for balance-of-payments measures are thus no longer major political headaches, it is difficult to appreciate the problems raised by this set of issues. But to the negotiators of the 1940s, they were central. They had first of all led to an International Monetary Fund based on fixed exchange rates and tough criteria for adjusting those rates. They now had to address the trade dimension of the IMF rules and the system set up by them. From the outset, this was the crunch issue, made more real by the fact that the United Kingdom and Europe faced a chronic balance-of-payments problem, which, though evident even before the war, had been exacerbated by the heavy costs of the war and the gradual erosion of British overseas investments. The difficulties were evident not only in the ITO negotiations but in continuing discussions about emergency financial assistance—finally resolved by the Marshall Plan—and in difficulties in making the IMF regime operational.[77]

In many ways, the discussion of the balance-of-payments regime colored much of the rest of the negotiations and the approach to them. Two sets of issues were involved: determining the criteria that would authorize resort to quantitative restrictions for balance-of-payments reasons and the extent to which those restrictions could discriminate to accommodate the division of the world into a sterling block and a dollar area. Throughout the next two years of negotiations, the United States resisted tooth and nail any relaxation of its proposed tough discipline, while the United Kingdom and other Europeans worked equally hard to relax it. The differences were not only practical; they also reflected a fundamentally different approach to rule making. The United States was looking for an international economic constitution that set out in considerable detail what governments could and could not do;[78] the United Kingdom, reflecting its more fluid approach to constitution making, sought agreement on a broad set of principles, the detailed application of which would be fleshed out as circumstances dictated. The Americans were wary of an agreement that did not spell out the rules in detail; the British were wary of one that did.

There were, of course, other issues. At the London meeting, Australia's concerns about full employment policies became a major issue. Wilcox portrays Australia as the great champion of stabilization and employment policy at every turn.[79] Flowing from this, Australia argued the classic infant-industry case to justify continued protection and exemption from the tough rules proposed by the United States. On restrictive business practices, Canada and the United States sought strong anticartel provisions, but these were opposed by the United Kingdom, Belgium, and the Netherlands, which saw a need for some relaxation of anticompetitive practices in order to foster companies within their jurisdictions to regain the prominence they had lost as a result of the war. On commodities, the issue revolved around whether to separate out agricultural products. Central to all of these issues were attitudes toward the role of government in the economy as well as concerns about discrimination. The United States, the great champion of free enterprise and nondiscrimination, defended its approach with vigor, except where Congress had passed laws at odds with these principles, as in agriculture. In its approach, it could usually count on Canada, which saw its interests as best protected in a code that would discipline various protectionist practices.[80] On imperial preferences, however, Canada could not accept the American position in the absence of a commitment by the United States to lower its own tariffs by a substantial margin. At the same time, Canada insisted that trade in agriculture should be subject to the same disciplines as applied to other sectors, a point that American negotiators could not accept.

Over the course of the five weeks that the preparatory committee met, other countries who were prepared to see a much larger role for state-controlled trade and for discrimination fought to provide wiggle room within the rules of the draft charter. As a result, many provisions were enlarged and adapted to accommodate their needs and preoccupations. Nevertheless, the United States succeeded in ensuring that the charter maintained its basic character. It also agreed to the addition of a chapter on economic development in which the issue of international investment would be addressed. American business had long insisted that there should be tough rules on international investment. But the State Department, knowing how sensitive these were for other governments, had resisted such measures. It now agreed to include such rules, but starting from considerations directly opposite to those of American business: the promotion of economic development in poorer countries, rather than the promotion of American investment in such countries. At the close of the meeting, a drafting committee was established to continue the work on technical issues having to do with voting and organizational matters and to clean up the text as a whole in preparation for a second session to be held in Geneva the following April.[81]

In keeping with its two-track approach, the United States proposed during the course of the London meeting that the committee use the commercial-policy chapter of the draft charter, with the addition of a few other articles, to create a general agreement to cover the proposed tariff negotiations. The preparatory committee further agreed that these negotiations would take place during its second session in Geneva and approved a memorandum setting out how these were to be conducted.[82]

During the early months of 1947, the State Department engaged in extensive congressional and public preparations for both the tariff negotiations and the enlarged and amended draft charter and received continued business support.[83] Concurrently, at Lake Success, New York, the drafting committee not only cleaned up the charter text but also produced the first draft of a general agreement.[84]

By the spring of 1947, therefore, considerable progress had been made in putting together the basis not only for the ITO charter but also for a multilateral tariff conference and a general agreement. The United States had successfully maintained a tough line in many areas but had been prepared to compromise on some issues or allow competing drafts to go forward in difficult areas, such as the balance-of-payments issue. In areas where the vested interests of the major parties were less entrenched, hard obligations had resulted. Where vested interests were entrenched, various exceptions had been built in, based on generally agreed criteria, creating a pattern others would seek to exploit. Poorer countries, for example, sought exceptions on "development" grounds, looking for a relaxation of obligations for developing countries as a group subject to another set of criteria, and spelled out the circumstances that would trigger access to them.[85]

The preparatory committee met again in Geneva at the end of April 1947 and settled in for a six-month session. The delegates had set themselves three interrelated tasks and had come up with the requisite resources to carry out all three concurrently: to continue preparation of the text of the charter for an international trade organization; to negotiate a series of bilateral tariff-cutting agreements among the members of the preparatory committee, plus six more countries that had been invited to participate; and to conclude a general agreement that would tie the various bilateral agreements together into one multilateral tariff-cutting accord. For the United States, the second and third task had acquired some urgency, because the current version of the Reciprocal Trade Agreements Act expired on June 12, 1948; if the administration was to take advantage of it and create a basis for recommending its more ambitious proposal for an ITO to Congress, it would have to be able to demonstrate the advantages that had already accrued to the United States as a result of the tariff negotiations. For the other members of the preparatory committee, the tariff negotiations would provide tangible proof of what could be achieved through an ITO by anticipating some of the benefits that would accrue more widely, once the charter was adopted by a sufficient number of states.

The first task continued in the mold established at London and Lake Success. Delegates toiled away at completing the draft text of the charter for an international trade organization. The seventeen members of the committee proper completed this task by the end of August. Over the course of four months "the text of the Charter was reorganized, obscure passages were clarified, inconsistencies were removed, and the appearance of the document was generally improved."[86] Virtually all amendments proposed by the United States as a result of its consultations with Congress and business interests were accepted. New articles were added on motion picture film and investment. Canada, over the objection of the United States, managed to get agreement that export subsidies could not be used without the prior approval of the ITO.

Balance-of-payments issues again proved troublesome, with the United Kingdom and France continuing to push for a greater degree of discretion in the use of quotas to defend balance-of-payments measures. The United States reluctantly agreed but in return insisted on more criteria, as well as a requirement that the IMF approve resort to such quotas. Australia and some of the lesser developed countries continued to push for the right to use import quotas for economic development reasons, and the criteria allowing such a departure from the basic rules were further clarified. Issues relating to voting, the functioning of the organization, and the relationship between members and nonmembers remained unresolved, but these were issues that could be readily postponed for consideration at the conference itself, scheduled to convene in Havana, Cuba, in November.[87]

The second task involved the negotiation of a series of bilateral tariff-cutting agreements. In effect, the United States successfully organized what had been considered impossible in 1934, a multilateral tariff negotiation, by arranging a huge jamboree of bilateral, item-by-item negotiations, including those between countries that had already exchanged concessions and were thus looking for deeper, more sensitive cuts.[88] By harnessing the power of the unconditional MFN rule as well as the principal and substantial supplier rules, it proved possible to negotiate 123 such agreements containing reductions and bindings affecting some 45,000 items in the tariff schedules of the twenty-three participating countries.[89] The result for the United States was a further 35 percent reduction in its tariff protection. To provide rough balance, particularly for smaller countries and low-tariff countries, negotiators accepted that a binding could be as valuable as a reduction. It thus proved possible to meet the U.S. congressional requirement for reciprocity.[90] In effect, the United States successfully harnessed the mercantilist attitude of most governments to trade (maximize export opportunities and minimize import exposure) in a multilateral tariff-cutting procedure that provided for the gradual reduction of tariffs on a politically acceptable basis.[91]

To tie the various individual bilateral agreements together into a single set of rights and obligations, the delegates had agreed in London the previous year to take most of the provisions of chapter 4 of the draft charter— the commercial policy chapter—add a few articles to hold them together, provide final provisions, and call it the General Agreement on Tariffs and Trade (GATT). The text of this GATT had been fleshed out at Lake Success and was now further refined to reflect the continued evolution of the draft charter. The amalgamated results of the 123 tariff agreements were now added as schedules to article 2, providing for the tariff concessions traded among the participating countries.[92]

Both in the text and in the bilateral tariff negotiations, the issue of tariff preferences was addressed pragmatically. The American preoccupation with the evil of discrimination was satisfied by stating unequivocally in article 1 that member countries owed each other unconditional MFN treatment in all matters relating to protection at the border, particularly the tariff. The United Kingdom and the Commonwealth, which had not been satisfied by the overall depth of the U.S. tariff cuts and the fact that the United States had successfully resisted establishment of a multilateral tariff approach as well as a relatively low ceiling on tariff rates, succeeded in grandfathering existing preference schemes with the proviso that existing margins of preference could not be increased. In effect, therefore, they agreed to a long-term commitment that would see their margins of preference erode as tariffs came down.[93]

The agreement thus put together was never intended to function as an organization; the participating countries agreed that it would be an interim agreement that would shortly be subsumed into the ITO. The ITO would then supply the institutional muscle to guide international commercial policy and provide the framework within which further tariff negotiations would be organized. Since the American delegation did not have congressional authority to enter into a trade organization but did have authority to negotiate a trade agreement, members of the preparatory committee were consciously seeking to conclude what could be achieved while also laying the groundwork for a more ambitious approach. In fact, in face of congressional criticism that the draft GATT as it stood at the end of the Lake Success meeting contained too many organization-like provisions, American negotiators had successfully insisted on some necessary cosmetic changes at Geneva to make the final text more acceptable.[94]

To provide a basis for bringing the new agreement into force before the expiry of the 1945 renewal of the RTA act and before news of the agreement on significant tariff cuts began to leak, the negotiators invented the Protocol of Provisional Application. Parts I and III of the GATT were judged to be fully consistent with the RTA and could be brought into force definitively. Part II, which contained many of the trade rules and amended many of the clauses of earlier bilateral agreements, would be brought into force only insofar as it was not inconsistent with existing legislation. Once the ITO charter was concluded, it would provide the vehicle for bringing part II of the GATT into force definitively. The protocol would thus allow the interim GATT to fit the mold and time frame prescribed by the RTA and allow the U.S. administration to implement it without seeking further legislative authority. In effect, rather than tailoring its suit to fit available cloth, the U.S. administration decided to tailor two suits—one out of available cloth and another in the event that more cloth should become available. Seven other participants joined the United States—including the United Kingdom and Canada—and agreed to bring the new accord into force by January 1, 1949, on the basis of the protocol. Other participants agreed to take the necessary steps to bring it into force on the same basis as soon thereafter as possible.[95]

By the end of October 1947, therefore, the preparatory phase of the negotiations had come to a satisfactory conclusion. The seventeen members of the preparatory committee were satisfied with the draft charter they had prepared. While a wide range of compromises had been necessary between the free-enterprise ideology of the United States, shared by Canada and a few others, and the more state-centered enterprise favored by the United Kingdom, Australia, and most of the developing countries, these had not been such as to breach the basic ideals and objectives first discussed in 1941 and again in 1943. Additionally, they had made a good start at reducing tariffs by means of the GATT and its supporting 123 bilateral agreements. The GATT had been hailed as a major accomplishment in world capitals, and they had reason to be satisfied and optimistic about concluding the rest of their work successfully. The challenge now was to take this draft and sell it to a wider audience so that the international trade organization would have as universal an appeal as possible. The delegates assumed that this would be their main task at the conference scheduled to start in Havana in a few weeks. Many proceeded directly to Havana from Geneva, without touching base in their capitals first.

With hindsight, they would have been well advised to postpone the opening of negotiations for a few weeks, or even months, to gain a wider appreciation of where matters stood at home. Circumstances had changed, and, while the GATT negotiations were widely hailed as a major breakthrough, the urgency of reaching agreement on a charter for an international trade organization seemed to have become more remote and of greater interest to the delegates than to their political masters at home. By this time, the ITO was seen as an American proposal and an American creature, even if U.S. negotiators found it a far cry from what they had originally proposed. If they hoped to conclude a charter that stood a reasonable chance of entering into force, they needed to make sure they had solid support at home. Not enough delegations took this precaution.[96]

The summer of 1947 had not been a propitious time to negotiate trade agreements. Political courage was in short supply. It followed a hard winter, which had contributed to deteriorating economic and political conditions in Europe. Against this background, U.S. strategic interests in eliminating discrimination increasingly had to be tempered by the reality that it was in the United States's interest to shore up the economies of Europe and promote intra-European integration, to provide a bulwark against communist expansionism. By the following spring, conditions had reached such a point that the United States agreed to put the Bretton Woods agreements on ice for a while and tackle Europe's problems with a massive infusion of aid (the Marshall Plan). In many capitals, the conclusion of the charter for an international trade organization could not compete for attention, particularly since in most capitals attention was focused on immediate problems and not on the long-term goals that underpinned the draft charter.[97]

It came as a major disappointment to the veterans of Geneva, therefore, to discover that the thirty-three delegations that now joined them in Havana for the U.N. Conference on Trade and Employment did not share their assessment that the charter needed little more than polishing.[98] Instead, it came under wholesale attack by the developing or poor countries, particularly the Latins led by Argentina, who had not participated in the preparatory meetings and therefore had both general and particular views on the charter. They had concluded that the charter was too one-sided and served the rich at the expense of the poor. They took up the theme that India, Lebanon, and others had unsuccessfully pursued in the preparatory work. As a result, they made more than 800 proposals for improvements, many of which would have emasculated the carefully developed compromises worked out at Geneva.[99]

The Geneva veterans, however, held tough and would not depart from the basic contours and principles agreed at Geneva. They did, however, accept various changes, some cosmetic, some real. For example, they adjusted the more objectionable aspects of the investment provisions; they accepted the principle of one country, one vote; they clarified the relationship of the charter to the IMF; they spelled out members' obligations to nonmembers; and they once again tackled the thorny issue of the criteria for discriminatory balance-of-payments measures and economic development measures.[100] The result was an increasingly complex and increasingly compromised document.[101]

By the end of March, the work was completed, and fifty-three delegations signed the charter. Only Argentina and Poland refused. Turkey agreed to sign later. The adventure that had started with the Atlantic Charter almost seven years earlier had finally reached a successful conclusion. The charters for the International Monetary Fund and World Bank had been agreed at Bretton Woods, in the summer of 1944. A year later, the charter of the United Nations had been concluded at San Francisco. Various specialized agencies had been set up or revitalized, including the Food and Agriculture Organization (FAO) and the International Civil Aviation Organization (ICAO). With the Havana Charter for an International Trade Organization, the final piece would fall into place. The world community could count on an appropriate and powerful tool to ensure cooperation in every sphere of international activity.

Explaining Outcomes

Reality turned out to be somewhat different from the confident hopes of the negotiators. While many of the delegates to the Havana Conference may have retained their enthusiasm for institution building, the world had changed and the problems that needed to be addressed seemed to fit poorly into the mechanistic world of universal organizations. The Soviet

Union, which had signed up at the San Francisco conference that launched the United Nations, had been conspicuous in its absence at both Bretton Woods and Havana, and plans were now being laid for a North Atlantic defensive alliance to contain what was perceived as a growing Soviet threat to world peace. The problems of European recovery were proving more stubborn and difficult than originally envisaged, and talk had turned to plans for a European economic union. The United States had promised massive aid—the Marshall Plan—if Europeans would take more steps to help themselves. Canadian balance-of-payments problems had led first to restrictions and then to bilateral discussions with the Americans, looking toward a more comprehensive bilateral trade agreement.

Important as the conclusion of the conference seemed to the members of each delegation, therefore, it must have appeared anticlimactic and out of touch with changing reality in the members' capitals. The conclusion of the Gatt negotiations in October 1947 had been generally well received. The conclusion of the ITO negotiations was either not noticed at all or received critically. Only Liberia ratified the charter. The reaction in Britain was hostile, and debate in the House led to a decision to defer a decision on ratification until after the United States had ratified. In Canada, it was not even debated. Australia agreed to ratify the charter, with the proviso that it would only take effect after it had been ratified by the United Kingdom and the United States. The rest of the world did not go even this far. The charter was by now firmly identified as an American document that would only work if the United States ratified it and took steps to make it real.

Those steps were never taken. In Washington, the final product was regarded as a severely compromised document. Accordingly, no political champion of any stature stepped forward to advance the cause of the ITO. Cordell Hull had resigned in 1944; Will Clayton, who provided the most senior link to Hull's views, had resigned as assistant secretary for economic affairs soon after the conclusion of the Geneva meetings. General Marshall, Robert Lovett, and Willard Thorpe, respectively secretary of state, undersecretary of state, and assistant secretary for economic affairs at the beginning of 1948, had not been part of the planning and carried no special brief for an ITO. General Marshall fell ill at the end of 1948 and was replaced by Dean Acheson, who was somewhat skeptical about the importance of the grandiose plans hatched by Cordell Hull for postwar economic organizations. Other matters were more pressing. As a result, the United States waited more than a year to take the first step toward ratification of the charter, did little to promote it politically or in other capitals, and quietly withdrew it from congressional consideration a year later. During this period, other governments also did little to promote it, either in the U.S. Congress or elsewhere.

While no credible political champion stepped forward in the United States, those who had participated in the planning and negotiations did defend it vigorously. Clair Wilcox, the deputy head of the American delegation, published his *Charter for World Trade* soon after the charter was tabled in Congress. William Adams Brown, who had been part of the wartime planning staff but had since moved to the Brookings Institution, wrote his *The United States and the Restoration of World Trade* the following year. In articles and speeches, others joined in and echoed the basic message that the charter, though not perfect, offered a solid prospect for creating a more ordered and predictable world of international commerce. It was hardly a case to inspire confidence. Supporters in the academic and think-tank community all pitched in, but their arguments were also quickly squeezed between the more passionate cases put forward by perfectionists and protectionists alike. The former argued that the charter had departed too far from the ideals that had originally motivated the United States, while the latter insisted that the charter imposed too many obligations on the United States. The more clever protectionists, in fact, clothed their arguments in words that appealed to the perfectionists and thus added to the appeal of those who wanted nothing to do with the charter. It did not take long to conclude that the ITO was a dead duck, the product of utopian idealism outrunning political reality, not just in the United States but also in other countries.[102]

But while the ITO would never see the light of day, its proxy lived on. As early as March 1948, at the conclusion of the Havana conference, the twenty-three signatories to the GATT had met to consider whether to reflect the changes made at Havana in the GATT text. Interestingly, they decided to reflect some but not all. Only those that the major delegations considered improvements were incorporated. The GATT was already beginning to take on a separate, more permanent character as its viability as an alternative started to develop.[103] Over the next three years, as it met regularly in Geneva under the chairmanship of Dana Wilgress of Canada and the guidance of Eric Wyndham-White, its first executive secretary, this conviction was strengthened. Ten more countries joined. New tariff concessions were exchanged. Disputes were resolved. It is not surprising, therefore, that when, at the end of 1950, the Truman administration quietly withdrew the charter from Congress, other governments readily acquiesced in that judgment. Only a few academic scribblers expressed regrets, largely because it was difficult for them to appreciate the extent to which the "interim" GATT could serve as a flexible and pragmatic substitute.

By the end of 1950, therefore, it was clear that the postwar commercial policy negotiations had resulted in both a success and a failure: a successful multilateral trade agreement and a failed international trade organization. What ingredients had led to those different results within the confines of a single negotiation?

Why the GATT Negotiations Succeeded

From the outset, the United States had set out to negotiate a multilateral trade agreement that would provide a framework within which tariffs could be gradually reduced and other barriers could either be contained or eliminated. Such an agreement was intended to build on the successful model of the reciprocal trade agreements negotiated between 1934 and 1942 and extend to other countries the U.S. vision of trade conducted largely by private enterprises on the basis of nondiscrimination and transparency. Such a multilateral agreement was consonant with the administration's recent experience and had the support of Congress, U.S. business and leading American intellectuals.

Coalitions. In pursuit of this goal, the United States exercised consistent and determined leadership and built a core coalition of countries that shared its principal objectives. It was largely the work of five delegations: the United States, the United Kingdom, France, Canada, and the Benelux countries, together the five most important economic powers of the day. These five delegations were not unhappy with the way GATT obligations differed from those in the ITO, and they resisted all efforts by the smaller countries to dilute the GATT with some of the gains they had made in the ITO charter. While their ideas may have varied as to the detail of such an agreement and as to the areas in which the rules needed to be firm or flexible, the limited scope of the GATT fit in well with each of their objectives.

Issue Decomposition and Sequencing. The trade agreement negotiated in 1947, based on six years of careful discussion and preparation, was a pragmatic but limited instrument that successfully imposed discipline where governments were prepared for discipline and accepted flexibility where they were not. It was an agreement consistent with the best experience in negotiating trade agreements and involved acceptable compromises in politically tricky areas such as preferences and balance-of-payments measures. It dealt with only one of the four sets of commercial policy issues that the planners had set out to address: trade in goods.

Bridging and Bargaining Strategies. Negotiations, however, were not easy, because the negotiators had to find a middle ground between the two conflicting philosophies about the role of government in society and between the U.S dislike of discrimination and others' concern with high U.S. tariffs and anxiety that the 1934 reversal in U.S. trade policy would not hold. The solution was a set of measures that would increase the volume of trade by reducing barriers, at the same time allowing various discriminatory policies in the pursuit of full-employment goals. These departures from the basic rules were hemmed in by criteria aimed at reducing the potential for abuse. This compromise was gradually strengthened by the American-British resolve to use the GATT as a framework for further negotiations. The GATT could thus become the basis for a new treaty system, more enduring than the first, ushered in by the Cobden-Chevalier treaty.[104]

Crisis and Consensual Knowledge. The negotiation of this limited agreement succeeded because it reflected careful, step-by-step preparation in the United States and in the other core countries. Identification of the basic issues flowed from shared analysis—in governments and think tanks alike—of the crisis generated by the economic problems of the 1920s and 1930s and reflected the negotiating experience of governments and the intellectual tradition of the think tanks. Consensus on the preferred solutions was built gradually. It coalesced first around monetary issues and subsequently around trade policy.

The GATT negotiations thus succeeded in large part because they built on experience that had been successful, ideas that had been thoroughly discussed, and objectives that were widely shared. The road to negotiation involved careful preparation and discussion among the principals, both at home and collectively. To achieve their objectives, the principal participants were prepared to make some concessions in the course of negotiations but did not waver too far from the basic contours they had first discussed in 1943–45. The obligations were limited to a range of closely related policy issues.

Leadership. The United States provided the drive and leadership but could count on the United Kingdom, Canada, France, and the Benelux countries to maintain the necessary momentum. Efforts by other delegations to divert them into extraneous issues, such as those dealing with economic development, were successfully resisted, contained within a set of special rules, or addressed in the charter rather than in the GATT. Together, they ensured that the agreement was economically meaningful by exchanging a wide range of specific concessions among themselves. As a result, it did not prove difficult to implement the agreement and put it to work and gradually increase the number of interests that had a direct stake in its continued success.

Why the ITO Negotiations Failed

Where the GATT succeeded, the ITO failed. American planners did not set out in 1939–40 to create an international trade organization. They reached the conclusion that such an organization would be a productive way to address postwar commercial policy issues late in their planning, and only after their British and Canadian colleagues had suggested it. The latter had reached this view not because they had a strong conviction that a trade organization with a broad mandate was an important objective in its own right, but because they believed that such an organization would provide a better means of ensuring American participation in postwar trade arrangements and might prove a better means for effecting deep cuts in U.S. tariffs than a series of bilateral agreements. It might also provide a better setting within which to resolve the difficult issue of imperial preferences. Similarly, British and Canadian thinking had introduced the idea of an organization into the discussion of financial and related matters.[105]

The idea of an international trade organization to enforce a multilateral code of conduct gained increasing currency in the context of discussions about a United Nations organization as well as ongoing consideration of how best to address more specialized problems, such as food production, trade in raw materials, and cartels. Within a year after the conclusion of the hostilities, the United States and its allies had successfully concluded international agreements on finance and reconstruction (the IMF and the International Bank for Reconstruction and Development, in 1944), food production (the FAO, in 1944), civil aviation (the ICAO, in 1944), political cooperation (the U.N., in 1945), education, science, and culture (UNESCO, in 1945), and health (the World Health Organization, in 1946), each of which involved establishment of an international organization. The momentum of that success led naturally to the conviction that international trade should be similarly blessed and resulted in the proposal that the various strands of commercial policy planning—trade, employment, cartels, and commodities—should all be brought together under the aegis of a single organization.

The GATT and the ITO thus represented two complementary strands in U.S. policy. The GATT marked the logical continuation and even culmination of the narrowly conceived trade policy of the RTA program. The ITO represented a more ambitious effort involving not only trade policy but also broader geopolitical goals. These broader goals were clearly evident in the Atlantic Charter, in Article VII of the mutual aid agreement, and in various speeches by Cordell Hull and other senior State Department officials equating economic cooperation with peace. Congress was prepared to back the Atlantic Charter, but there is little evidence that it supported these other broader schemes, particularly after the end of the war and the return to respectability of traditional congressional isolationist tendencies. While Congress might be prepared to tolerate international organizations in the president's areas of competence, it was not prepared to go so far in areas of congressional jurisdiction.[106]

State Department planners thus did not pay sufficient attention to the fundamental difference between creating a supranational organization to address trade issues and establishing international institutions to address diplomatic relations, civil aviation, health, culture, and science. The latter in many cases involved the establishment of mechanisms to promote co-operation and did not threaten deeply entrenched domestic economic interests (and where they did, as in aviation, these were not touched). A trade organization involved legal obligations requiring changes in domestic law and congressional approval. The same held true in various other countries. The intellectual appeal of an international trade organization thus had to stand up to the varied special interests in each country and their ability to appeal to concerns about sovereignty, if it was to survive.

How had the negotiators arrived at such an unsatisfactory and politically unacceptable conclusion? A number of factors suggest themselves:

Lack of Consensus and Support for New Ideas. The idea of an organization to enforce a universal code of behavior in the trade field was a revolutionary idea for which the ground had not been sufficiently well prepared. The importance of preparation—both in terms of ideas and in terms of support—is borne out by the fact that the GATT succeeded where the ITO failed. The GATT was the direct linear descendant of the RTA program. Its ideas had been thoroughly tested in earlier negotiations as well as in domestic consensus-building efforts. The ITO, on the other hand, was the direct linear descendant of nothing but failure. Previous efforts by the League of Nations to explore similar ventures had not succeeded. The necessary preparatory work to translate ideas into pragmatic and politically realistic proposals was not carried out widely enough by any of the participants. When it came time to translate the proposals into treaty language, the well of intellectual capital soon ran dry. Even the example of the IMF was not edifying. While the ITO negotiations proceeded, the IMF was going through a very difficult period, when its major participants expressed little faith in its rules and procedures.

Failure to Apply Issue Decomposition and Sequencing Tactics. As negotiations proceeded, the agenda became overloaded. The United States had expanded the original proposal for a trade organization devoted to commercial policy issues to one that also addressed commodity trade, restrictive business practices, employment, and investment. It involved extensive in-stitutional provisions. The charter thus moved well beyond the traditional confines of commercial policy. There was little enthusiasm for such a grandiose scheme in many quarters, especially since it had not been part of the original discussions.

Inability to Forge a Core Coalition. American leadership led to a core coali-tion that supported U.S. goals for a limited trade agreement. It could not craft one for the more ambitious ITO. The ideal of universalism, so preva-lent in the political discussions that led to the United Nations, did not carry over into the field of trade and economics and made it virtually im-possible to craft an organization that would have broad appeal and would also serve as an effective instrument for reducing trade barriers and elimi-nating discrimination. By negotiating a charter that would have universal appeal and satisfy both the U.S. free-enterprise approach and the state-led approach favored by others, the negotiators created an instrument that was both politically and intellectually flawed.

Failure to Develop Bridging Solutions. On a related point, the architects of the ITO had from the beginning labored under the difficulty of reconciling two sometimes conflicting sets of objectives. Their short-term objective was to resolve the difficulties of the immediate postwar period. At the same time, they wanted a charter that would be applicable to the more normal circumstances they knew would eventually return. In the United States, the emphasis was placed on these longer term objectives. In the United Kingdom and elsewhere, there was a much more acute sensitivity to the shorter term problems.[107]

The delegations of smaller countries, like Canada and the Benelux coun-tries, proved essential in helping to bridge the differences that made it pos-sible to bring the negotiations per se to a successful conclusion, but they were powerless in moving either the United States or the United Kingdom to ratification, because their own governments shared, in one way or an-other, the misgivings expressed in London and Washington and were thus unwilling to expend any diplomatic coinage on a matter of relatively little consequence to them.

Incompatible Objectives between Key Coalition Partners. As the negotia-tions gained a momentum of their own, the delegates began to confuse ends and means. The United Kingdom had proposed the ITO as a means to an end; the United States made it into an end in itself. In practical terms, most U.S. concessions would have had little immediate impact on trade, because the most important prewar competitors (Germany, Italy, and Japan) were devastated and were not party to the negotiations. Most of the other participants were not geared up to start trading extensively. They saw benefits as potential rather than immediate. The unstable postwar economic situation, in both trade and monetary affairs, domestically and internationally, was thus poorly suited to the codification of a detailed set of rules; there was greater need for a diplomatic instrument capable of responding flexibly to changing circumstances. The GATT, precisely because of its weak constitutional base, proved a more suitable diplomatic instrument. Only over time would it overcome its constitutional handicap and assume a stronger institutional role at the same time as it gained stronger support as a code of enforceable rules. With hindsight, it was a better compromise.

Lack of Crisis. The economic crisis of the 1920s and 1930s that the negotiations sought to address was resolved at a politically satisfactory level with the conclusion of the GATT. Other solutions—such as the Marshall Plan—were being found to address more immediate problems. The availability of more practical alternative solutions and a sense that the immediate crisis had passed thus undermined support for the idealistic solution of the ITO. The major participants in the negotiations were, in the end, willing to accept only minor modifications in existing obligations and very little in the way of supranational supervision of their commercial policies. Narrow domestic interests were clearly judged to be more important than international interests. Where narrow interests were not engaged, however, they were willing to accept significant, legally binding obligations. The ITO, on the other hand, was left to linger on the back burner and from there to pass into historical obscurity.

Missed Communications. Missed communications among some of the delegations provided a false sense of what could be accomplished. For example, British willingness to explore ideas that did not necessarily carry political commitment may have conveyed the wrong signal to American officials about the degree of British commitment to their vision of a postwar commercial policy. Similarly, British officials wrongly interpreted positive statements made by American officials as commitments to fight for those issues in Washington. In addition, American officials always harbored their congressional negotiating coin carefully. As a result, throughout the negotiations there seemed to be a constant sense of betrayal undermining confidence between the two principal delegations. Worst of all, the American delegation repeatedly overplayed the hand that political and economic circumstances had dealt it, creating a corrosive resentment within other delegations.[108]

Absence of Domestic Coalitions. The major delegations appeared not to have paid sufficient attention to the need for supportive domestic coalitions. The need for and habit of secrecy during the war had prevented the kind of public diplomacy and coalition building in the principal capitals that might have overcome the initial urge to oppose the ITO. Within the administration, and supported by American political, business, and academic elites, there was a strong consensus in favor of an activist, forward-looking foreign economic policy. American negotiators, therefore, felt little need to build strong congressional or more broadly based support for their approach. The result was a charter that not only suffered from lack of public consensus building but one that, after all the compromises were made, was too far removed from basic American values. It carved out or allowed too large a role for government and provided too many opportunities for statist intervention. A similar lack of coalition building was evident in the other major capitals.

Lack of Political Consensus. Finally, the lesson of the ITO negotiations is that bureaucratic priorities are not necessarily political ones. For the postwar officials involved in the negotiations, faced with a host of problems and memories of the flawed policies of the 1930s, the ITO charter represented a neat package that would provide a code and an organization attuned to the need to address these problems systematically and thoroughly. It fit in well with the emerging consensus that governments now had a much larger responsibility for ordering national economic life. But it lacked a strong political consensus in any capital. Critics easily outnumbered defenders; only bureaucrats and their academic friends were able to make the case for the ITO. That was not enough, particularly when more pressing problems required more immediate solutions.

In the end, these problems and shortcomings doomed the ITO. In effect, the operation was a success, but the patient died. The negotiators did their job and concluded a charter, but in discharging their responsibility, they created a political curiosity that never stood a chance. As a result, the more limited GATT, originally negotiated as an interim agreement that would pave the way toward the ITO, became the successful alternative that the key delegations could accept.

Conclusions

Looked at narrowly, the ITO negotiations can be characterized as an exercise that succeeded at the level of the negotiators—fifty-three delegations signed the charter—but failed politically. Looked at more broadly, however, the seven years of international trade negotiations that created the

GATT and the ITO succeeded. In effect, the negotiations were aimed at finding the best instrument through which governments could pursue national interests and objectives; they were looking for a supranational code and organization within which countries would work together for their common good. That instrument proved to be the GATT, rather than the ITO. The GATT was possible because there was sufficient coincidence among the original signatories to make it work. The ITO, which tried to rise above this, required too many compromises in order to have broad appeal and ended up satisfying no one.

The lessons learned in London, New York, Geneva, and Havana deeply colored the approach to commercial policy by the United States, the United Kingdom, France, Canada, and the other major participants in the years that followed. They pursued their interests conservatively and proved wary of schemes to expand international obligations in the trade field too broadly and universally. Efforts by the United Nations through its Conference on Trade and Development (UNCTAD) to address issues that had been lost when the ITO failed to come into being were never embraced by the major trading countries. Efforts by smaller countries to expand the GATT's mandate were similarly resisted. Politically sensitive issues, such as trade in agriculture and textile products, were isolated by means of special rules. This conservatism and caution allowed the more limited GATT to gradually mature and gain the momentum and respect required to make it work.

The GATT's conservatism was also evident in the low political profile trade policy gradually assumed in the years following 1950. Until then, trade policy had been a politically sensitive issue, figuring prominently in the electoral strategies of politicians in most countries. The GATT, however, allowed trade policy to recede from high to low politics. Trade policy became an issue that preoccupied bureaucrats, and Geneva became a place where officials solved international trade problems. Trade policy retained that profile because the bargain struck in Geneva in 1947 made it possible for governments to address trade issues incrementally and cautiously. The spectacular growth in trade from 1950 to 1974 confirmed for most governments that this conservative approach had been the right one. Not until the 1980s, when new trade frictions flowing from the changing nature of the global economy exposed new problems, did trade again begin to assume a high profile.

7   The GATT Uruguay Round, 1986–1993: The Setting and the Players

By the middle of the 1980s, the GATT had been in existence for nearly forty years. During those years, its founding members had amply demonstrated that their judgment in 1948–50 to live with the "interim" GATT was not as foolish as it may have appeared to some at the time. Over the years, periodic negotiating conferences, or rounds, as well as day-to-day decisions, gradually gave the GATT both a permanence and an institutional structure that, while not as robust as originally envisaged for the ITO, proved pragmatic and enduring. Seven rounds of successful negotiations consolidated and extended the original agreement's reach and ensured that its rules and procedures contributed to the rapid expansion of world trade during the postwar years. For most of that period, global trade in goods and services grew twice as fast as production, to reach 20 percent of world GNP, worth more than three trillion dollars annually.[1]

To further strengthen the GATT's rules and procedures and expand its disciplines to a wider range of international economic activities, its membership launched an eighth round of negotiations at Punta del Este, Uruguay, in September 1986.[2] As in the 1940s, the United States was the prime mover in initiating this round, looking for a revitalized agreement that would have broad appeal and would satisfy the specifics of the U.S. trade agenda. Other players brought varying perspectives, ranging from a strongly supportive Canada to a cynical European Community (EC) to disapproving developing countries like India and Brazil. Nevertheless, all participants saw some potential benefit in a new round while emphasizing vastly differing issues as key to satisfying their needs. The wide range of both issues and players thus promised from the outset to make the negotiations the most complex and protracted commercial negotiations ever undertaken.

The negotiations successfully concluded in December 1993. Ministers met in Marrakech, Morocco, in April 1994 to give their final blessing to the result and to adopt the round's Final Act. The results, encompassed in some five hundred pages of text and thousands of pages of schedules, came into effect on January 1, 1995. The GATT ceased to exist as a separate agreement; instead it now was subsumed into the new World Trade Organization (WTO), which provides the management of world trade with new institutional muscle. The GATT, as well as the new General Agreement on Trade in Services (GATS) and the other agreements adopted at Marrakech, all come under the umbrella of the WTO.

Reaching agreement on the more than thirty separate agreements that make up the results of the Uruguay Round proved a formidable undertaking. Originally scheduled to end in December 1990, the round struggled through two more missed December deadlines before finally concluding on December 15, 1993. The on-again, off-again Uruguay Round negotiations thus offer a compelling second example for examining the factors that influence success or failure in multilateral commercial diplomacy.[3]

The Setting

The setting within which the Uruguay Round negotiations were played out could not have been more different from those that prevailed when the GATT was negotiated in the 1940s. The discontinuity from the past resulting from depression and war provided the architects of the GATT with a strong motive to try new approaches as well as the room to experiment. The result was a surprising degree of optimism about what could be achieved. Today, almost fifty years since the end of the Second World War, we can look back on an era marked not by the failure of policy but by its success. In Canada, the United States, Japan, and Europe, the growth in both the domestic and international economies has underpinned a tripling in the standard of living. And yet, the beginning of the 1990s seemed to be characterized not by hope but by pessimism. Despite the end of the Cold War and the expansion of prosperity to many more corners of the globe, the prevailing view appears to be that conditions will deteriorate for most people in years to come.

This widespread pessimism was reflected in the trials and tribulations of the multilateral trade negotiations. While the world did not experience the same kind of discontinuity as was evident in the 1940s, there was widespread evidence of a substantial transformation in the way national economies function and relate to the global economy. This transformation seemed to have undermined the confidence of both governments and their electorates in internationalist and outward-looking solutions. Despite the success of the multilateral order, government after government, but particularly those in the United States and Europe, appeared reluctant to make deeper commitments to multilateral economic rules and procedures, in large part because their citizens were not convinced that such a further cession of national political authority would be in their interest. Ironically, therefore, the misery of war and depression appear to have predisposed governments to take a bolder and more optimistic approach to the economic problems of their day than the economic problems generated by the domestic fallout of globalization, the success of forty-plus years of economic cooperation notwithstanding. Grassroots democratic movements, which insist that the combination of international agreements and multinational firms has robbed governments of their capacity to respond to new problems such as the environment, appeared to have spooked the willingness of governments to respond broadly to the challenges posed by changes in the technology and organization of production and the resultant acceleration of globalization.

Looking back over the past forty-five years, it is not difficult to conclude that the GATT has been a positive force in the international economy. It was instrumental in providing a forum within which the industrialized countries could substantially reduce barriers to trade among them and pave the way for a tremendous expansion in trade and investment. It created the conditions necessary for the pervasive economic integration of the economics of the members of the Organization for Economic Cooperation and Development (OECD). Its rules, both as originally envisaged and as adapted and expanded over the years, provided private investors with the necessary confidence to expand their horizons. Its periodic negotiating rounds maintained the momentum toward increasing trade liberalization and rule making.[4] For the OECD countries, its rules and procedures, again as originally envisaged and then as adapted and strengthened over the years, helped to shape domestic policy so as to improve general economic welfare, reduce the ability of domestic special interests to influence policy to meet narrow interests, and provide an agreed basis for resolving conflict between competing interests, at home and abroad. As a result, the domestic legal regimes covering trade and economic matters in OECD countries had become broadly similar and widely accepted by their populations and underwrote the ability of firms in one jurisdiction to do business in another relatively easily.

But the GATT had not been an unqualified success. Problems left unresolved at the beginning continued to hamper harmonious trade relations. New problems that had cropped up over the years had received inadequate attention. Martin Wolf has characterized trade as economic war and the GATT as a peace treaty among mercantilist states.[5] While the mercantilist states had agreed to peace, they had not fully disarmed, nor were they averse to the odd skirmish. They had, for example, kept tariffs in place that served little useful economic purpose other than as payment for future trade concessions; they had imposed new barriers in order to increase their bargaining leverage or to force concessions from weaker states; and they had appeased protectionist pressures with GATT-illegal measures, so we were told, in order to safeguard the system as well as to provide payment for future concessions. Thus, while the GATT may have provided a rationale for a rearguard battle against protectionism, some critics were beginning to conclude by the mid-1980s that the compromises had begun to overwhelm the system.[6] Robert Gilpin went so far as to conclude that the postwar multilateral institutions had become irrelevant monuments to the past:

A significant transformation of the postwar international economic order has occurred. The Bretton Woods system of trade liberalization, stable currencies, and expanding global economic interdependence no longer exists, and the liberal conception of international economic relations has been undermined since the mid-1970s. The spread of protectionism, upheavals in monetary and financial markets, and the evolution of divergent national economic policies among the dominant economies have eroded the foundations of the international system. Yet inertia, that powerful force in human affairs, has carried the norms and institutions of a decreasingly relevant liberal order into the 1980s.[7]

Unquestionably, the system had become increasingly complex over the years in order to compensate for the failure of the more ambitious ITO to come into being, to address new problems, and, most important, to take account of the continuing decline in enthusiasm for commercial disarmament and the principles embodied in the original peace treaty. The thirty-five original articles had become encrusted with a range of ancillary or supporting arrangements, including codes, protocols, understandings, derogations, regional agreements, and ad hoc institutional arrangements. Many qualified and changed the original bargain, and some undermined progress toward the fundamental GATT objective of freer and less discriminatory trade. Additionally, the GATT had become a multilayered instrument with various members accepting different degrees of rights and obligations.[8] GATT legal scholar John Jackson warned that GATT law, because of its studied ambiguity backed up by an inadequate constitutional structure and flawed dispute settlement provisions, tended to be very slippery and could be bent and abused with relative impunity by its more powerful members.[9]

Despite these difficulties, the GATT could lay claim to many achievements. Trade had been liberalized; tariffs had been cut; old-fashioned quantitative restrictions had been virtually eliminated; and many potentially harmful practices had been restrained by its rules. In many ways, therefore, the arguments about whether the GATT had been beneficial were about whether the glass was half-full or half-empty. By the 1980s, the challenge was to come to grips with the realities of the more demanding global economy and the inadequacy of mercantilist bargaining. For many, that was the principal objective of the Uruguay Round.[10]

Thus by the mid-1980s, as preparations began for a new, ambitious round of multilateral trade negotiations, the experience of negotiating and living with a rules-based multilateral trading order had brought mixed results. The system had underpinned steady liberalization and growth, particularly in OECD economies, but it had not adapted quickly enough or thoroughly enough to new problems and challenges, nor were its negotiating techniques and dispute settlement procedures attuned to the changing requirements of a rapidly globalizing economy. Finally, public support for multilateral rule making was not strong in leading OECD economies, even as it was increasing in smaller countries. Against that background, the call for a new round of negotiations that would revitalize and expand the multilateral trading order provided a daunting challenge.[11]

Ideas and Objectives

The original GATT negotiations in the 1940s were based on the broadly shared perception that the economic problems of the interwar years had been exacerbated by the absence of international rules and agreements, as government after government adopted beggar-thy-neighbor policies. The solution involved the negotiation of an innovative multilateral trade and payments system built around the IMF and the GATT. By the 1980s, the success of that system had institutionalized multilateral decision making and established the convention that the effective functioning of the system required periodic negotiations to reform, expand, and deepen rules and obligations. A new round of multilateral trade negotiations, therefore, would follow down a well-trodden institutional path geared more to incrementalism than to innovation.

It is within that context that we must look for the kinds of ideas and objectives that first convinced governments to initiate a new round of negotiations and then to carry them through to a conclusion over the course of an extended period of time. What problems did governments perceive could best be addressed in the context of a major negotiation? Who and what animated governments to pursue the negotiations? Which groups in society saw their interests advanced by a negotiation? Which groups felt threatened?

The Issues

The issues that seemed uppermost in the minds of governments and their advisors in considering the desirability of initiating a new round fell into three broad categories:

- *Systemic.* Maintaining the integrity of the system loomed large in the priorities of many participating governments, particularly in the light of the growth in so-called gray-area measures (e.g., voluntary export restraint agreements) and the rise of the new protectionism (i.e., reliance on a broad range of nontariff measures to control the flow of imports). A popular image used to explain this objective was that of the bicycle theory: unless governments maintained the momentum of trade liberalization and regime integrity, the system would collapse. These systemic concerns were reflected not only in the conviction that negotiations were a desirable end in their own right but also in the focus on such issues as dispute settlement, institutional reform, and functioning of the GATT system.
- *Trade in goods.* While much had been achieved in seven rounds of GATT negotiations between 1947 and 1979, there remained—or had developed—a number of thorny issues that by the early 1980s cried out for resolution. Most prominent among them was the extent to which trade in agriculture and in textile products was not covered by the same rules as those for other goods. Other prominent problems involved subsidies, antidumping and countervailing duty proceedings, remaining tariffs, customs procedures, and other aspects of the existing framework of rules where there was room for clarifying or deepening commitments.
- *New issues.* The increasing integration of the international economy, the changing nature of international business, and changes in the comparative advantage of the GATT's members had identified a number of areas of international economic activity that were not covered to the same extent by rules and obligations as trade in goods. Increases in the international exchange of services, the greater prominence of direct foreign investment flows, and the growing importance of knowledge-intensive activities all pointed to the desirability of an international code of conduct to cover these activities, building on existing GATT concepts.

The approach adopted by various governments to these concerns, however, and the priority assigned to each varied considerably and ensured, first, a protracted preparatory phase and then an equally protracted negotiation. The United States, for example, placed greatest emphasis on the second and third set of issues and was convinced that progress on these issues—defined as new rules and greater liberalization based on the American market model—would ensure that the first concern could be managed. Developing countries, on the other hand, were much more concerned about regime maintenance and strengthening and consolidating the existing framework than about expanding the system, illustrated by their desire for a standstill and rollback of GATT-illegal measures. The EC's inclination was to emphasize the first and third set of issues, arguing that there were good reasons why there continued to be unfinished business; these were the sensitive issues, which, if not handled carefully, would undermine support for the system as a whole. Within each set of issues, there were similar divisions and nuances in approach. Reducing such a potentially extensive agenda to manageable proportions and then developing broad consensus on the issues among the more than one hundred participating players thus posed an awe-inspiring challenge.

Two sets of issues illustrate the complexity and ambition of this emerging agenda: agriculture and the new issues. In the case of agriculture, negotiators would need to take on a perplexing set of issues that had proved resistant to change in every previous trade negotiation dating back to the GATT's origin. The new issues presented a different challenge. Negotiators would need to devise not only proposals about *what* to negotiate but also think through *how* to negotiate. In short, changes in the global economy suggested that the old way would not necessarily work in the new circumstances. Each set of issues offered more than enough complexity to challenge any negotiator; combined, the challenge was formidable.

The problems facing trade in agriculture were deep seated. Given the vagaries of weather as well as of supply and demand, farm prices and incomes can fluctuate enormously. The collapse of the farm economy throughout the world in the 1920s, coupled with the specter of hunger, depression, and war in the 1930s and 1940s, had taught governments a healthy respect for the demands of farm voters and the havoc that could be wrought by the free operation of the market. In response, governments had instituted a variety of measures to promote both domestic price and income stability and national self-sufficiency. The GATT provided for such policies from the beginning or took steps to accommodate those that did not. The result is that in most temperate-zone countries, the agriculture sector had strayed further and further from the discipline imposed by markets and the rules that ensure its operation. To complicate matters further, governments were intervening with very different instruments and different priorities, and thus market distortions in each country affected different subsectors and flowed from different policies.[12]

Whatever the techniques adopted—price supports, supply management, production subsidies, guaranteed minimum prices—farmers were encouraged to produce more than what the market would bear. The result was enormous surplus production for many farm commodities, which were then dumped on world markets at distress prices or disposed of with the help of export subsidies. Since many markets were either closed or had disappeared because of subsidy-induced excess capacity, there were by the 1970s few temperate-zone agricultural commodities for which there existed a reasonably free world market where prices dictated supply and demand. Despite various efforts at reform, that was the situation governments faced in the mid-1980s and throughout the negotiations.

The distortions in world markets induced by various government programs had created at least four major problems: they cost consumers huge amounts, either directly in the form of high prices or indirectly in high taxes to pay for various support programs; they had created tremendous inefficiencies in farm production; they had placed great strains on the environment by inducing both nonsustainable intensive cultivation and inappropriate use of marginal lands; and they had destroyed the economies of efficient, export-based agricultural sectors.

Any one of these problems would have been enough to warrant a major international negotiating effort. Governments desperately wanted a framework of rules that would allow them gradually to reintroduce sufficient discipline on a collective basis to undo the worst distortions. Given the interdependence of national economies, none could do it alone. The extent of government interference and its longevity meant that there were powerful interests with a direct stake in current production and consumption patterns. Undoing any of the national regimes, therefore, required large doses of political courage as well as clear evidence of offsetting benefits.

Nowhere did this hold more true than in the European Community, where the Common Agricultural Policy (CAP) had provided much of the glue that had held the European Community together for its first thirty-five years. The CAP served not only agricultural goals but also important social and political objectives. While EC politicians may have had their internal reasons for reforming the CAP—particularly fiscal reasons—they were loathe to see the terms of that reform dictated by demands by the United States and others, unless they could point to clear benefits in other areas of the negotiations.

Similarly, in the United States, where the Reagan and Bush administrations were keen to effect major reforms as part of a large global package, many farm-state legislators remained convinced that the problems were overseas and should not be borne by American farmers. Canadian politicians faced the unpalatable choice of balancing export-oriented Western grain interests with import-competing dairy and poultry interests in Ontario and Quebec. Thus, while the intellectual case for reform may have been compelling, political reality suggested from the beginning that the road to reform would be fraught with risk.

The so-called new issues presented a different set of problems and challenges. In many of the OECD economies, traditional manufacturing industries were going through a major transformation, in part because of the success of previous GATT negotiations. Barriers for most industrial products had been reduced to such an extent that many manufacturing sectors needed to adjust constantly if they were to remain competitive on both domestic and international markets. These adjustments involved a variety of developments that at bottom comprised a gradual transformation in the technology and organization of production: new products and processes were making production much more knowledge intensive; the disaggregation of manufacturing was leading to the death of old firms and the emergence of new ones; shortening product-life cycles and increased competition had placed a premium on innovation; the high cost of innovation was stimulating the development of various new alliances and risk-sharing arrangements; and standard-technology production was migrating to developing countries, while knowledge-intensive production had become the basic ingredient for success in OECD countries.[13]

Coupled with the development of a service economy—itself a product of improvements in manufacturing efficiency—these changes were radically altering the economic profile in many OECD countries. Industries on the rise were those with a high knowledge and service dimension, while those on the decline were largely standard-technology manufacturing industries. The trade policy implications of these developments were clear: traditional liberalizing policies created problems for those industries in decline, while they did little for those on the rise. Indeed, traditional industries were clamoring for protection from the competitive pressures of a more global economy, while the new industries complained that their export growth prospects were being hampered by a range of policy measures that were not subject to the same kind of multilateral rules as trade in goods.

Three particular aspects of the new economy had become clear by the middle of the 1980s. Trade in services—such as banking, insurance, tourism, consulting, engineering, architecture, education, and medicine—offered tremendous potential for growth internationally but was hemmed in by domestic regulatory requirements that either discriminated on the basis of nationality or residence or varied so much as to constitute a barrier to expansion. Perhaps even more important, the potential for future protectionist actions loomed large in policy-makers' thinking. Direct foreign investment had become the most important agent of international integration, as firms sought ways to expand, build strategic alliances, and locate production facilities in the most advantageous places. Again, however, discriminatory regulatory regimes, as well as various incentive programs, particularly in developing countries, distorted investment decisions and hampered the most efficient allocation of resources. Third, exponential growth in new products and process technology placed a great premium on the protection of proprietary knowledge and the need for international norms, both to protect such knowledge and to punish those who did not. Thus, for the industries of the future, international rules that addressed barriers to trade in services, impediments to foreign direct investment, and the protection of intellectual property would provide them with a much firmer basis for growth.

For most of the OECD countries, therefore, reforms in the trade regime had to satisfy three political imperatives:

- it had to include a package on agriculture that addressed the rising fiscal problem as well as the distortions in export markets but still leave some room for domestic income and price support programs;
- it had to include rules on the most important barriers to growth for the industries of the future; and
- it had to tread delicately on the existing rules by allowing continued adjustment by traditional industries but at a pace that would not undermine political support for the maintenance of an open multilateral trade regime. While such traditional issues as safeguards, subsidies, antidumping and countervailing duties, textiles, tariffs, and customs procedures would obviously need to be addressed, they required delicate handling. In some cases, traditional concession swapping would work; in others, rule writing would be required, with some industries interested in liberalizing rules and others looking for tighter rules.

That was the view from the industrialized end of the telescope. Most of the developing countries had a different view. Their economies were also being transformed by the twin forces of globalization and changes in the technology and organization of production. For them, the key to future growth lay in gaining better and more secure access to rich OECD markets for the export-oriented traditional manufacturing facilities now locating in their territories. This would require further liberalization along traditional GATT lines. To what extent they needed to open their own markets was a subject of some controversy. Some agreed that the discipline that came with an open economy would work as much for them as for OECD countries; others believed that they were not yet ready and were certainly not ready to open up their service sectors. Rules that impinged on their ability to use investment and technology policies as instruments of development also raised serious political difficulties. Many of them were food importers and were not at all worried about the availability of cheap surplus agricultural products, while food exporters among them were desperate for a regime that would bring order to the current chaos. Thus, while the developing countries were keen to participate in the negotiations and had something to offer, their perspective was such as to guarantee difficult and protracted negotiations.

Old and New Bargaining Strategies

In the closing stages of the Tokyo Round, U.S. negotiators had already suggested that the GATT's rule-making experience should be extended to the new issues. The U.S. analysis of the changing global economy was generally accepted; the prescription, however, raised serious concerns, not least of which was how to address the issues and where. U.S. negotiators assumed that the GATT approach—both its principles and its bargaining strategies—could be readily adapted to these new challenges. Little serious analysis was undertaken, however, to test this assumption.[14]

The traditional approach to the GATT negotiations involves two reinforcing bargaining strategies. The first revolves around a set of negative prescriptions. The GATT rules respecting nondiscrimination,[15] tariffs, quantitative restrictions, balance-of-payments measures, and trade remedies all involve self-denying ordinances: governments agree not to engage in certain policies and practices and thus let the market determine winners and losers. These negative prescriptions are susceptible to the exchange of concessions, that is, each government can deny something in return for another government denying something of similar value. In this way, governments are able to exchange politically risky increases in import competition for politically rewarding increases in export opportunities within a fixed-rule order that guarantees stability.

The second strategy is grounded in the commitment to MFN and the organization of negotiations around the principal-supplier rule. It means that bargaining about exchanges of concessions is based on market power: the largest economies exchange concessions among each other, which are then multilateralized for the benefit of all the other participants. Smaller countries, having little to offer in terms of economically significant markets, are marginalized both in terms of the concessions they can offer and the specific concessions they can seek. Nevertheless, they gain considerably from the concessions traded among the larger economies, and the overall effect of the process is liberalizing. Following the lead of the major powers thus makes both political and economic sense for the smaller powers and ensures commitment to a regime dominated by a few major players.[16]

These two fundamental characteristics of the GATT trade relations system of the 1950s through the 1970s, however, seemed less well suited to the trade policy requirements of the 1980s and 1990s. The issues that had become critical to trade and investment were domestic regulations rather than border measures. Substantive obligations in such areas as intellectual property, investment, and services require governments to go beyond self-denying ordinances and enter into positive obligations, that is, not merely to refrain from interfering in the market but also to conform to international standards. As had been demonstrated in the negotiation of the Tokyo Round trade remedy codes, they address not only limits but also entitlements. The 1980s saw a tidal wave of trade remedy actions because governments had armed themselves with these new devices and industry had learned how to use them. The Tokyo Round experience suggested the extent to which rule writing is neither necessarily liberalizing nor readily susceptible to the traditional exchange of concessions.[17]

Bargaining about norms and standards is also not as easily organized on the basis of market power. In most cases, the norms are those of the major powers which insist that they do not have to make major adjustments.[18] It is the smaller powers that are now asked to make the most significant concessions, but without the politically critical counterweight of gaining additional access to the markets of the large powers. Most of that access has been gained; what remains is more secure access, as well as access to the most politically sensitive sectors of the larger markets, such as for textiles and clothing, footwear, and agriculture. Opening those sectors—which will bring only limited new economic benefits, in return for huge commitments on sensitive domestic policy issues—creates a difficult bargaining scenario. While there may be clear benefits to expanding the reach of a fixed-rule international economic order, such benefits are likely to be perceived more in intellectually than in politically persuasive terms.[19]

Complicating matters even further, the number of countries actively participating in the negotiations had vastly increased. By the end of 1993, a dozen or so countries followed the GATT's rules on a de facto basis, and 117 countries were members. Many of these are small countries with a high stake in a successfully functioning multilateral trading order but with little to offer to make it work better or to unblock stalemate. Additionally, they have a greater interest in consolidating the old order than in building a new one.

The impact of globalization and the transformation of production thus had a double, sometimes conflicting, impact. It underlined the economic need for a revitalized global trade regime and raised fears about the political cost of further global integration. From one perspective, the overriding challenge was to consolidate and strengthen the existing regime; from another, it was to modernize and revamp the regime to reflect the new reality. In the Uruguay Round, the need for trade-offs between these two priorities would tax the capacity of the bargaining process, threaten stalemate, and delay the conclusion of the round by three years, almost doubling its length. The apparent inevitability of globalization and the resultant need for adjustment by societies, particularly by business, labor, and government, sharpened political debate and returned trade policy to the realm of high policy. The comfortable days when trade negotiations were the concerns of professionals in government and elsewhere and only rarely escaped the business pages of daily newspapers was replaced by a strident public debate calling into question both the objectives and means of trade negotiations. Farmers in the European Community, the fishing industry in Canada, and environmental activists in the United States transformed trade policy into a controversial issue and made politicians leery of the conventional advice emanating from the professional elites who for many years dominated the negotiation and implementation of international trade rules. Ironically, in the larger, industrialized countries, this phenomenon made politicians cautious about further international commitments, while it fostered the opposite attitude in smaller countries, particularly developing countries, leading to a historic reversal in approaches to a multilateral trading order.[20]

The Players and Their Objectives

Unlike the original GATT negotiations, which started with a relatively small group and then gradually expanded to include fifty-six countries, the Uruguay Round proceeded within the established framework of the GATT and on the basis that the negotiations would need to meet the interests not only of the GATT's members but possibly of nonmembers, like the People's Republic of China, as well. From the start, therefore, the Uruguay Round involved a diverse group of players with a broad range of interests and priorities. As can be expected, the negotiations were dominated by the big three—the United States, the European Community, and Japan; but a significant number of second-level participants, both industrialized and developing, played critical roles in developing the agenda, defining the negotiating parameters, and maintaining pressure for an ambitious outcome. The stake in the health of the international trading system had significantly expanded during the GATT's first forty years. In the end, however, the results were dictated by the requirements of the major players, particularly the United States and the European Community.

The United States

As in previous negotiations, the United States was the prime mover both in initiating the round and in setting the pace, but less successfully than in the past, as it struggled with growing ambivalence at home about the value of multilateral trade rules. A number of factors contributed to this ambivalence. Internationally, the economic renaissance of Europe and Japan had reduced the dominance of the United States in both the international economy and in bargaining about the international economic order. In the closing stages, the end of the Cold War further removed the political rationale that underpinned American leadership in that order, both at home and abroad. As long as the Cold War proved a threat to U.S. security, it disposed the United States to exercise leadership and balance economic with geopolitical considerations. The absence of this threat had made the United States less certain about the benefits of exercising leadership along these lines and made the rest of the players less convinced that they would benefit from their followership.

At home, slow economic growth in the 1970s and early 1980s had unleashed a virulent new strain of protectionism. Import-competing industries increasingly sought ways to insulate themselves from more competitive Japanese and developing countries' firms, while export-oriented firms expressed growing frustration with the pace of multilateral negotiations and the absence of internationally agreed solutions to the problems they were experiencing in the global market. Allied with labor and populist groups unhappy with the impact of international trade rules on American freedom of action, they found a sympathetic ear in Congress, which responded with legislative solutions not always consistent with U.S. international obligations. The real source of American trade problems in the 1980s may have lain in macroeconomic factors, but both Congress and the administration found it easier to address them through protectionist or aggressive export-enhancing actions, many of which aggravated U.S. trade relations and undermined American leadership in the round.[21]

To counter the protectionist pressures flowing from the 1981–82 recession and maintain momentum for multilateral liberalization, the Reagan administration had worked with a new export-oriented coalition of service, knowledge-intensive, and advanced technology industries to gain support for a work program aimed at revitalizing and expanding the GATT. The chosen vehicle had been a meeting of the GATT at the level of ministers, the first since the 1973 meeting that had launched the Tokyo Round. The failure of the 1982 meeting to reach consensus on any issues of significance to the United States channeled U.S. trade policy energy into a variety of directions including free trade with Israel and Canada as well as greater resort, under section 301 of the Trade Act of 1974, to unilateral action to counter unfair trading practices, leading to the punishment of trade partners for falling afoul of American, rather than international, rules. These latter actions more often than not resulted in the United States hurting itself as much as the target countries, further fueling resentment about international trade and undermining confidence in the system and in American leadership, both at home and abroad.

These developments all found expression in the various strains of U.S. trade policy advocated in Washington. One represented the traditional multilateral orthodoxy that had inspired American leadership in the erection and maintenance of the multilateral trading system and drove the U.S. position in the round. A second was based on a resurgence of unilateralism and protectionism, disdainful and distrustful of the multilateral trading system. A third favored the negotiation of regional or bilateral agreements with selected countries, notably Canada, Mexico, and those of the Pacific Rim, either on their own merits or as a complement to multilateral trade negotiations.[22]

It is, of course, possible for a superpower like the United States to ride off in several directions at once for a considerable period of time. Nevertheless, the multilateralist position had lost some of its potency; it was no longer the preeminent and unchallenged position; the geopolitical impulses that had successfully subordinated trade policy to U.S. foreign policy had lost their authority.[23] The unilateralists, while paying lip service to the multilateral ideal, appealed to deeply embedded U.S. mercantilism and struck an emotionally powerful chord in the American psyche. For their part, the regionalists and bilateralists were struggling to find a patch of secure ground by marrying the liberal virtues of the traditional multilateral approach to a recognition that the future might lie in tailor-made trade agreements with particular countries and regions. To add to the confusion, the Byzantine complexity of the U.S. decision-making process often made it difficult for the rest of the world to determine who was in charge and what was in vogue at any one time.

As it struggled to respond to these competing strains, the United States' traditional leadership role proved less effective than in previous negotiations. Too often, American officials mistook posture for leadership. Much of their rhetoric had strong moral overtones, expressing anxiety about fairness, level playing fields, and the need for disciplines. Having been burned by the 1982 ministerial meeting, American officials approached the round with caution. Still eager to see the launch of a new round, particularly one that would address the concerns of the new free-trade coalition, American officials were less prepared to make the necessary concessions to stimulate the interests of its trading partners and maintain the momentum of the round, particularly once the end of the Cold War decoupled trade and foreign policy considerations. Wary of potential congressional hostility, American officials advanced a negotiating agenda made up of a delicate mix of market-opening and market-protecting objectives aimed at creating and maintaining U.S. industry support for a trading system that would be more open than closed and a round that contained more pluses than minuses. For example, for the services, farm, and advanced technology sectors, the United States sought market-opening rules; for the traditional manufacturing sectors, the initial objectives were geared to regime maintenance.

The U.S. agenda seemed built up more from individual irritants than a broad vision of a future, more comprehensive and better functioning global trade regime.[24] American politicians seemed to have difficulty coming to grips with the challenge to U.S. economic leadership from Europe and Japan and with the profound changes that were taking place in the trade relations system. American officials repeatedly indicated that significant U.S. contributions to earlier rounds should now be matched by others. As a result, they seemed unable to galvanize other GATT members into forward-looking commitments that provided a balance between narrow, short-term political interests and broader, long-term economic interests.[25]

The European Community

The European Community was the second most dominant participant in the round, often playing the role of spoiler as its primary energies continued to be preoccupied with consolidating the internal market. Europe was buffeted by tremendous changes in the 1980s and, like the United States, brought a somewhat schizophrenic approach to the problems of more global competition. At the beginning of the 1980s, the prevailing mood was summed up in the word *Eurosclerosis*. By the end of the decade, however, that mood had been transformed into a Europhoria, flowing from successful efforts at completing the single market and the buoyant response to new competitive challenges from within and without. The collapse of communism added to this new mood, even as it brought new challenges from the east involving a united and dominating Germany—a strongly motivating and uniting factor for the rest of Europe—and a need to find ways to accommodate the aspirations of the emerging market economies of Central Europe. By the early 1990s, in the face of a global recession and even higher unemployment, the mood swung again. The potential expansion of the European Community to include the remaining European Free Trade Agreement (EFTA) countries (Sweden, Switzerland, Norway, Finland, and Austria) as well as some of the former Council for Mutual Economic Assistance (COMECON) countries required tremendous policy ingenuity and energy and provided expanding competence and prestige to Brussels and the Eurocrats. Additionally, fiscal pressures forced a major adjustment in the CAP, an issue particularly sensitive in France, the most committed Europhile among the major countries.[26]

These developments created an extraordinarily charged policy agenda in Brussels that sucked up much of the available creativity and political commitment. Little wonder, therefore, that U.S. insistence on a new GATT round attuned to its agenda and based on its internal policy requirements initially fell on ambivalent ears in Brussels. While not averse to a new round and prepared to address many of the same issues as the United States and for many of the same reasons, the European Community was not prepared to go either as fast or as far as the United States and found U.S. pressure tactics increasingly irritating and counterproductive, particularly given its newfound confidence and economic importance. During the later stages, EC officials repeatedly had to remind American officials that the era of the European Community as an American protectorate was over. Europeans no longer considered themselves beholden to the United States on either security or economic grounds and resented any suggestion that past dependence should make them grateful and accommodating to U.S. interests.

From the perspective of the round, the EC-92 program marked the most important development in Europe. Fears that it indicated a major move to EC inwardness proved unfounded, but this fear was high on the list of concerns of the negotiators from other countries in the round's early phases. Events proved that the European Community has too large a stake in the markets of the rest of the world to wish to turn its back on them, but its actions, like those of the United States under section 301, often gave the false impression that it would be prepared to do just that.

The EC-92 program may have started out as another exercise in Euroguff containing significant elements of Eurobluff and Eurothreat, but it soon captured the imagination of business and opinion molders and took off because it responded to some real problems, internal as well as external. Most of the round, therefore, was played out against the background of a major restructuring of the European market, severely limiting the scope for the European Community's negotiators to consider new obligations at odds with this movement. It equally cooled the ardor of the negotiators on agriculture, because too large an erosion of this traditional glue would undermine progress on the other elements, creating a more united and more integrated Europe, much as the Maastricht accords (agreements to strengthen the political cohesiveness of European Community members) aimed at political and monetary union.[27]

The number one EC objective in the round was thus to keep new GATT rules from impeding progress toward a more integrated and united Europe. Second, the European Community looked to the round to put in place rules and procedures that would constrain the U.S. penchant for unilateralism, for example, as a result of section 301 procedures. Neither was a wholly negative stance; it involved export-oriented objectives, in services, for example, as well as the traditional Eurocratic interest in using multilateral negotiations to enhance the competence of the commission. Nevertheless, EC participation in the round was essentially conservative or passive, an approach that extended even to the Nordics and the central Europeans looking to their eventual entry into a pan-European federation. EC conservatism colored, for example, its approach to standards, procurement, rules of origin, and trade-related investment measures (TRIMs). Most of all, however, pan-European ambitions placed tight constraints on what the European Community was prepared to do in agriculture. It was prepared to factor internally driven CAP reforms into the negotiations, but it was not prepared to let U.S. demands dictate further changes in the CAP and thus open up a Pandora's box of political problems. The problem was not just with French farmers and the mountains of surplus wheat, wine, and butter they produce. It also involved inefficient German farmers facing the potential of increased competition from the east, as well as militant farmers in Ireland, Greece, Italy, and Spain, equally unprepared to give up their protected markets.

Within the European Community, however, attitudes toward the round were not monolithic. The United Kingdom, Denmark, and the Netherlands were generally keen, while France and the Mediterranean countries were not. Germany straddled the fence, disposed to address most of the issues in the round but unprepared to run too far ahead of France and isolate it, particularly on agriculture. As a result, U.S. pressure tactics usually worked to increase French intransigence and German ambivalence, rather than persuading them to see things as the United States did. The primacy of pan-Europeanism, as well as internal divisions, thus made it difficult for the European Community to assume the kind of leadership in the round that its economic importance and increased stake in global trade seemed otherwise to indicate.[28]

While EC participation was thus hemmed in by the realities of pan-European institution building, it would be false to characterize the European Community as more protectionist than liberal in its approach to trade issues. Evidence to the contrary is too compelling. For example, EC expansion to the Mediterranean countries (Greece, Spain, and Portugal) was accompanied by efforts to ensure that these countries became more open and competitive. Similarly, the European Community moved to open its markets to the central European economies on a nonreciprocal basis and has had long-standing arrangements extending one-way preferences to many of its former colonies. EC conservatism, therefore, may have constrained its capacity to lead and its ability to make major concessions on sensitive issues, but it did not prevent it from participating in the making of a broad and deep new multilateral trade agreement, particularly one that would help in the management of future EC-U.S. and EC-Japan trade relations.

Japan

Japan played a leading role in the preparatory and early stages of the negotiations, but in the closing stages, as it became clear that a successful round would call for some serious concessions, Japan seemed to be retreating to its more normal defensive shell. Like Germany, Japan developed rapidly in the postwar years, with the significant difference that Germany opened its market while Japan did not. Part of the explanation for this deep-seated mercantilist isolationism lies in the peculiar nature of Japanese society and part in the way Japan has been treated by its major trading partners. Japan learned its trade policy in response to the U.S. and EC penchant for taking GATT-illegal measures. In a rearguard action to counteract Japanese competitiveness, both the United States and European Community as early as the 1950s restrained Japan's exports of low-cost products such as cotton textiles. The habit formed then continued over the years, culminating in restraints on trade in automotive and electronic products in the 1980s and the aggressive use of antidumping actions on a wider range of products. Throughout this period, U.S. and EC complaints about the unfairness of Japanese competition and the closed nature of the Japanese economy had a hollow ring in the face of anemic U.S. and EC business efforts to penetrate the Japanese market.

Japan responded to EC and U.S. complaints with a strategy of accommodation to the extent necessary while keeping its own market as closed as possible. While nominally following GATT principles, Japan used the ingenious device of administrative guidance to deny in reality what it might accept formally. Its goal in multilateral bargaining was to ensure that the United States and the European Community did not adopt policies harmful to Japanese interests. Whenever possible, policy issues raised by its trading partners were pursued bilaterally and dealt with in bilateral agreements that avoided nondiscriminatory commitments. Starting in the mid-1980s, however, Japan also began to use its GATT rights to fight back and showed a willingness to open its market in the context of a major negotiation. As early as 1983, Prime Minister Nakasone was among the first to call for a new round of negotiations; but this early leadership was not sustained, and Japan failed to take full advantage of its economic importance to contribute to the modernization of the trading system in a manner that would properly reflect Japan's stake in the system.[29]

Japan's primary interest in the Uruguay Round remained defensive. It found multilateral negotiations to be an effective means of containing or limiting the impact of U.S. and EC protectionism. As a consequence, its principal objectives included tightening discipline on antidumping actions, rules of origin, and TRIMs, all favorite EC and U.S. measures to harass Japanese competition. It shared an interest in effective intellectual property rules and generally favored the establishment of a GATT-like regime for services. Defensively, Japan was anxious not to see much erosion in its agricultural protection. Its attitude to the integration of developing countries into the GATT system was ambivalent.[30]

The Developing Countries

The hesitant leadership and lack of vision of the big three was to some extent offset by the active and often constructive role played by an increasing number of developing countries. Although it would be misleading to regard developing countries as a monolithic group, until the mid-1980s most developing countries in the GATT were preoccupied with the concept of special and differential treatment. They sought the rights of GATT membership but were less prepared to accept its obligations and over the years succeeded in achieving this objective. But they also found that when they became too competitive, such as in standard-technology goods like textiles, clothing, and footwear, the industrial countries found ways to deny them their GATT rights. The result was that the domestic trade policies of many developing countries were frankly mercantilist, justified on the basis of a branch of development economics that has at best a fragile intellectual foundation.[31]

During the preparatory phases, India and Brazil represented the prevailing orthodoxy of the developing countries: industrial countries were responsible for the problems of the trading system and should take steps to resolve problems; developing countries were not responsible and, while prepared to support a new round, should not be expected to liberalize to meet industrial country concerns; the special status enjoyed by the developing countries should be preserved and strengthened, industrial countries should move quickly to liberalize trade in agriculture, textiles, and tropical products and to discipline the use of gray-area measures as safeguards; and trade in services and other new issues were not part of the GATT agenda and should be addressed elsewhere. In the early 1980s, this was the litany that characterized many interventions by the developing countries. Members of industrial countries welcomed the more active interest shown by the developing countries in GATT affairs, but they bemoaned the rhetoric, the UNCTAD-like obstruction and group solidarity, as well as their fascination with texts and political statements. For the first half of the decade, it led to stalemate and rising frustration with the GATT process.[32]

As discussions proceeded, however, more and more of the developing countries began to see their interests being served by a more open, rules-based system that imposed obligations on them as well as on their industrial trading partners. This more pragmatic strategy reflected changing attitudes and approaches to economic development. The politicized approach of the 1960s and 1970s was, by the late 1980s, widely regarded as inadequate and counterproductive. In its place, a consensus appeared to be developing around a policy that accepted that sound macroeconomic management and disciplines on various microeconomic policies were as important for developing countries as for industrial countries.[33] The debt crisis of the 1980s and the role of the IMF in restructuring helped many developing countries realize the extent to which the statist, inward-looking import-substitution strategies of the past had helped to keep them poor. In fact, the absence of strong traditions of democracy allowed some developing countries to practice this new orthodoxy more effectively than did many of the OECD countries.

The tigers of East Asia (Korea, Taiwan, Hong Kong, and Singapore) exemplified this new pragmatism. All experienced steady growth in the 1980s and either practiced an open trade policy or were moving rapidly in that direction. All needed more open and more secure access to the markets of the United States, the European Community, and Japan to maintain their economic development. From the beginning, they were thus keen supporters of the round. Their interests were generally supported by the countries of the Association of Southeast Asian Nations (ASEAN) and increasingly by countries in Latin America. Many countries in that region also accepted that liberalization is an important ingredient in fostering growth and development, and many (e.g., Mexico and Chile) adopted unilateral liberalization programs. Collectively, the countries of East Asia and Latin America thus demanded that they be heard and that the United States and the European Community take their GATT obligations seriously. As a result, the developing countries for the first time played a major and constructive role in a round.[34]

The export profile of most developing countries indicated that the most important categories after fuel and resources—food, textiles, and clothing—were among the most protected in OECD countries, suggesting where the specific interests of many of the developing countries would lie in the negotiations. Liberalization of world trade in both agriculture and textiles and similar products would help the developing countries address both their debt and development problems, but only if both OECD and developing countries liberalized. Thus the developing countries agreed on the need for a broad and deep result across the full spectrum of issues. In effect, a natural—if somewhat superficial, difficult, and old-style—bargain developed between rules on trade in services and other so-called new issues to satisfy the needs of industrial countries, on the one hand, and the liberalization of trade in textiles, agriculture, and tropical products to satisfy the needs of developing countries, on the other. In addition, many of the more advanced developing countries were also prepared to open their own economies to a greater extent, for example, by lowering and binding their high tariffs in the context of a comprehensive agreement that addressed their interests.

By the closing stages of the round, many of the more advanced developing countries in Asia and Latin America were acting on the understanding that their economies had reached a stage where they could add economic clout to moral and political arguments. As a result, they had learned to maximize their limited bargaining leverage through alliances, such as the Cairns Group, and a shrewd willingness to make trade-offs. In effect, they had learned how to use the bargaining strategies of smaller industrial countries like Canada, Australia, and Switzerland.

The Coalition Builders

For the smaller industrial countries, the arrival of the leading developing countries on the stage of serious trade negotiations proved a godsend. A number of them had found themselves increasingly marginalized as the role of middle powers eroded, first in the face of the sterile East-West and North-South confrontations of the 1950s and 1960s and then with the development of a triadic economic world. Most of the smaller industrial countries in Europe had disappeared into the smothering embrace of the European Community either directly or by means of various free-trade or association agreements. By the mid-1980s, only Canada, Australia, and New Zealand remained as small, fully independent industrial countries, with the EFTA countries not sure whether their interests were best protected as independent voices or as EC satellites. Only Canada had found a channel for ensuring its views were heard as a junior member of the Summit Seven and its offshoot, the periodic quadrilateral trade ministers' meetings (Quads).

The realization that the developing countries were prepared to participate in the negotiations in order to advance specific economic interests, rather than on the basis of posture and theology, made it possible for the smaller industrial countries to dust off their alliance-building skills and find common causes. During the early preparations, they came together in Geneva in various informal groups and plotted strategy and tactics. From the beginning, Australia and Switzerland proved they had the sharpest elbows and keenest noses, and Colombia, as a result of its able representation in Geneva, emerged as the voice of consensus for the more pragmatic developing countries. Canada, trading on its status as a member of the summit and of the Quads, proved an indispensable link between the smaller players and the big three and learned to play this card with great care, pursuing its traditional role of enthusiastic cheerleader for any agreement that advanced the cause of international rule making. Its energies and attention, however, were somewhat diverted by first the Canada-U.S. free-trade agreement and then its expansion into a North American free-trade agreement including Mexico.[35]

Various alliances grew out of early efforts at smaller country cooperation. At Cairns, in Northern Australia, in the summer of 1985, Australia hosted the first meeting of a group of thirteen agriculture exporting countries, which came to be known as the Cairns Group and which throughout the negotiations ensured that agriculture would be addressed seriously. For most of its members, the round would have little meaning and value if trade in agriculture were not liberalized and the rules strengthened.[36] In Geneva, Switzerland hosted a regular lunch for a group of smaller countries, which became known as the de la Paix Group, after the hotel where some of the lunches were held. The Quad countries met regularly to exchange information with each other, as well as with the smaller industrial countries, in a group known as the Dirty Dozen. Developing countries continued to meet in their own caucus, and over the course of the 1980s, its deliberations gradually evolved from an UNCTAD-like approach to the issues to one that reflected the new pragmatism. The Rio Group provided opportunities for informal discussion among industrial and developing countries, as did discussions in the Asia-Pacific Economic Cooperation (APEC) Forum. This coalition-building process proved critical in moving the negotiations along and also helped draw the GATT's smaller members more fully into the process and increased their stake in and commitment to a successful outcome.

Activist coalition building by the smaller countries was, on the whole, welcomed by the big three delegations. They found these new counterweights both a challenge and a help in managing the difficulties imposed on them by the ambivalence and schizophrenia evident in their capitals. There were occasions when U.S. and EC delegations alike looked to the Cairns Group or the de la Paix Group or the developing countries' caucus for help, either in isolating one of the other big three delegations or in dealing with a problem of support or issue development at home. Officials in Washington and Brussels paid more attention than in the past to the views of smaller countries and devoted considerable energy to efforts aimed at influencing opinion in their capitals. While they may not have viewed the role of the Cairns or de la Paix Groups in terms of leadership, they recognized their members as potentially useful allies in advancing their own interests and thus added to the ability of these countries to place their stamp on the negotiations.

The capacity of the group of more than forty smaller countries to build and maintain issue-specific and process-oriented alliances thus became the engine that kept the round going in the face of faltering U.S. and big three leadership. The kinds of issues that mattered to these countries were not always the same as those that mattered to the big three. As a result, the contours and content of the final agreement would need to be truly multilateral, reflecting not only the big three agenda but also that of the lesser players.

While the coalition builders had become an important and even indispensable force in the negotiations, in the end they collectively possess neither the political authority nor the economic clout to dictate success or failure. These smaller countries made it possible to make progress on issues where the big three could not lead but could acquiesce. They could ensure that the necessary intellectual leadership and creativity was present to get the round started and keep it going, but the ultimate success or failure of the agreement would still revolve around the United States and the European Community and, to a lesser extent, Japan. In effect, a successful conclusion of the negotiation would require a package that satisfied all four major participants: the big three and the preponderance of the coalition of smaller members. That package would require not only progress on the traditional agenda to satisfy the smaller players but also a way through the thicket of new issues advanced by the large players.

The Director General and the Secretariat

From the outset, Arthur Dunkel proved he would be a much more activist director general than his predecessor, Olivier Long, who had seen his role strictly as a neutral international public servant. While Long had made active use of his office—for example, in so-called seven-plus-seven meetings, informal meetings involving roughly equal numbers of industrial and developing countries—he was more inclined to place pressure on delegations to meet informally on their own to resolve issues than to do so under his leadership. Dunkel took a different approach. He saw himself as a catalyst. In that role, he proved a tireless participant in the negotiations, cajoling delegations, encouraging the development of coalitions, building public support through speeches and a much more active publications program, traveling to capitals, presiding at informal meetings in the "greenroom" next to his office, hosting dinners at his home, and invoking one-on-one meetings with recalcitrant delegations. Long's style had suited the era of GATT negotiations dominated by the big three, where the views of the secretariat were neither sought nor appreciated. Dunkel's style was more suited to a GATT with a much broader active membership, one prepared to welcome a director general who could help the process of coalition building and move the big three in directions likely to benefit the membership as a whole.

Dunkel was backed up by a secretariat that grew considerably during the 1980s and was capable of providing the analysis and advice required by the smaller members. Small by U.N. standards but widely recognized as a capable international secretariat, the GATT's permanent staff proved during the 1980s that they had the necessary expertise and analytical skills to move beyond their traditional service function, and they became a constructive contributor in the negotiations.

What was less clear was how well they understood the implications of the new issues. Schooled in discussions and disputes arising out of the GATT's traditional agenda, the secretariat had little capacity for long-term or speculative analysis. Even the small group of economists charged with preparing regular assessments of global trade issues had spent little effort looking at the interaction between trade and investment, the growing importance of trade in services, the kinds of barriers to growth faced by knowledge-intensive industries, and other aspects of the emerging global economy. In response to the demands of the United States at the GATT ministerial meeting in 1982, work began to develop the necessary analytical capacity, but throughout the round, the secretariat's expertise was more evident on the old issues than on the new.[37]

Dunkel and the secretariat proved indispensable in the agenda setting and developmental stage as well as a positive force during the enervating negotiation of texts. They could not, however, generate the necessary political will to close. That final ingredient was provided during the final six months of negotiations by a new, more political director general, Peter Sutherland. Appointed to replace Dunkel on July 1, 1993, Sutherland brought the experience of the rough and tumble world of EC and Irish politics, which was by then more needed than Dunkel's bureaucratic experience and intellectual leadership. Sutherland was more interested in results than in the fine points of the negotiations. He could bully where Dunkel could only cajole. He could sit down with EC, U.S., and other politicians as an equal rather than as an international civil servant. As such, he demonstrated that the base built by Dunkel of an actively involved director general could be put to good but different use by a man with Sutherland's talent and temperament.

Ideas and Their Brokers

In preparing for and pursuing the round, negotiators could count on a plethora of information and analysis on every possible dimension of the issues under consideration. More so than during any previous negotiation, the problem was not a shortage of information and analysis but a surfeit. The past fifty years had seen the development of epistemic communities with interests, specialized knowledge, and a stake in the outcome of multilateral trade negotiations. The growth in bureaucracies ensured that each major delegation could count on a wealth of internally generated analysis and advice. In addition, the success of the GATT-based trade regime in informing and underpinning domestic trade regimes in the OECD countries had resulted in the development of a variety of epistemic communities and interest groups outside governments. By the early 1980s, these groups possessed the necessary detailed knowledge to provide both general and specific advice on the issues under consideration.[38] In developing negotiating objectives and ideas, therefore, the negotiators needed to take account of this information and advice and factor it into their own more immediate requirements.

For purposes of our analysis, four groups with overlapping interests and knowledge bases stand out: government officials, lawyers and legal scholars, academic analysts, and business groups. The pertinent issues in each case are why these communities sought negotiations, what they hoped to gain—or feared losing—from the negotiations, and what values and ideas they advanced over the course of the negotiations. Their examination should yield a better appreciation of the intellectual capital available to help negotiators move the issues from broad concerns into specific rules and obligations, as well as a sense of the political dynamics of the negotiations in the major capitals.

Government Officials

The successful functioning of the GATT trade regime during the postwar years had led to the establishment in most governments of a cadre of officials with a direct stake in the preservation and expansion of that regime. For these officials, regime maintenance had become one of the overriding goals of trade policy and negotiations. From their perspective, therefore, the principal objective of the round was the strengthening and expansion of the GATT into an even broader, better functioning global trade regime. Regime maintenance at times even translated into the conviction that process considerations were as important as substantive commitments. As a result of such attitudes, GATT meetings in the early 1980s became consumed with agenda issues and led Martin Wolf to complain:

A cynic might conclude that the prospect of lengthy negotiations may be regarded by some as a "consummation devoutly to be wished" rather than as a distressing fact of life. The lengthier the negotiations the longer politically difficult decisions can be avoided. Indeed permanent negotiation can itself be a strategy, albeit a profoundly conservative one. . . . To postpone problems, though, is not necessarily to solve them. An agreement to negotiate can as surely be associated with further decay as failure to reach such an agreement, even if the process of decay is slowed. What is negotiated and how is also important.[39]

Modern bureaucrats love systemic issues. Institutional provisions help to provide a framework to tie the politicians down; dispute settlement makes it easier to deal with aggrieved interests; and frequent meetings build consensus and give the appearance of purposeful movement. In the preparatory phase of the negotiations, until such time as broader consensus had developed on the substantive issues that needed to be tackled, the emphasis on such bureaucratic priorities tended to dominate the discussions. They were uppermost in the minds of those officials who prepared the ground for the 1982 ministerial meeting and were reflected in the writings of former officials and think-tank analysts closely associated with the work of those officials.[40] These concerns became the focus for negotiation in the groups reviewing the GATT's articles, examining the function of the GATT system, and considering the institutional and dispute settlement procedures. In each of these, the objective was to put in place institutional and procedural obligations that would enhance the role of multilateral decision making in domestic trade law and policy.

Trade officials were, of course, thoroughly familiar with the traditional terrain of the GATT negotiations and had little difficulty in identifying the issues that needed to be addressed. But as the agenda moved beyond the familiar, they needed increasingly to widen their circle and invite in issue specialists familiar with the domestic regulatory regimes now also being discussed. These officials, in turn, were unfamiliar with the principles and processes of trade negotiations. Each group, jealous of its prerogatives, found it difficult to learn from the other and build common approaches.[41] Thus within official circles, turf considerations became an important element in the negotiations and added a new layer of complexity both to building domestic consensus and to pursuing national interests. The round thus proved a laboratory for testing new ways for developing domestic and multilateral bargaining strategies more attuned to the new agenda.

Lawyers and Legal Scholars

Economics had been the leading academic discipline for many of the architects of the original GATT. By the 1980s, the dominating academic paradigm had become law, and legal training was increasingly appreciated as an important background for trade negotiators. For outside advice, negotiators were more likely to turn to lawyers and legal scholars than to any other professional group. The preeminent position of legal scholarship in discussions about the GATT and the Uruguay Round negotiations can be directly traced to the judicialization of trade relations that flowed from the

Tokyo Round negotiations. American legislators discovered earlier in this century that they could satisfy their constituents' complaints about foreign competitors by giving the U.S. courts the right to try cross-border trade disputes and prescribe trade remedies such as antidumping and countervailing duties. Rather than one government addressing the complaints of its citizens to another government on the basis of international treaty rights, citizens could address their complaints directly to quasi-judicial domestic panels or to the courts, which would try the issues on the basis of domestic law. Sparingly used before the 1970s, these private rights became the instrument of choice in the 1980s and, as a result, altered the nature of intergovernmental trade relations and the interest of the legal profession in trade issues.

Judicialization and legal interest in trade issues had its origins in the United States,[42] but by the early 1980s, EC, Canadian, Australian, and other legal professionals had also discovered the international trade regime; the result was a torrent of literature and advice on the legal dimensions of international trade.[43] Three sets of issues preoccupied legal scholars: systemic, procedural, and legal remedies. On the first, legal scholars have generally added precision to the work on institutional and related issues and have been at the forefront in seeking a stronger constitutional base for the GATT.[44] The negotiation of a series of procedural codes during the Tokyo Round made GATT obligations more sophisticated and alerted legal scholars to the potential for more negotiations along these lines, as governments began the process of gradually translating the GATT's broad obligations of principle into a code of detailed rules and procedures.[45] Finally, the prominence of trade remedies such as antidumping and countervailing duties in the trade policy of the 1980s provided the legal community with a rich opportunity to explore how the international rules governing these remedies could be made more lawlike.[46] The direct stake of lawyers in much of the detail of what was being negotiated, their capacity to reach officials, legislators, and ministers, and the precision of their knowledge and advice made the legal profession a formidable factor in the negotiations. Their influence was evident in the fact that for the first time delegations to the negotiations consciously included officials trained in the law and frequently sought advice from legal scholars. It is also illustrated by the fact that the decision documents that emerged from the negotiations were by far the longest and most detailed ever to emerge from a GATT negotiation.[47]

Legal training also proved a critical dimension in pursuing the agenda of new issues. The process of legislating positive international norms and standards was ideally suited to the talents of legal scholars and practitioners. Thus, many of the ideas on how to pursue agreements on intellectual property protection, subsidies, services, and investment were first suggested in legal periodicals, at conferences of legal practitioners, and in studies prepared by legal scholars. More than any other group, they could see benefits in the development of international codes laying out detailed codes of behavior. It was no accident that Peter Sutherland, United States trade representative (USTR) Mickey Kantor, and EC trade commissioner Sir Leon Brittan, the three individuals who dominated the final six months of discussions, were all lawyers.

Academics and Think Tanks

Economists, who had been the principal intellectual influence on trade policy matters and trade negotiations in the 1940s, had by the 1980s lost that influence. Business and government attitudes to international trade from the 1940s through the 1970s had reflected the prevailing economic theory that international trade flowed from comparative advantage, a relatively static condition based on national endowments of the principal factors of production: resources, capital, and labor. Government policies that distorted the most efficient allocation of these factors of production were likely to lower national and global welfare, while the removal of such barriers was likely to raise them. Similarly, trade and investment were considered to be alternative ways of pursuing comparative advantage; the establishment of a foreign branch-plant was thought to replace production in the home country that would otherwise have been exported to the foreign market.

By the 1980s, prevailing theories about economic growth and international exchange had become much more sophisticated and varied and had robbed governments of the moral and intellectual certitude that had underpinned the trade regime of the 1950s and 1960s. New ideas about dynamic comparative advantage, the international division of labor, the complementarity of international trade and investment, the role of technology, the importance of trade in services, the management and organization of production, and the role of government policies challenged the conventional theoretical foundations of trade policy and made governments less certain about the direction of future domestic and international policies and arrangements.

Busy as academic analysts were in developing a more sophisticated understanding of trade and investment, they had little advice to offer on policy issues. Instead, their work concentrated on theories, games, and models.[48] Strategic trade policy, for example, which has in recent years dominated much of the academic discussion of trade issues, seems remote from the real world of trade negotiations.[49] Thus, while mainstream economists may still have upheld the benefits of an open economy and a fixed-rule order, few of them offered advice on the policy implications of their more integrated views of industrial organization and international trade or of their more sophisticated understanding of the role of technology and management in economic development.

As a result, the policy specialists associated with think tanks, rather than those associated with universities, have become most influential. Many of these may have been trained as economists, political scientists, or lawyers, but their knowledge of and experience in applied policy gave them much greater ability to talk the language of government officials and negotiators. Some of the most influential literature on the negotiations was prepared by such practical scholars in Europe, North America, Latin America, and East Asia.[50] They provided specialists with a much greater range of analysis and approaches, in keeping with the growing sophistication of the social sciences and its disaggregation into various disciplines. At the forefront of economic modeling, for example, there were those who sought to find ways to predict the dynamic effects of changes in the international trade regime or to factor in the impact of changes in nontariff barriers.

The combined work of academic and think-tank analysts concentrated on all three sets of issues—systemic, traditional, and new—thus providing negotiators and lobbyists with useful information and analysis to carry the issues forward. This information can be divided between the broad, generally disinterested analytical work examining, for example, the economic impact of various possible negotiating outcomes and the more polemical work advocating specific approaches and priorities and geared more to the requirements of business and lobby groups. From a negotiating point of view, this work was most important in informing and consolidating public support for various negotiating objectives, particularly among business and lobby groups.[51]

Again, however, the policy advice emanating from the think tanks tended to be conservative. It extolled the virtues of the existing GATT regime and generally assumed that it could be extended with little difficulty to the new issues. Few questioned the difficulties involved in taking a set of rules and bargaining strategies developed for trade in goods among a relatively homogeneous group of countries and applying those same rules and strategies to a much wider and more diverse range of issues to be applied to trade within a much larger and more heterogeneous group of countries.[52] The further complication of moving from negative to normative prescriptions, from shallow to deep integration, was not even touched on and is only now beginning to be discussed.[53]

Limited as it was, the concentration of this kind of knowledge and analysis in the OECD countries and a few of the major developing countries meant that negotiators from these countries could count on a much broader range of views. In the absence of home-grown expertise, developing countries and some of the smaller industrialized countries tended to rely on international secretariats at the GATT, the World Bank, and UNCTAD, at regional banks and commissions such as the Economic Commission for Latin America and the Caribbean (ECLAC) and the Asian Development Bank (ADB), and at internationally recognized think tanks such as the Institute for International Economics in Washington. Given the strong bias in most of these organizations in favor of open markets and fixed-rule regimes, the result was to reinforce their commitment to an open, rules-based multilateral trading system.[54]

Business and Lobby Groups

Organized lobbying has developed as a major factor in the politics of the late twentieth century, and governments have responded by organizing business and lobby groups into formal advisory committees.[55] The result is a more informed and detailed dialogue between government and business on trade issues than ever before, ensuring that trade negotiations continue to be dominated by producer interests rather than consumer or broad economic considerations, particularly in industrial countries. Unlike previous negotiations, however, where focus on the highly specific tariff led to particular industry views, business groups in the 1980s tended to provide more broadly based aggregate advice and to rely heavily on the work of lawyers and think tanks for the details of their views.

Two broad strains of advice emanated from business groups. For those firms already involved to a significant degree in international business, the advice tended to favor open markets and more rules that guaranteed nondiscriminatory and predictable treatment. For firms operating in import-competing segments, advice tended to favor regime maintenance and greater scope for addressing the problems raised by foreign competition. Broad horizontal business groups tended to be outward-looking, whereas sector-specific groups tended to be more nuanced in their advice. Those with a stake in existing regulatory schemes, such as agricultural groups, tended to be very specific in their advice, as did groups dissatisfied with their treatment in foreign markets, such as pharmaceutical firms. Think-tank organizations provided business groups and individual firms alike with the sophisticated information needed to influence governments on the details of specific negotiating issues.

For those firms who had become involved in the global economy and whose horizons reflected global rather than any particular national interests, the round offered the prospect of breakthroughs that would make doing business on a global basis easier. Their advice to national delegations emphasized the importance of the round and the need to make progress on the new agenda. Often, however, they were frustrated because they found progress on the new issues slow and much of the posturing irritating. By the end of the round, their views wavered between dismissing the round as irrelevant and insisting that progress had to be made, depending on the latest view of these matters by think-tank articles in the *Harvard Business Review* and similar business publications. A clear trend, however, was visible: most of them were more interested in what was happening in regional negotiations than in the round; they found what was being achieved in new regional agreements more directly related to their concerns and less confusing. The number of players and issues seemed more manageable, and the results more predictable.

Businesses geared to local and regional economies, on the other hand, found further liberalization on a global basis threatening. If there were going to be liberalizing agreements, they also preferred that this be done on a regional basis, where they could adjust to new competition on a more limited basis. In North America and Europe, regional agreements offered the bonus of excluding the Japanese and thus placing a *cordon sanitaire* around the most competitive firms in many sectors, justified on the grounds that the Japanese were unfair competitors. Much of their advice on specific issues in the round tended to favor incremental changes and continued scope for protection. Changes to antidumping and countervailing duty procedures, for example, or to the textile and clothing regime were regarded with some trepidation. For politicians, their advice had the added attraction that many of these firms had strong roots in national economies and could not be dismissed as rootless global corporations.

More so than with other interest groups, the concerns of business tended to focus on substantive rather than systemic or process issues, ranging from government procurement, subsidies, and tariff issues to the operation of trade remedy regimes. Two highly committed sector-specific groups stood out for much of the negotiations: the agriculture community and the new coalition of service and knowledge-intensive industries, each with different agendas and priorities. Each made extensive use of the academic and think-tank communities to develop detailed and sophisticated positions on the issues, ensuring that these would have to be addressed whatever the predilections of officials and politicians.[56]

Conclusion

Among the four groups mentioned, officials were of course the most influential in determining the course and content of negotiations. Ministers dispose, but officials propose, and when the issues are as complex as a modern multilateral trade negotiation, outcomes are critically dependent on what is proposed. Among officials, however, the multilateralists responsible for much of the conduct of the negotiations no longer enjoyed the luxury of being able to assume that ministers would accept the traditional argument of the Kennedy and Tokyo Rounds, that multilateral agreements were their own reward. Two sets of other officials had gained sufficient legitimacy to make such a proposition no longer automatically acceptable.

First, in the United States, Canada, Europe, and elsewhere, there had developed an increasingly influential cadre of officials who were no longer convinced that multilateral agreements were necessarily the only or always the best way to make progress on all aspects of the trade agenda. While governments continued to pay lip service to the virtues of multilateralism, they in fact hedged their bets by also pursuing a range of unilateral, bilateral, and regional approaches. Billed as complements rather than alternatives to the multilateral order, they nevertheless illustrated to embattled politicians that there were alternatives and that some of the hard choices they faced could be put off or addressed with more certainty and specificity on a regional basis, at least in the short run and on issues of more relevance to a geographically integrated area. They could pursue some of the same issues on a more limited basis and not lose the support of influential business lobbies.

Thus throughout the round—during both the preparatory period and the actual negotiations—alternative strategies were deployed. In Europe, the EC-92 program and efforts to extend the European Community to the rest of Western Europe solidified pan-Europeanism. In North America, first the Canada-U.S. Free Trade Agreement (FTA) and then the North American Free Trade Agreement (NAFTA) proved that some of the difficult new issues were susceptible to the negotiation of rules of general application. In Latin America, subregional agreements, as well as tentative overtures to extend NAFTA into a Western Hemisphere FTA (WHFTA), indicated the infectiousness of regionalism.[57] In Asia and the Pacific, unilateral liberalization paved the way for a number of regional experiments, including a much more ambitious Australia-New Zealand FTA and preparations for an ASEAN FTA.[58]

Second, a range of officials not steeped in the values and folkways of the GATT negotiations were of necessity involved in issue development and consensus building as the agenda expanded. Many of these were prepared to question whether liberalism, multilateralism, and nondiscrimination were necessarily virtuous. Some resented trade officials poaching on their territory, while others had a stake in regulatory regimes that had long histories and required either discrimination or protection. Transport officials, for example, saw no reason why the cozy international air regime should be offered up on the altar of the GATT. Finance officials were leery of agreements that would undermine their ability to maintain control over their fiduciary responsibilities. Government procurement officials were not confident that internationally open bidding procedures were necessarily good, while industry policy officials did not warm to the idea of subsidy codes that reduced their capacity to promote winners and cosset losers. All of them saw difficulties in applying GATT-like principles to their areas of responsibility.

Thus the round, by its ambition and complexity, raised formidable problems in the development of positions and the internal and public consensus building necessary to carry them forward. Stepping through the minefields required a level of analysis and debate not previously required in trade negotiations and opened tremendous scope for well-prepared epistemic communities. While the broad contours of the negotiations were publicly debated, detailed discussion took place within these communities. The more informed and detailed the views, the more likely a particular group was to be influential. The agricultural community, for example, had a direct stake in the outcome of the negotiations. It is not surprising, therefore, that in every major country, members of that community—in government, think-tanks, and lobby groups—worked hard not only to advance their interests in agriculture but to influence the direction of the negotiations as a whole. Similarly, the pharmaceutical industry, with a particular interest in the intellectual property regime, proved influential in setting the agenda and in directing outcomes.

In the face of the debased coinage of multilateralism within governments, groups who couched their views in broad systemic terms found their influence waning as the round progressed. While such views were helpful in creating a climate receptive to beginning negotiations, they had little to add to the difficulties that must be resolved in the closing stages of a negotiation. To close, ministers needed to hear why a particular solution was superior to the status quo in addressing problems that domestic measures alone would not solve.

Unlike the original GATT negotiations, when powerful ideas held by persuasive epistemic communities organized and drove much of the negotiations, the Uruguay Round was more a proving ground for testing the ideas of a much wider and diverse range of epistemic communities without the benefit of a single integrating idea. The presence of a single integrating idea might have made it possible to overcome some of the difficulties arising from the complexity of grafting the new agenda to the old. In its absence, the negotiators faced an uphill struggle in putting together a package that had the kind of broad appeal necessary to overcome the inevitable criticism from highly focused disaffected groups.[59]

8   The GATT Uruguay Round, 1986–1993: The Negotiations

In the GATT's forty-five year history, each new round of negotiations has taken longer to prepare and longer to conclude than the last. The Uruguay Round proved no exception. The earliest antecedents of the round can be traced back to the closing stages of the Tokyo Round, when discussions began on the need to address some of the new issues as well as business that would be left unfinished. It took seven or eight years, however, to translate those early soundings into a consensus on the agenda and approach. Formal negotiations consumed more than seven years, and the results did not come into force until January 1, 1995, that is, some fifteen years after preparations began. By way of contrast, the Tokyo Round, using the same criteria, took approximately eleven years (five years of preparations, from 1968 to 1973, and six years of negotiations, from 1973 to 1979) and the Kennedy Round, five (1962–63 and 1963–67).

Each step in the Uruguay Round required laborious preparation and discussion. Throughout the negotiations, the difficulties identified in the previous sections suggested that there would be nothing inevitable about these negotiations. It took from 1979 to the middle of 1985 to reach sufficient consensus among the GATT's core members that a new round would be desirable, and even then it took rare resort to a formal ballot to isolate the dissidents. Negotiating a declaration that provided the political commitment of governments to the round's objectives took a further year, much of it marked by un-GATT-like drama. Detailed issue identification and the elaboration of specific texts proceeded in two stages, marked in the middle by another ministerial meeting in Montreal in 1988, and again involved arduous horse-trading within and among issues. A ministerial meeting in Brussels at the end of 1990 to crunch the various elements into a final package proved premature. Efforts for the following two years struggled to find the elements of a package that could bring the various disparate segments together into a whole with which all the major participants could live. By early 1993, the task looked hopeless, and the betting was that it could not be done on any basis other than a face-saving, minimalist package.

Throughout 1993, however, various straws in the wind began to come together to form the basis not only for a successful conclusion but for a bigger package than had seemed possible earlier. The arrival of new administrations in both Washington and Brussels provided for a new chemistry among the principal players, while the appointment of a new director general with the drive and confidence of a successful politician added momentum. The successful passage of the North American Free Trade Agreement (NAFTA) through the U.S. Congress put the naysayers on the defensive and provided the final impulse. As a result, December 15 saw the director general strike the gavel on the biggest, most ambitious, and most comprehensive trade deal ever negotiated, with a commitment by the more than 100 participating governments that they would meet in Marrakech, Morocco, in the middle of April to adopt the Final Act, bringing the negotiations to a formal conclusion.

Over the course of this protracted period, the GATT members formally met at the ministerial level five times, with only two of those meetings— the 1986 meeting launching the round and the 1994 Marrakech meeting— reaching its stated objective. That fact alone stands out as eloquent testimony to the difficulties to be surmounted. Throughout, the round required an extraordinary amount of political reinforcement to avoid crumbling under its own weight. The need to constantly fortify political will was also evident in the ritual statements declaring the importance of the round in the communiqués issued at the end of economic summits, OECD ministerial meetings, EC Ministerial Council meetings, Cairns Group ministerial meetings, APEC ministerial meetings, and more. Many of them began to assume an unreal and hollow air as the prospect for early success faded. Unraveling the story of the negotiations is thus a complex, if revealing, undertaking.

Prenegotiation

The beginnings of the Uruguay Round can be found in the closing stages of the Tokyo Round. Few major negotiations ever succeed in satisfactorily addressing every issue and demand. In the end, compromises are made, and matters left for another day. The Tokyo Round was no exception. It did not prove possible, for example, to conclude a code on safeguards, to address the myriad problems afflicting the agricultural sector, or to address a late proposal from the United States to negotiate an agreement about counterfeiting practices. Thus, as the ink dried on the Geneva Protocol (1979) capturing the results of the Tokyo Round, work proceeded on unfinished business, some in the vain hope that it could be concluded on its own merit, others in the clear knowledge that it constituted preparatory work for a new, as yet undefined, negotiation.[1]

That work would proceed under the direction of a new director general. Olivier Long, who had directed every stage of the Tokyo Round from its earliest beginnings through the first year of its implementation, was succeeded at the end of 1980 by Arthur Dunkel, a fellow Swiss with long experience as a national participant in GATT affairs. Dunkel's first major challenge as director general came in managing the renewal of the GATT multifibre arrangement (MFA). Since 1961, GATT members had managed trade in textiles on the basis of a derogation from the GATT's basic rules. This temporary expedient, which chose the lesser of two evils—an organized and agreed derogation rather than a flood of GATT-illegal measures—had by 1981 been in place in various manifestations for twenty years. The challenge that faced Dunkel was how to extend it in a manner that satisfied both industrial and developing countries. In these negotiations, he indicated the extent to which he was prepared to play an active and personal role. As chairman of the Textiles Committee, he pioneered the use of the "greenroom" informal process to successfully challenge the members of the committee to find the means to extend the MFA for a further period. By the end of 1981, it was clear that the Long era was over and the Dunkel era had begun.[2]

Renewal of the MFA was played out against the background of the deteriorating economic conditions of the 1981–82 global recession. The Tokyo Round had seen a constant rise in so-called gray-area measures and an attempt to negotiate a code of conduct that would bring such measures under control. That effort had failed, and the end of the round as well as the economic problems of 1981–82 had unleashed a renewed spate of such measures, including efforts by the United States and Canada to control imports of Japanese cars and disputes between the United States and the European Community about trade in steel.[3] In response, in various capitals and at meetings of the GATT's Consultative Group of Eighteen and the OECD Trade Committee, the idea developed that management of these pressures would be easier if there were a more formal, political commitment both to the principles of the GATT and to a work program to further elaborate these principles. While discussion was not couched in terms of launching a new round, there was a broad consensus that the absence of a round made it more difficult to keep protectionist sentiments in check. Thus at the November 1981 meeting of the contracting parties, members decided that the 1982 meeting would be held at the ministerial level. Its purpose would be "to examine the functioning of the multilateral trading system and to reinforce the common efforts of the contracting parties to support and improve the system for the benefit of all nations."[4] But the 1982 ministerial meeting proved a disappointment. Chaired by Canada's Secretary of State for External Affairs Allan MacEachen, it achieved nothing of substance.[5]

The response in various capitals, but particularly in Washington, was that the GATT was no longer at the forefront in addressing real problems. The deteriorating U.S. fiscal position resulting from the introduction of Reaganomics was beginning to be reflected in a growing trade deficit, further fueling protectionist sentiment. The administration had hoped that an aggressive and forward-looking GATT work program would have provided a constructive signal to help contain protectionist pressures, but as long as its purpose and agenda remained unclear, GATT considerations would not be central to U.S. policy. American policy makers—congressional and administration alike—thus felt no qualms in aggressively pursuing contingency protection measures (antidumping and countervailing remedies), bilateral gray-area measures (voluntary restraint and orderly marketing agreements), and unilateral section 301 actions, all geared to satisfying immediate political needs. Congress added to the air of unease by beginning work on new trade legislation.[6]

The United States also turned to bilateral negotiations, openly welcoming a Canadian overture in 1983 to explore bilateral sectoral arrangements, negotiating its first Free Trade Agreement (FTA) with Israel in 1984, and entering into preliminary discussions with Canada the following year toward the negotiation of a full-fledged FTA.

In October 1984, the U.S. Congress passed the Trade and Tariff Act of 1984, the first major piece of trade legislation foisted on an unwilling president by an insistent Congress since presidents and congresses had decided to work together on the development of U.S. trade policy in 1934. The new act not only authorized the president to negotiate bilateral and multilateral trade agreements but also included a wide range of amendments to the trade remedy system, adding to the ability of American producers to gain import relief and that of the administration to pursue export issues. The act also had a strong flavor of unilateralism, particularly in the enhanced section 301 procedures.[7]

In September 1985, the day after the G-5 countries succeeded in establishing a coordinated approach to monetary matters to help the embattled U.S. dollar by sharply raising the value of the yen and the Deutschmark—a measure known as the Plaza Accord—President Reagan announced an even more far-reaching willingness to consider bilateral arrangements. In the future, the United States would get tough with its trading partners and explore bilateral solutions. While committed to a new round of GATT negotiations, the United States was not going to sit around waiting for others to come around to its views.[8]

The same kind of skepticism and cynicism was apparent elsewhere, but particularly in the European Community. It soon began to imitate the United States, aggressively pursuing its rights and using both GATT-legal and GATT-illegal measures to force solutions to its short-term trade policy problems. Trade relations soured between the United States and the European Community, the European Community and Japan, Japan and the United States, and the United States and Canada. Attitudes toward the need for developing countries to participate more fully in the trading system similarly hardened.[9] The willingness of industrialized countries to extend special and differential treatment to developing countries was beginning to wear thin, particularly for rapidly industrializing countries like the four Asian tigers.

To help cut through the malaise, Arthur Dunkel, on his own initiative, appointed a blue-ribbon group in November 1983, headed by Swiss banker Fritz Leutwiler, to examine the trading system.[10] The idea of such a group preparing the ground for a new negotiation was not unusual. In preparation for the Tokyo Round, for example, the OECD Council of Ministers had appointed a commission headed by Jean Rey.[11] But it was unusual for an international civil servant to appoint such a group on his own initiative.

The trade bureaucrats were not amused; discussing what ailed the trading system was their prerogative; if they needed help, they would decide where to seek it. Dunkel prevailed, however, and the Leutwiler Commission reported in February 1985 recommending, among other things, a new round to address a range of old and new issues.[12] Much of the report was ignored, but it confirmed that the idea of a round to refocus trade discussions had by now gained increased currency and acceptance beyond the United States and Canada. Within the European Community and in Japan, Australia, and elsewhere, business and academic voices were beginning to call for a new round, and governments were beginning to see some merit in moving beyond the sterile confrontation and process discussions to a negotiation. By the middle of 1985, the countries of the G-7 economic summit collectively endorsed the idea of a round at the Bonn Summit, although the French expressed strong reservation. What was less clear was what a new round would achieve.[13]

The lack of clear focus on traditional issues added to suspicion among some developing countries, particularly Brazil and India, that a new round would concentrate on new issues while leaving older problems unresolved. They insisted that a new round would result in the industrial countries gaining new rights and disciplines at the expense of the interests of developing countries. To slow down any move toward a decision a number of developing country delegates in Geneva, schooled in the salami-slicing techniques of UNCTAD, used every procedural trick in the book to frustrate efforts to launch a new round.[14]

Without considering the merits of the India-Brazil case—which rests on a branch of development economics that assumes that the terms of trade and the rules of the game are biased against the interests of resource-producing economies at the periphery of the global economy—the ability of India and Brazil and a few others to block the will of the majority demonstrated the changes that had taken place in the GATT. Their voice—made more powerful by the Geneva habit of maintaining solidarity among developing countries—was sufficiently important that it could no longer be ignored. Their ability to block consensus, of course, was helped by the lukewarm support the idea of a new round still had in Europe. While the European Community could see advantages in negotiating new rules for services and investment, it was not prepared to pay for these new rules on the basis of a major reform of agricultural trade.[15]

The combined impact of India-Brazil recalcitrance and EC ambivalence added to American frustration with the GATT process and fueled its interest in non-GATT solutions. Ironically, the United States' resort to section 301 procedures aimed at India and Brazil, its pursuit of bilateral solutions, and the rise in trade remedy cases gradually helped to bring some of the more moderate developing nations out of the India-Brazil camp. It also suggested to some EC member states that there was more to be gained than lost from a new round; section 301 could as well be trained at them. The nasty trade disputes in the first half of the 1980s had indicated the length to which American interests were prepared to go.

Moving toward Consensus

In June 1985 in Sweden, at a meeting of the Rio Group attended by twenty-two trade ministers, American officials again explored attitudes toward a new round and found a much higher level of support than discussions in Geneva had suggested. Even the Indian and Brazilian ministers proved more supportive than their officials in Geneva. The meeting indicated the extent to which the Geneva process was handicapped by the migration of veterans of the North-South dialogue from UNCTAD to GATT meetings.[16] If there was to be progress, their hold on the GATT decision-making machinery had to be broken. This became painfully apparent when what was achieved in Stockholm was rapidly undone by the Geneva delegations of the recalcitrant developing nations. In response, the United States called their bluff and sought a rare postal ballot to convene a special session of the contracting parties in September.[17]

This time, the United States had done its homework and made better use of its allies. It got the necessary two-thirds vote in the postal ballot and thus succeeded in convening a special session. Discussion at the special session was bitter and protracted, and it again took a majority vote, rather than the normal consensus, for the contracting parties to set up a meeting of senior officials to prepare the ground for the establishment of a preparatory committee (Prepcom). The Prepcom, in turn, would prepare for a ministerial meeting in September 1986 to kick off a new round.[18] In a foretaste of things to come, the French delegation temporarily held up EC agreement, thus strongly signaling French hesitation about the whole project. Preparations would thus proceed amid U.S. bluster about achieving its objectives by other means, Indian and Brazilian pique that the Prepcom had been established on the basis of threat, and a forced vote and EC efforts to make haste slowly.[19] With the disaster of the 1982 ministerial meeting still fresh in their minds, the trade policy professionals in Geneva and in capitals knew that the next ministerial conference had to be better prepared, with a clear set of objectives and the means to get there.[20]

The committee of senior officials met in October and November and the preparatory committee was duly established at the regular November 1985 meeting of the contracting parties.[21] It began its work in January 1986 under Dunkel's chairmanship, building on the results of the 1982 ministerial work program.[22] Additionally, however, key countries pursued the issues in various bilateral and plurilateral meetings with a view to gradually fleshing out a consensus on the issues. Political momentum was added by making preparations for the new round a major focus of the annual G-7 economic summit, as well as at OECD, nonaligned, and regional meetings.

The Prepcom focused on a range of interrelated issues including:

- the broad objectives to be pursued in the new round;
- the issues to be considered, building on progress in pursuing the 1982 work program;
- the general approach to be taken to new issues, such as the protection of intellectual property, trade in services, and investment;
- whether there existed a basis for agreement on a standstill on GATT-illegal measures and a rollback of existing illegal restrictions;
- the position that developing countries and their concerns would play in the round;
- the relationship of the GATT's program to other international economic activities, largely with an eye to addressing the concern of a number of countries with debt and other macroeconomic problems and the need to ensure that such problems were not addressed exclusively with trade measures and vice versa; and
- organization of the round.[23]

These prenegotiations involved the usual high degree of posturing as various participants positioned themselves and staked out untouchables and bottom lines. The European Community, for example, declared its

CAP to be off-limits, while the United States insisted that this time it would not retreat from a major reform on agriculture.

The prenegotiations served a number of functions. They not only helped forge the necessary consensus to launch a round and determine the major contours of the negotiation but also framed the basis for the political management of the round and public perceptions about its potential and importance. Markers were being put down that would be used later to determine success or failure and establish what would or would not be politically acceptable. Governments cannot easily make grandiose claims about the significance of something, walk away from those claims later, and still declare success. Some of the markers laid down during this period, however, would come back to haunt governments as they tried to see their way to a politically acceptable conclusion.[24]

Agreeing on the Scope and Agenda of the Negotiations

Throughout the first half of 1986, Dunkel chaired periodic meetings of the Prepcom where delegates continued the process of formally stating their positions and voicing their concerns and misgivings. The real work, however, took place at lunches and dinners and in smaller meetings held in delegation conference rooms throughout Geneva. This is where the critical alliance building and networking was being pursued and the real temper of the negotiations could be gauged. At the same time in the major capitals, other officials worked at the critical tasks of fleshing out proposals and building consensus among business and other interest groups on national objectives and priorities.

In Geneva, two facts stood out: little progress was being made in reaching agreement on the content and organization of the round in the Prepcom, and the posturing by the major players was beginning to take on an irritating life of its own. The United States, the European Community, India, and Brazil were repeating set positions and seemed incapable of advancing imaginative solutions to their problems; nor did they seem eager to take on board the views of others. On a more positive note, however, private meetings had clearly indicated that Brazil and India did not speak for all the developing countries. A significant number of moderate developing countries expressed interest in making progress. They were ready to participate in a new round that would address both old and new issues. They could see real economic benefits in a round that addressed the mess in agriculture and tackled such old issues as safeguards and textiles. If the price was the negotiation of new codes on services and trade-related investment measures, they were prepared to see what that would involve.[25]

In an effort to harness this new pragmatism, the Swiss, Swedish, Canadian, Australian, and New Zealand delegations used their newly developed networks to begin work with other smaller industrial countries and some of the leading moderates among the developing countries, such as Colombia, Chile, Uruguay, Hong Kong, Korea, and the ASEAN countries on a draft declaration that would be acceptable to the big three but could not be sponsored by any of them. They demonstrated that success for smaller countries does not depend on cleverness at the end of the process but on painstaking preparations and consensus building at the beginning.[26]

In July, when it became clear that the Prepcom was still far from agreement, delegations from some forty countries convened at the EFTA headquarters in Geneva to prepare a draft declaration based on a draft first advanced by a group of twenty countries under the chairmanship of Switzerland. This text had proved generally acceptable to most of the other participants and thus formed a basis for hammering out a text that would enjoy the widest possible support. In developing the text, the moderate developing countries had insisted that in the negotiations, there could be no progress on services without substantial progress on goods. This proved acceptable and cleared the way for a declaration that anticipated a major expansion of the GATT's mandate.[27]

Not surprisingly, agriculture proved the most difficult issue. There were three basic approaches: an EC view, supported by the other Europeans, which preferred a go-slow approach; the views of the emerging group of agricultural exporters—who would the following month constitute themselves as the Cairns Group—who wanted a breakthrough on agriculture but accepted the fact that if the European Community was pushed too hard, there would be no deal at all; and the United States, which wanted a big deal or no deal. The major issue was the extent to which new rules would discipline export subsidies. The major problem was France. The deadlock within the group in the EFTA building was finally broken by a new text drafted by Colombia and Switzerland (cochairs of the group) with the help of New Zealand, which reflected the emerging Cairns Group approach.[28]

With the breakthrough on agriculture, the way had now been cleared for the text to be introduced to the Prepcom by Switzerland and Colombia on behalf of the group of forty-seven countries. Brazil and India, on behalf of ten other countries, introduced a much shorter text that stuck to the GATT's traditional agenda. Argentina, in an effort to be helpful, tabled its own text. The United States indicated that it could work with the Swiss-Colombian text, but the European Community, due to French intransigence on agriculture, announced that it could not support any text, suggesting once again the delicate position within the European Community and the degree of its ambivalence toward the project as a whole.[29]

Little more could be done at the Prepcom level. It was now up to the ministers. Unlike the disappointing 1982 meeting, the professionals had worked hard and carefully and produced a realistic draft declaration that provided a solid basis for ministerial discussion and decision. While issues remained to be negotiated, they had been reduced in number and proportion to be manageable in the unwieldy setting of a ministerial meeting where the political egos of nearly a hundred countries had to be massaged and satisfied.

The Punta del Este Declaration

At Punta del Este, a resort city at the mouth of the Rio de la Plata in Uruguay, some 1,200 delegates from seventy-eight countries accompanied by 300 journalists convened in the San Rafael Hotel on September 15, 1986. At the formal conference, U.S. trade representative Clayton Yeutter told the gathered delegates that the "GATT can be responsive to the rapidly-changing requirements of international commerce," while Indian Finance Minister V. P. Singh opined that the conference could "take effective measures for preserving and strengthening the system." Japan's Foreign Minister Kuranari tried to strike a middle ground by emphasizing that a new round could "build a more open and viable trading system, one which will effectively counter the mounting protectionist pressures and make GATT responsive to new challenges confronting international trade."[30] The real discussions, however, took place in smaller rooms and hotel suites, where ministers worked hard to resolve the final differences. In this sense, the Punta del Este meeting was very different from the Tokyo meeting that had launched the Tokyo Round almost a generation earlier. There, the only debate had been symbolic. At Punta del Este it was real, and a positive result was not guaranteed.

Building consensus again provided opportunities for leadership for the coalition of smaller industrial countries and moderate developing countries. The bullying tactics of the United States were, as often as not, counterproductive, while the European Community was hamstrung by the depth of French dissatisfaction. The potential for, and fear of, failure was a strong motivating force for both the coalition and others. GATT could not afford another failed ministerial conference. While a solid motive for bringing a difficult meeting to a close, it was an insufficient basis for launching a very ambitious and complex round of negotiations.[31]

The Swiss-Colombian consensus text set forth a series of objectives, the majority of which proved noncontroversial and were adopted by ministers without much discussion. The difficult issues involved agriculture and the new issues (trade in services, investment, intellectual property protection, and a commitment on a standstill and a rollback). On agriculture, the determination of the Cairns Group and American willingness to support them isolated the European Community and led to debate as to whether the objective of the negotiations would be the liberalization of trade in agricultural products (Cairns-U.S.) or its management at the international level (the European Community). In the end, the way through the maze was to postpone decision by finding compromise language that made it possible for both sides to interpret it as they needed and leave the tough decisions for another day.

The United States had contended that agriculture had to be a central element in both the Kennedy and Tokyo Rounds, but each time, the results were anemic, with the United States itself not prepared to make the necessary concessions to warrant a breakthrough.[32] Thus U.S. insistence on agriculture in the lead up to Punta del Este had fallen on cynical ears in Brussels and in other EC capitals. This time, however, there were signs that things might turn out differently. Pressure from the Cairns Group, the enormity of the distortions that were destroying world agricultural markets, the increase in intellectual capital that questioned the benefits of existing policies, and public concerns about costs and prices all suggested that the issue might be treated more thoroughly this time. The fact that the European Community in the end agreed to a broader mandate than at first seemed possible was also a positive sign, even if that breadth suggested that much could be hidden within it. From the EC perspective, however, breadth ensured that the sins of others would be equally targeted.

The second crunch issue at Punta del Este was whether the declaration would involve a meaningful commitment to a standstill and rollback. This was a litmus test for the developing countries of the seriousness of the United States and the European Community in launching a new round. On it, India and Brazil were not isolated. The draft declaration looked impressive, but it was carefully drafted to provide the necessary wriggle room and avoid contractual commitments that could be subject to dispute settlement. In the end, language was found that limited the commitment to GATT-illegal measures and multilateral surveillance. Both the United States and the European Community chose to take a narrow perspective of what that meant, while for the developing countries it was something to build on. Nevertheless, it represented a significant achievement. It symbolized the extent to which the developing countries had learned to participate actively and successfully in setting the mandate of the round and ensuring that their concerns would be addressed as an integral part of the negotiations.[33]

Efforts by the European Community to include a Japan-bashing paragraph were successfully resisted by Japan but added a sour note to the whole proceeding. The issue was confined to a statement from the chair but provided a negative note for the future.

The last issue, services, was settled on the basis of a procedural compromise providing that services would be negotiated on a separate track, with the decision as to whether a services code would be part of the GATT left to the conclusion of negotiations. Agreement on the other two new issues—intellectual property protection and investment—had been forged earlier, with the understanding that negotiations would be limited to trade-related measures and without any commitment that the developing countries would be asked to liberalize measures.

All three compromises, while diplomatically clever, were not dissimilar to the agricultural compromise: they swept the real issues under the rug for later decision. In the case of agriculture, this was a widely accepted piece of chicanery. In the case of the new issues, as much ignorance was involved as sophistry. Many delegates had not yet grasped what needed to be negotiated and how. The requirements of a multilateral trade order that involved deep rather than shallow integration remained only dimly understood among many of the delegates, even those who were at the forefront in proposing this substantial expansion in the GATT's mandate and approach.

The broadly agreed draft declaration finally emerged from the back rooms late on September 19 and was adopted the following day. It set out an ambitious agenda and time frame that promised to tackle some of the deep-seated problems undermining the continued viability of the GATT, extend its discipline to agriculture, textiles, and gray-area measures, continue the process of liberalization, modernize it to bring it into line with the changing nature of the global economy by addressing trade-related intellectual property and investment issues, and launch negotiations on services.[34] It identified sixteen specific areas for negotiation, which can be categorized as follows:

- *Systemic issues.* Four areas were set out where negotiations would seek to improve the architecture and operation of the GATT-based trade relations system: a standstill and rollback of GATT-illegal measures; a review of the GATT's articles, particularly those addressing balance-of-payments measures and state-trading practices; consideration of ways to streamline and strengthen the GATT's dispute settlement procedures; and a general review of the functioning of the GATT system, including its role in reviewing the trade policies of members and the relationship between the GATT and other international institutions, as well as the constitutional basis for the GATT.

- *Traditional issues.* A broad range of both functional and sectoral areas consistent with the GATT's traditional agenda were identified for negotiation: tariffs, nontariff measures (particularly customs practices), subsidies and countervailing duties, the operation of the Tokyo Round codes (including the antidumping, standards, customs valuation, and government procurement codes), safeguards, trade in agricultural products, tropical products, natural resources-based products, and textiles and clothing.
- *New Issues.* All three issues were included on the agenda, albeit in somewhat more reduced form than originally envisaged: the trade-related aspects of investment and of intellectual property protection and trade in services.

While a significant diplomatic achievement, the declaration carefully papered over or concealed some critical differences between the parties, both about the desirability of a new round and about its principal objectives. It left most of the difficult issues to be resolved in the negotiating process and even left issues of organization and process unresolved. Nevertheless, it provided a clear statement of commitment by the participating countries to begin a new round with an ambitious agenda and time frame and recognized more explicitly than previously the interconnection between trade and other economic policy issues. At the same time, by embarking on such an ambitious agenda, the GATT had created expectations that might prove difficult to realize, particularly since the challenge of grafting a wholly new order to an existing order steadily losing credibility seemed to be only imperfectly appreciated.

The Punta del Este Declaration set up four bodies to manage the negotiations: a trade negotiations committee (TNC), a group for negotiations on goods (GNG), a group for negotiations on services (GNS), and a surveillance body to monitor the standstill and orchestrate the progressive dismantling of existing illegal trade restrictions.[35] During the remaining months of 1986, delegations in Geneva worked out how to organize for the negotiations. They agreed that Arthur Dunkel would chair both the TNC and the GNG, while Felipe Jaramillo, Colombia's ambassador to the GATT, would chair the GNS. The GNG was further subdivided into fourteen negotiating groups to address each of the objectives set out in the declaration (see fig. 8.1). By the end of January 1987, the TNC approved "guidance" documents for each of the negotiating groups as well as for the surveillance body. In effect, by the beginning of 1987, the preliminaries were over, and substantive negotiations could begin.[36]

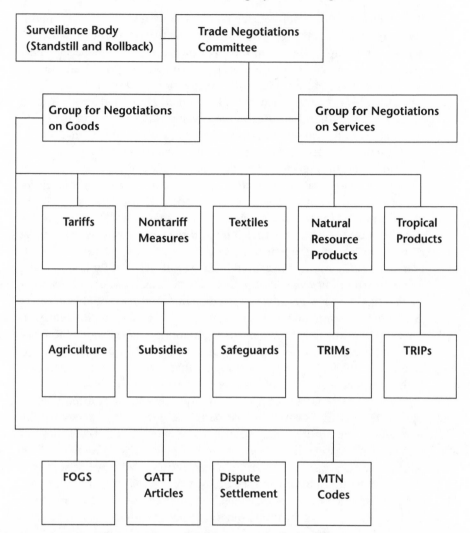

Fig. 8.1. Organization of the GATT Uruguay Round Trade Negotiations, 1987

Negotiations

Looking for an Early Harvest

The intense preparatory work that had characterized the period from early 1985 to the end of 1986 had created a momentum that proved hard to stop. All the major participants had built up political will, interests, and ideas that now fed the machinery set up by the Punta del Este Declaration. As a result, the round moved ahead with almost unprecedented speed. In-

dividual negotiating groups pursued their tasks with dispatch and commitment and made steady progress in defining the issues, building intellectual
capital, and clearing the ground for specific proposals. They began to develop the broader level of consensus on the negotiating issues assigned to
each group necessary for substantive negotiations. Many of the proposals
being discussed were far-reaching and radical and indicated a wide level of
participation. Rather than predictable developed-developing or big coun-
try-small country differences, the early discussions generated fluid alliances reflecting specific rather than broadly shared interests.

From the beginning, Dunkel made the most of the greenroom process to
build both procedural and substantive progress, using it to organize negotiations, appoint chairs for each of the groups, review proposals, maintain
momentum, and make sure no significant delegation was left out. In this
way, he was able to ensure that the big three would provide the smaller
delegations maximum opportunity to influence the negotiations. As a veteran of a small-country delegation, he knew full well that for these smaller
countries, the early stages are the most critical. That is when they can put
forward good ideas and influence the direction of the negotiations. Larger
countries take longer to build consensus and are more easily influenced in
the early than the later stages of the negotiations. Dunkel wanted to make
sure that the Uruguay Round, unlike previous rounds, would be a true exercise in multilateral diplomacy, engaging the interests of every delegation
with a significant stake in the outcome.

The first few years of the negotiations also saw a flurry of dispute settlement activity. Various countries, but particularly the United States and the
European Community, rushed to bring complaints to the GATT, both to
resolve issues and to create negotiating leverage. Agricultural measures
were a favorite target: thirteen of nineteen panels established between the
launch of the negotiations and the Brussels ministerial meeting in December 1990 addressed agriculture issues. For example, the United States initiated a series of complaints the primary purpose of which seemed to be to
test the limits of the exemption for agriculture provided by Article XI.[37] It
also launched complaints against the European Community on oilseeds
and against Canada on salmon and herring.[38]

The proliferation of dispute settlement cases demonstrated a number of
points: the GATT's existing procedures could be used to discipline agricultural trade; dispute settlement could be used to create negotiating leverage;
and there was a limit to what the big three would tolerate from one another or from others. The fact that other contracting parties participated in
a number of these cases and supplied the panels with briefs and pleadings
further underlined the importance of these proceedings, both in their own
right and as part of the Uruguay Round negotiations. While many of these

cases created political discomfort in those countries whose practices had been found wanting, on balance they created a positive momentum underlining the fact that rule making was important and beneficial. They also suggested that it was important to resolve issues in the negotiations on the basis of clear and detailed texts. Ambiguity would only fuel more disputes and allow issues to be settled on a basis beyond the control of national governments. These disputes also illustrate the continuing ambivalence among politicians about the value of a rules-based system: to the extent the GATT findings confirmed their views or political needs, such a system was beneficial; to the extent it did not, it was irrelevant.

The heat generated by both disputes and negotiating controversies in 1987 in some ways provided a false picture of the health of the trading system. In fact, 1988 marked the sixth year in a row that world trade had increased at a robust rate (8.5 percent by volume, 14 percent by value), again outpacing growth in world production. Global exports of merchandise reached US$2.88 trillion; services exports added another US$625 million.[39] At the annual session of the contracting parties at the beginning of November, chairman Alan Oxley of Australia took an optimistic view of developments in the round and in the trading system. He concluded that the standing and authority of the GATT had been enhanced by the round and pointed to the effective and frequent use of dispute settlement and the number of new accessions and unilateral reductions in trade restrictions by the developing countries and others as illustrative of the GATT's new vitality.[40]

The United States shared in this expanding world market, but this fact was obscured by the continuing budget and current-account deficits flowing from Reaganomics. The 1985 Plaza Accord had in no way tackled the fundamental economic problem in the United States. Trade thus continued to be a negative issue in Washington. Japan was widely regarded as the main culprit, but other countries were also being branded as systematic "unfair" traders, the main evidence for this being large bilateral trade deficits. As a result, Congress continued to be preoccupied with the trade file. At the end of 1986, the House of Representatives passed a frankly protectionist new trade act, and the Senate continued work on its own version. Administration efforts to dampen the mood fell on deaf ears as Congress continued to work throughout 1987 and into 1988 on a new trade bill. A massive Trade and Competitiveness Act, drafted by the administration and introduced early in 1988, disappeared as quickly as it had appeared. Congress had its own ideas and was not looking for administration advice. It finally delivered its own Trade and Competitiveness Act in May of 1988, minus the worst excesses of the various bills under consideration but more protectionist and nationalistic than any trade act since 1930.

It was within this embattled atmosphere that USTR Clayton Yeutter and his advisors hit upon the idea of a midterm review of the round and an early harvest of decisions and commitments. Reports from Geneva indicated that good headway was being made and that the pace of negotiations was far more positive than the sour preparatory period would have suggested. It seemed to make sense to take advantage of these positive developments and use them as concrete evidence in Congress that the negotiations were a good idea and would result in tangible benefits for the United States.

Informal discussions with think-tank advisors and friendly delegations indicated general support for the idea, and USTR officials began to draw up a list of candidates for an early harvest. In the opening months of 1987, Yeutter raised the idea of a midterm review at meetings of the Quad, with Arthur Dunkel, and in March at an informal trade ministers meeting in Lake Taupo, New Zealand. Suggestions for an early harvest included reform of dispute settlement procedures, decisions on the functioning of the GATT system (FOGS), a framework on services, the tariff-cutting formula, and interim agreements to reduce agricultural protection.[41]

Yeutter found support in Canada, Australia, and, to some extent, Japan, who saw a midterm review as a way of deflecting pressure from the perennial favorite U.S. and EC blood sport, Japan-bashing. The European Community, however, was not amused. Having barely made it through the Punta del Este meeting and only now beginning to work through the agenda, it felt that a midterm review would detract attention from the tough work ahead. An early harvest would erode the principle that nothing was agreed until everything was agreed and could put additional pressure on the European Community on agriculture and thus further erode EC willingness to address the full range of issues. Various developing countries expressed similar concerns, worrying that progress on new issues would limit progress on old issues.[42]

Despite these misgivings, the United States and its allies continued to push for a midterm review, and by the beginning of 1988, a basis for it began to emerge, with indications that agreement on dispute settlement procedures and FOGS issues would be relatively uncontroversial. Additionally, however, the United States and the Cairns Group insisted that there had to be something on agriculture. The European Community matched this ambitious demand by insisting that there also had to be something on services, calculating that this rather woolly area could be used effectively as a roadblock to agreement on agriculture. In February, the TNC formally agreed that there would be a midterm review and accepted Canada's invitation to hold it in Montreal in December. Ministers would be asked to gauge progress on the full range of issues on the basis of reports from each of the negotiating groups and to make decisions where progress warranted.[43]

Consistent with this decision, Dunkel asked all chairs to ensure that their groups produced progress reports indicating the approach to, and the parameters of, the negotiating issues. In effect, he asked each group to prepare a mandate for the next phase of the negotiations for consideration by ministers. Dunkel's request represented a demanding task for some groups, where both substantive and tactical considerations made such a document nearly impossible to prepare, such as services, intellectual property, and agriculture. Even tariffs proved tough, with the United States insisting that it would only engage on an offer-request basis on individual items, while the European Community, Canada, Japan, and others preferred an across-the-board formula approach with detailed negotiations on exceptions and better-than-formula cuts.[44]

Throughout the summer and fall of 1988, Dunkel made extensive use of the greenroom process and, through attrition, gradually forced agreement on many of the issues, sometimes in effect starting negotiations that had been virtually stalled for months, leaving the difficult issues in square brackets for later discussion. Prospects began to improve for a possible early harvest on a range of issues. Not surprisingly, agriculture proved immune to this process. Even commitments by leaders at the annual economic summits in Venice in 1987 and Toronto in 1988 had little impact.[45]

Early Signs of Trouble

The midterm review team convened in Montreal on December 5 at the Palais des Congrès, with more than 90 ministers and 1000 delegates in attendance dogged by over 600 journalists.[46] As in Punta del Este two years earlier, ministers were tasked to chair groups and negotiate away square brackets. Almost two years of negotiations and careful preparation at first paid off with early breakthroughs on tropical products, dispute settlement, and the functioning of the GATT system. As well, far-reaching texts on services and tariffs were quickly agreed. Four issues, however, proved particularly knotty: textiles and clothing, safeguards, intellectual property, and agriculture.[47] The media emphasized agriculture as the main dividing issue due to high-profile differences between the European Community and the United States, but the other three issues were equally taxing, both in their own right and as tactical considerations. A number of Latin American delegations, for example, made it clear that until all issues were agreed, none was agreed. They were exercising their new muscle as individual delegations and as members of coalitions like the Cairns Group.

On agriculture, the United States wanted a commitment to the objective of complete liberalization, while the European Community would commit to no more than gradual reduction in support levels. No basis existed for bridging this gap, particularly since the European Community was not all that interested in an early harvest. The United States was the *demandeur* on most issues but had little to trade that would interest the European Community. Additionally, the U.S. delegation represented an outgoing administration. While President Bush represented Republican continuity, it remained to be seen who would be part of his new team and whether it would pursue the same policies. The new president had, after all, run a campaign in which he tried to put some distance between himself and President Reagan.

After three days and nights of tough discussions, ministers admitted defeat and went home.[48] To stave off the potential disaster of another failed ministerial conference, Dunkel suggested that senior officials continue work in Geneva after further reflection in their capitals. Ministers agreed, and over the next four months Dunkel pursued discussions in capitals and in Geneva and gradually prepared the ground for the deadlocks to be broken. Consensus was achieved on agriculture, for example, by agreeing that the long-term objective was to reduce agricultural support substantially, without specifying what was meant by either "long-term" or "substantially." By April, Dunkel felt confident enough to convene a meeting of senior officials who worked out the necessary package of early harvest and negotiating mandates to bring the midterm review to a successful conclusion.[49]

While Dunkel in the end succeeded, with little help from Yeutter and the Americans, it is questionable whether the decision to hold a ministerial midterm review was a tactic that had made much sense.[50] A review that provided renewed political momentum would have been one thing; to insist on formal conclusions on some issues but not others was something else. With an agenda as complex and ambitious as that of the Uruguay Round, with different participants pursuing different priorities, it did not make much sense to break up the package at midpoint and reach some agreements but not others in order to satisfy the short-term political requirements of one participant. The timing—after the U.S. election—had dissipated any potential political advantage, and given the mood in Congress, nothing was likely to have satisfied in any event. In the previous forty-odd years, Congress had never yet found time to find a kind word for the GATT negotiations. Additionally, the review forced decisions on issues that were far from ready. The resulting texts created straitjackets that robbed negotiators of the necessary flexibility to try out new ideas. While some issues were helped along by the political direction provided by ministers, on balance the decision to reach some early agreements undermined capacity to craft a satisfactory package at the end.

Two of the decisions taken, however, did have the benefit of providing constructive fuel for future negotiations. The Trade Policy Review Mechanism (TPRM)—which would subject the trade policies of member states to periodic scrutiny in a series of published documents—would create pressures to counter the normal bias for protection, while the streamlined dispute-settlement procedures further underlined that GATT law was becoming a more serious and reliable basis for resolving conflict and keeping member states' practices in line.[51]

The Negotiations Get Real

With the Montreal interlude behind them, the negotiators could now get back to the painstaking professional task of working out detailed negotiating proposals, ranking the issues, and looking for common ground among positions. From May 1989 through to the summer of 1990, that task preoccupied most of the negotiators, and they made significant technical progress. Texts were tabled, studied, recast, and gradually worked into composite negotiating texts. The round had now reached the critical stage when posturing had to be translated into concrete proposals and the differences in position reflected in bracketed language amenable to detailed negotiations.[52]

In the group on tariffs, for example, discussion first concentrated on finding an agreed approach to tariff cutting to reach the ministerial target of a one-third overall reduction. The majority of delegations favored a formula approach, and the European Community, Japan, and Canada all tabled formula proposals that would reach that target. The United States, however, continued to insist that it would only negotiate on an offer-request basis, arguing that it had already made a lot of concessions in earlier rounds and that a formula would not be balanced. In January 1990, the group finally agreed that it would proceed on both formula and offer-request bases and invited delegations to start making specific proposals. By the middle of the year, despite the general preference for a formula approach, the negotiations had in fact evolved into an offer-request exercise, with critical meetings taking place on a bilateral basis, as delegations began to assess the value of the various proposals.[53]

In the prenegotiations and early stages, intellectual property had been viewed as a difficult and barely legitimate issue for the GATT.[54] To get it on the agenda, it had been covered with the figleaf that the negotiations would only address the trade-related aspects of intellectual property protection. By the time the midterm review rolled around, it was one of the areas where the earliest substantive results were coming together. An increasing number of governments had begun to recognize that the world was changing and that the trade system required appropriate rules geared to the needs of the knowledge-intensive industries. India, for example, recognized that its huge film industry might benefit from better copyright rules. The midterm review decision had cleared the way for delegations to table a large number of detailed proposals on both substantive intellectual property standards and enforcement provisions. These were fully discussed; by the beginning of 1990, five competing draft legal texts had emerged (from the United States, the European Community, Japan, Switzerland, and a group of fourteen developing nations). These provided a basis for the chair of the group, with the help of the secretariat and individual delegations, to start crafting a chair's text that would provide a basis for detailed negotiations. This was tabled in July 1990 and proved an acceptable basis for initiating the final phase of the negotiations. Much of the detail borrowed from existing intellectual property agreements, with the difficult issues being the extent to which the GATT's nondiscrimination principles applied, the extent to which substantive standards would be included in the text, and the extent to which dispute settlement and sanctions could be used to enforce compliance with these standards.[55]

The agriculture group was even busier, meeting frequently to try to unravel the various proposals and cobble them into a basis for negotiations.[56] In effect, the agricultural negotiations involved three distinct elements identified as such in the April 1989 ministerial decision:

- a commitment to effect a substantive long-term reduction in support and protection and not increase current levels of support and protection;
- efforts to reduce the ability to use sanitary and phytosanitary measures as disguised barriers to trade; and
- efforts to improve access to markets, impose discipline on internal farm support measures, and discipline export competition.

The first element lent itself to endless debate but offered little scope for agreement. Fortunately, agreement in this case was more a political than a practical matter. The second element was technically daunting but did not offer much scope for useful political debate. It was a matter of rolling up sleeves and getting to work looking for creative ways to solve real problems. The final issue was the heart of the matter. Each of its three elements lent itself to negotiation, and if delegates could turn their attention away from the debate on the first issue, there was significant scope for practical proposals.

The United States, still committed to radical reform, proposed to deal with internal support and market access by requiring that all current measures be converted to tariffs and bound against further increase, while all derogations from current GATT rules be eliminated, as would protection afforded by Article XI. GATT members would then enter into negotiations aimed at progressively reducing tariffs to reasonable levels. It further proposed that all export subsidies and restrictions be phased out and eliminated over five years. Although draconian, the U.S. proposal had the merit of being direct and easy to grasp.

The Cairns Group generally supported the U.S. proposal but wanted to add a few subtleties. It suggested, for example, that current domestic support be frozen and reduced on the basis of an agreed timetable (ten years), leaving only income support measures decoupled from production levels. It further indicated that all existing nontariff measures should be made consistent with GATT rules, while all nonconforming measures should be eliminated.

The European Community continued to prefer that the agricultural negotiations be deferred until it had completed its internal reforms and was better placed to put forward proposals it could live with. In December 1989, however, it did finally table a framework within which it was prepared to negotiate. It suggested that internal support and border measures be made more transparent and expressed in terms of the OECD formula for aggregate measures of support (AMS). This would provide a basis for negotiating a progressive reduction in each member's AMS level while leaving some room for governments to determine for themselves which mix of policies was appropriate to its circumstances. It agreed that there should be a tightening in the rules but felt that there should be sufficient flexibility to allow some differentiation between domestic and imported production. It was similarly prepared to enter into negotiations to reduce the impact of all measures that distorted trade, but on the basis of a reasonable timetable that allowed for a review after a few years and ensured a balance of benefits. It also suggested that in a few areas, the European Community would wish to increase protection to ensure that it started from an equitable position in negotiating the future reduction of protection.

Various other delegations added their own ideas. The EFTA countries' proposals provided variations on the EC proposal; Canada, Japan, and Korea were interested in expanding and clarifying the scope for the application of Article XI; and food-importing countries were not at all keen to see an end to subsidized food exports.

Over the course of the fall and winter 1989–90, these proposals were explained, clarified, and debated until the point was reached that the chair of the group felt he needed to bring things to a head by putting forward a detailed proposal within which more focused negotiations could proceed. To that end, he tabled a text early in the summer of 1990 consisting of the following elements:

- a commitment to reduce internal support on the basis of the AMS formula;
- the imposition of tariffs on all border protection and the progressive reduction of those tariffs;
- the progressive reduction of export subsidies;
- clarification of the GATT rules to ensure that they would fully apply to trade in agriculture; and
- country-specific market access negotiations based on offers and requests to determine the specific commitments and a timetable for complying with the first three elements.

Once the Houston economic summit in 1990 had endorsed this text as a practical basis for proceeding, there was nothing left for the agricultural negotiators to do but get on with the task of tabling specific offers and requests. These, however, proved both slow in coming and disappointing in their degree of commitment. As the deadline for the closing ministerial meeting approached, it was clear that only by means of a major breakthrough on the part of the European Community in tabling a proposal that would capture the imagination of others could the chair's text be translated from an empty framework into a basis for a satisfactory settlement. Key to this would be the extent to which the United States and the European Community could reach agreement on satisfactory levels of reduced support, tariffication and reductions in export subsidies.

The dispute settlement group, having contributed to the early harvest, continued its examination of a wide range of proposals that would not only further streamline and strengthen dispute settlement but also help to depoliticize GATT procedures. The United States and the European Community, for example, put forward proposals aimed at ensuring that panels would be selected from a roster of competent and experienced officials with a minimum of jockeying for advantage by the disputing governments; other proposals included the establishment of permanent tribunals, measures that would make it easier for private parties to trigger dispute settlement procedures, and the establishment of an appellate tribunal for rogue panels. By September 1990, these various reform proposals had been massaged into a broadly agreed text for ministerial consideration, with only a few issues left for ministerial debate and decision.[57]

Other groups similarly busied themselves with the task of testing proposals. Gradually, texts began to emerge on textiles, subsidies, tariffs, customs issues, TRIMs, and the more than two dozen discrete agreements under consideration.

While the working groups went about their task, the TNC continued its task of plotting grand strategy and maintaining momentum. In late July

1989, still flush with the euphoria of having successfully cobbled together a satisfactory midterm review in April, it decided that a final ministerial meeting would take place in Brussels, December 3–7, 1990. The Punta del Este Declaration had committed governments to a four-year negotiation, and the TNC was determined to live up to that promise. Uppermost on its mind was the fact that the United States's fast-track authority would run out on May 31, 1991, requiring the president to notify his intent to enter into any new agreements by the beginning of March. A December 1990 ministerial meeting would leave sufficient time to work out the technical details within that time frame.

To meet the December 1990 deadline, the TNC envisaged three phases for the remaining eighteen months. It suggested that the tabling of national positions in the negotiating groups be finished by the end of 1989, while leaving some leeway for further proposals to be tabled at later stages. From January to August 1990, each negotiating group would seek to reach broad agreement on its set of issues, while the remaining three-month period would be devoted to preparing legal texts. By July 1990, however, it had become clear that these plans were somewhat ambitious; a lot of groups were behind schedule. In response, Dunkel began to use the green-room process to force the pace and ensure progress. Group after group was subjected to marathon sessions in a determined effort to create a basis for ministerial negotiation and decision. More and more was agreed at the level of senior negotiators. What was not agreed was placed between square brackets for ministerial consideration.[58]

Intense efforts in September and October removed roadblocks on most of the less controversial issues, and advanced texts were ready for ministerial consideration (e.g., on reform of various GATT articles, functioning of the GATT system [FOGS], and the Tokyo Round codes). There remained, however, significant gaps in many areas and some chasms in problem areas such as agriculture. By late fall, it was clear that it would not be possible to bridge all the differences that remained or clean up the texts that had been agreed. Instead, the TNC reluctantly agreed that it would have to send ministers a draft Final Act rather than a more polished document. Even then, the document prepared by the secretariat on the basis of the texts in play in each of the negotiating groups totaled more than 400 pages of closely typed text, which did not include any country-specific commitments on market access, agricultural issues, government procurement, services, and more. As well, there were no texts from the agriculture and TRIMs groups and the antidumping subgroup. Ministers would have their work cut out for them when they arrived in Brussels and would have to be prepared for significant political movement, or there would not be agreement. The script was ready, but was it the right one?[59]

The Negotiations Flounder

Deadlines are a necessary evil. Without them, negotiations can go on forever; there is always some reason for at least one major participant to slow
things down, such as an inconvenient election. Unrealistic or artificial
deadlines, however, can also pose a problem. Crafting a complex, multiparty agreement takes time; forcing the pace is likely to lead either to
agreements that cannot stand the test of time or to failure.

In multilateral trade negotiations, deadlines are often the product of
U.S. trade legislation. The president negotiates on the basis of a time-lim-
ited delegation of authority from the Congress, which automatically forces
deadlines. In the case of the Uruguay Round, the U.S. delegation operated
on the basis of the so-called fast-track procedures set out in the Trade Act
of 1974 as extended by subsequent acts. The effective deadline for negotiations was the first week in March, so that the president could notify Congress of his intent to enter into the resulting agreements at least ninety
days before the expiry of his authority, on May 31, 1991. While there was
provision for a two-year extension, neither the administration nor the
United States' trading partners were eager to learn what price Congress
might exact for an extension.[60]

Based on the state of the text of the Final Act, however, it was clear that
December 1990 was too early. It in effect meant that the professional negotiators dedicated to the task had had only four years to put together one
of the most complex international agreements ever contemplated and to
gain the approval of the more than one hundred governments participating. Available time had been reduced by the time and energy devoted to
the midterm review in Montreal. Four years may have seemed long enough
in September 1986, but in the months leading up to December 1990 it
looked like a very short time indeed. Large and significant gaps remained.

Despite these gaps, it could still have been possible for ministers to have
come prepared to make the necessary concessions to reach agreement, giving the professionals almost three more months to conclude a reasonably
polished Final Act. Events proved, however, that neither Carla Hills, for
the United States, nor Frans Andriessen, for the European Community,
came equipped to make those concessions. Both were prepared to close
only on their terms; neither appeared ready to conclude on the basis of the
compromises necessary to achieve consensus; neither saw sufficient political advantage in the package as a whole to make the necessary concessions
on the difficult files to reach agreement. Thus for the third time in less
than a decade, the GATT would host a ministerial meeting that failed to
meet expectations.[61]

This time the scene was Brussels, the seat of the EC Commission, where on December 3, 1990, some 90 ministers, 1500 official delegates, as many more advisors and hangers on, accompanied by nearly as many journalists, gathered to put the finishing touches to a 400-page draft text that represented the distillation of some 1300 proposals and working papers and five years of work. The text was full of square brackets indicating where political guidance was needed before technical solutions could be found. The meeting was scheduled to last four days and thus left no time for political gamesmanship; the name of the game was negotiation. As at Punta del Este and Montreal, various ministers were tasked to lead negotiations on selected issues based on the draft Final Act. In some areas, such as services, textiles, and nontariff measures, they made rapid progress; in others, such as agriculture and tariffs, stalemate stared them in the face.[62]

The biggest stumbling block was clearly agriculture. The gap between the United States and the European Community, however, could not be bridged. Not only were their approaches to the issues too different, but the baggage of four years of negotiations, as well as jockeying for leverage through dispute settlement procedures, had loaded the process to the point where no amount of brokering and arm-twisting could create the necessary trust to build consensus. The United States continued to insist that it had to get the whole loaf, while the European Community was equally adamant that it could not go beyond its commitments on CAP reform, which at this stage was still in a formative, rather than agreed, stage. To underline the point, farmers from all over the European Community staged ugly demonstrations throughout Brussels, which, if they did not impress Hills, certainly impressed the EC commissioners and the world media.

After four days of trying, the conference chair—Uruguay's foreign minister, Gros Espiell—announced that while much progress had been made, more time was needed to build the necessary consensus in certain key areas. Dunkel was again charged with undertaking intensive consultations and reconvening the process when he felt there was sufficient consensus to ensure a successful conclusion. He was instructed to work on the basis of the draft Final Act arrived at in Brussels. Swedish trade minister Anita Gradin summed up the missing ingredient: not enough delegations, particularly major ones, had prepared their publics for the kind of changes required to make the kind of progress ministers had pledged to make four years earlier, in Punta del Este.[63]

Gradin had a point but there was more to it than that. In addition to the problem of time, the package on offer, even with the gaps filled in, missed an even more important ingredient: it had little political appeal for either of the major players, in part because the critical market-access commitments had yet to be filled in; without them, the package was more theoretical than economically real.[64] While most of the other participants would have been prepared to close if the European Community and the United States were prepared to do so, without the United States and the European Community on board the meeting was doomed. From both the U.S. and EC perspectives, however, the package as it stood could not be sold. Even if they had gained every change sought, it remained a political orphan. The very fact that it was a professional tour de force made it a major political albatross. Its complexity and comprehensiveness made it too easy for the losers—such as EC farmers—to zero in on their problems but difficult for the winners to explain what they had gained and why they cared. Thus in neither the United States nor in the European Community were there sufficient communities with clout prepared to stand with the government and provide an effective counterweight to the inevitable wailing and gnashing of teeth that would come from the losers. The challenge to Dunkel and his Geneva colleagues, therefore, was only partly to continue negotiating a Final Act in which they could take professional pride. It was also a matter of finding the elements that would make the product politically salvageable. For ministers and their colleagues from capitals, that was the main challenge. They had to find countervailing forces at home to offset the negative voices; without them, no amount of further consultation and negotiation could rescue the round.

Alarms and False Starts

The disappointment in Brussels took a while to sink in. There was brave talk of still trying to finish within the existing U.S. fast-track authority, but reality soon intervened; the differences were too profound. Officials could not quickly erase gaps that had defeated the pressures generated by a ministerial meeting. Delegations, however, were getting used to adversity, and by February they were ready to soldier on. Much of that activity, however, took place in capitals, as senior officials from the major countries consulted among one another to find the basis for restarting negotiations. The American administration, for its part, agreed that it would seek a two-year extension as part of a package that would include authority to negotiate a North American FTA. That hurdle was eventually passed with most of the attention focused on the Mexico negotiations rather than on the round.

Once the hurdle of a two-year extension—in effect, to March 2, 1993—was passed, the first order of business was to come to a common understanding that the differences that had led to failure in Brussels were not matters of a few details; they were profound and needed hard work. The key was agriculture, and it did not take long to agree that a breakthrough would require progress along all four fronts: domestic support levels, market access commitments, discipline on export competition, and rules covering sanitary and phytosanitary measures. More generally, however, work

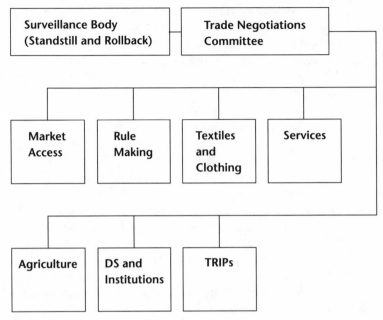

Fig. 8.2. Organization of the GATT Uruguay Round Trade Negotiations, 1991–1992

would be required along the full range of negotiating issues. In order to ensure a fresh look at the issues, the TNC decided to reorganize the fifteen negotiating groups into seven: agriculture, textiles and clothing, services, rule making (subsidies, antidumping, safeguards, rules of origin, preshipment inspection, GATT rules, GATT codes, and TRIMs), Trade-Related Intellectual Property Rights (TRIPs), dispute settlement and institutions, and market access (tariffs, nontariff measures, and tropical products) (see fig. 8.2).[65]

In the first half of 1991, little substantive progress was made. Only the agriculture group met to try to search for the road to success. It soon became clear that it lay in Brussels and Washington: the United States needed to obtain a two-year extension of its negotiating authority, while the European Community needed to make progress on CAP reform and the negotiation of farm prices for 1991–92. At midyear, high-level statements of political commitment emanated from both the June OECD annual ministerial meeting and the July Summit Seven meeting in Paris, but without the desired result.[66]

By September, however, Dunkel was confident that behind-the-scenes efforts over the previous months could now be translated into results, and he began an intensive effort aimed at meeting an end-of-the-year deadline.

In some areas, the negotiators completed their task with provisionally agreed texts with no square brackets, many substantially improved over the draft texts tabled in Brussels (e.g., those on services). The structure of an agreement on agriculture was also beginning to emerge. The TRIPs negotiation was close to a satisfactory conclusion. Offers on specific commitments on services started to make the services agreement (GATS) economically real. The textiles negotiation was virtually finished. Problems, however, had emerged on subsidies, antidumping, safeguards, and other issues. The extra time afforded by the Brussels failure was being used to improve the texts and had also given some governments an opportunity to rethink their position. The United States, in particular, was beginning to backtrack on some issues, encouraging others also to revisit their pet peeves.[67]

In order to prevent further unraveling and encourage delegations to look at the negotiations as a seamless web rather than as a series of independent agreements, Dunkel decided to issue a revised Final Act that took account of the changes and improvements that had been agreed in the previous months and filled in gaps and solved problems where delegations had been unable to resolve their differences. While he consulted closely with key delegations and worked with the chairs of each of the seven negotiating groups, a text was prepared on his own authority, which did not commit any delegation. Rather, Dunkel and his advisors tried to capture a balanced, hopefully satisfactory, outcome.

On December 20, Dunkel gave each of the 108 participating governments his version of a new and revised draft Final Act. Some five hundred pages long, it set out draft agreements on twenty-eight specific items—the whole agenda, with the exception of commitments on market access for goods and for services.[68] The text responded admirably to the objectives set at Punta del Este, Uruguay, more than five years earlier. Dunkel called on governments to determine whether they could live with it as a whole, rather than focusing on individual details at this stage. In effect, he challenged governments to proceed now to a final push involving the negotiation of two protocols on market access and services and agreement on the Final Act. "This has not been a Round in which initial objectives have been steadily whittled away to produce 'diplomatic,' but impractical solutions to difficult and complex problems. Quite the contrary; ambitions have risen with time, not fallen. The results we have already secured are relevant, precise, balanced and urgently needed answers to some of the biggest economic challenges of the day. They are results from which every trading nation will gain."[69]

The Dunkel text contained a significant number of technical improvements over the Brussels text. Virtually every individual agreement had been clarified and improved. The total product constituted a formidable professional result, but it could not address the fundamental divide. The United States and the European Community had by now developed a bunker mentality, particularly on agriculture. Neither was prepared to make meaningful concessions to the other; both had created critical hostages in their bilateral consultations, in their public pronouncements, and in their highly publicized disputes. Rather than becoming easier, finding the basis for agreement had become more difficult. The good work of Dunkel and the other negotiators was helpful but by now a successful outcome was totally dependent on the European Community and the United States finding the basis for a bilateral settlement. Frustrating as it may have been for the remaining governments, this was the reality they all had to accept. While technical work proceeded, particularly among a select group of legal advisors looking at ways to clean up the text and remove any unnecessary ambiguities, the negotiations proper were, by the beginning of 1992, on hold. The momentum that had been there at the end of 1990 and again at the end of 1991 gradually began to dissipate.

Groping for a Solution

In January 1992, the TNC agreed to streamline negotiations even further. Dunkel and his advisors reasoned that the stage had been reached where further technical discussions in individual negotiating groups were more likely to derail than assist the process of concluding the negotiations. The TNC itself would be the place where the Dunkel text would be discussed and further negotiations on all the main issues pursued. Three subsidiary bodies would carry on the remaining technical work: a market access group would concentrate on negotiating the specific commitments on tariff and other market access issues, including both industrial and agricultural goods; a services group would continue the negotiation of specific access commitments to be included in the schedules to be attached to the General Agreement on Trade in Services (GATS); and a legal drafting group would proceed with the task of preparing a cleaned-up version of the Final Act. Formally, the surveillance body established to oversee the standstill and rollback commitments would also continue, but its function served a more political than a negotiating requirement (see fig. 8.3).[70]

The real work of the negotiations, however, was now taking place in Brussels, Washington, and various other locations in the United States and Europe, where the USTR and senior officials from the European Community Commission and the U.S. Agriculture Department sought to bridge the gap between the two major delegations. Periodic Quad meetings provided the cover that it was more than strictly a matter of U.S.-EC negotiation. The European Community had finally reached internal agreement early in 1992 on CAP reforms and was now in a position to negotiate. As a

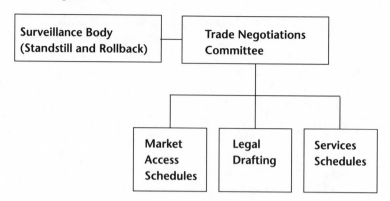

Fig. 8.3. Organization of the GATT Uruguay Round Trade Negotiations, 1992–1993

result, the United States continued to press hard to gain EC commitments on market access, support levels, and export markets. The time-bomb on oilseeds planted three years earlier was an important stick being used to beat the European Community into seeing things the U.S. way. The United States was not satisfied with the European Community's plans for implementation of the panel's findings and threatened to use its retaliatory authority to force compliance.

Other delegations were essentially helpless, knowing that whatever the two giants decided would largely decide their fate. Whatever influence most of them had been able to exert had by this time been exerted. Insistence by various delegations that they still had problems that needed fixing—such as Japanese, Canadian, and Korean preoccupations with Article XI—had in essence become sideshows for domestic consumption and of little relevance to the fate of the round.[71]

With the deadline of the extended U.S. fast-track authority rapidly approaching in the final months of 1992, efforts by U.S. and EC agricultural negotiators intensified, with the United States upping the ante by threatening to use its retaliatory authority from the oilseeds' case by imposing punishing tariffs of up to 200 percent on a range of products, particularly French wines. EC officials found themselves in an increasingly untenable position, buffeted between defiant French politicians, blustering U.S. negotiators, and increasingly nervous British, German, and other politicians. In this atmosphere, senior officials gradually whittled away at the differences, setting the stage for a high-level showdown in November in Chicago involving EC External Relations Commissioner Frans Andriessen and EC Agriculture Commissioner Ray MacSharry and USTR Carla Hills and U.S. Agriculture Secretary Edward Madigan. The meeting ended in high drama; the two sides succeeded in overcoming their differences, only to have the deal repudiated by EC President Jacques Delors because it was unacceptable to the French. A furious MacSharry, who had worked tirelessly for more than two years to find the very narrow zone of agreement that would allow the European Community to reform the CAP and respond to U.S. demands, now found himself in an untenable position and resigned as the negotiator.[72]

Throughout the round, but particularly since the ill-fated 1990 ministerial meeting in Brussels, EC negotiators had found themselves stuck between the rock of the United States and the hard place of French intransigence. Not convinced that much in the round would serve traditional French industrial interests and under intense pressure from French farmers not to give an inch, France had been the spoiler not only on the round but also on CAP reform. French negotiators in Brussels skillfully used the ace of the French referendum on the Maastricht accords (on the European Community's political and monetary future), as well as EC disdain for U.S. heavy-handedness, to keep MacSharry and his Brussels colleagues on tenterhooks. The Maastricht ace had disappeared in September with a narrow victory for the European ideal, and French negotiators had now turned to the March 1993 parliamentary elections in France as the next problem, cynically playing on Delors's ambition to return to France and succeed François Mitterand as president in 1995. American insensitivity to these European currents had not made things any easier for EC negotiators. It was, therefore, not surprising that MacSharry's patience had finally snapped.

Back in Brussels, however, MacSharry found surprisingly strong support among his fellow commissioners and most of the member states, many of whom had by now grown weary of French grandstanding and U.S. bluster and wanted to bring this file to a conclusion. A chastened Delors backtracked and took MacSharry back into the fold, while sending Andriessen back to Washington to see if some slight revisions would save EC face and at the same time ensure an end to the negotiations. Andriessen succeeded in a series of meetings at Blair House in November, thus paving the way for a last-ditch effort to bring the round to a conclusion while George Bush was still in the White House. French politicians expressed anger and despair and threatened to use a rare veto to block EC adoption of the Blair House agreement, but commission officials now had the bit in the teeth, and the basis for a deal on the whole round now appeared to be in the making.[73]

In Washington, U.S. interests in the round had been managed by three successive USTRs. Bill Brock had provided the push and vision at the beginning, seeing it as the best way of managing growing protectionist pressures while simultaneously responding to the requirements of the industries of the future. He had seen the collapse of the traditional U.S. free-trade coalition during the 1981–82 recession, and he had skillfully begun the work of crafting a new coalition made up of service, high-tech, and other knowledge-intensive firms. He had been succeeded in 1985 by Clayton Yeutter, whose Nebraska cornpone hid a shrewd mind and a determined will. Yeutter's strong interest in agriculture had ensured that agriculture would join the new issues as the backbone of American objectives for the round. He pursued that interest with zeal as secretary of agriculture during most of the Bush administration and had only recently moved to the White House to work on the president's reelection campaign. He had been succeeded at USTR by Carla Hills, whose experience as an antitrust litigator had translated into a strong interest in the trade remedy system and a conviction that there should be no erosion in U.S. ability to deal with "unfair" trade. She had also added the litigator's dogged determination to win each and every point to the usual U.S. confidence that only its point of view has much to recommend it. Compromise and sensitivity to the political problems of others were not a normal part of her brief.[74]

Brock, Yeutter, and Hills were all Republicans. While their tasks may have been made more difficult by Democratically controlled Congresses, all three had enjoyed the full support of business. The 1992 election, however, had brought the Republican era to a close with a resounding Democratic victory. While the new president had carefully avoided being identified with the protectionist wing of his party, his views on trade were somewhat of an enigma. If ever there were an incentive for others to conclude the negotiations, Clinton provided it. He let it be known that he would be happy to see the round conclude on President Bush's watch and offered few hints of what he would do if he inherited the round.

Thus in the closing weeks of 1992, delegates again trooped to Geneva in an effort to bring the round to a successful conclusion. The omens looked reasonable: the Dunkel text had been further cleaned up and clarified; the access negotiations had produced what promised to be some major breakthroughs, including some sectors where the negotiators had refined a Canadian proposal of zero-for-zero tariff cuts (i.e., tariff-free trade in whole sectors); service negotiators had similarly put together some specific commitments on access; and the United States and the European Community appeared to have solved their agriculture conundrum at Blair House and thus paved the way for more general negotiations on access commitments. There were, of course, some tough issues that various delegations were still worried about, and, if there was wriggle room, they wanted these addressed. Canada, for example, was looking to solve a problem in the subsidies text that seemed inequitable for a federal state, and it was still looking for accommodation on Article XI on agriculture. These problems, however, could easily have been swept under the rug in some way if the will to close had been there. The smaller delegations, while chagrined that they had been kept waiting for a year while the European Community and the United States sorted out their differences, stood ready to work for as long as it took to conclude. The European Community was ready to close. The secretariat had all the necessary apparatus in place to close, if that were the will of the delegates.[75]

Dunkel could not be blamed for expressing some optimism. As late as December 18, he had received a message signed by American President Bush, European Community Commission President Jacques Delors, and British Prime Minister John Major, acting in his capacity as the European Community president, urging that the negotiations be speeded up with the aim of concluding a "balanced and comprehensive agreement by the middle of January."[76] Within a matter of days, however, it was clear that 1992 would also not be the year of the Uruguay Round. The U.S. delegation had taken another close look at the whole package—agriculture, new issues, systemic issues, and traditional issues—and found it wanting. Interesting as its various parts were, the Americans believed that the package as a whole held insufficient political appeal. The agriculture community was not ecstatic, arguing that it was giving up more than it was gaining as a result of the Blair House agreement; the intellectual property lobby saw some fatal flaws in the TRIPs package and now liked what the United States had been able to negotiate bilaterally much better; environmentalists were unhappy with the standards provisions; the services companies were not impressed; steel and other import-sensitive industries were worried about erosion in the trade remedy system; and the market access provisions were not good enough—the European Community and Japan would not move far enough to satisfy U.S. demands, and the United States would not meet their needs. Even the systemic issues failed to excite, with American negotiators finding flaws in the proposed provisions for a multilateral trade organization. With the exception of think-tank cheerleaders, few American interests were prepared to give the prospective Uruguay Round results an enthusiastic thumbs up. American negotiators, while they would like to have closed within the time frame of the Bush administration, did not believe that they could sell the package as it stood to Congress.[77]

The U.S. dilemma, however, was compounded by the character of its chief negotiator. Rather than work with the other delegations to find acceptable compromises, she preferred to insist on changes that would meet each and every objection raised by American lobbyists and their congressional allies. Rather than rising above the detail and exercising broad leadership, she chose to dig in her heels. She was prepared to let the perfect be the enemy of the good. Her lack of political vision was matched on the other side of the table by Frans Andriessen, who felt uncomfortable with his file. In the face of U.S. truculence, he withdrew into a defensive shell. As in 1990 and 1991, neither could rise above their narrow briefs to seize the moment.

Efforts by the American delegation to make last-minute changes across a wide spectrum of issues thus fell on hostile ears. Not only was the European Community offended, but so were many of the other delegations; they had worked hard and in good faith with the United States over a period of close to seven years to put together an impressive set of agreements; they were not prepared to have the United States dictate new terms for a settlement. The deal would be made on a basis close to the text as it stood, or there would be no deal, at least at this time. There was a willingness to accommodate a few points, but not the long litany of U.S. complaints. Making resistance easier were a number of members of congress in Geneva as observers. They let it be known that there would be no problem getting an extension of the fast-track authority, allowing a Clinton team to take a fresh and more reasonable look at the issues. Once again, Dunkel was charged with a mandate to consult and cajole, while the delegates returned to capitals to work the phones and see if there was still some way to finish the round.

New Blood

On January 17, 1993, during the final days in office for the Bush administration, Dunkel made one more stab at concluding the round. He had again pursued a series of informal bilateral, plurilateral, and multilateral meetings, which indicated that the differences between delegations were not insurmountable. He wanted to give the process one more chance and had called a meeting of the TNC at the level of senior officials. He need not have bothered. American negotiators no longer had the stomach for concluding. The Uruguay Round would not be a legacy of the Reagan-Bush years. It would now be up to President Clinton and his newly appointed USTR, Mickey Kantor, to decide what priority to assign to the round.

January 1993 marked the close of twelve years of Republican administrations in Washington, as well as the practical end to its fast-track negotiating authority. The new administration indicated it owed nothing to the past. While the new president had hinted that he was prepared to see the round conclude in the dying days of the Bush administration, in which case he had intimated a willingness to live up to its commitments, the new administration felt under no compulsion to conclude an agreement on the basis of its predecessor's approach. It had its own priorities and concerns, such as environmental and labor adjustment issues, which it felt had not been addressed adequately in trade agreements. The more populist elements in the Democratic Party were pressing for a "fair" trade agenda, which the rest of the world perceived as protectionist and destructive of the existing trade regime.[78] Nevertheless, furious diplomatic efforts in the opening weeks of the new administration confirmed that it was not hostile to the round, would seek congressional authority for an extension of the fast-track authority, and was prepared to entertain ideas on how the package could be improved.[79] The round was not dead. Success remained a possibility, although the parameters of what that would involve had become even murkier.

There was also a changing of the guard in Brussels. A new commission took office in January 1993, and while many of the faces were the same and Jacques Delors was still president, its priorities were different. Sir Leon Brittan, previously responsible for competition policy, had been put in charge of the trade portfolio. He had his work cut out for him. The delicate agriculture reform package that had been key to putting the European Community in position to close would not hold forever, nor were EC industrial leaders any more impressed than their American counterparts with some parts of the package. Sir Leon had no difficulty appreciating the intellectual appeal of the package as it stood, but he too was aware that its political appeal was fragile and could begin to unravel at any moment. Other priorities were pressing. With the largely successful conclusion of the EC-92 program, as well as CAP reform, the commission had to turn to the challenges to the European Community's further political cohesion and expansion. Additionally, the end of the Cold War had profoundly altered the EC-U.S. relationship and added a new toughness and confidence to the European Community's approach to trans-Atlantic, as well as global, issues.

For both Kantor and Brittan, however, the first order of business was to establish their credentials as tough trade negotiators who would not blink or give the other side any comfort. Fortunately, the agenda of available trade irritants allowed them both to show their teeth, not only to each other, but also to their counterparts in Canada, Japan, and leading developing countries.[80]

To add to his credentials, Kantor delivered a further extension of the fast-track authority to December 15, 1993—enough time to get the job done but not enough to allow further unraveling of the delicate package beginning to come together or to respond to cries by various interest groups to add emerging issues to the agenda. At the same time, Kantor made clear there would be no negotiations in Geneva until issues between the United States and the European Community and between the United States and Japan had been resolved and the North American Free Trade Agreement had been put to bed.

There remained one other important piece of new business. The new blood in Washington and Brussels needed to be matched by new blood in Geneva: Dunkel would have to go. He had indicated a desire to retire at the end of a successful round in 1991. That had not happened, and he had accepted a renewal of his contract for a year. For some time there had been talk of elevating the profile of the GATT by appointing someone with the political clout of a former senior politician to succeed Dunkel. The European Community and the United States now decided that the time had come to follow through. They needed a new director general to bring the round to a conclusion, rather than to implement it. While not unhappy with Dunkel's stewardship over the previous decade, they now wanted someone fresh with greater public stature and clout.[81]

By the end of June, Dunkel's place was taken by a very different kind of director general. The Europeans had successfully insisted that the job belonged to them and pushed forward the candidacy of Peter Sutherland. A former attorney general of Ireland and EC commissioner for competition, Sutherland was at the time chair of Allied Irish Banks in Dublin and possessed of the credentials, contacts, youthful vigor, and dominant personality to fit the profile sought by the United States and the European Community. He radiated a no-nonsense confidence and was more interested in results than in debating points. He had superb business and political contacts on both sides of the Atlantic and was not shy about using them.[82] By July 1, he was in place, together with three new deputies, Warren Lavorel of the United States, Anwarul Hoda of India, and Jesús Seade of Mexico, all Geneva veterans steeped in the lore of the Uruguay Round and ready to add to the new push.

Recapturing the Initiative

The new director general wasted no time in establishing his presence. Even before moving into his new office, he had been working the phones to reinforce ongoing work based on a Canadian suggestion that the Summit Seven meeting in Tokyo at the beginning of July provided an opportune time to do something more useful than the ritual call for a successful end to the round; they should agree on a concrete market-access package that would provide the momentum he needed for his first meeting as chair of the TNC. They agreed, and by the end of June, when the Quad countries met in Tokyo, they had begun to put together a respectable market-access package. By building public expectations, failing to meet them, and then delivering on a package at the summit, the principal players created just the right kind of tension and result to breathe new life into the round. The details of what was achieved mattered little. A carefully orchestrated media campaign convinced those who needed to be convinced that the new

American president was a fellow to be reckoned with, that his USTR could deliver, and that Sir Leon Brittan was a tough guy prepared to make a good deal. Additionally, Peter Sutherland and his new team were confirmed as the kind of brokers who could make things happen. The round was definitely on again.[83]

The following week, more careful press briefings suggested that the road ahead would be a tough slog, but both the United States and the European Community now had shoulders to the wheel, and the new director general was ready to put the rest of the apparatus to work with a view to concluding within the new time frame. At the July meeting of the TNC, momentum was restored, and the hundreds of delegates working at the mineface of the negotiations could return with renewed purpose to the painstaking work of crafting market access commitments and honing the texts of the several dozen agreements in play.[84]

Building Momentum

Now that both the media and the delegates were convinced that the round was back on track and the timetable firm, Sutherland turned his attention to one of the most critical deficiencies in its prosecution up to that point: the development of politically powerful constituencies committed to a big result. While there had been improvements and there continued to be room for more, the essential contours of a successful outcome for the round had been clear since the end of 1990. What had been missing, and was still missing, was the political will to cut through the inevitable difficult issues and reach the necessary compromises. That political will would not emerge in either the United States or the European Community until U.S. and EC political leaders became convinced that there were sufficient interest groups committed to a successful outcome to outweigh the hue and cry from those who felt threatened by more open, rules-based international trade and investment, such as farmers, textile workers, and economic nationalists. Sutherland's political experience told him that no agreement could survive on its professional merit alone; it also needed the committed and sustained support of politically powerful audiences. National delegations had not done enough to build such audiences.

In the absence of adequate national efforts, Sutherland set out to develop the necessary constituencies himself. He and his staff, working in harmony with other international organizations, took the wealth of available material that would make the point and repackaged it for much broader and politically useful consumption. A flurry of press releases and studies developed two mutually reinforcing themes: a successful outcome would add a significant percentage to the world's wealth, while failure would usher in a period of rancor that would subtract an even more significant portion from existing wealth. Culling studies pursued by international secretariats (the World Bank and the OECD), national think tanks, and university scholars, as well as the GATT's own economic analysts, the media were given the necessary material to write stories about the direct benefits that would accrue to ordinary consumers throughout the world, as well as the dire consequences they would face if the round failed. Various studies suggested that global economic wealth would increase by more than US$200 billion by the year 2000 or soon thereafter. The figures were in turn carefully broken down to indicate how much of this bonanza would accrue to individual national economies. To make the case even more politically persuasive, examples of benefits were drawn from the more embattled sectors, such as the costs to consumers of continued protection in the agriculture and textiles and clothing sectors and the benefits that would flow from liberalization, all tailored for consumption at the local level.[85]

Once the stories had been given wide circulation, Sutherland followed with a full court press on opinion molders and political leaders in the capitals of the major players. A flurry of phone calls, letters, speeches, and visits served the double purpose of raising the stakes and pressing home the message that a successful outcome brought political benefits while failure would bring trouble.[86] By the end of September, he had succeeded in creating the necessary atmosphere within which to put pressure on the European Community and the United States to get serious and cut through their differences. These differences, of course, remained profound, if not in economic terms, at least in political terms. France continued to find the Blair House agreement unacceptable. Neither the European Community nor the United States was satisfied with the market access offers made by the other side. The United States was not happy with the changes in the antidumping code and some thought that the subsidies code went too far. Both were worried that the textile text committing them to end the discriminatory MFA regime was not balanced enough by access commitments by the leading low-cost supplying countries. The United States still did not like some of the compromises that had been inscribed in the trade-related intellectual property text, nor was it satisfied that countries were making sufficient market access commitments in the services agreements, particularly on telecommunications and financial services. The European Community was not impressed by the United States's own effort on services, particularly on maritime services. The list went on, and when multiplied by the more than 100 participating countries, it was clear that failure would be much easier to orchestrate than success. The key, however, was for the United States and the European Community to craft, bilaterally, an agreement they could live with; this was the message that the director general pursued and others seconded.[87]

For the new American administration, however, the first real test on the trade front would be to get NAFTA through Congress. Like the Uruguay Round, NAFTA had been inherited from the Bush administration, and there were those in the new administration who believed that the president should not expend much political capital on it. There were others, however, who were prepared to see it pass on the basis of a series of side agreements that responded to the criticisms raised by Democrats in Congress and their natural constituencies, such as labor, environmentalists, and other populist groups. Clinton had chosen the second path, and over the course of the spring and summer Canada and Mexico had shrewdly accommodated his interests in negotiating two anodyne but symbolically important side agreements on the environment and labor. As a result, by the early fall NAFTA had been transformed from a Bush agreement into a Clinton agreement. The president now had little choice but to pull out all stops to gain congressional approval.

For most of October and well into November, NAFTA occupied center stage in Washington, with politicians, pundits, and lobbyists all concentrating on the benefits and perils of a free-trade agreement with a poor country. Both sides used all available rhetorical flourishes; based on media appearances and polling, the anti-NAFTA forces moved somewhat ahead. However, the administration and its congressional allies steadily worked to shore up support for NAFTA among Republicans and to court sufficient support among Democrats to ensure passage. The vote in the House, on November 17, provided the first real legislative test for the new president; formidable forces were arrayed against him, largely from within his own party; equally formidable forces were marshaled to support him from among Democrats and Republicans, former presidents, and other political icons, as well as business and academic leaders. The result was a stunning victory for the president. NAFTA passed by a solid majority.

The message for the Uruguay Round negotiators was crystal clear. The Clinton administration was committed to trade liberalization and international rule making and could deliver the Congress in the face of formidable and sustained opposition. Any deal that had the full support of the administration was not likely to be frustrated by Congress. Both Clinton and Kantor had achieved stature as serious players in Geneva.

To put a point on his new stature, Clinton flew to Seattle, Washington, the day after the House vote to host a summit meeting of Asia-Pacific leaders. The main topic for discussion was a proposal, developed by an expert's group chaired by Fred Bergsten of the Institute for International Economics, that the Asia-Pacific countries begin to lay the foundation for an Asia-Pacific free-trade agreement.[88] The meeting did not endorse the proposal. Rather, it laid emphasis on the need to concentrate on concluding a good agreement in Geneva. The subtext, however, was clear. The United States was prepared to expand its regional approach to trade liberalization, should the GATT process falter; sufficient other leaders shared this view to make this more than an idle threat.

While the United States concentrated on getting NAFTA through Congress, the European Community worked on defining a closing mandate that could accommodate the French and everyone else. A series of summits of trade, foreign, and agriculture ministers, as well as detailed staff work, gradually provided Sir Leon Brittan with a measure of the possible. The French government abandoned its posturing and agreed that a successful round was worth fighting for. Heavy pressure from the United Kingdom and the other market-oriented member states kept the bottom line honest. Behind the scenes, discussions with the Americans, the Japanese, and other leading delegations filled in the details and prepared the ground for the final push.[89]

The way had now been cleared to bring the round to a successful conclusion. The underbrush had been largely cleared away by the negotiators in Geneva, Brussels, Washington, and elsewhere. It was time for the two principals, the United States and the European Community, to come to some agreement and to do so on a basis that would carry at home as well as with the other delegations. This was the task to which Kantor and Brittan now bent themselves on a virtual full-time basis. Shuttling between Brussels and Geneva, they began to put together the final details of their bilateral package. While the two ministers and their closest advisors struggled to find the various zones of agreement, their staffs worked with the director general, other delegations, and the critical players in EC capitals and in Washington to work out reactions to various possible compromises and scenarios. Slowly, the package began to come together. By judicious softening of the Blair House package on agriculture, French intransigence was transferred to culture. By dropping audiovisual services in tandem with maritime services, two sources of strident opposition were neutralized. Some give-and-take on subsidies cleared the way for accommodation on the antidumping code. Improvements in market access for goods were balanced by some withdrawals on financial services. The horse-trading went on for days and well into the nights, but by December 14, the deal was essentially done.

All that remained was to hold the line for twenty-four hours while the details were communicated to the other delegations and put together into a final package to be considered by the TNC. Good staff work throughout the final three weeks ensured that other delegations were largely ready to conclude. With some necessary drama to cement the agreement in place and accommodate those delegations who needed to demonstrate their distaste for the way big powers feel they can railroad their wishes through a multilateral conference, the substantive negotiations of the round came to an end. Late in the afternoon of December 15, well before midnight in Washington, Peter Sutherland brought down the gavel and declared the negotiations over. Mickey Kantor could in good faith advise the president to send the necessary notifications to Congress of his intention to enter into the agreement within the time frame and procedures laid out by the fast-track authorization.

Assessing the Results

There remained work to be done, but the basic deal was now cast in stone. Over the next three months, before the final conference of ministers in Marrakech, officials and lawyers polished the text, filled in some of the missing details, removed as many ambiguities as possible, and ensured that the Final Act reflected the agreement reached on December 15. What had been agreed was monumental by any standard. It involved no less than a complete overhaul of the multilateral trading system, providing a new framework within which to consolidate and strengthen a broad range of new and old obligations, which together would put international trade on a much firmer and more open foundation.

The deal reached in Geneva involved some thirty separate agreements collectively amounting to the largest commercial agreement ever negotiated on such a universal basis. In order to provide an integrated set of obligations and at the same time remove the institutional ambiguity that had hampered the GATT in its first forty-plus years, the centerpiece of the new trade regime is a World Trade Organization (WTO). It provides the organizational framework within which members will pursue rights and obligations set out in three main agreements: an amended General Agreement on Tariffs and Trade, dubbed the GATT 1994; a new General Agreement on Trade in Services (GATS); and a new Agreement on Trade-Related Intellectual Property Rights (TRIPs). Fleshing out the rights and obligations contained in the revised GATT are a series of codes (most of which are revised versions of the Tokyo Round codes, in some cases radically revised, as in the case of subsidies) and decisions and understandings on a range of important matters, including dispute settlement, the trade-policy review mechanism, and the interpretation of various GATT articles.[90] Appended to the revised GATT and the new GATS are detailed schedules setting out in specific terms the market access commitments of individual members. The schedules appended to the GATT 1994 contain not only traditional tariff bindings but also commitments on other product-specific border measures. On the thorny issue of agriculture, a detailed agreement was worked out involving the imposition of tariffs on all border measures, minimum access commitments, reductions in export and production subsidies, and clear discipline on domestic support measures. Finally, to overcome the problems, created at the end of the Tokyo Round, of a hierarchy of obligations resulting from the less-than-universal adherence to the codes, the Final Act enters into force on an all-or-nothing basis. With the exception of four so-called plurilateral agreements (on procurement, aircraft, dairy products, and bovine meat products, which apply to only a few signatories), signature of the Final Act meant acceptance of all the agreements.

From a trade policy perspective, the agreements reached in Geneva have much to recommend them, including:

- *Breakthroughs.* The conclusion of multilateral agreements on agriculture, subsidies, intellectual property, and services represent major advances in international rule making and should provide an improved basis for the continued development of an open global economy. Some of these agreements are experimental in nature and will require continuing negotiation and clarification. Indeed, experience may demonstrate that some are insufficient or even wrong or too ambiguously worded and may eventually require wholesale revision. What is important, however, is that these agreements either provide a basis for resolving long-standing and festering problems (such as trade in agriculture and subsidies) or introduce general rules of nondiscrimination to areas of increasing importance in international trade (such as services and intellectual property). The objection of some of the leading developing countries to the expansion of the GATT to these new areas was neatly overcome by integrating the new and the old into a new world-trade body with a broad mandate.
- *Strengthening of the GATT system.* The agreements on safeguards and textiles and clothing ensure that the erosion of the GATT's basic principles flowing from the proliferation of gray-area measures and the cynical regime for textiles and clothing will now be reversed. Agreement to establish a World Trade Organization (WTO) to provide oversight, improvements in the dispute settlement procedures, and the introduction of a permanent Trade Policy Review Mechanism provide a basis for believing that the more ambitious set of rights and obligations contained in the Final Act can in fact be implemented and become the basis for a dynamic and more modern trade relations system.
- *Improvements in market access.* The protocols providing for specific commitments on reductions and bindings in tariff schedules and other

product-specific border measures, access to most services markets, and enhanced commitments on government procurement all suggest that the momentum of multilateral trade liberalization has been restored. Reductions in overall tariff levels are close to 40 percent, bringing tariffs among the industrial countries down to little more than a nuisance in all but a few sectors. Of particular interest is the extent to which developing countries have agreed to take on hard obligations for the first time, the extent to which members were prepared not to protect preferences established by the new regionalism, and the number of sectors in which industrial countries have agreed to move to tariff-free trade. While there remains room for improvement, the urge to manage rather than liberalize trade appears to have been largely resisted.

- *Clarifications and modernization of the GATT system.* A range of agreements, such as those involving rules of origin, preshipment inspections, improvements to the codes on import licensing, customs valuation, government procurement, and technical barriers, provides a more secure basis for trade and continues the transition from general to specific rules and procedures. These agreements should also encourage the further transition to a more lawlike and less political approach to dispute settlement.

- *Disappointments.* Looked at from the perspective of the GATT's principles and the values of an open, nondiscriminatory international trade and investment regime, there are a number of disappointments, which will provide continued work for the future. The revisions in the antidumping code and the countervailing duties procedures, as well as the new agreement on trade-related investment measures, fail to come to grips with the fundamental problem of fair competition in an open global economy. While perhaps politically necessary to keep the United States and to some extent other major traders on side, they maintain in place a set of rules that favor power-based trade relations based on flawed economic thinking. The growing conflict between competition and trade policies will thus need to be addressed in a future round.[91] The negotiation of a services agreement represents a major breakthrough, but the actual amount of trade liberalized is disappointingly small. Additionally, the TRIMs agreement fails to capture the importance of foreign direct investment as an agent of international integration and economic development. There is still need for a multilateral investment code that addresses the full range of issues related to discriminatory regulation of the conduct of business. The comparable chapter in the North American FTA is much further along in capturing the reality of the global economy.

Despite the disappointments, the round established an expanded and revitalized GATT-based trade relations system. It reverses the gradual shift from multilateral agreements to regional ones and reestablishes the primacy of a universal set of rules and institutions. As such, it provides a stronger framework for the continued evolution of a trade relations system based on the principles of nondiscrimination, transparency, due process, consultation, and cooperation. It lays an impressive foundation for continuing the process of applying these principles to a wider range of international economic transactions, and it should continue the transition from a set of broad principles and general rules aimed at shallow integration to a much more detailed and complex set of rules capable of fostering deep integration. It demonstrates that it is possible to negotiate, on a multilateral basis, rules of general application involving positive norms that go well beyond the self-denying prescriptions of the original GATT. Finally, it signals that it is possible to negotiate international agreements of some scope and significance in the absence of effective, sustained leadership by the major players.

The Final Act thus involves an impressive set of achievements commensurate with the ambition and goals set out at the beginning. The very ambition and complexity of these goals, however, suggest why it proved so difficult to reach agreement.

Explaining Outcomes

As we have seen, much of the round was a success as early as December 1990 and no later than December 1991, at least at the professional level. The subsequent three years were used to clean up and improve the text and add to its professional quality, particularly the service agreement and market-access commitments. The result is a Final Act establishing a solid new framework within which to proceed. In each of the substantive areas covered by the final text, a combination of specific concessions and general rules provides a means of gaining both immediate benefits and future order and stability. The fact that the professional and largely anonymous negotiators in Geneva were able to achieve this highly satisfactory result can be attributed to a number of factors:

Consensual Knowledge

Forty-five years of experience in negotiating and maintaining a trade regime had developed a large and committed epistemic community of trade experts in a sufficient number of governments and related institutions to ensure a professionally committed and competent negotiating process. The literature on the round alone attests to the depth and commitment of these epistemic communities. On most of the issues tackled by the negotiators, a wealth of analytical work inside and outside government ensured that the negotiators could count on an impressive range of intellectual capital, which in turn fostered creative solutions to difficult problems.

Crisis and Public Diplomacy

Trade policy came out of the obscurity of low policy to the intense scrutiny of high policy in the 1980s, and many of its practitioners were ill equipped to address the need for building broad public support for a trade negotiation. The public was given three images of the round: the increasingly hollow rhetoric of the G-7 Summit, OECD, and similar declarations, which stressed the importance and commitment of governments to the round at a high level of abstraction but did not explain why these same governments could not negotiate solutions to specific problems; the strident claims and counterclaims of the European Community, the United States, and smaller countries on the need to address the sins of others without any effort to address one's own; and finally, an image of the GATT, projected by both politicians and interest groups, as a faceless international bogeyman responsible for destroying the family farm and other icons. Rather than strengthening the capacity of negotiators to address issues at the table, public diplomacy during the first few years undermined the ability of most governments to reach satisfactory outcomes. A predilection for short-term political-issue management resulted in a public more likely to be hostile or indifferent to the round than convinced that it could make a positive contribution to solving real problems. This dismal experience was largely reversed in the final six months in the hands of a new director general, who organized a blitz of positive public diplomacy that provided the necessary air of crisis, as well as a more balanced public appreciation of the dangers of failure and the benefits of success.

Coalitions

The range of countries that actively participated in these negotiations ensured that this round would be more multilateral, and thus potentially more broadly supported, than any previous GATT negotiation. Organizing the negotiations and maintaining momentum was immensely aided by the development of fluid, issue-oriented and process-oriented coalitions, rather than the sterile ideological groupings that had previously characterized economic negotiations between industrial and developing countries—for example, the Cairns Group, the Rio Group, and the de la Paix Group. The developing countries no longer behaved like a herd but joined forces with one another and with other players to advance specific national interests.

Issue Decomposition and Sequencing

The professional negotiators approached the issues systematically, beginning with agenda setting and issue identification procedures, effectively breaking down a complex agenda into a manageable set of issues for negotiation in fifteen separate groups, initially finding trade-offs within each issue set before gradually brokering thirty separate agreements into a comprehensive whole.

Bridging and Bargaining Strategies

Work at this level was largely concentrated between 1985 and the end of 1991. While the professional negotiators continued to be busy over the subsequent two years, they did not materially alter what had been largely conceived and achieved by them by the end of 1991. But their product—contained within the draft Dunkel text—lacked the necessary level of political appeal to bring the round to a successful conclusion; it needed delicate compromises on a range of politically ticklish issues if the round was to come to a successful conclusion. The Dunkel text may have been intellectually sound, but it was not politically marketable.

While the American political process set out the differences between professional and political assessments of the Dunkel draft in sharpest relief, other countries faced similar difficulties. In the European Community, the French had not become reconciled to the result and were not convinced that the overall benefits outweighed the political pain that would flow from the agriculture results. As late as the beginning of 1993, French political leaders were calling for the end of the round and a fresh start.[92] Their concerns were shared by the Mediterranean countries and not wholly offset by the support of the Northern Tier, whose electorates were not clamoring for the round to conclude. Politicians in other countries could point to similar difficulties. Despite these difficulties, however, it proved possible to bring the round to a successful conclusion at the end of 1993.

Leadership and Representation

Both the original GATT negotiations and subsequent rounds had been initiated and driven to a successful conclusion under American leadership. As the dominant economic power with both economic and political considerations to guide it, the American vision, although not always shared, was sufficient to ensure successful conclusion. In the Uruguay Round, not only was the United States unable to exert this kind of leadership, but it also frustrated efforts by others as it struggled with the psychology of having to share leadership. The early attitude that past concessions should be sufficient to pay for new concessions by other players illustrated this lack of firm leadership. Neither the European Community nor Japan proved ready to assume leadership on its own, while the potential collective leadership of the G-7 countries and the Quads was undermined by the fact that the most intractable problems lay among its members. When the United States was ready to deal, the European Community was not; when the European Community was ready, the United States had new problems; and Japan continued to raise suspicions, rather than providing the kind of bridging leadership its stake in the system should have fostered. While the smaller players did partially fill the leadership vacuum, they were unable to overcome problems between the principal players, and without agreement among the principal players, the round could not be concluded. In the final months, however, new political leadership in Brussels, Washington, and Geneva, unencumbered by the rhetoric of the past, showed that it could be done. Both sides finally exhibited a willingness to compromise and thus provided the determination and political judgment to rise above the detail and grab the opportunity offered by success.

A number of other factors and lessons can be drawn from the last two years of effort.

Institutional Setting

The institutional setting provided an agreed basis and venue for addressing the issues. It was not necessary for those interested in advancing rule making and liberalizing trade to invent either the place or the means to pursue their interests. The GATT provided a forty-five year history of relatively successful trade management and a record of seven earlier successful multilateral trade negotiations.

The Need for Developing New Negotiating Techniques

Much of the round marked a continued effort to apply the negotiating technique developed for trading tariff concessions on goods—mercantilist bargaining—to the more complex job of writing rules of general application. The political arithmetic that had made mercantilist bargaining an effective strategy proved less suited to the task of developing normative codes. The new kind of trade-offs are more likely to be seen as politically acceptable in more limited agreements, in terms of either the number of players or the number of issues. Agreement to establish a WTO, first proposed by the European Community and Canada and long resisted by the United States, should provide an improved basis for developing new techniques in tune with the broader membership and more complex range of issues now on the international trade agenda.

The Problem of Politically Viable Alternatives

For too many of the principal players, success in pursuing alternative means to solving immediate trade problems, leading to acceptable second-best results, made it difficult for decision makers to maintain credibility in their claims that the round was important. The consequences of failure could only be explained in terms that were professionally, rather than politically, persuasive. While trade policy professionals billed second-best solutions as complementary efforts, to politicians and their publics they were in fact alternatives that further undermined governments' ability to take on the politically difficult commitments necessary to conclude the round. One of the most pressing issues that will now need to be addressed by the WTO is how to integrate regional and multilateral rule making into a coherent whole that avoids this complication in future negotiations.

The Need to Narrow the Gap between Epistemic and Political Communities

The texts developed by the negotiators represent a significant achievement in international legislation, but they are so complex and interrelated that the political decision makers—and their publics—have difficulty grasping the extent and significance of the issues that they must decide. As a result, politicians can too easily be cowed or diverted by the slogans and fears of narrow interests. Their refuge is stalemate. It used to be that trade liberalization could best be achieved in a broad negotiation allowing for broad trade-offs of narrow interests. The complexity of the Uruguay Round suggests that it may now be easier to reach consensus on a few related issues in order to avoid becoming hostage to a few deeply entrenched but unrelated narrow interests.

Ambiguity and Lowest-Common-Denominator Solutions

In some areas, services, for example, parts of the text are still very woolly, because players with insufficient stake or understanding felt constrained to seek words that would render obligations meaningless. While multilateral agreements have much to recommend them, the need to achieve consensus among a large number of players means that the lowest common denominator will prevail. In a number of cases, it means that the gap between the negotiated product and business perceptions of what is required is still too wide. For many firms in the new economy, interested in a set of rules that will make international commerce easier, the convoluted negotiating process made it easy to accept the GATT-is-dead syndrome advocated by some analysts. Too few of these firms have as yet experienced the impact of protectionist measures after they have made significant investments.

Thus, while the round ultimately succeeded, these are some of the issues that will need to be addressed and considered in capitals and by the new WTO if the promise of the new multilateral regime is to be translated into a vibrant reality. Throughout the GATT's history, various commentators have been quick to conclude that the trading system is in crisis or that the GATT is dead. The nature of the bargain struck in 1947 and the manner in which it was achieved virtually guaranteed a perpetual crisis in confidence in the GATT's constitutional capacity to address the problems of the day. Despite this handicap, however, the GATT-based trade relations system has survived. It has adapted to changing circumstances by means of various artful procedures and compromises. The rules and procedures have never measured up to the ideals of its most ardent admirers and advocates. Rather, governments prefer to give it just enough room to do the job they want done, and no more.

By the mid-1980s, these jerry-built compromises and procedures were beginning to look very fragile, as the trading regime needed to address an increasingly complex world of international business transactions and a fragmented range of international rules and procedures. The gap between the reality of international business and the framework of intergovernment rules that regulated it had widened to the point that cynics were prepared to dismiss the GATT as hopelessly outdated and irrelevant. The temptation on the part of government trade officials and their supporters in think tanks to solve the problem with an ambitious program of reform is readily understood. What was forgotten in the zeal of pursuing reform was that there have to be sufficient politically powerful constituents favoring such reform to offset the wailing and whining of groups that would lose from changes in the system.

Most of the energy expended over the first years of negotiations concentrated on the tough and necessary work of negotiating a sound professional product. During that time, insufficient attention was paid to how to make the ambitious package in the making a politically marketable package. The conventional wisdom that only a big package would attract sufficient support, while true on previous occasions, may this time around have been too simple an answer. The key requirement of success was to ensure throughout the negotiations that politically active and interested publics had a stake in the negotiations and were aware of both the costs and the benefits of a big deal.

It took a further three years for the negotiators and their governments to find the ingredients that would allow them to build the necessary political will to translate their ambition into a package that had broad appeal and appeased the most strident opponents. In this they finally succeeded, with the infusion of new blood in Washington, Brussels, and Geneva.

Both the original ITO negotiations and the Uruguay Round are good examples of what happens when expert opinion and ideology develop substantive and institutional goals that are too far ahead of public opinion and political acceptability. Without a major effort at public education and at forging broad support, governments find it impossible to reach compromises that are both workable and politically acceptable. In the end, however, it proved possible to put together a package that is both professionally and politically acceptable. The enduring lesson of the Uruguay Round, therefore, would seem to be that better ways will have to be found to negotiate the increasingly complex trade rules that the globalization of the economy dictates.

IV Multilateral Environmental Negotiations

9   The Ozone Accords

Negotiations leading to the Vienna Convention for the Protection of the Ozone Layer (1985), the Montreal Protocol (1987), and subsequent Helsinki agreements amending the protocol (1990) represent a landmark in international diplomacy and environmental cooperation. The depletion of ozone in the upper atmosphere because of manmade emissions of ozone-harming gases poses a threat to global survival, and it was recognized early on that it would require unprecedented levels of international cooperation to address the problem.

Although some argue that these treaties were concluded "through the influence of epistemic communities" ("transnational networks of knowledge-based communities that are . . . politically empowered through their claims to exercise authoritative knowledge"),[1] it would be erroneous to explain the success of these agreements solely in terms of the influence (or impact) of science on policy. First, public opinion fueled by fears about the links between ozone depletion, growing levels of ultraviolet radiation and skin cancer played a crucial role in bridging the gap between science and politics by forcing the issue on to the political agenda. Second, a growing sense of crisis (coupled with the "dread factor") moved the issue from the national to the international stage, especially as the Green movement took hold of the issue in Europe and other countries. Third, once the issue became a subject of international discussion and negotiation, the exercise of skillful leadership and mediation by a variety of different actors, including the United States, the executive director of UNEP (United Nations Environment Programme), and several smaller states, helped to sustain negotiations, bridge key bargaining impasses, and bring the parties to agreement.

Although science helped promote convergent expectations and was crucial in propelling negotiations forward as new knowledge and information came to light, much of the hard bargaining was not about science but about how to deal with questions of equity, efficiency, and distribution, not only between advanced industrial countries but also between North and South. What ultimately accounts for the success of these negotiations, particularly in meeting the concerns of developing countries, was the promotion of a sense of social justice embodied in a new set of principles and institutions that explicitly recognized the responsibility of industrial countries to help developing countries cope with the costs of adjustment to a new regulatory regime. On the one hand, extranegotiatory influences in the form of epistemic pressures and public opinion were crucial in bringing the ozone issue to the negotiating table and sustaining negotiations once they formally got under way. On the other hand, mediation and political leadership were crucial to resolving key differences among the players at critical junctures in the negotiation process, particularly when competing values and notions of fairness were at the core of the debate. The complex interplay between the external environment and the negotiating table thus helps to explain not only how but also why these agreements were negotiated.

Issues and Stakeholders

Chlorofluorocarbons (CFCs) and halons, which are used as refrigerants, are the primary pollutants identified with ozone depletion, although other gases may also contribute to the problem. They have been called the "boy scouts of industrial chemicals." In the United States alone, CFCs are used as refrigerants in more than 100 million household refrigerators and freezers, not to mention virtually every supermarket, grocery, and restaurant. CFCs are also used in 10 million home air conditioners, more than 60 million automobile air conditioners, and the cooling systems of most public and commercial buildings.

The United States is the world's largest producer and consumer of CFCs, in 1987 accounting for 29 percent of global consumption and 34 percent of global production. Much of the research on ozone depletion was conducted by U.S. scientists, and public awareness and concern about the issue first peaked in the United States. The United States was a strong advocate of large-scale reductions of ozone-harming substances, as were Canada and the Scandinavian countries (the Toronto Group).[2]

The second major stakeholder in the ozone story is the European Community (EC), which in 1987 accounted for approximately 20 percent of CFC global consumption, with one-third of its production going into exports. At the time negotiations leading to the Montreal Protocol began, the European Community favored a freeze on production, reflecting the interests of its own chemical industries. The strongest opposition within the European Community to international controls came from the United Kingdom and France. The United Kingdom's position changed with the "greening" of Prime Minister Margaret Thatcher, initially one of the strongest opponents to CFC reductions, who subsequently endorsed proposals for drastic cuts in CFC usage and their eventual ban.

As of 1987, Japan was the world's third largest producer and consumer of CFCs, after the United States and the European Community. Japan's position was initially aligned with the European Community. It was not an active player in the negotiations, although it eventually joined the Vienna Convention and signed the Montreal Protocol.

The third set of interests were the developing countries, which in 1987 accounted for 14 percent of global consumption. They were led by Mexico and Brazil during the negotiations. Although China and India initially refused to participate, they subsequently joined the negotiations. The developing countries were concerned about the effect CFC cutbacks would have on their own economic development; they felt they should not be unduly penalized by a problem that, in their view, had been created by industrial countries. Their condition for participation in the convention was that the protocol contain provisions allowing for limited increases in consumption of CFCs, along with financial assistance and transfers of CFC substitutes and recycling technologies.

Industry was the fourth major stakeholder. In 1987, the U.S. du Pont de Nemours & Company was the largest developer and producer of CFCs, controlling some 26 percent of world production. Other major industrial producers of CFCs included ICI (the United Kingdom), Allied Signal (the United States), Forbwerke Hoechst (the Federal Republic of Germany), and ATOCHEM (France). Initially opposed to controls, Du Pont came to support a global ban on CFCs.

Environmental nongovernmental organizations (NGOs), a fifth stakeholder, were also strong supporters of a CFC ban. The Green movement in Germany and the United Kingdom eventually came to exert a strong influence over the national policies of these countries. In the United States, the Natural Resources Defense Council (NRDC) played a major role in politicizing the issue and in using the legal system to force the Environmental Protection Agency (EPA) to confront the issue. Although NGOs were not formally represented in the negotiations, they had an observer status, and their presence gave the issue a high profile in the media, through press conferences, briefings, and circulation of position papers.

Prenegotiation

The problem of depletion of stratospheric ozone was first raised at the 1972 Stockholm Conference on the Human Environment. Scientists had expressed concern about the threat posed to the ozone layer by high-flying supersonic aircraft, but in 1974 two scientists, Mario Molina and F. Sherwood Rowland, drew attention to the dangers of CFCs and their possible link with stratospheric ozone depletion.[3] During this early stage of policy formulation, "CFC-induced stratospheric ozone depletion emerged as a major environmental and political issue primarily in the United States. While other nations (Canada and Scandinavian countries) were concerned about the problem, most European countries (particularly the EC countries) showed little interest."[4] The politicization of the issue of ozone depletion in the United States was the result of a combination of factors: strong opposition, especially among environmentalists, to the American supersonic transport aircraft program, the growing importance of environmental issues generally in the early 1970s, and widespread public concern about cancer and the factors that might cause it.

Although the link between CFCs and stratospheric ozone depletion was by no means proven, "the fear of skin cancer from the depletion of stratospheric ozone due to the use of CFCs as aerosol propellents in spray cans personalized the risks for many people." As Peter Morrisette explains further, "through the media, the public learned that such nonessential products as aerosol hairsprays and deodorants could pose serious future environmental and health risks. The public came to view the risks of using CFC-based aerosols as unacceptable. As a result, even before the aerosol ban of 1978, the sale of aerosol products fell sharply."[5] In response to pressure from consumers, the use of CFCs and aerosol propellants was cut back in some countries. In the United States, regulations banning the nonessential use of CFCs in aerosols were introduced by the EPA and the federal Food and Drug Administration (FDA) in 1978. CFC used in aerosols was also banned in Canada, Sweden, Norway, and Denmark. The Netherlands and the Federal Republic of Germany also took measures to reduce CFC use in aerosols. There were regular meetings of representatives of the major CFC-producing nations. The European Community adopted measures to freeze the level of production of CFCs and to reduce CFC use in aerosols, even in the face of resistance from two of its members, the United Kingdom and France.

In the late 1970s, the CFC-ozone issue moved from the national to the international arena. In 1977, a UNEP-sponsored meeting of intergovernmental experts was formally charged with developing an action plan to protect stratospheric ozone. The meeting also led to the establishment of the Coordinating Committee on the Ozone Layer. One of the committee's chief functions was to bring together industry, scientists, and government officials to study and report on the risks of ozone depletion. In the absence of conclusive scientific data about the problem, the World Meteorological Organization (WMO) recommended the reactivation of a British monitoring device at Halley Bay in Antarctica, which in 1985 revealed the ozone hole over the South Pole.[6]

Concerns about ozone depletion were by no means widespread, however. Although the EPA proposed limiting domestic production of CFCs in 1980, for a variety of political and scientific reasons the proposal was never adopted. As Allan Miller and Irving Mintzer explain, "the Administration that took office in 1981 looked unfavorably on most regulation, and researchers' perceptions of the seriousness of the problem changed. Modelers reduced their estimates of depletion based on revised reaction rates, and CFC producers and users argued that the risks did not justify the high costs of alternatives for non-aerosol uses, particularly when many other countries were still using CFCs."[7]

Negotiations

In April 1980, UNEP's governing council urged governments to reduce national use and production of CFCs. Then in January 1982, UNEP also convened an ad hoc working group of legal and technical experts to lay the foundations for a global framework convention for the protection of the ozone layer. In 1983 a coalition of countries known as the Toronto Group, which comprised Canada, Finland, Norway, Sweden, and Switzerland, first proposed the idea of reducing CFC emissions by banning aerosols. Although the United States initially was not supportive of this proposal, it eventually came around and joined the Toronto Group. The strongest opposition to a CFC aerosol ban came from the European Community, followed by Japan and the Soviet Union. The European Community favored a cap on CFC production capacity, which would benefit its own producers, who enjoyed a sizable surplus capacity and would therefore be able to continue to increase their production of CFCs. U.S. producers, like du Pont, who enjoyed no surplus capacity would therefore find themselves at a competitive disadvantage vis-à-vis European producers under the European plan.

Negotiations in the ad hoc working group eventually culminated in the Vienna Convention for the Protection of the Ozone Layer, signed in 1985 by twenty countries and the EC Commission. The convention contains twenty-one articles and two technical annexes spelling out the obligation of states to control activities that might have adverse effects on the ozone layer and to cooperate in scientific research and data exchanges. However, the convention did not identify ozone-depleting substances, nor did it set any legally binding targets or control measures. At the initiative of the Toronto Group, a resolution was carried committing UNEP to resume diplomatic negotiations on a legally binding control protocol within two years and for UNEP to convene a workshop to that end. In the words of

UNEP's executive director, Mostafa Tolba, this was the first global convention "to address an issue that for the time being seems far in the future and is of unknown proportions."[8] But as one friendly critic notes, "a framework convention is a little like an author selling a book on the basis of a table of contents and a statement of intent to write the text at some later date."[9] In this case, the manuscript was not long in coming.

New Scientific Findings

Between the signings of the Vienna Convention in 1985 and the Montreal Protocol in 1987, new data and improved methods of modeling and forecasting played an important role in narrowing scientific disagreement about the causes of stratospheric ozone depletion. These scientific developments in turn helped to create a political consensus for a stricter international regulatory framework to address the problem. Key in this debate was the 1985 publication of a report by the WMO and NASA presenting a comprehensive multilateral scientific assessment of the growing dangers that CFCs posed to the upper atmosphere. The report concluded that "there is now compelling observational evidence indicating increases in the concentrations of gases which control the atmospheric ozone. These gases, which include chlorofluorocarbons . . . catalyze the destruction of ozone in the stratosphere."[10]

The WMO-NASA study was followed by the release, in June 1986, of the report of EPA-UNEP-sponsored conference on stratospheric ozone depletion and climate change by some 300 scientists and policy makers from twenty countries, which reached similar conclusions. At the conference, held in Leesburg, Virginia, some scientists argued that a freeze on CFC production would not be enough and that these chemicals would have to be phased out in ten years.[11] According to David Doniger, the Leesburg conference paved the way for subsequent negotiations by making headway in several areas: convincing major industrial producers of CFCs, like du Pont, that the issue was one of price, not chemistry, in developing safe substitutes for CFCs; getting Japan and Europe to admit that production rates of CFCs were rising; and achieving widespread agreement that some sort of international measures would have to be taken, even on an interim basis, to cut CFC emissions.[12] The EPA also conducted its own independent risk assessments through its Stratospheric Ozone Protection Plan and concluded that "continued increases in the concentrations of a variety of trace gases in the atmosphere are likely to modify the vertical distribution and column of abundance of stratospheric and tropospheric ozone," which could eventually lead to over 150 million additional skin cancer cases resulting in more than three million deaths in the United States alone by the year 2075.[13] The EPA, along with the State Department's Bureau of Oceans, Environment, and International Science (OES), called for a 95 percent worldwide cut in production of CFCs, to be followed eventually by a complete ban.[14] In June 1987, after a prolonged bureaucratic battle within the administration, the policy was formally endorsed by President Reagan himself. As Peter Haas explains, this shift in policy was brought about by pressures from the scientific community and the compelling weight of scientific evidence.

> Both the UNEP and the American position were shaped by the views of a transnational epistemic community of atmospheric scientists. These individuals accepted the Rowland-Molina hypothesis, developed models to elaborate it and began monitoring for actual ozone depletion, while also publicly supporting policies that would ban CFCs. Further, this group of scientists shared causal beliefs that related stratospheric ozone depletion to the infusion of chlorine and CFC use. . . . Because of their desire to protect the environment, they advocated anticipatory action, despite the remaining scientific uncertainties.[15]

The Road to Montreal

Protocol negotiations began in Geneva in December 1986. At the time they began, the only governments to have ratified the Vienna Convention were Canada, Finland, Norway, Sweden, the United States, and the Soviet Union; the European Community and Japan had not yet ratified the convention. No protocols would go into effect until the convention had been ratified by at least twenty countries. Three negotiating blocs emerged: the European Community, led by France, Italy, and the United Kingdom, wanted some form of limits on production but were still reluctant to ban CFCs in aerosols; the Toronto Group was joined by Switzerland, which wanted stringent controls and an aerosol ban, New Zealand, Australia, and Austria; and a number of developing countries, represented by Argentina, Brazil, Egypt, Kenya, and Venezuela, were uncommitted but increasingly came to favor international regulations.[16]

At the first round of negotiations in Geneva, Canada, the United States, and the Soviet Union each offered their own draft or "illustrative" text. According to U.S. negotiator Richard Benedick,

> the U.S. text was the most comprehensive, covering not only control measures but also provisions for periodic assessments and adjustments, trade restrictions, and reporting. Three Nordic nations—Finland, Norway, and Sweden—jointly offered an amendment to the U.S. text, calling for immediate cuts rather than an initial freeze. . . . The Soviets seemed unfamiliar with,

and sharply critical of, the scientific rationale for new controls. They suggested national allocation based rather vaguely on population and CFC production capacity, with a complete exemption for developing countries.[17]

The Canadian plan took the middle road: an immediate freeze on the production of CFCs, short-term cuts, and an option on longer-term cuts, based on future assessments of the danger to the ozone layer. The proposal was based on a complex formula for quotas on national emissions, which took into account a country's gross national product and population.[18] However, the European Community indicated that it would negotiate a cap only on production capacity.

The second session was held in Vienna in February 1987. Canada and the Nordic countries, along with Egypt, Mexico, New Zealand, and Switzerland, adopted a proposed U.S. text outline. The European Community continued to argue that a freeze on production would not be acceptable, but the Federal Republic of Germany, which was increasingly unhappy with the EC position, threatened to break ranks and unilaterally ban aerosols.

In an effort to break the growing impasse, the United States asked scientists to test their models for the future effects of alternative regulatory strategies. A meeting of scientists from four countries was convened by UNEP in April in Würzburg, Federal Republic of Germany. Their report, as Haas notes, "provided consensual support for the position already promoted by the United States and UNEP. Given the authority of the scientists involved, this report was sufficient to compel the recalcitrant Europeans to accept the need for speedy controls over a wide variety of CFCs—a position they had previously opposed."[19]

At the third round in Geneva in April 1987, negotiations began to move forward. The number of participating countries had risen to thirty-three. Based on results of the Würzburg meeting of scientists, UNEP's executive director, Mostafa Tolba, argued that "those who oppose action to regulate CFC releases [can no longer] hide behind scientific dissent" and called for tough international regulations.[20] Tolba organized a series of small closed meetings out of the political limelight to discuss appropriate control measures. The negotiators worked out a secret text, the countries involved being Canada, Japan, New Zealand, Norway, the Soviet Union, the United States, and the European Community, along with Belgium, Denmark, and the United Kingdom (the presidential troika). The group produced an unofficial draft, which became the basis for subsequent discussions at the meeting of delegation heads in Brussels in June 1987. The emerging protocol text was also studied by a group of legal experts in The Hague.

At the Brussels meeting, however, the European Community and the United Kingdom unsuccessfully tried to alter Tolba's text and water down the emerging protocol. These efforts were strongly resisted by Tolba, even though much of the draft text was to become the subject of heated negotiations in Montreal in September 1987.

By the time of the final round of negotiations in Montreal in September, the number of participants had grown to sixty, of which half were developing countries. Tolba and conference chairman Winfried Lang, an Austrian diplomat, were responsible for hammering out many of the compromises. The new international accord was unveiled on September 16. The Montreal Protocol on Substances That Deplete the Ozone Layer, as it is formally known, called for CFC reductions of 50 percent by the year 2000. The protocol set out a schedule, for both the short and the long term, to control these substances. For the short term, it established phasedown requirements to reduce emissions of specified ozone-depleting substances. For the long term, flexible mechanisms by which control measures can be periodically assessed and adjusted to reflect the latest scientific findings were set out. The protocol also provided for trade sanctions against nonparty countries who fail to sign the agreement or deny their obligations to protect the global environment.[21] The protocol was signed by sixty-two countries and ratified by thirty-six countries and the European Community.

Key Issues

The key issues in the negotiations from December 1986 to September 1987 were (1) what chemicals to include in the protocols; (2) where production or consumption of these substances would be controlled; (3) the base year from which reductions would be calculated; (4) the timing and size of cutbacks; (5) how the treaty would enter into force and be revised, including the question of weighted voting; (6) restrictions on trade with countries not participating in the protocol; (7) treatment of developing countries with low levels of CFC consumption; and (8) special provisions for the European Community.[22] Of these, the most contentious were the production-versus-consumption issue, the stringency and timing of reductions, and the question of special treatment for the European Community. In each case, bargaining impasses were broken through a combination of diplomatic skill and leadership and the invention of novel bridging proposals, which not only appealed to basic principles of equity and fairness but also allowed for new political coalitions to form that cut across traditional Toronto Group–EC lines.

The issue of whether to restrict production or consumption of controlled substances saw stark divisions between the European Community, which favored controls on production, and the Toronto Group, joined by the Soviet Union and Denmark, which favored a consumption-related formula. This issue was especially controversial because of the commercial implications of each approach. The European Community argued that (1) production was administratively easier to control than consumption, and (2) as consumption was cut back, U.S. chemical companies, then operating at full capacity, would be left in a highly favorable position, having an exportable surplus at the same time that European companies, which had spare production capacity and dominated world exports, would be forced to cut back their production. The other countries argued that production controls would give European producers an unfair competitive advantage unless other producers cut back on their supplies to domestic markets to meet foreign demand. Furthermore, if European demand continued to grow, European producers would have to cut back their exports, which would leave foreign CFC-importing countries high and dry and bearing the brunt of the burden of regulatory controls.

The alternative was an "adjusted production" formula (suggested by the United States and other members of the Toronto Group) based on production-plus-imports-minus-exports, which took into account the European Community's concerns about the difficulties of controlling consumption but eliminated any monopoly based on existing export positions.[23] Under the formula, national production would also be allowed to be slightly higher than national consumption, in order to meet the import demands of developing countries. Although the European Community resisted the idea, according to U.S. negotiator Benedick, "the logic and equity of 'adjusted production' proved to be compelling, and opposition to a 'production only' formula . . . became implacable."[24] Countries which produced less than their quota could also transfer their production quotas to another country and meet imports from that country under an "industrial rationalization" clause proposed by Canada.

The timing and stringency of reductions were visibly the most contentious issues in the protocol negotiations, and again the United States and the European Community found themselves in diametric opposition. The United States favored an immediate freeze followed by mandatory phased cutbacks, which would be periodically reviewed and based on updated scientific assessments. The European Community, on the other hand, agreed to a freeze but wanted reductions on a more relaxed schedule, and only if they received the approval of at least a two-thirds majority of the signatories to the convention. The U.S. position was supported by Egypt, New Zealand, and the members of the Toronto Group. As negotiations continued, it became evident that some parties wanted reductions up to 50 percent, and the European Community split, with Belgium, Denmark, the Federal Republic of Germany, and the Netherlands opting for a more stringent approach to reductions. In particular, the Germans were increasingly concerned about new scientific evidence and had decided that they would opt for major reductions, regardless of what the European Community decided. As Benedick reports, "the Würzburg scientific meeting in April had major repercussions on this debate. The scientists demonstrated that serious damage to the ozone layer would occur under the weaker control options being considered by the negotiators. . . . By the time of the Geneva meeting later in April, more governments had moved in the direction of favoring 50 percent cutbacks."[25] At the same time, Mostafa Tolba convened an informal consultative group of the ten delegation heads from Canada, Japan, New Zealand, Norway, the Soviet Union, the United States, the European Commission, Belgium, Denmark, and the United Kingdom. The group thrashed out a text that became the basis of final negotiations in Montreal. Largely under pressure from the Toronto Group and the European Community under its own pressure from Germany, which was threatening to break ranks by supporting the more radical schedule for cutting production of ozone-depleting chemicals, the final protocol put a cap on CFCs at 1986 levels for a twelve-month period followed by automatic 20 percent cuts over the next twelve-month period, to be followed in turn by 30 percent cuts later on.

A final irritant, which almost derailed negotiations at the final hour, concerned special concessions demanded by the European Community in order to deal with evolving political and economic relations within the union. The European Community wanted to be treated as a single political unit under the protocols, but other countries were concerned that this would allow reductions planned in one country to be offset by increases in another. As Winfried Lang, the Austrian chair of the Montreal conference, noted, "the aggregated accounting for EC consumption enables individual states to lag behind in their [treaty] obligations to the extent that other EC states undertake their reductions more rapidly than required by the Protocol."[26] The United States indicated that it would not sign a treaty that gave some states the advantage of membership in a convention without having to abide by its rules in the same way as other states. Compromise was achieved when New Zealand's environment minister, Philip Woolaston, suggested that the protocol allow EC members to be treated as a single unit for the purposes of consumption but not of production, provided that all members of the community plus the European Community itself become parties to the protocol. This formula neatly addressed both sets of concerns and thus broke the bargaining impasse.

As Edward Parsons notes of the Montreal Protocol negotiations,

> it was not science, but bargaining that determined the decisions adopted in Montreal. The 50 percent cut that was agreed had no particular scientific prominence. Indeed, the distribution of expert opinion at the time seemed

strongly divided; either much more, or much less stringent controls were warranted, depending on your point of view of the then-partial Antarctic evidence. The Wurzburg workshop had provided a strong scientific push away from the freeze-only position, but the 50 percent cut was essentially a bargained outcome between the EC's proposed freeze and the US's 95 percent cuts. On the vexed question of controlling production or consumption, it was agreed to do both.[27]

More New Findings

New scientific data soon revealed that the Montreal Protocol, in its existing form, was inadequate to protect the ozone layer. On September 30, 1987, just two weeks after the signing of the Montreal Protocol, a NASA-NOAA (National Oceanic and Atmospheric Administration) team released an interim report based on findings from their Antarctic expedition, which revealed that ozone depletion over Antarctica was much worse than had been earlier noted by British scientists.

On March 15, 1988, the Ozone Trends Panel (which had been set up in October 1986 by NASA, the NOAA, the U.S. Federal Aviation Administration, the WMO, and UNEP and cosponsored by the Federal Republic of Germany and the European Commission, involving more than one hundred scientists from ten countries) released its final report. This panel had reevaluated ground-based and satellite data to determine if they would support modeled predictions. It concluded that "there is undisputed observational evidence that the atmospheric concentrations of source gases important in controlling stratospheric ozone levels . . . continue to increase on a global scale because of human activities." The scientists also reached a consensus that "global emissions of CFCs and halons need to be reduced in excess of 85 percent to arrest the depletion of the ozone layer."[28] Under the phaseout schedule of the Montreal Protocol, the ozone layer would continue to suffer significant depletion unless more drastic reductions were undertaken.

The Ozone Trends Panel report led to new calls for the elimination of ozone-harming substances. Du Pont announced that it would phase out its production of CFCs by the end of the century and accelerate research into substitutes. In September, EPA administrator Lee Thomas called for the complete elimination of CFCs, halons, and methyl chloroform (MCs), an industrial solvent, and in December 1987 the EPA proposed new regulations that were in accordance with the Montreal Protocol. In February 1988, the congressional Office of Technology Assessment (OTA) issued a study on the potential impacts of the protocol on global CFC and halon production and consumption, noting that if every nation signed the treaty, CFC and halon consumption could decline by as much as 45 percent by the year 2009, but if only the original signatories complied, consumption might actually increase by 20 percent.[29]

Given these and other findings, many environmental groups called for renegotiating the protocol. However, UNEP's first priority was to get as many countries as possible to sign and ratify the protocol before tightening its provisions.[30] Some countries, however, facing strong domestic pressure, decided that they would actually move ahead of the provisions in the protocol. In the summer of 1988, the Federal German Republic announced that it would unilaterally move to a 95 percent reduction of CFCs and halons. They also called for the protocol to be revised to achieve 85 percent reductions by 1995. The British government, in a striking departure from its previous policies, announced that it would accelerate its own schedule for achieving reductions and would press the European Community to accelerate the Montreal timetable and enact an 85 percent reduction as soon as possible. The change came about partly because the United Kingdom's Stratospheric Ozone Review Group concluded from its own review of the Ozone Trends Panel report that reductions under the Montreal Protocol would be inadequate to halt the depletion of the ozone layer. At the same time, Margaret Thatcher's government found itself under increasing pressure from environmental groups to adopt more progressive environmental policies. With the change in policy, Britain announced that it would host an international ministerial meeting, in March 1989, to address the problems of ozone depletion and climate change.

North-South Issues

In March 1989 the London Conference on Saving the Ozone Layer was hosted by the United Kingdom, with some 123 countries in attendance. This conference underscored that the rate of ozone depletion was far more rapid than earlier thought and produced a consensus that the ultimate objective had to be the elimination of the production and consumption of CFCs and halons. The conference also stressed the link between the depletion of the ozone layer and global warming and the special threat climate change presents for low-lying countries. The conference spurred the pace of government ratifications, adding another eighteen countries to the treaty by the end of 1989, including fourteen developing countries. At the same time, the conference underscored North-South divisions and the serious problems confronting developing countries under the terms of the protocol. Many developing countries called for promises of financial aid and technology transfer from the North to help them develop substitutes for products and industrial processes reliant on CFCs. Many of them also expressed concern that substitutes would be too expensive or would not be available soon enough.

These issues were taken up at Helsinki the following year. In May 1989, eighty-six countries, comprising the thirty-six initial parties to the Montreal Protocol and fifty countries attending as observers, met at a UNEP-sponsored forum in Helsinki. The meeting was significant in several respects. First, in a nonbinding document, the parties pledged to eliminate production of CFCs and other chemicals that threaten the ozone shield by the year 2000.[31] This commitment went well beyond the Montreal Protocol. Second, the accord called for industrial countries to create a special United Nations fund to help developing countries industrialize without CFCs, and a working group was established to work out the details of this fund. Norway's environment minister pledged 0.1 percent of his country's gross national product to this fund if other countries would agree to follow suit. Third, the parties agreed that developing countries could not increase exports of CFCs under the treaty's provisions, which allowed countries with low levels of CFC consumption to expand their use of controlled substances to meet domestic needs. The meeting endorsed the establishment of four panels for scientific, environmental, technical, and economic assessment. These panels would report to an "open-minded working group," which would prepare draft proposals for any amendments to the Montreal Protocol and develop any work plans called for by the Protocol.[32]

Finally, the meeting dealt with the difficult issues of reporting and compliance with the treaty. Under the terms of the agreement, each party would be required to report its annual production, import, and export of each controlled substance. However, the parties submitting data on controlled substances would receive a guarantee that the data would be treated confidentially. In preparing reports on controlled substances, it was agreed that the secretariat "shall aggregate data from several parties in such a way as to ensure that the data from parties deemed confidential is not disclosed."[33] This was intended to address the concerns of those countries worried about unrestricted access to national data from other countries or by nongovernmental groups. However, national data would be available for examination by other countries on a confidential basis.

The reports of the four panels to the Open-Ended Working Group provided the basis for subsequent negotiations on revising the Montreal Protocol. These recommendations were contained in the *Synthesis Report*, which argued on the basis of new scientific studies that CFCs, along with other chlorine-based substances (carbon tetrachlorine and methyl chloroform), would have to be eliminated even earlier than anticipated to alleviate growing stresses on the ozone layer.[34] The report stressed the urgency of phasing out all ozone-depleting substances and the need to develop substitutes as soon as possible. Although the chemical industry warned that the costs of phasing out these chemicals would be high, especially for manufacturers who would have to redesign or scrap their old equipment in order to make the switch, the main point of contention concerned the schedule for phasing out carbon tetrachlorines (CTs) and methyl chloroforms (MCs). This was because industry was increasingly substituting these chemicals in production processes for CFCs. Environmentalists warned that failure to regulate MCs and CTs would lead to rapid increase in the use of these chemicals. Industry argued that the phaseout of these chemicals would lead to plant closures and shutdowns. These and other issues were taken up during meetings of the Open-Ended Working Group for eventual consideration at the June 1990 meeting in London, to decide on revisions to the 1987 Montreal Protocol.[35]

The other main issue taken up by the working group concerned the question of assistance to developing countries in making the conversion to new non-CFC-based technologies. Although most developing countries were low on the scale of both consumption and production of CFCs, they were concerned that rapid phaseout might impose undue burdens on their economies, particularly if they were forced to import high-priced substitutes or use costlier products in their own industry. However, nonparticipation in the CFC regime by developing countries could delay rehabilitation of the ozone layer, especially since some countries, like China, were experiencing rapid rates of growth in CFC consumption. Developing countries, led by Mexico and Venezuela (who were parties to the Montreal Protocol) and China and India (who were not), pressed for the establishment of a multilateral trust fund within UNEP to help them with the costs of compliance with the protocol. Such a fund would be financed by industrial countries and would come from new funds and not out of existing aid flows (in keeping with the principle of additionality). Developing countries would also be guaranteed free access to ozone-friendly technologies. Initial costs for such a fund were estimated to be $400 million annually over a ten-year period.

Although the United States balked at the proposal, preferring to create the multilateral fund out of existing aid contributions, it came under strong pressure from Japan and the European Community, who felt that the fund should be financed out of new contributions. The Bush administration also came under intense pressure from its own domestic critics (particularly Congress, which began to prepare its own separate legislation for U.S. assistance), who felt that it was in the United States' self-interest to assist developing countries in a worldwide effort to protect the ozone layer.[36] Once the United States had accepted the principle of additionality, it was agreed that the fund would be jointly administered by the World Bank, the United Nations Development Programme (UNDP), and UNEP, although the issue of mandatory, as opposed to voluntary, national contributions to the fund, and at what level, remained unresolved.

When the London meeting convened, the unresolved issues on the negotiating table were: (1) the timing and phaseout of CFCs, halons, CTs, MCs, and hydrochlorofluorocarbons (HCFCs); (2) the actual mechanisms and voting procedures for a fund to help developing countries; (3) voting procedures for future changes to the protocol; and (4) procedures to deal with noncompliance, especially as regards new amendments to the protocol. Each of these issues was marked by a different constellation of actors, coalitions, and interests, sometimes across industrial, sometimes across North-South, lines. On some issues compromise was achieved by simply splitting the difference between competing interests and points of view. On others, recognition of certain principles of equity and fairness helped bridge key differences and produce agreement. Still others required ingenuity in crafting new formulas that redefined core issues and thus broke bargaining impasses. According to Richard Benedick, the story unfolded this way.

CFCs and Halons. At the outset of the London Conference, Japan, the Soviet Union, and the United States were the strongest supporters of a compromise proposal, engineered by Mostafa Tolba, calling for a CFC freeze and gradual reductions (20 percent by 1993; 85 percent by 1997) leading to a total CFC phaseout by the year 2000 (the reduction schedule, but no freeze, would apply to "new" CFCs not previously covered by the Montreal Protocol); and a 1992 freeze on halons, with phaseout by the year 2000. In contrast, Australia, Austria, Canada, New Zealand, the Nordic countries, and Switzerland favored a more rapid phaseout schedule and tighter controls. The final agreement settled on a 50 percent reduction by 1995; 85 percent by 1997; and total phaseout by the year 2000. However, thirteen countries, including the Federal Republic of Germany, Belgium, Denmark, and the Netherlands from the European Community, committed themselves to phasing out CFCs by 1997.

Other Chemicals. Under a compromise formula, again worked out by Mostafa Tolba, phaseout of MCs would follow a freeze in 1993 and cuts of 30 percent in 1995, and 50 percent in the year 2000. The same coalition of smaller industrial countries, however, joined by the Federal Republic of Germany and the Soviet Union, pressed for an accelerated timetable (85 percent reductions by the year 2000). Although the solvents industry was strongly opposed to reductions, the passage by Congress of the Clean Air Act, which included an accelerated schedule for MC phaseout, made U.S. industry more supportive of an international agreement that would subject its international competitors to similar tough regulations. Norway and the smaller industrial countries also put pressure on the United States by withholding approval for the U.S. position on a new ozone fund in order to secure U.S. support for stronger controls. The European Community (which was held up by British opposition to stricter controls) was brought on board by U.S. willingness to no longer "oppose an EC amendment that would allow the Community members to transfer production facilities for controlled substances within the New European single market." Japan also agreed to the new consensus.[37] Agreement on tougher controls covering HCFCs was not achieved because of EC opposition.

Developing Countries. The London meeting led to the establishment of an ozone fund that would be located in Montreal.[38] The initial fund, based on voluntary contributions, would be between $160 million and $240 million for the first three years of its operations, depending upon which developing countries would become parties to the protocol during that period. The executive committee of the fund would be comprised of seven representatives from each donor and developing country. Although there was some wrangling between North and South over decision-making procedures for the fund, the final compromise allowed for voting rules based on consensus or, failing that, a two-thirds majority, including a majority of each group of seven, giving both donors and recipients a veto. At U.S. insistence, the amendment specifically states that the financial mechanism is "without prejudice to any future arrangements . . . with respect to other environmental issues."[39]

The issue of technology access and linkage to the protocol was far more contentious. As Benedick explains:

> The problem was that both sides wanted ironclad guarantees. . . . Developing countries wanted to build into the protocol an assurance that, if they did not receive sufficient financial and technical help, they would not be obligated to implement the reduction schedules. For their part, industrialized nations recognized the reality of a linkage between external aid and the capability to renounce usage of CFCs and the other substances. But the donor countries would agree neither to a blank check nor to a situation in which any party could unilaterally claim that it had received insufficient aid and therefore would not fulfill treaty obligations. Underlying the debate was a difference in degree of confidence in the ability of the international market mechanism to transfer modern technology fairly and efficiently.[40]

India led the developing countries in demanding advance commitments from industrial countries for technology transfer on favorable terms. She was supported in her demands by other developing countries, including

Brazil and China. Under the terms of the Indian proposal, developing countries would have the right to withdraw unilaterally from their treaty commitments if they felt they had not received adequate financial and technological assistance from industrial countries. However, with Mexico serving as a mediator, some Latin American countries, along with Ghana, pressed the view that developing countries would be able to achieve access to new technologies via the market and that the language of the treaty calling for industrial countries "to take every practical step . . . to ensure that the best available, environmentally safe substitutes and related technologies are expeditiously transferred . . . under fair and favorable conditions" was adequate.[41]

In turn, developing countries would be expected to fulfill their treaty obligations subject to the "effective implementation" of the financial mechanisms and technology transfer. A country could notify the secretariat if it could not comply with the control measures, and the matter would be decided by the parties according to established voting procedures, but no sanctions or penalties would be imposed against the country in the interim. As Benedick concludes, "the parties and nonparties to the Montreal Protocol had accomplished far more than significantly strengthening controls over ozone-depleting substances: they had created a financial mechanism dedicated to the protection of the global environment, and, for the first time, the governments of industrialized countries had accepted a responsibility to help developing countries with modern technology.[42]

Explaining Outcomes

The story of the ozone accords is one of a complex interplay of variables, each of which exercised a decisive influence on negotiations at different phases or stages of the negotiation process.

Crisis

During the prenegotiation phase of the ozone diplomacy, a growing sense of crisis, accompanied by what Morrisette calls the "dread factor," pushed the ozone issue to the forefront of the environmental agenda. At first, it was feared that high-flying supersonic transport might damage the ozone layer. But as a result of further research, scientists then postulated a link between CFCs (widely used in aerosols and refrigerants) and stratospheric ozone depletion. Even before scientists had reached definitive conclusions about CFCs (and well before there was concrete scientific evidence), the public clamor for controls on aerosols and other ozone-harming substances had already prompted action from policy makers. Underlying the public outcry were fundamental concerns about human health and the perceived link between ozone depletion and increased risks of skin cancer and cataracts. In response to consumer pressures to "ban the can," industry also began to develop substitutes for CFCs.

What began as a national sense of crisis in the United States, Canada, and Scandinavian countries soon blossomed into an international one, as scientists in other countries began work on the ozone problem and a transnational scientific and public movement to ban CFCs emerged. In this respect, the ozone crisis had an integrative impact on international cooperation, and formal negotiations began when UNEP convened an ad hoc working group of experts to lay the foundations for a global convention to protect the ozone layer. These efforts culminated in the Vienna Convention, which was followed by the Montreal Protocol negotiations to implement controls on CFCs and other ozone-harming chemicals. Although the 1985 discovery of the hole in the ozone layer over Antarctica was treated cautiously by negotiators, there can be little doubt that it crystallized public fears about the harmful effects of CFCs on the ozone layer and gave added impetus to negotiations.

Consensual Knowledge

The scientific community and a growing consensus about the CFC-ozone link played a key role in negotiations, making it increasingly difficult for those who opposed action to "hide behind scientific dissent." This transnational scientific consensus did not emerge automatically but was carefully fostered by the UNEP and the United States and other countries, who commissioned expert reports at key junctures in the negotiations to persuade holdout countries of the need for controls. Thus, in both the prenegotiation and negotiation phases, science helped develop an international consensus about the nature of the problem and the need for controls. However, science could not solve thorny questions about what chemicals to include in the protocols, how they should be controlled (i.e., by consumption or production strategies or some combination of the two), the timing and size of cutbacks, and the treatment of developing countries with low (but growing) levels of CFC consumption. Different regulatory options had different distributional consequences (both economic and social) for each country and each set of interests.

At the heart of the ozone debate also lay fundamental questions of equity, fairness, and distribution. Clearly, these debates could not be resolved by science alone, nor could any one country impose its own preferred solution, since no single country (or coalition) controlled a sufficient share of CFC production. Moreover, even those countries with relatively weak political influence, like some of the developing countries, had an important negative veto over negotiations and the future of the ozone convention. By threatening not to participate in the convention, they could effectively wipe out any gains from cutbacks achieved by the advanced industrial countries. This point was not lost on the industrial countries and was one of the reasons why they finally agreed to a financial and technology transfer mechanism to help developing countries cope with the costs of transition to a new regulatory regime.

Representation

Bargaining in the successive rounds of negotiations leading to the ozone accords was facilitated by the formation of three distinct coalitions: the Toronto Group, led by the United States, who favored swift international measures to combat ozone depletion; the European Community, led by the presidential troika of Belgium, Denmark, and the United Kingdom, and Japan, who were initially not predisposed to strict controls; and the developing countries, led by Mexico and Brazil, which joined negotiations when it became apparent that the Montreal Protocol would have far-reaching implications for their own economic health and future.

Bridging and Bargaining Strategies

The success of negotiations in developing an international regulatory framework to protect the ozone layer depended upon political leadership and the development of a series of bridging proposals, which first addressed outstanding differences between the United States and the Toronto Group countries and the European Community and Japan, and subsequently the concerns of developing countries vis-à-vis the industrial world. No single country or individual was responsible for devising formulas and breaking bargaining impasses. Rather, different actors intervened at different points in the negotiation, offering compromises and bridging solutions to outstanding issues. On the key issue of whether to restrict production or consumption of controlled substances, which pitted the European Community against the Toronto Group countries, agreement was eventually achieved through a compromise, based on the simple principles of equity and fairness, that eliminated the possibility of special advantages being conferred on any one side. This formula was devised by the United States in collaboration with its Toronto Group partners.

When negotiations were in danger of being derailed at the eleventh hour by EC demands to be treated as a single unit in the Montreal Protocol, New Zealand's environment minister stepped in with a compromise solution that satisfied competing interests. During the London negotiations, Mexico also played a crucial mediation role, not only in representing developing country interests but also in creating support for a compromise financial and technology transfer proposal being offered by the industrial countries. Finally, the decision by the Federal Republic of Germany to opt for a stricter regulatory regime on a number of key issues facilitated bargaining processes by creating a crosscutting coalition, which made the interests of the European Community and the Toronto Group overlap.

Issue Decomposition and Sequencing

Incremental bargaining strategies and issue decomposition and sequencing tactics were also crucial ingredients in paving the road to increasingly stringent and comprehensive controls on a wide variety of chemicals. Early agreements, like the Vienna Convention, were vague and open-ended but were structured in such a way as to allow room for continuing negotiations and future controls once there was a firmer scientific basis for undertaking them. So, too, did the Montreal Protocol allow for monitoring and revisions to the protocol in the light of new scientific assessments.

During the difficult round of negotiations leading up to the Montreal Protocol, UNEP's executive director, Mostafa Tolba, worked hard to keep negotiations out of the political limelight in order to prevent grandstanding and allow for greater bargaining flexibility among the participants. Issues were dealt with in separate working groups, although all were eventually incorporated into a single draft negotiating text. Once the advanced industrial countries had signed the Montreal Protocol, the challenge was to secure the agreement and participation of developing countries in the convention and to tighten its provisions. Again, the strategy was to deal with these issues in separate working groups but to incorporate their recommendations into a single document, the *Synthesis Report,* which set out the issues for the 1990 London Conference.

Compliance and Verification

Verification procedures in the Montreal Protocol were weak, and mechanisms to ensure compliance virtually nonexistent. An open-ended, ad hoc working group of legal experts was set up to discuss and develop procedures and institutional mechanisms for determining noncompliance with the protocol and for treatment of parties who failed to comply with its terms. Under the original accords, each party is required to report its annual production, import, and export of each controlled substance to the secretariat. Parties submitting data on controlled substances receive a guarantee that the data will be treated with confidentiality. In preparing reports on controlled substances, the secretariat "shall aggregate data from several parties in such a way as to ensure that the data from parties deemed confidential is not disclosed."[43] This formula essentially places the onus of responsibility on each government to provide reliable data, with no provisions for verifying compliance with the treaty.

During the negotiations, the European Community sought to focus on production limits, on the grounds that they would be easier to verify than consumption limits. (This proposal would have helped protect EC markets from overseas competition.) The United States and other members of the Toronto Group, as noted above, resisted the idea. The compromise formula, based on production-plus-imports-minus-exports, took account of the European Community's concerns about verification, because all three elements of the formula could be measured reliably.

The London amendments extended the data-reporting requirements to other substances, including other halons, and also provided incentives (in the form of financial and technical assistance and feasibility studies to foster compliance) for developing countries to join the regime. An implementation committee was also established to review compliance issues. The committee can receive, consider, and report on submissions made by parties to the secretariat on noncompliance. It is also responsible for preparing reports on national data submitted to the secretariat with the assistance of technical and scientific reports prepared by experts.[44]

Arguably, the lack of strong and effective compliance mechanisms is the Achilles' heel of this regime (as it is with other environmental regimes). Nevertheless, the strengthened monitoring and transparency provisions of the London amendments through closer reviews of national policies can serve as a check on noncompliance through what Alan Beesley calls the instruments of "national embarrassment" or "international odium."[45]

Leadership

Leadership, defined in terms of innovative thinking, inventiveness, and problem-solving skills, was evident throughout the course of negotiations. UNEP's executive director, Mostafa Tolba, obviously played a key leadership role in the negotiations by structuring and shaping the agenda, moving negotiations forward, and inventing novel solutions to what at first glance seemed to be intractable problems. So too did the chair of the Montreal conference, Austrian diplomat Winifried Lang. At the same time, other heads of delegations provided critical input to the negotiations at crucial junctures, including the head of the American delegation, Richard Benedick. Without such leadership, which was exercised by a variety of individuals at different points in the negotiation, it is unlikely that the negotiations would have met the ambitious goals the negotiators set for themselves.

Like some of the other cases of successful negotiation examined in this volume, the ozone accords were the product of a combination of factors. These included growing consensual knowledge in the transnational scientific community about the dangers of ozone depletion, coupled with a looming sense of crisis; support for a new regulatory regime from citizens' groups and industry (support that, in certain key respects, was ahead of scientific opinion); incremental bargaining strategies, leadership, and active scientific input, which sustained the bargaining process once the issues were on the negotiating table; and the identification of resolving formulas based on shared principles of equity, which sought to bring together competing interests—not just along West-West but also along North-South lines—in a fair and balanced manner. The verification issue surfaced early in the negotiations because it had a direct impact on concerns about economic competitiveness. Although initial verification mechanisms in the treaty were weak and compliance mechanisms virtually nonexistent—for which the treaty has been justifiably criticized—subsequent measures have sought to strengthen and improve reporting and verification mechanisms in the treaty. Finally, although scientists played a critical role in these negotiations, the final debates were not so much about science as about ways to satisfy competing interests within the context of a new global regime to protect the ozone layer. In this latter stage, political leadership and distributional considerations played a crucial role in international efforts to strike a new global bargain that would extend the ozone regime to the newly industrializing states of the South.

10 Hazardous Wastes

The problem of hazardous waste shipment from industrial to developing countries began to receive worldwide attention in the 1980s. In a series of highly publicized cases, the world became aware of the potentially lethal consequences of the growing international trade in toxic wastes whereby industrial countries were using developing countries as illicit dumping grounds.

In 1986 the freighter *Khian Sea* carrying a load of highly toxic incinerator residues tried to unload its cargo in the Bahamas where it was refused entry. After several unsuccessful tries at other ports in the Caribbean, the ship crossed the Atlantic for repairs in Yugoslavia where it changed its name to *Felicia*. The captain headed the ship for the Philippines via the Suez Canal trying unsuccessfully to dump his cargo on the way in Sri Lanka and Indonesia. When the ship arrived in Singapore its hold was empty and its name had been changed yet again to the *Pelicano*. Somewhere along the way the ship had surreptitiously disposed of its cargo in spite of denials by the ship's captain.

In 1988 the Italian government commissioned the toxic waste freighter the *Karin-B* to pick up a lethal mixture of toxic wastes which had been secretly dumped in Koko, Nigeria by a group of Italian companies. The Nigerian government jailed those who were responsible and seized an Italian freighter in retaliation until the wastes were removed. The *Karin-B*, filled with her unwelcome cargo, was denied entry to ports in Spain, France, the United Kingdom, the Federal Republic of Germany, and the Netherlands. The Italian government was eventually forced to accept responsibility for the cargo over the objections of protestors and port authorities at Livorno, Italy, who blocked the ship's entry. The ship eventually found anchor off the port of Ravenna.

In the summer of 1988, hundreds of leaking barrels which were found on a wharf in Bangkok were found to contain toxic wastes. They had been sent there from Singapore to non-existent Thai firms.

In 1988 environmental groups discovered that a New York firm was planning to export asbestos to Guatemala on the pretext that it would be recycled to manufacture brakes—even though the material was unfit for brake manufacture.

In 1989 it was revealed that a British company had contracted with the government of Benin to import 5 million tons of European wastes per year to be dumped in a landfill site. The wastes included a rich menu of herbicides, solvents, and other toxins. Such wastes can only be disposed of safely through incineration at very high temperatures.[1]

There were outcries against such waste traffic and more than 100 reported proposals in the 1980s to regulate or ban traffic in hazardous waste from industrial to developing countries. The Organization of African Unity (OAU) unanimously passed a resolution condemning dumping of potentially hazardous wastes on African soil. The European Parliament passed a resolution condemning all significant exports of hazardous wastes from the European Community to any country with a developing economy. In addition, legislation was introduced in the U.S. Congress that would prohibit the export of any waste, with the exception of certain recyclable materials, unless a special permit (export license) were granted stipulating that the waste would be disposed of as if it were in the United States. Many individual countries also restricted or prohibited imports of waste or hazardous waste. By 1989 some forty countries had declared their territories off limits to foreign wastes.

This chapter traces the negotiating history of the efforts by UNEP to develop a global Convention on the Control of Transboundary Movements of Hazardous Wastes and Their Disposal, which was adopted in Basel, Switzerland, on March 22, 1989. Although the convention did not ban international traffic in hazardous wastes, it contained measures for the identification, notification, and control of movements of certain wastes. The convention also declared that transboundary movement of such wastes should also be minimized and that the disposal of these wastes be performed so that humanity and the environment will be protected from "the adverse effects which may result from such wastes."[2]

Unlike the other environmental cases examined in this volume, negotiations did not come to the table as a result of the efforts of scientists to shape the prenegotiation agenda. Although a number of environmental nongovernmental organizations, like Greenpeace International, were instrumental in publicizing the dangers of international traffic in hazardous wastes, the international scientific community did not play a key role, since the dangers and health risks associated with hazardous waste shipments were generally well understood. Negotiations to address the problem began as the result of the intense lobbying efforts of a coalition of environmental nongovernmental organizations and developing countries led by the African states, which had been the most recent victims of illicit trade in hazardous wastes. At the same time, the issue began to receive attention within the OECD and the European Community, and independent initiatives were undertaken in these bodies to develop regulatory measures to control the shipment and disposal of hazardous wastes.

Once formal negotiations began under UNEP auspices, it played a crucial role in spearheading and shaping the negotiating agenda. In particular, UNEP Executive Director Mostafa Tolba assumed a direct and crucial role in the negotiations, helping to push the negotiations through to their conclusion. Negotiations took place primarily between two major contending coalitions: the advanced industrial or OECD bloc of countries, which represented one set of interests, and developing countries of the Group of 77 (a group of less developed countries that formed a coalition in the 1970s to advance their collective interests on trade and economic interests), which represented the other. The key issues in the negotiations concerned developing countries' demands for strict controls on hazardous waste shipments and an international regime that would address their distributional concerns versus industrial countries' desire for a somewhat looser set of international arrangements that would not create unnecessary obstacles to international trade and would be relatively easy to administer. Much of the discussion centered on these core issues, and both sides drove as hard a bargain as they could. Agreement was reached by moving discussions into informal working groups that worked out of the political spotlight, with many of the key bargains struck at the eleventh hour under the pressures of the final conference deadline. Leadership by the conference chair was also crucial to the negotiating process and helped to move the negotiations forward, although some critics argue that the arbitrary decision-making procedures adopted by the chair undermined the possibility of negotiating a fairer and ultimately sounder agreement.

Prenegotiation

Arguably, the prenegotiation phase of the Basel Convention began with Principle 21 of the Declaration of the United Nations Conference on the Human Environment in 1972, which states that each country has "the responsibility to ensure that activities within . . . [its own] jurisdiction or control . . . [do] not cause damage to the environment of other States or of areas beyond the limits of national jurisdiction." This was the first time that the international community formally recognized that extraterritorial waste disposal should be conducted safely.

The more immediate precursors to the Basel Convention were the efforts by the many OECD countries in the early 1980s to adopt regulatory measures to enable government authorities to monitor the management of hazardous wastes. It soon became evident that national monitoring mechanisms were not adequate to deal with transfrontier movements, since countries did not have sufficient information about wastes being imported into their territory. In the autumn of 1982, the Waste Management Policy Group of the OECD proposed that guidelines be developed for the export and import of hazardous wastes. On February 1, 1984, the OECD Council, the governing body of the OECD, decided that "member countries shall control the transfrontier movements of hazardous wastes and, for this purpose, shall ensure that the competent authorities of the countries concerned are provided with adequate and timely information concerning such movements."[3] The council also recommended a comprehensive set of guiding principles concerning such control to its member country governments. With the assistance of the Swiss government, the council's seminar, the Legal and Institutional Aspects of Transfrontier Movements of Hazardous Wastes, met in Paris, June 12–14, 1984.

In March 1985, the OECD environment ministers, the EC commissioner responsible for environmental matters, and senior policy officials participated in the Conference on International Cooperation concerning Transfrontier Movements of Hazardous Wastes, hosted by Switzerland in Basel. Also attending were representatives of UNEP, the World Health Organization, the Council of Europe, and representatives of various nongovernmental organizations. The conference reaffirmed that the basic principles for the management of wastes (including hazardous wastes) must be, first, to prevent and reduce, as far as possible, the generation of wastes; and second, to increase the proportion of waste that is recycled or reused in order to reduce its hazardous character. It also recommended that OECD countries should establish appropriate disposal facilities for the management of hazardous waste at the national level in order to reduce the need for transfrontier shipments of such waste. The conference recommended that an effective international system for the control of transfrontier movements of hazardous waste should be developed by the OECD and that this system should address issues concerning the definition and classification of hazardous waste; notification, identification, and control procedures; common technical standards for management and control; relations with non-OECD countries; and legal and regulatory frameworks.[4]

At the OECD Environment Committee meeting in June 1985, governments declared their intention to "strengthen control of the generation and disposal of hazardous wastes and establish an effective and legally binding system of control of their transfrontier movements, including movements to non-member countries."[5] This declaration was transformed into an action program by the OECD Council, which instructed the Environment Committee to undertake the necessary work to implement the resolution. For the next three years, the Environment Committee would work intensively on this problem, its efforts paralleling those of UNEP and the European Community.

In adopting a series of directives aimed at monitoring and controlling transfrontier shipment of hazardous waste, the European Community collaborated closely with the OECD, electing to adapt certain results achieved in the OECD to EC needs and requirements. Thus, a directive on the supervision and control within the European Community of the transfrontier shipment of hazardous waste, which was adopted by the European Community in December 1984, largely transposed the principles included in the OECD Council decision-recommendation into a legally binding form for use within the European Community. Further directives providing details of precisely how the notification of transfrontier shipments of hazardous waste should occur and conditions governing controls of exports of hazardous waste from the European Community area closely resembled earlier OECD counterpart recommendations.[6]

In 1987, UNEP established the Cairo Guidelines and Principles for the Environmentally Sound Management of Hazardous Wastes to assist countries in developing policies for the environmentally sound management of hazardous wastes. These guidelines did not provide for specific binding regulations on the transboundary shipment and disposal of hazardous wastes. However, the governing council of UNEP also authorized the executive director to prepare a global convention to regulate transboundary shipment of hazardous wastes. This decision marked the launch of formal negotiations on a global Convention on the Control of Transboundary Movements of Hazardous Wastes and Their Disposal. The governing council also approved the London Guidelines, designed to increase chemical safety by achieving an information exchange on the shipment of chemicals from one country to another. UNEP's International Register of Potentially Toxic Chemicals was the designated focal point for the exchange of information called for under the guidelines, but countries were also asked to exchange information directly concerning the shipment of chemicals or other toxic substances. The general procedures of the guidelines stated that participating countries "taking measures to regulate chemicals with a view to protecting human, animal or plant life or health, or the environment, should ensure that regulations and standards for this purpose do not create unnecessary obstacles to international trade."[7]

At the meeting of the governing council, a coalition of African countries headed by Senegal, Ghana, and Kenya, backed by a coalition of nongovernmental lobbying organizations (the most vocal being the Pesticides Action Network, an adversary of chemical industries; the International

Baby Food Action Network, which led the international boycott of Nestlé; and the International Federation of Consumers' Federations, based in Kuala Lumpur, Malaysia) forced through a resolution on the question of "prior informed consent," which would give importing countries the right to refuse shipments of potentially toxic chemicals from developed countries. The resolution also called on countries to develop systems and alternative procedures with respect to banned systems and alternative procedures with respect to banned or severely restricted chemicals and to step up North-South information exchange and financial assistance for developing countries.[8]

This issue quickly became a major point of contention. Western countries, with the exception of the Netherlands, which supported the viewpoint of developing countries, strongly opposed the principle of prior consent on the grounds that most developing countries lacked the infrastructure to handle the consultation procedures that would be required, and that such action would strangle the free flow of chemicals from North to South (which was obviously the intention).

Negotiations

Under the auspices of UNEP, the first meeting to prepare the global Convention on the Control of the Transboundary Movements of Hazardous Wastes and Their Disposal was hosted by the government of Hungary and held in Budapest on October 17–29, 1987.[9] This meeting was attended by fifty-two experts representing twenty-five countries and twelve international and nongovernmental organizations. The report of the meeting laid the foundations for preparation of a draft convention to be submitted by the UNEP secretariat to the working group at its first session, scheduled for February 1988 in Geneva, Switzerland. The report underscored the fact that while virtually all governments agreed that there should be a convention on hazardous wastes, there was fundamental disagreement on whether the treaty should be general in character, leaving technical issues to future protocols or to bilateral and regional accords, or should contain comprehensive and detailed controls. UNEP was urged to draft a convention that would build on the experience of the OECD and the European Community. It was also evident that there were major differences about how to define hazardous wastes and whether the treaty should try to define a hazardous waste or refer to it simply as being defined by national legislation. The matter of whether there ought to be a written prior consent procedure between the exporting and the importing countries and whether this principle should be extended to transit countries was also marked by differences of opinion between industrial and developing countries.

Five rounds of negotiations were held, in Geneva, Switzerland, February 1–5, 1988; Caracas, Venezuela, June 6–10, 1988; Geneva, Switzerland, November 7–16, 1988; Luxembourg, January 30–February 3, 1989; and Basel, Switzerland, March 20–22, 1989.

The February working group chaired by Alain Clerc, head of the International Organizations Division of the Swiss Federal Department for the Environment, worked on a draft twenty-five-article text. The text covered such issues as wastes and their definition; responsibilities of exporting, importing, and transit countries; notification procedures; and the rights of countries to refuse entry and to reimport wastes. The meeting addressed a number of key issues, including the question of "prior informed consent" under which both the nation accepting the shipment of wastes and the country shipping them have to agree before a shipment can be made.[10] Developing countries were insistent that the principle of prior consent be included in the proposed treaty.[11] It remained open to question how a transit country would handle such permissions and whether it would have the right to require its written consent before a shipment of hazardous wastes crosses its territory. A proposal that every state has the right to refuse shipment of hazardous wastes into its territory was deleted from the text. The question of whether exporters should have the obligation to receive hazardous wastes back into their territory was also a matter of continuing discussion.

On the definition of hazardous wastes, the meeting agreed to the European Community's definition that "wastes are substances and objects which the holder disposes of, intends to dispose of, or is required to dispose of by the provisions of national law."[12] However, the United States wanted the term "holder" to be defined more precisely. This issue was contentious, because few countries other than the industrial country members of the OECD have precise national legislation on the subject. It was decided to consider the OECD's "core list" of hazardous wastes at the next meeting.

Another hot topic was the issue of disposal and how and where disposal should be handled. Final disposal of wastes was defined to include both reprocessing wastes and disposing of them "definitively" through burial at sea, incineration, or other "terminal processes."[13]

The next session was held in Caracas, Venezuela, June 6–10, 1988, and was attended by experts from forty countries, twenty-one of whom were developing countries. The key issues were once again definition of hazardous wastes, disposal, and verification procedures for importing and transit countries. The growing urgency of the problem at hand was underscored by evidence received by UNEP of ongoing or planned practices, and malpractices, concerning transfrontier shipment and disposal of hazardous wastes. Nigeria had charged in early June that some Italian industrial waste that had been dumped in the country was radioactive and threatened to execute fifteen persons who were arrested following seizure of the ship that allegedly dumped the waste (see above). The African state of Guinea-Bissau had called on Norway to remove 15,000 tons of unidentified industrial waste that had been dumped on an island off the capital city of Kassa. There were also reports that the Congo, Togo, Chad, and Guineau-Bissau had been recipients of toxic waste in Africa, and that Brazil, Argentina, Guyana, Venezuela, Peru, and Mexico had been recipients of toxic waste in Latin America.[14]

UNEP Executive Director Mostafa Tolba highlighted four sets of issues that had been brought to the attention of the secretariat:

- *Definition of hazardous wastes.* In some instances, wastes not defined as hazardous in legislation of exporting countries appeared to be hazardous under the conditions they had been transported and disposed of in developing countries that had no national legislation dealing with hazardous wastes. If the definition of hazardous wastes relied on the existing national definitions of exporting countries, it would not necessarily address this problem.
- *Assessment capacity of developing countries.* Some developing countries do not have the capacity to ascertain the true nature of the substances being sent to them for disposal. The rights of these countries to receive proper information and mechanisms to ensure that they have the technical and knowledge-based capacity should be considered.
- *Responsibility for environmentally sound disposal.* Recent cases demonstrated that hazardous wastes shipped to developing countries are often not treated or disposed of properly because of poor institutional and receiving capacities in the receiving country. Tolba suggested that industrial countries should be assigned responsibility not to begin shipment until disposal sites and technical capacities in the importing country had been assessed. However, importing countries might be loathe to have their own internal disposal assessments called into question.
- *Illegal disposal.* Tolba asked the group to consider the growing problem of traffic in contravention of national legislation and traffic not carried out in compliance with internationally accepted guidelines and principles and whether specific penalties governing illegal movement of hazardous wastes should be included in the convention.[15]

The meeting agreed to base the definition of hazardous wastes on a core list of some forty-four categories and substances that had been approved in May by the OECD group working on international waste shipment. It was also agreed that the definition would not include nuclear waste, which falls under the jurisdiction of the International Atomic Energy Agency. However, there was no agreement on the actual definition of a hazardous waste.

There was general agreement on the requirement of advance notification of transboundary shipment of hazardous wastes to countries of import and transit, on the establishment of a prior-informed-consent mechanism for importing countries, and on the responsibility of the exporting country to reimport wastes when shipment could not be completed as foreseen. However, the question of a prior-informed-consent mechanism for transit countries was not resolved. The group also decided on the establishment of a mechanism, in the form of a secretariat to the proposed convention, for information exchange, technical assistance, training, monitoring and control, emergency response in case of accident, and transfer of technology. The United States and other industrial countries were not opposed to the concept of a secretariat but were unwilling to make commitments to finance such an institution. The secretariat would also have enforcement powers, but the United States expressed reservations about giving the secretariat too much investigative authority, and developing countries made it clear that they did not want to have a U.N. police force to check on their disposal of hazardous waste.[16]

The issue of third parties in the shipment of wastes was also a major point of continuing controversy. The United States changed its position on the concept of prior informed consent, suggesting that a third country should have a certain period of time, for example, fifteen days, to express its objections to a shipment passing through it. If it objected, then a shipper and consignee would have to make new arrangements; if the allotted time period passed without any objections being raised, the shipment would be allowed to proceed. Developing countries challenged this position. While accepting the idea of a time limit, they took the view that if a country did not reply to the transit within the allowed time period, it would be assumed that it had objections to the shipment. The principle was of particular concern to island countries, such as those in the Caribbean, which claimed that their territorial waters are part of their national territory and that ships carrying toxic wastes should not be able to transit those waters without their express permission.

Developing countries also demanded a technology transfer mechanism in the convention that would help them acquire the necessary technology from industrial countries to build hazardous waste disposal plants. Senegal was at the forefront of demands for such a mechanism, which would include the sharing of recycling technologies; Japan and the United States, which have highly developed recycling laws, were strongly opposed to the inclusion of recycling technologies in the convention, arguing that present legislation is more than adequate.

Fundamental differences were also emerging between the accords governing the transport of hazardous wastes being finalized by the OECD and those of UNEP. At meetings of the Waste Management Policy Group on October 3–6 in Paris, the OECD reached near agreement on provisions governing formal notification of hazardous waste shipments involving OECD members. Central to those proposed agreements were the requirement that exporting, importing, and transit countries be notified about all shipments of hazardous wastes and according to a strict timetable. If notification was by mail, responses would have to be made within fifteen days of receipt allowing an additional fifteen days for reply for a total of thirty days. If notification took place by courier, the response would be required within fifteen days after receipt, allowing three days for courier time for a total of eighteen. If notification was by telex, telecopy, or other electronic mail, the response would have to be within fifteen days of receipt, allowing one day for transmission. Thus, whereas UNEP after the Caracas conference was moving toward a more embracing concept of prior consent because of pressure from developing countries, the OECD was moving toward a more streamlined approach based on tacit consent procedures. Under the UNEP proposal, the shipper would be required to notify each transit country and could not proceed until receiving approval. The problem with this provision for industrial countries was that there are literally thousands of transborder shipments each week (for example, a truck with twenty tons of waste crosses a European border every five minutes), and the administrative requirements of such a system would be unwieldy, if not unworkable.[17]

The summer of 1988 was marked by growing interest, particularly among African states, in the issue of hazardous waste dumping. A resolution of the Interparliamentary Conference on Health of the Organization of African Unity appealed to African states "to continue tirelessly their efforts at the national and international levels in order to prevent the African continent from becoming a dumping ground for industrial, radioactive, and toxic wastes" and to industrial countries "to take immediate measures aimed at preventing companies located within their borders from dumping such wastes in Africa."[18]

A fourth draft of a Convention on the Control of Transboundary Movement of Hazardous Wastes and Their Disposal, consisting of twenty-nine articles and five annexes, one of which contained a list of wastes to be controlled under the convention, was examined in Geneva from November 7 to 18, 1988. The draft treaty was heavily bracketed, reflecting divergent points of view among the delegates representing some fifty states. General obligations under Article IV of the draft convention were expanded and strengthened. It was agreed that exporters of hazardous wastes have an obligation to take back a shipment if the arrangement with the consenting country falls through for whatever reason. An exporter's notification to an importer must state that wastes are being shipped and in sufficient detail so that the importing country and any transit country can assess what the effects of the movement of the waste are on local health. The concept of limited ban was also accepted, whereby no contracting party to the treaty may export or import hazardous waste to or from a country that has not ratified the treaty. It was also agreed that only signatories would benefit from the technical assistance, training, and technology exchange provided for by the treaty.

There was also some progress on the principle of prior informed consent as a result of the first experts meeting on the subject, held in Dakar on September 19–23, 1988, hosted by Senegal with financial assistance from the Netherlands, Norway, Sweden, Switzerland, and the European Community Commission. Some twenty governments (half industrial, half developing countries) participated in the meeting. A second meeting was held on November 2–3 in Geneva along with NGO, UNEP, and FAO representatives. The participants accepted a corollary to the question of prior informed consent that no hazardous waste could move until the recipient country put in writing its willingness to accept the shipment. It was also agreed that transit countries should enjoy the same advance information on shipments of hazardous waste passing through their territory. However, agreement could not be reached on the meaning of tacit consent of the transit country. Industrial countries argued that a transit country's failure to say either "yes" or "no" implied tacit consent. Developing countries argued that no reply meant no transit.

Other remaining obstacles included (1) the status of "off-shore" or "dependent" territories, such as the British Channel Islands, which are subject only to the United Kingdom's foreign and defense policies and not to environmental protection legislation (other countries with dependent territories include the United States, the Netherlands, and Denmark); (2) criteria for allowing transboundary movement of hazardous waste and criteria for approval or disposal sites or facilities; (3) the issue of territorial seas and whether a country can exercise sovereignty over the exclusive economic zone of 200 miles offshore and the right to refuse a ship carrying hazardous waste to pass through its waters or whether vessels would enjoy the right of innocent passage; and (4) how to deal with ships registered under flags of convenience.

The fifth draft text of the Basel Convention to emerge from the Geneva meeting contained almost as many bracketed phrases as the previous version, indicating that there were many outstanding points of disagreement. A meeting of legal experts, hosted by the European Community, was scheduled to be held in Luxembourg from January 30 to February 3, and an eleventh-hour session was planned in Basel from March 13 to 17, just before the ministerial-level Plenipotentiaries Conference on March 20–22. Mostafa Tolba also announced that he would hold informal consultations with government representatives holding opposing points of view in January and February, in an effort to find common ground.

The Luxembourg meeting reached agreement on a number of issues. It was agreed that the question of offshore territories, such as the British Channel Islands or the U.S. Virgin Islands, would be dropped from the proposed text for the Basel meeting. The meeting also dropped the question of flags of convenience. The original text said that ships flying flags of convenience, such as those of Panama or Liberia, should not be allowed to transport dangerous goods from one country to another. However, there was continuing disagreement about whether silence from a transit country would represent tacit consent for such shipments. The question of prior informed consent would be taken up at a meeting of technical and legal experts in New York on March 8–10, just ten days before the signing date for the convention. Some countries, like Nigeria, also wanted the question of liability and compensation to be dealt with before the Basel conference, whereas other countries (notably the advanced industrial countries) felt that the issue could not be settled before Basel and should be the subject of thorough negotiations and considered later by the contracting parties themselves once the convention had come into force.[19]

When delegates representing 116 countries (including 41 African states) assembled in Basel on March 20, 1989, for the conference to sign the convention, it still looked as if the treaty would not be ready for their signature. The list of outstanding issues was a lengthy one, reflecting (1) the desire of some developing countries for a complete ban on hazardous waste exports, which the OECD countries opposed; (2) developing countries' desire to make the exporter responsible for "illegal" shipments under the terms of the treaty and for the exporting country to take back (or assume responsibility for the disposal of) wastes that had been shipped illegally; (3) developing country interests in strong liability and compensation rules, which would compensate them for accidents and improper or illegal disposal of wastes on their territory; (4) monitoring and enforcement provisions and the degree to which the secretariat would have responsibility and power of enforcement; and (5) developing country insistence on a well-funded secretariat and provisions for technical assistance and technology exchange under the convention. Mostafa Tolba and representatives of Switzerland, the host country, therefore had to work late into the night to reach a compromise. Much of the final language was drafted at the eleventh hour and in informal negotiating groups formed at the request of the conference chair. According to Brian Wynne, both at Luxembourg and at Basel the chief characteristic of the negotiating process was that it "fragmented into sub-committees on different topics, and plenary debating sessions were suspended. The conclusions of the unrepresentative subcommittees were deemed by the Chair to be sovereign. The result of these extraordinary procedures was a significantly weaker version than that which had been taking shape in Luxembourg."[20]

The general outlines of the treaty are as follows. Article I defines the scope of the convention, which applies to hazardous wastes as well as a list of some twenty-seven other wastes also considered to be hazardous. Wastes are also defined as being hazardous if the domestic legislation of the exporting, importing, or transiting country considers them to be hazardous. Radioactive materials are excluded from the convention. (The United States voiced its strong objections to including them in the convention.)

Article II of the convention defines "wastes" as "substances or objects which are disposed of, are intended to be disposed of, or are required to be disposed of by the provisions of national law." A transboundary movement "means any movement of hazardous wastes or other wastes from an area under the national jurisdiction of one State to or through an area under the national jurisdiction of another State." Article IV of the convention describes the general obligations of the parties to the convention. Article VI describes notification procedures governing the transboundary movement of wastes. Article IX deals with illegal traffic of hazardous and other wastes. Article XII addresses the matter of consultations on liability. Other articles address such matters as procedures governing the transmission of information, financial aspects of the treaty, conference of the parties, functions of the secretariat, and provisions governing amendments to the convention. The principal points of the convention are as follows:

- a signatory state cannot send hazardous waste to another signatory state that bans imports of it (more than forty nations ban the import of hazardous wastes);
- a signatory state cannot ship hazardous waste into any country that has not signed the treaty;
- every country has the sovereign right to refuse to accept a shipment of hazardous waste;
- before an exporting country can start a shipment on its way, it must

have the importing country's consent, in writing, and the exporting country must first provide detailed information on the intended export to the importing country to allow it to assess the risks;
- no signatory state may ship hazardous waste to another signatory state if the importing country does not have the facilities to dispose of the waste in an environmentally sound manner;
- when an importing country proves unable to dispose of legally imported waste in an environmentally acceptable way, then the exporting state has a duty either to take it back or to find some other way of disposing of it in an environmentally sound manner;
- the treaty criminalizes illegal traffic in hazardous wastes;
- bilateral agreements may be made by signatory states with each other and with a nonsignatory country, but these agreements must conform to the terms of the Basel treaty and be no less environmentally sound;
- the treaty calls for international cooperation involving the training of technicians, the exchange of information, and the transfer of technology in an effort to assist developing countries;
- the treaty establishes a secretariat to supervise and facilitate its implementation;
- the treaty asks that lower levels of hazardous waste be generated and that generated waste be disposed of as close to its source as possible.

The definition of hazardous waste was a key point of contention in the negotiations leading up to the Basel Convention. Some countries did not want the convention to define hazardous waste at all, whereas other countries wanted a strict definition of hazardous waste in the convention. Because of conflicting views on this matter, it was decided to rely on national definitions of hazardous waste. Thus if a country shipping wastes did not define them as hazardous but the importing country did, then the importing country could prohibit importation of the waste materials. From the point of view of the convention, a waste is considered hazardous if it is deemed to be such by the exporting, importing, or transit party. Radioactive wastes are excluded from the convention, on the grounds that they are subject to other international controls, as are wastes from ships, which fall under international maritime marine pollution controls.

The convention contains detailed provisions on reporting and consent requirements prior to export. On the contentious issue of prior informed consent, the compromise to emerge was that export states have to obtain written consent from states of transit prior to shipment but that this consent provision can be waived if the transit state is silent for sixty days after notification. Furthermore, the specific notification provisions in Article VI can be avoided if hazardous wastes are shipped regularly to the same disposer through the same customs office; general notice is sufficient if repeatedly shipped wastes have consistent physical and chemical characteristics.[21]

The convention does not contain any specific penalties for parties in violation of the agreement. However, parties to the convention are required to introduce national legislation to prevent and punish illegal traffic of hazardous waste; illegal traffic being defined as transboundary movements of hazardous waste that occur without the notification of the exporting party, without the consent of the importing or transit state, via shipments that are misrepresented or falsely reported, or in contravention of the convention and international law. Illegally transferred waste must be returned to the country of export if alternative arrangements to dispose of the waste in an environmentally sound manner cannot be made within ninety days. The convention also does not address the problematic issue of liability, simply stating that parties shall adapt rules and procedures governing liability and compensation for damage resulting from the transboundary movement and disposal of hazardous wastes.

The convention also requires parties to cooperate in the management of hazardous wastes and to make information available to each other that will harmonize technical standards and practices. At the same time, industrial countries are committed to helping developing countries adopt sound management policies and low-waste technologies. Although the convention does not contain concrete measures to promote technology transfer, it does recognize the need to establish centers for training and technology transfer. Article XIV of the convention calls on parties to fund these activities voluntarily and to help with interim funding for any emergencies.[22] Financial responsibilities were deemed to be voluntary, because industrial countries would not agree to formal financial commitments in the convention.

Finally, under Article XX, covering dispute settlement procedures, parties can opt for voluntary international arbitration or a hearing before the International Court of Justice if they cannot settle matters between them through peaceful negotiation. Decisions of the arbitration panel (made up of representatives chosen by the parties) are binding and final. The convention's provisions regarding monitoring and enforcement are weak, because these were major issues of disagreement in the negotiations. Thus it was decided to leave these matters up to future discussions, although for many countries the lack of strong enforcement mechanisms was a compelling reason not to sign the convention.

Critics of the convention argued that it failed to ban exports of hazardous waste from industrial to developing countries, which was the objective of several intergovernment groups like the Organization of African Unity and the African, Caribbean, and Pacific (ACP) group of countries, as well as nongovernmental organizations like Greenpeace International (which had attended every treaty negotiation session since June 1988) and the Natural Resources Defense Council. Greenpeace charged that "the Basel Convention has failed to incorporate such a ban because the heavily industrialized countries want to maintain waste exports as a legitimate waste disposal option" and that "the convention [is] . . . a mere duplication of recently adopted laws and directives in the U.S. and the EEC that require waste exporters to notify governments of any exporting and importing countries before any shipment takes place." Greenpeace believed that "power politics prevailed in the critical final week of negotiations" and that the convention "was not drafted in the spirit of compromise and cooperation."[23]

Another critic, Brian Wynne, argues that "the formal resolution to reduce international waste trade to a minimum is without substance unless the means to exert practical pressure at the right points in the system is agreed." Furthermore, "Article IV's requirements [which prohibit exports to or imports from non-contracting countries] . . . are undermined and potentially negated by Article II, which allows toxic waste trade between contracting and non-contracting countries to the Convention 'so long as they do not derogate from environmentally sound management as intended under the Convention.'" According to Wynne, "this standard is nowhere specified, so countries are free to make deals with anyone and to define them as 'sound' within very permissive limits." Wynne also argues that the Luxembourg version of the convention, which contained provisions obliging exporting countries to ensure "'the availability of adequate disposal facilities for environmentally sound management of hazardous wastes'" and to reduce transfrontier shipments "to a minimum," was "reduced to a much weaker requirement for the parties to agree that disposal under an export deal would be according to 'environmentally sound management.'"[24]

Supporters argue that the accords do in fact ban the transfrontier shipment of hazardous wastes to countries that do not want to import them or do not have the facilities to dispose of them properly. At the same time, according to one legal scholar, "because the UNEP Convention allows for the possibility of hazardous waste export (at least in theory) it provides an incentive for developing nations to advance their environmental regulations, and thus goes further than a complete ban in attempting to even out the world's divergent hazardous waste management regulations. [This is because under a complete ban, companies in developed nations would still face higher disposal costs than companies located in countries with less strict environmental regulations.] The result will be a more equitable world in the long-run." The convention also affects "the competitiveness of private companies by making it harder and more costly for them to export their hazardous waste in the short-run" while making it "equally more difficult and costly for all companies located in the countries which are parties to the UNEP Convention to dispose of their hazardous waste."[25] This is an important argument because it recognizes the importance of the accord's impact on economic incentives and the fact that it will encourage companies to dispose of their hazardous wastes abroad rather than at home if regulatory standards are the same worldwide. However, compliance and enforcement are obviously crucial for a regulatory regime to achieve this effect, and these are unfortunately areas where the Basel Convention is weak as noted above.

Explaining Outcomes

Crisis

Negotiations leading to the Basel Convention were prompted by a growing sense of crisis, particularly from the point of view of developing countries, who feared becoming a dumping ground for the hazardous wastes of the industrial countries. These fears were dramatized in several well-publicized cases, notably the *Khian Sea* and *Karin-B* incidents. The sense of crisis was rendered more acute through the well-publicized campaigns of environmental nongovernmental organizations, who used the media and other forms of publicity to press demands for an outright ban on international traffic in hazardous wastes. At the same time, industrial countries shared some of these concerns, and some of the more progressive governments (e.g., the Netherlands) supported the idea of a complete ban on international shipments of hazardous wastes. Thus, the perception of a crisis was integrative, insofar are governments around the world saw the need for some kind of regulatory action to address the hazardous waste problem, but there was little consensus about how the problem should be tackled. Industrial and developing countries brought different interests and regulatory philosophies to the bargaining table, which were not easily reconcilable.

Consensual Knowledge

The Basel Convention is striking as a story of international regime creation insofar as scientists and epistemic communities were absent in the prenegotiation and negotiation processes. In part, this is because the risks of traffic in hazardous wastes were reasonably well understood by the negotiators themselves, although certain kinds of expertise were obviously useful and necessary to discussions revolving around the definition of hazardous waste. However, the decision to rely on OECD and national definitions of hazardous waste circumscribed the need for additional expert advice on this aspect of the regulatory problem. The case suggests that epistemic communities are not necessary to negotiations where the negotiators themselves are familiar with the risks and uncertainties associated with an issue. Epistemic knowledge is more important to discussions where risks are poorly understood and negotiators feel the need to turn to experts for advice.

Coalitions and Representation

The presence of two well-defined competing coalitions characterized the Basel Convention negotiations from the outset through to their conclusion. Developing countries (the Group of 77) represented one distinct coalition; the OECD or group of advanced industrial states the other. Developing countries held together as a bargaining unit throughout the negotiations, and there were no observable defections from this group—unlike the climate change or ozone negotiations, which were marked by the fairly rapid disintegration of the Third World bloc of the Group of 77 countries. However, the maintenance of this coalition did not appreciably strengthen Group of 77 bargaining capabilities or their ability to wrest more favorable concessions from the advanced industrial countries. Many developing countries did not sign the Basel Convention right away, because they felt that its provisions did not go far enough to restrict international traffic of toxic wastes. A series of last-minute amendments proposed by the OAU and a number of Asian countries were also rejected after pressure from some Western nations. (These amendments would have made countries that produce waste liable for its disposal; prevented the import of wastes to countries that did not have the same level of facilities and technology as exporting nations; and insisted on sophisticated verification procedures, including inspection of disposal site.)[26]

The coalition of advanced industrial states, which had largely worked out its own positions within the OECD beforehand, also functioned as a coherent bargaining unit, although a number of smaller countries (e.g., the Netherlands and Switzerland) indicated their support for some of the concerns being put forward by developing countries. There were some minor disagreements between the United States and the EC members over certain definitions in the negotiating text but nothing like the fissures that opened in the Uruguay Round of the GATT (General Agreement on Tariffs and Trade) or in ozone and climate change negotiations.

The OAU was prominent in representing the interests of developing countries in the negotiations. In part this was because the problem of toxic-waste dumping was especially acute in several African states. The

OAU passed a number of independent resolutions condemning dumping, spearheaded efforts to get UNEP to address the problem, and played a key role in coordinating developing countries' positions once negotiations were underway. Among the advanced industrial countries, the United States and the European Community were key players in defining bargaining positions and developing guidelines that were compatible with OECD interests. The Netherlands, Norway, Sweden, and Switzerland were the most supportive of developing country interests within the OECD bloc.

Bridging and Bargaining Strategies

On the key issue of prior informed consent, one of the most contentious points in the negotiation, a bridging formula was slow to emerge because developing countries were adamant that the consent of importing and transit countries be given before any transport of hazardous wastes could be allowed. Industrial countries opposed the concept on the grounds that it would lead to complicated administrative procedures that would strangle transborder shipments of wastes between industrial countries (where the volume of trade is much higher than between industrial and developing countries). The OECD's decision to adopt streamlined tacit-consent procedures for hazardous waste shipped between its members added a further complication. At the Dakar meeting held in September 1988, some progress was achieved in accepting the principle of prior informed consent by recipient countries of hazardous waste. It was also agreed that transit countries should enjoy the same advance information about shipments. However, there was no agreement about whether prior informed consent would apply to transit countries at subsequent meetings in Geneva and Luxembourg. Compromise was only reached at Basel when it was agreed that the consent provision would apply to transit states but could be waived if the transit state did not reply to a request sixty days after the request had been received. In addition, the notification provisions could be waived in the event of regular shipments to the same disposer, thus satisfying the interests of industrialized countries.

Compromises were also reached on matters concerning technical assistance and secretariat responsibilities. However, liability and compensation, monitoring and enforcement, and technology exchange provisions for the exchange of technologies in the convention were weak, because developing countries lacked adequate bargaining power to wrest concessions for a compromise.

Issue Decomposition and Sequencing Tactics

Issue decomposition and sequencing tactics characterized much of the negotiation. Although negotiations began with a single draft negotiating text prepared by the conference chair, different subgroups dealt with different sections of the text, and discussions in plenary session were kept to a minimum. Divergent viewpoints were presented in bracketed portions of the text, and these typically became the focus of discussion at subsequent sessions. When agreement could not be reached on certain issues, a decision was sometimes made to simply drop the matter from the proposed text (e.g., the outstanding question of offshore territories such as the British Channel Islands or U.S. Virgin Islands, flags of convenience, etc.). The watered-down provisions of certain items in the convention, for example, articles regarding liability and compensation, simply meant that these matters would be deferred to future negotiations. Issue decomposition techniques—or what might uncharitably be referred to as a divide-and-rule strategy—were also evident in the final hours of the negotiation, where much of the final language in the treaty was drafted by informal subcommittees working independently on key items in the text and making decisions that were deemed by the chair to be binding. However, the lack of consultation and consensus almost proved to be the convention's undoing, because only 34 of the over 116 countries attending the conference signed the treaty when it was tabled, and of those signatories, many have yet to ratify the convention.

Leadership

Leadership was exercised by different actors and interests at different phases in the negotiation, and it is difficult to point to a single source of innovative thinking and constructive problem-solving talent. During the prenegotiation phase, environmental nongovernmental organizations helped to publicize the plight of developing countries that had been the recipients of illegal shipments of hazardous waste. NGOs were also important behind the scenes, in providing advice and information to developing countries at the bargaining table. Within the Group of 77, African countries played both a representational and a leadership role in championing common causes and putting pressure on industrial countries to take developing country concerns seriously. A key driving force at the negotiating table was UNEP executive director Mostafa Tolba and the Swiss chair of the drafting group, Alain Clerc, who sustained the momentum of negotiations and tried to broker compromises where possible. Depending upon whether the outcome at Basel is viewed as favorable or not, their leadership roles can be viewed in a positive or negative light, although it is indisputable that the shape of the final treaty bore the clear imprint of the chair's interventions.

Compliance and Verification

There are no explicit verification and compliance provisions in the Basel Convention. Responsibility for enforcing the provisions in the convention lie with the parties to the convention, although the secretariat can inform parties about violations through its access to information on manifests, shipment notifications, and yearly reports submitted by the parties concerning their respective transboundary shipments of hazardous wastes. Various meetings have been held by the ad hoc working group of legal and technical experts to develop elements that might be included in a protocol on liability and compensation for damage resulting from hazardous waste shipments.[27] However, negotiations on such a protocol have not yet been concluded.[28]

Like so many of the other cases in the volume, the prenegotiation phase of the Basel Convention began with a perceived crisis that developing countries were becoming the victims of toxic waste imperialism. This crisis prompted UNEP and the OECD to take up the issue and initiate negotiations in the hopes of devising a regulatory approach to the problem. Although epistemic communities did not play an important role in the evolution of negotiations, environmental NGOs did. The timing and substance of negotiations were significantly shaped by (1) a series of well-publicized toxic-waste disasters, particularly in Africa; and (2) parallel negotiations within the OECD and the European Community (who, as industrial countries, reached agreement among themselves on certain issues and created their own special constraints on UNEP-sponsored negotiations). Negotiations in UNEP were thus significantly affected by external events and pressures on the extranegotiatory environment.

Issue sequencing and decomposition tactics, as well as strategies that sought to move negotiations to more informal and loosely structured settings (thus allowing greater room for maneuver and compromise) played a key role in moving negotiations forward to closure. Deferral of irreconcilable issues for future discussion and negotiation also limited the scope of the treaty to those areas where agreement could be reached. The outcome was in a real sense a convention that satisfied no one—neither developing nor industrial countries. The convention has also been heavily criticized by environmentalists for not banning international trade in toxic wastes, although supporters of the treaty contend that the treaty will lead to a more level playing field, which will stem the flow of toxic wastes of developing countries. There are also positive signs that a protocol on liability and compensation for damage resulting from the transboundary movement and disposal of hazardous waste will soon be included in the treaty.

But monitoring and enforcement provisions in the treaty will have to be strengthened if the treaty is to achieve its intended goals. The achievement at Basel was, by most standards, a modest one, but it committed parties to a series of regulatory commitments that were better than none, as well as to new rounds of discussions and negotiation aimed at strengthening the original treaty.

11   Climate Change and Global Warming

The summer of 1988 marked a turning point in public consciousness about the looming dangers of environmental catastrophe from human pollution of the atmosphere. The fear that humanity's own actions somehow lay behind the hottest recorded summer of this century—a summer that brought searing droughts to the American and Canadian Midwest and violent cyclonic storms in Asia, the Pacific, and the Caribbean—galvanized public demand for governments to address the problems of global warming and climate change. At the same time, there appeared to be a growing consensus within the scientific community that the burning of fossil fuels, the destruction of tropical rainforests and temperate-zone forests, and the addition of manmade chemicals to the atmosphere were not only threatening the earth's ozone layer but also leading to a dangerous buildup of carbon dioxide (CO_2) and other greenhouse gases (GHGs) such as nitrous oxide, methane, and surface ozone.

According to scientists, the buildup of CO_2 and other GHGs that keep heat from escaping into outer space could lead to a rapid and unprecedented rise in global mean temperatures—by some estimates, anywhere from 1.5 to 4.5 degrees Celsius—in the next fifty years.[1] The rise in temperatures would be greater in higher latitudes than in the tropics, perhaps by a factor of two or three. Warming would affect global precipitation and weather circulation patterns and would be accompanied by rising sea levels of possibly up to a meter or more. Although temperature changes would be less pronounced in tropical areas, developing countries would be hard hit by the adverse consequences of global warming. A 50-centimeter rise in sea levels, for example, would bring the sea 25 kilometers inland in the country of Bangladesh, one of the world's most densely populated coastal states. In South America the effects would be particularly severe in such heavily populated areas as Rio de Janeiro, Brazil, and Mar del Plata, Argentina. Rising sea levels would pollute surface and ground water and threaten deltas, coastal marshlands, and tropical embankments.

Climate change, in turn, could lead to a dramatic increase in the number of "environmental refugees," people fleeing flooded homelands or regions that could no longer sustain marginal agricultural production because of fresh water shortages. World food supplies might also be threatened by changing precipitation and climatic conditions consequent to temperature warming. In middle and higher latitudes, global warming might cause a fall in crop yields because of reduced precipitation (despite the longer growing season). Traditional grain exporters, like Canada, the United States, and Argentina, could find their surpluses diminishing with the loss of arable land to persistent drought.

Given such dire predictions, it would seem that governments would be prompted to undertake dramatic and immediate actions to reduce emissions of GHGs that contribute to global warming. However, they have moved slowly and chosen to act cautiously, although some industrial countries have committed themselves to freezing or lowering carbon and other greenhouse-gas emissions. An epistemic consensus of sorts has emerged on the scientific aspects of global warming and climate change, which has moved it forward from the prenegotiation to the negotiation stage. But because scientists cannot, as yet, fully predict the consequences of global warming because of the unusual difficulties of modeling and prediction associated with the science of climate change, negotiations have proceeded slowly.

Although scientific research into global warming has raised public consciousness and forced the issue onto the agenda of governments around the world, the level of public concern has not been as intense as it has, say, in the case of the ozone depletion, and there is no sense of impending crisis (even though some say there should be). In other words, at the psychological level the "dread factor" has been lower and less acute. Part of the reason is that the adverse consequences of climate change may not be experienced for many years to come, some forty to fifty years hence. That may not be a long time in the course of world history, but it is for most individuals and governments.[2] The costs of actions taken now are calculable, but the benefits are uncertain and will only be experienced by future generations. This presents substantial difficulties in calculating the trade-offs of appropriate responses and policy actions, insofar as the intergenerational aspects of climate change and the transfer of costs and benefits from one generation to another are not easily handled by current economic models and approaches to decision making.[3] Governments have, therefore, tended to accord the problems of climate change and global warming lower priority than other environmental issues, and this has slowed progress on international accords to combat the problem.

Climate change and global warming cut to the heart of major social equity and distributional concerns in world politics. For many developing countries confronting diminished natural-resource bases, runaway population growth, and declining per capita incomes, there are far more immediate and pressing problems than global warming.[4] Governments, industrialists, and consumers in these countries are reluctant to divert scarce resources to the problems of global warming, which they see as being the responsibility of advanced industrial countries (although recent evidence indicates that some developing countries, like Brazil, are responsible for significant greenhouse-gas emissions). Developing countries argue that the advanced industrial countries should provide financial and technological assistance to help them meet their obligations under an international convention. The success of current and future international discussions on climate change hinges on the willingness of the advanced industrial countries to address these distributional concerns.

Given this array of obstacles, namely, lingering scientific uncertainties about the magnitude and severity of climate change, issue complexity, an absence of a shared sense of crisis, a low "dread factor" in public opinion, and major questions of equity and distribution that cut across the North-South divide, it is perhaps surprising that international negotiations to address the problems of climate change and global warming did not stop dead in their tracks. However, a framework convention on climate change was tabled at the Earth Summit in Rio de Janeiro, Brazil, in June 1992. The convention sets out the key objective of stabilizing GHG concentrations at a level preventing dangerous anthropogenic interference with the earth's climate system, commits industrial countries to adopt policies and measures on mitigating climate change by limiting GHG emissions with the aim of returning to 1990 emission levels, and sets up mechanisms for providing developing countries with new additional financial resources to meet the incremental costs of addressing the climate change problem.[5] Later protocols to the convention might establish levels for CO_2 emissions and perhaps also methane and tropospheric ozone, but no formal targets to reduce emissions of GHGs have been agreed to. Nonetheless, some twenty-two countries, including the European Community and Canada, have pledged to stabilize or reduce GHG emissions. After fifty ratifications (estimated to take from one to two years), the convention will come into force.

To the extent there has been progress in negotiating an international convention on climate change, it is the result of a number of factors, including (1) the exercise of effective leadership by the UNEP and the international scientific community; (2) the active involvement of particular countries who pushed the climate agenda forward, served as intermediaries and brokers, devised compromise formulas, and sustained negotiations; (3) incremental bargaining strategies, which deferred outstanding issues and moved ahead on those on which a consensus could be reached; (4) growing recognition that international agreements are necessary to help states share the risks and burdens of adjustment to global warming, establish a basis for reciprocity, and provide information; and (5) the momentum of the negotiation process itself and the fact that states committed themselves to a deadline (the 1992 U.N. Conference on the Environment and Sustainable Development) for tabling a convention on climate change. But the process of social learning is incomplete, and unresolved value conflicts, which cut across societies and cultures, still remain. As one study explains,

> managing global climate change may require significant alterations in existing social, economic, and political structures. These changes could have major impacts on established power interests as to forestall radical ameliorative measures. The necessary steps may also not generate sufficiently immediate payoffs to political leaders dependent upon electoral support or other forms of popular support to spur them to effective action. . . . Social learning is a process of managing a long time-scale, high-uncertainty problem. The long time scale presents problems for . . . the community or institution undergoing change.[6]

Prenegotiation

The formal prenegotiation phase of the climate change negotiations began on December 6, 1988, when the government of Malta introduced a resolution, which was passed by the U.N. General Assembly, formally requesting UNEP and the World Meteorological Organization (WMO) "immediately to initiate action leading, as soon as possible, to a comprehensive review and recommendations with respect to . . . elements for the inclusion in a possible future convention on climate."[7] The resolution directed UNEP and WMO to coordinate these activities through the Intergovernmental Panel on Climate Change. This action followed a number of major scientific conferences that had drawn attention to the link between the buildup of GHGs in the atmosphere and global warming.

The greenhouse effect was first described in the early nineteenth century by the French mathematician Baron Jean Baptiste Fournier. In 1896, a Swedish scientist by the name of Svante Arrhenius was the first to postulate a link between rising levels of CO_2 in the earth's atmosphere and global temperature increases. In 1970 a group of researchers at the Massachusetts Institute of Technology recommended that CO_2 levels in the atmosphere be continuously measured in order to study the effects of such a buildup over the long term. In 1979, the First World Climate Conference, sponsored by the WMO and held in Geneva, Switzerland, declared that there was a link between the burning of fossil fuels, deforestation, and changing land-use patterns and increasing levels of CO_2 in the atmosphere. It postulated that this could contribute to a gradual warming of the atmosphere that would be pronounced at higher latitudes.[8]

In the 1980s scientists began to devote considerable attention to possible future climate changes resulting from the accumulation of GHGs. At a joint conference organized by UNEP, the WMO, and the International Committee of Scientific Unions (ICSU) held in Villach, Austria, in October 1985, scientists from twenty-nine industrial and developing countries agreed that "increasing concentrations of GHGs are expected to cause a significant warming of the global climate in the next century."[9] The participants also concluded that results obtained from climate models indicated that a doubling of CO_2 levels in the atmosphere would have a profound impact on the biosphere.[10]

Two subsequent workshops held in Villach and Bellagio, Italy, in the fall of 1987—initiated by the Beijer Institute (Stockholm), the Environmental Defense Fund (New York), and the Woods Hole Research Center (Massachusetts) and sponsored by UNEP and a variety of other private and government funding agencies—further underscored growing scientific concerns about climate change. The report of the two workshops argued that "the common assumptions underlying many past decisions in the social and economic sphere that past climatic data are a reliable guide to the future is no longer valid" and that "if present trends continue, climate change will be more rapid in the future than it has been in the last few millennia."[11] The report called for immediate steps to limit greenhouse gas increases in the atmosphere, including ratification of the Montreal Protocol (see chapter 7), a reexamination of national energy policies worldwide and intensification of research into nonfossil energy systems, measures to reduce tropical and extratropical deforestation, and measures to limit growth of other non-CO_2 GHGs. In addition, the report called for an increase in global monitoring activities and further development of climate models to better understand climate change. The recommendations of the Bellagio meeting were presented to the Advisory Group on Greenhouse Gases (AGGG) of the WMO, UNEP, and the ICSU at their meeting in Paris in December 1987.

The Villach and Bellagio workshops were followed by the Toronto Conference on the Changing Atmosphere sponsored by UNEP, the WMO, and Environment Canada and attended by some 300 scientists, policy makers, and representatives of nongovernmental and government organizations from forty-six countries. The conference played a key role in underscoring a growing consensus within the scientific community that human activities are leading to a dangerous buildup of CO_2 and other GHGs in the atmosphere and set out the following detailed elements for a comprehensive global strategy to address the problems of climate change, including:

- an international framework convention that would encourage other standard-setting agreements and national legislation to provide for the protection of the global atmosphere;
- a comprehensive global energy policy to reduce emissions of CO_2 and other trace gases in order to lessen the risks of future global warming (such reductions would be achieved from national commitments to greater energy efficiency, conservation, and modifications in supplies);
- reduction in CO_2 emissions by approximately 20 percent of 1988 levels by the year 2005 as an initial global goal;
- establishment of a world atmosphere fund, financed possibly through a tax on fossil-fuel consumption, to mobilize the resources necessary to achieve energy efficiency improvements;
- establishment of continuing assessments of scientific results and government-to-government discussion of responses and strategies; and
- a worldwide plan to reduce deforestation and increase afforestation by establishing an international trust fund to provide adequate incentives to developing nations to manage their tropical forests and achieve sustainable development.[12]

Although the idea of setting an actual target for emission reductions was the subject of active debate behind the scenes and in the plenary session of the conference, the conference approved the target in the interests of setting concrete goals that governments could actively pursue. The conference also assigned responsibility to the industrial world as "the main source of greenhouse gases" and having "main responsibility to the world for ensuring measures are implemented to address the issues posed by climate change."[13]

The Toronto Conference was followed by numerous other international workshops and conferences intended to focus international attention on the problems of global warming and, at the same time, raise the profile of this issue on the political agenda of national governments. Some of the key international meetings and conferences to be held over the next year were as follows:

- the Meeting of International Legal and Policy Experts, Ottawa, February 1989, attended by experts from twenty-five countries and eight international bodies. The group examined different frameworks for and approaches to devising a convention on climate change. The conference adopted the Ottawa Declaration, which recognized that the atmosphere is "a common resource of vital interest to mankind" that should be protected by all states.[14]

- the Heads of Government Meeting, The Hague, the Netherlands, March 1989, sponsored by the Netherlands, France, and Norway and attended by representatives from twenty-four countries. The final declaration stressed that the climate-change problem "has three salient features, namely, that it is vital, urgent and global; we are in a situation that calls not only for implementation of existing principles but also for a new approach through the development of new principles of international law including new and more effective decision-making and enforcement mechanisms."[15]

- the G-7 Summit, Paris, France, July 1989 (dubbed the Green Summit). The environment and the twin problems of ozone depletion and global warming were major items of discussion at this annual summit meeting of the G-7 heads of state. In the final communiqué, the leaders "strongly advocate[d] common efforts to limit emissions of CO_2 and other greenhouse gases, which threaten to induce climate change, endangering the environment and the economy." The communiqué stressed that "decisive action is urgently needed to understand and protect the Earth's ecological balance" and urged "all countries to give further impetus to scientific research on environmental issues, to develop necessary technologies and to make clear evaluations of the economic costs and benefits." The communiqué also emphasized the need to "help developing countries deal with past damage and to encourage them to take environmentally desirable action." Finally, the G-7 leaders expressed their belief that "the increasing complexity of issues related to the protection of the atmosphere calls for innovative solutions. . . . The conclusion of a framework or umbrella convention on climate change to set out general principles or guidelines is urgently required."[16]

- the Ministerial Meeting on Atmosphere Pollution and Climate Change, Noordwijk, the Netherlands, November 1989. Environment ministers from some sixty-eight countries called for a convention on climate change as soon as possible, although a Dutch proposal for countries to limit CO_2 emissions to current levels by the year 2000 was rebuffed by the United States, the Soviet Union, and Japan.

- the White House Conference on Global Warming, Washington, D.C., April 1990. At a gathering of international decision makers and experts, President George Bush announced that further research on global warming is required before decisive action can be taken. The White House tried to secure international support for a go-slow approach to global warming in the face of scientific uncertainty.

In addition to the above meetings, various conferences and meetings were held (some under UNEP-WMO auspices) that examined the regional implications of climate change and global warming, particularly for developing countries.[17]

The principal mechanism for coordinating scientific assessments and devising response strategies to climate change (at least until the beginning of formal intergovernmental negotiations) was the Intergovernmental Panel on Climate Change (IPCC). The panel was formed in November 1988 at a meeting organized by the WMO and UNEP in Geneva, Switzerland, in which thirty countries participated. The IPCC's agreed mandate was to provide a firmer assessment of the scientific basis for climate change, including the impact of emissions of GHGs on the earth's radiation balance and the environmental and socioeconomic consequences of climate change, and to formulate "realistic response strategies for the management of the climate change issue."[18] The panel set up three working groups: the first, to conduct reviews of the state of knowledge of the science of climate change with special emphasis on global warming; the second, to review programs and conduct studies of the social and economic impacts of climate change; and the third, to develop and evaluate possible policy responses by governments to delay or mitigate the adverse impacts of climate change.

At its second meeting held in Nairobi in June 1989, the IPCC established a Special Committee on the Participation of Developing Countries to promote the participation of developing countries in the work of the panel. The panel also agreed to present its first assessment report in September 1990. At its third session, held in Washington, D.C., in February 1990, the IPCC also agreed to a request of the Noordwijk Ministerial Conference on Atmospheric Pollution and Climate Change to examine the feasibility of various options to stabilize or reduce emissions of CO_2 and other GHGs. Because of the tight schedule, the working groups and the special committee worked in parallel, rather than together, which led to criticism of the lack of proper coordination among the different groups.

Working Group I followed clear procedural rules and very quickly reached a consensus on the science of climate change. Working Group II had a less well developed method of arriving at decisions and followed a somewhat different management style; nonetheless, it too was able to reach a consensus. Working Group III, by contrast, had greater difficulty separating discussion of general issues from individual country positions and achieved the least amount of consensus of the three groups. This was especially true when oil-producing countries began to realize that climate change was not a meteorology issue but a policy issue. Every sentence in Working Group III's draft report became the subject of vigorous and sometimes heated debate.

The release of the first reports of the IPCC's various working groups in the summer of 1990 generated intense controversy.[19] Working Group I released a general summary of its findings predicting (on the basis of current model results) that the rate of increase of global mean temperatures during the next century would be about 0.3 degrees centigrade per decade. (This would result in a likely increase in the global mean temperatures of about 1 degree centigrade above the present value by 2025 and 3 percent or more before the end of the twenty-first century.) The group was criticized for releasing its results before explaining how it had arrived at its general conclusions. Working Group II's report was criticized for containing outdated predictions and unsustainable qualitative assumptions. Working Group III's report was also criticized by environmental groups for failing to call for stringent cuts in greenhouse-gas emissions,[20] even though Working Group I's final report predicted that emissions of GHGs would have to be cut by more than 60 percent to stabilize atmosphere concentrations at existing levels.[21] As one group of critics notes, the report "failed to pick up the conclusions from the scientific and impact assessments and follow through with clear recommendations for action by nations, groups of nations, and the international community as a whole. Chaired by the United States and dominated by diplomats, it was unable to bridge the growing gap between a majority of industrialized nations wanting to move ahead on global warming and a small minority of industrialized and Gulf states wanting to postpone action indefinitely."[22]

The IPCC's reports were tabled at the Second World Climate Conference held in Geneva, Switzerland, October 29–November 7, 1990. The first part of the conference was attended by some seven hundred scientists from around the globe, and the second part by heads of state and ministers from one hundred thirty-seven countries and the European Community. The scientists' concluding statement proved to be even stronger than the assessments of the IPCC, arguing that there are "technically feasible and cost-effective opportunities" for reducing CO_2 emissions for all countries and that industrial countries should take the lead by reducing their emissions 20 percent by the year 2005.[23] This view was not embraced by the ministers. The ministerial meeting was marked by major divisions between industrial countries, with the European Community, joined by the six members of the European Free Trade Area, agreeing "to take actions aimed at stabilizing their emissions of CO_2, or CO_2 and other greenhouse gases not controlled by the Montreal Protocol, by the year 2000 in general at the 1990 level," a similar if somewhat more ambiguous commitment to this goal by Japan, Canada, Australia, and New Zealand, and outright opposition from the United States, the Soviet Union, and the oil-producing states, who refused to take any immediate actions to reduce fossil-fuel emissions of carbon dioxide.[24] Developing countries took the position that the climate change problem was the responsibility of industrial countries and any actions taken by developing countries would depend on new financial and technology transfers from developing countries.

Nonetheless, conference participants were able to agree that negotiations on a framework convention on climate change should begin "without delay" and that it would be "highly desirable that an effective framework convention on climate change [that] contains appropriate commitments, and any related instruments as might be agreed upon on the basis of consensus, be signed in Rio de Janeiro during the United Nations Conference on Environment and Development."[25] The Intergovernmental Negotiating Committee for a Framework Convention on Climate Change (INC) was thus set up under the auspices of the U.N. General Assembly to establish a "single negotiating process . . . for the preparation of an effective framework on climate change."[26] The commencement of formal negotiations at the state-to-state level in the INC, in February 1991, marked an important shift away from the IPCC forum on the climate change issue. Although some of the same personnel have been involved in the activities of both organizations, these negotiations have taken place independently of the WMO, UNEP, the U.N. Conference on Environmental and Development (UNCED), and the U.N. General Assembly. As one participant in the INC noted, "when INC started the whole IPCC process was virtually aborted." The actors changed from scientists to diplomats and bureaucrats, and there was a corresponding shift in focus "from substance to process," as a picture of potential "winners and losers" began to emerge.[27]

Negotiations

Round I

The first session of the Intergovernmental Negotiating Committee (INC) was held in Chantilly, Virginia, outside Washington, D.C., on February 4–14, 1991, thus marking the onset of formal negotiations on the climate change problem.[28] As might be expected, the meeting dealt almost exclusively with procedural matters, although important substantive issues were reflected in the debate. Participating states were organized into regional groupings as recognized by the United Nations and the IPCC: Western European and Others Group (WEOG), East Europe, Asia, Africa, and the Alliance of Small Island States (AOSIS). In addition, several informal groups emerged: the "common concerns" group (Canada, Australia, New Zealand, and United States), "the common interests" group (members of the Organization for Economic Cooperation and Development, i.e., the advanced industrial states), and the Group of 77 (developing countries).

Sixty-eight countries spoke in the general debate, which lasted over two and a half days. Sharp differences quickly emerged between industrial and developing countries, particularly with regard to the nature of commitments, financial assistance, and the transfer of technology in a climate change convention.[29] The initial position of the developing countries was that industrial countries are the cause of 70 percent of the emissions problem and therefore must take the lead role in action and provide assistance comparable to their contribution to the problem. They argued that industrial countries should provide financial assistance, over and above traditional ongoing bilateral, multilateral, and other assistance programs, to assist developing countries meet their obligations under a climate change convention. Many also called for transfers of technologies to assist them with emissions reduction, enhancing sinks, increased energy efficiency, alternative energy development, and so on, although there was strong support for this principle among many of the advanced industrial countries.[30]

The European Community was the most vocal group among the advanced industrial states. The European Community wanted to move quickly on a draft text, and the United Kingdom, the Federal Republic of Germany, the Netherlands, Switzerland, Austria, and Finland presented draft recommendations and principles for the elements of a climate change convention. Some EC countries also recommended protocols covering greenhouse-gas emissions, CO_2 emissions, sinks, forestry, and adjustment and adaptation. Most EC countries had already established domestic targets for CO_2 emissions stabilization or reduction and were looking for ways to establish targets for other GHGs. Some EC members also recommended development and implementation strategies for sinks and reservoirs for CO_2, particularly in the area of forestry. EC countries also acknowledged the need for financial mechanisms to facilitate fulfillment by developing countries of obligations under a climate change convention, along with technical assistance and transfer of knowledge.

The "common concerns" group expressed its support for a comprehensive approach to climate change that would treat sources and sinks together. Australia and New Zealand supported assistance to the South Pacific Islands, which could be inundated by rising sea levels as a result of climate change. Canada expressed similar concerns and, along with Australia and New Zealand, indicated its support for measures that would limit CO_2 emissions.

The AOSIS group (with members from the Caribbean, the South Pacific, the Indian Ocean and the Mediterranean) was concerned about adaptation to the rise in sea level and the increased frequency and intensity of tropical storms. These states argued that they have limited resources to deal with a problem to which they have contributed (and will continue to contribute) little.

Eastern European countries, along with some NICs (newly industrial countries), noted that the dual differentiation between industrial and developing countries should not apply in the case of a climate change convention. (There was not opposition to this concept, although the criteria for determining types and degree of responsibility would prove to be controversial.) The Soviet Union did not see any reason to hurry, indicating in its opening statement that protocols to a climate change convention should be developed after 1992. However, it did support the concept of financial and technical assistance, technology transfer, and scientific data and information sharing.

The African states had a low participation rate at the meeting. African states were most concerned about desertification, dysfunctional economies, limited resources, and adaptation problems. The Africans were generally poorly organized and attended the meetings intermittently. In contrast, the Latin Americans were well organized and strongly in favor of action. They pushed hard on the issue of financial assistance and technology transfer to developing countries and were keen to have favorable results from the conference to complement the upcoming June 1992 UNCED meeting.

Overall, there was overwhelming support for action and the view that the precautionary principle (action now, despite not having all the scientific answers) should prevail. However, a few countries were not particularly anxious to move quickly. The United States came under fire from some environmental nongovernmental organizations (ENGOs),[31] and Brazil's ministry of science and technology was criticized for its own strategy and approach to the climate change issue, which was announced in *America's Climate Change Strategy* by the chair of the President's Council on Environmental Quality.[32] The report stated that GHG emissions in the United States would be equal to or below the 1987 levels by the year 2000 as a result of the implementation of existing energy and clean-air policies and emphasized the need for a comprehensive, adaptable, no-regrets approach to the climate change problem.

Process issues, which dominated much of the work of the first session, concerned the size of the conference bureau, the selection of a bureau chair, rules of procedure, and the establishment of working groups. Jean Ripert of France was elected chair of the INC by acclamation. The vice chairs were selected from the other four regional groups, although some concern was expressed by several delegations, particularly the AOSIS nations, that the bureau was not sufficiently diverse. There was considerable discussion in regional and informal groups about rules of procedure. An open-ended "contact group" was formed to resolve these issues, with the result that decision making by consensus continued to be emphasized, with recourse to voting in some circumstances.

There was further debate over the number of working groups and the mandates of these groups. The Group of 77 sought to minimize the number of groups. The EC member states were insistent on separating sources and sinks, while most other industrial countries were determined that these two subjects should be treated together. Eventually a consensus emerged on the establishment of two working groups: Working Group I would deal with commitments related to emissions reduction and sink enhancement, financial resources for and technology transfer to developing countries, and the special circumstances of developing countries with economies in transition; Working Group II would consider mechanisms, including legal and institutional mechanisms as well as mechanisms for scientific cooperation, and monitoring and the question of financial assistance to developing countries. These working groups would establish texts for consideration by plenary. No agreement on chairs for the working groups was reached at the first session.

There was also considerable discussion about the links between the INC and the IPCC. Most countries were keen to see the IPCC provide scientific and technical advice to the INC, although a few delegations were critical of the IPCC and its process and sought to minimize its influence on the INC. There was widespread agreement that the IPCC was not a forum for negotiations, although there were calls for the IPCC to give priority to the INC's needs for the negotiations, especially to balance its scientific assessments with economic analysis.

Round II

The second round of negotiations took place in Geneva on June 19–28, 1991.[33] Draft convention tests were circulated prior to and during the session; the most substantive of these were presented by the United Kingdom, India, Vanuatu, France, and New Zealand.[34] Some developing countries also circulated informal non-papers for the first time. The chairs of the two working groups were elected by acclamation: for Working Group I, Nobutoshi Akao (Japan) and Edmundo de Alba-Alacaraz (Mexico), for Working Group II, Elizabeth Dowdeswell (Canada) and Robert van Lierop (Vanuatu).

Discussions in Working Group I focused on the principles for a climate convention, what minimum commitments should exist in the convention, and issues of technology transfer and financial assistance. Working Group II dealt with legal and institutional mechanisms for a climate change convention, including entry into force, withdrawal, compliance, and assessment and review; mechanisms related to scientific cooperation, monitoring, and information; and mechanisms related to financial resources and technological needs of developing countries.[35]

In Working Group I, developing countries, led by India and China, argued for the following principles in a climate change convention: (1) the need for a differentiated response, that is, developing countries must reduce poverty, and their GHG emissions will have to increase in line with economic growth; (2) additionality, that is funding assistance to developing countries must be over and above other assistance; (3) technology transfer on a preferential and noncommercial basis; (4) recognition that measures of abatement and adaptation are the responsibility of countries with high per capita GHG emissions. The industrial countries indicated that they would accept only a convention embodying those principles that were included in the Ministerial Declaration of the Second World Climate Conference, as well as the following: (1) cost-effectiveness, that is, a country's emission-reduction actions should be based on the most cost-effective measures; (2) universality, based on the recognition that climate change is a global problem requiring global, cooperative solutions, including developing country commitments to minimize emissions (while maintaining growth) and to maximize sinks; and (3) a comprehensive approach that considers all GHG gases, their sources, and their sinks (a view shared by many developing countries as well).

The issue of commitments was just as contentious, marking clear divisions between industrial and developing countries. India, supported by China, argued that developing countries should not be required to undertake commitments until they had reached an appropriate level of economic development comparable to that of the advanced industrial countries. India also argued that developing countries should be compensated for the historical abuse of the environment by industrial countries, advocating the use of per capita emissions as a way of determining the basis of limitation commitments under a climate change convention. The European Community suggested a common but differentiated approach, under which commitments would be broken down into common and differentiated elements. The industrial countries generally favored a comprehensive approach to commitments, that is, stabilizing GHG emissions at 1990 levels by the year 2000. However, some countries (e.g., Sweden, Germany, and Austria) put greater emphasis on CO_2 emission reductions.

On the matter of technology transfer and financial assistance, industrial and developing countries' views were again polarized: developing countries talked about both in specific terms, whereas industrial countries were more interested in technology transfer. However, there was a convergence of views that technology transfer and financial assistance must be linked to obligations undertaken by countries toward the long-term stabilization of atmospheric concentrations of GHGs in the convention, in order to prevent dangerous anthropogenic interferences with the earth's climate.

Working Group II dealt with three issues: (1) the legal and institutional mechanisms regarding entry into force, withdrawal, compliance, and assessment for a climate change convention; (2) legal and institutional mechanisms related to scientific cooperation, monitoring, and information; (3) legal and institutional resources related to financial and technological cooperation and assistance for developing countries. On the first issue, there was general agreement that mechanisms should be flexible and adaptable, a Conference of the Parties should be the supreme decision-making body, and that some form of nonadversarial review mechanisms that did not focus exclusively on emissions would be appropriate for reporting and information purposes. There was disagreement, however, as to whether a dispute-settlement mechanism should be compulsory or voluntary, whether implementation and review mechanisms should be addressed in a convention or in protocols, whether reservations to the convention should be allowed, and whether entry into force of the convention would be based on a specified number of ratifications or on ratification by countries producing a fixed percentage of global emissions.

On the second issue, there was unanimous agreement that the convention must rest on a solid scientific foundation and that some form of scientific-advisory mechanism be built into the convention. The need to strengthen the indigenous scientific and technical capabilities of developing countries was also recognized. Drafting of the convention article on research and systematic observation was begun—the only such drafting to occur at this session.

Finally, with regard to the third issue, a number of common themes emerged: that transfer of technology and adequate and additional funding would be critical to allow developing countries to participate in the convention; that mechanisms supporting local and indigenous technologies be developed; that institutional mechanisms concerning transfer of technology and financial resources be based on a genuine partnership and be under the equitable and democratic decision-making control of the parties to the convention. However, there were key divisions on the matter of whether financial resources must be new funds separate from aid or development assistance, whether the Global Environment Facility (GEF) would be an appropriate mechanism for the transfer of financial resources in a climate convention, whether a separate climate fund should be established and whether it would be based on mandatory assessments or voluntary contributions, whether technology transfer should be provided on a concessional and noncommercial basis, and whether the question of intellectual property rights is an impediment to the transfer of technology. Draft convention articles provided by the United Kingdom, India, and Vanuatu were key in the discussions of the group. Working Group II decided that the two cochairs would be authorized to prepare a single text on the elements relating to the mandate of the group and that the text would be based on submissions received from the group's members. The text would include areas of convergence and present alternative versions where there were differences of opinion. The text would serve as the basis for the group's discussions at subsequent sessions.

In the second round of the INC, there was considerable discussion of technology cooperation and transfer, both formally, in the working groups, and in various informal meetings. The United States issued a non-paper on technology cooperation, which was the focus of these discussions. There was support for the concept of country studies that would identify specific technology needs and help developing countries prepare their response strategies. However, developing countries argued that the exercise should only be viewed as the first step to technology transfer and that the exercise should not dictate actual response strategies. A series of non-papers explored the concept of pledge-and-review, whereby countries would pledge themselves to GHG-reduction targets without undertaking specific obligations.[36] These pledges, in turn, would become the basis of some sort of (unspecified) international review process. Pledge-and-review proposals were circulated by the United Kingdom, France, Japan, Sweden, Australia, and New Zealand. The concept underwent considerable discussion, although much of it was focused on the review aspects and associated institutional requirements. Japan proved to be the strongest advocate of the concept, gaining some support from the European Community. However, interpretations of the nature of the pledge varied considerably, especially over whether the concept would include global targets, commitments, or minimum actions. India rejected the pledge-and-review approach on the grounds that it would not provide for firm commitments on emission limitations by industrial countries and therefore was not a useful basis for further negotiations. Many of the environmental nongovernmental organizations also criticized pledge-and-review (what they called "hedge and retreat") on the grounds that it would simply enable countries to avoid making any commitments whatsoever to reducing GHG emissions.

During the second session there were also a number of informal meetings among industrial countries on institutional questions. There was strong support for the view that existing institutional mechanisms to meet the needs of a climate convention were inadequate and that such a convention would require new, strong, credible, and neutral institutions, including a conference of the parties, a secretariat, and some form of scientific and implementation-review mechanism. In several key respects, the second session of the INC was marked by progress, because substantive discussions were launched on a climate change convention, a framework for future negotiations was established, and developing countries were fully engaged in the debate. However, the lack of general agreement in Working Group I on the nature of commitments threatened to stall negotiations in Working Group II, and developing countries continued to argue that climate change was a problem caused by industrial countries and therefore was their responsibility.

Round III

The third negotiating session was held on September 9–20, 1991, in Nairobi, Kenya.[37] The session was marked by some progress in both working groups. Working Group I narrowed down the range of possible commitments and gave the cochairs the mandate to develop a negotiating text that would serve as the basis for discussions at the next session. Working Group II got down to the details of options for mechanisms and associated functions in a climate change convention. A draft text was reviewed by Working Group II, and the cochairs were given a mandate to present a revised text at the next session.[38]

Generally speaking, the third round was marked by continuing and major differences between industrial and developing countries on a wide range of issues. However, the United States was alone among industrial countries in resisting the idea of including specific targets and schedules for GHG reductions in a climate change convention. Japan's position was somewhat ambiguous, while the Soviet Union continued to plead for special treatment. There were also differences among industrial countries on such matters as the amounts and modalities of financial and technology transfer mechanisms to be covered by the convention. Some of the more interesting ideas to emerge were Norway's suggestion for a "financial clearing house" that would involve emission credits and India's proposal for contractual and project-specific versus convention-based obligations.[39] There was also considerable discussion of pledge-and-review, although, as a result of continued opposition by the Group of 77, the concept was set aside while discussion of commitments continued. Delegates expressed frustration that there was not more progress, as well as concern that a convention might not be ready in time for the UNCED conference in Rio. A fifth negotiating session in February 1992 was added to the roster, and there was much talk that a sixth session might be required.

Working Group I had two rounds of discussion on principles and commitments related to sources and sinks, to financial resources and technology transfer, and to countries with special circumstances. Industrial countries wished to have either no statement of principles in the convention or at most a limited number of general principles. They preferred to allocate most of the suggested principles to either the preamble of the convention or to the provisions on commitments. Industrial countries were also opposed to principles that would go beyond the issue of climate change, such as the right to development and "polluter-pays" principles. Developing countries, however, advocated a wide range of principles to be set out in the convention. These principles would be linked to and reinforce specific commitments in the convention. Most developing countries also wanted to see explicit recognition of their special circumstances (e.g., those of small island states, newly industrial states, and the poorest or least developed countries) in the convention.

Some of the principles put forward by developing countries included non-conditionality (i.e., financial assistance and technology transfer would not be conditional on developing countries' adherence to common commitments in the convention); the "polluter pays" principle (with particular emphasis on the industrial countries' liability to pay compensation for past, present, and future interference with climate changes caused by their emissions); an attempt to enshrine the right to develop in the provisions of the convention; convergence of per capita emissions sometime in the future, thus enshrining the right of developing countries to increase their emissions up to levels attained by industrial countries; and sovereignty, mandating noninterference with sovereign rights and responsibilities, including unfettered use of natural resources and development of national emission strategies. By the end of the session there was a consensus on some principles, namely, the precautionary approach (act now, even if there are major scientific uncertainties), equity and the common but differentiated responsibilities of states, and the need to cooperate on an international scale. However, aside from these three principles there remained outstanding differences on what other principles ought to be included in the convention.

Almost all delegations supported a flexible and differentiated approach to commitments related to sources and sinks. Developing countries, led by China and India, generally called for concrete actions on the part of industrial countries, insisting that since emissions of GHGs come predominantly from industrial countries, these countries must shoulder responsibility and share liability for the consequences. Although most developing countries felt that they should not be obliged to take any actions under the convention to limited GHGs, some developing countries did recognize the need for them to consider limitations that would be within their means. India introduced the notion of contractual arrangements, whereby developing countries that limited their growth of GHGs would have the full incremental costs of doing so paid for by industrial countries. The concept of parties moving to a common level of emissions per capita was widely supported by developing countries, although the utility of the concept of net emissions of CO_2 was challenged by some coastal states, which argued that they were net sinks of CO_2.

With the notable exception of the United States, industrial countries were prepared to commit to targets and schedules for reducing GHGs. The European Community indicated that it believed that "a crucial part of the package to be agreed in the process toward Rio 1991 is the stabilization of CO_2 emissions by the year 2000 in general at 1990 levels by industrialized countries individually or jointly."[40] The United States argued against specific targets on the grounds that "the costs of achieving these targets may be quite high" and that "the benefits of taking these actions, while clearly in the right direction, are still uncertain with respect to their magnitude because of continuing scientific and economic uncertainties," adding that "if only industrial countries take these short-term actions, the effect on global atmospheric GHG concentrations, and on climate change, is likely to be small and transitory."[41] The Soviet Union indicated that it would have difficulty taking any action.

Most countries favored a comprehensive approach toward GHG reductions, with some countries suggesting a phased approach focusing initially on CO_2. However, carbon dioxide was the focus of many delegations' commitments in the near term, and most industrial countries supported the concept of net emissions, taking into account all sources and sinks of GHGs. The European Community, along with Sweden and Switzerland, while accepting the theoretical correctness of the concept of net emissions, expressed reservations about its political acceptability and the practicality of the approach and argued for a focus only on sources. Canada advocated early adoption of the net-emissions approach on the grounds that all countries implicitly include sinks of GHGs to a greater or lesser extent as offsets to gross anthropogenic emissions when assessing the contributions of various human activities to national inventories of greenhouse-gas emissions. However, Canada argued that allowable sinks should be restricted to those that are "new, incremental to background natural sinks, and quantifiable by internationally agreed upon methodologies."[42] Industrial countries supported the need for parties to formulate national and regional plans for dealing with climate change. New Zealand called for net emissions moving to a common level (either per capita or per unit of gross domestic product), and Australia proposed to remove all government subsidies for activities that would increase emissions of GHGs—a measure that was endorsed by the European Community.

Several oil-producing states, led by Saudi Arabia, raised the need to study the climate change problem further before taking action, while stressing the need not to interfere with the free market through a system of targets and schedules. Norway proposed that industrial countries should be given credit for sponsoring actions to reduce GHG emissions—a proposal that met with a mixed reaction from developing countries, some of which saw it as a constructive approach to a funding mechanism while others saw it as a way for industrial countries to avoid taking action. Developing countries were not unified on the matter of commitments relating to sources and sinks. India and China continued to take a hard-line approach, while the Alliance of Small Island States took a more moderate point of view. But most developing countries did not foresee the convention as requiring initial commitments from them.

On the matter of commitments relating to financial resources and technology transfer, developing countries continued to press with their demands that new funding would have to be over and above existing transfers and that industrial countries would have to pay the full costs of any obligations undertaken by developing countries to address climate change. Developing countries also expressed confidence in their ability to make use of indigenous technologies. In discussions about funding institutions (an issue that was outside the mandate of Working Group I), several developing countries expressed their opposition to the use of the Global Environment Facility as a funding mechanism.

While all industrial countries recognized the need for a transfer of resources to developing countries, some countries, like Norway, indicated their willingness to commit new funding to help developing countries deal with climate change. Norway also proposed that OECD countries commit themselves to contribute to the financial mechanism "with new and additional financial resources and that these responses be provided from budget sources that are *separate* and *additional* to development aid budgets."[43] At the other end of the spectrum, the United States maintained its position from previous sessions regarding the importance of "making maximum use of existing resources and multilateral and bilateral mechanisms before considering the creation of new entities."[44] The United States also made it quite clear that it would be willing to consider provision of adequate financial resources and technology transfer only on the basis of specific, costed needs, as identified by developing countries in plans they would have to produce to deal with climate change, that is, in a manner that would be consistent with the U.S. preference for the country-study approach to climate change. The European Community seemed prepared to commit "new and additional resources" but was vague as to whether this would include new financial resources. There was growing support among industrial countries for the Global Environment Facility as a funding mechanism, although there was also recognition of the need to address some of its shortcomings.

At the June INC session held in Geneva, the United States tabled a non-paper proposing a process for conduct of country studies, particularly in developing countries, for developing national plans to address the problems of climate change. These studies would have three main elements: (1) an inventory of greenhouse-gas emissions; (2) identification of alternatives to deal with climate change in the country; (3) prioritization of means, measures, and technology requirements to implement the plan. During the summer, several countries, including the United States and Finland, worked on refining the methodology for country studies. Working with the members of Working Group III of the IPCC, the United States drafted a common methodology for country studies.[45] During the discussions in Working Group I of the INC, the United States made it clear that it would link funding and technology transfer commitments to developing countries to the need for the recipient country to have participated in a country study. However, developing countries argued that they would need financial and technological transfers—up-front monies—before the country studies could be carried out; nor did they want country studies to impose specific national strategies upon them.

Finally, the cochairs of Working Group I, in cooperation with the secretariat and the bureau of the INC, were given a clear mandate to produce a consolidated text on principles and commitments that would serve as a basis for negotiations at the fourth session of the INC.

Working Group II began its deliberations by reviewing all areas within its mandate, considering concepts and functions related to mechanisms, identifying options, and producing some draft language for the convention. Industrial countries advocated similar positions while disagreeing on details. North-South differences loomed large on matters relating to financial resources and technology, research priorities, information exchange, access to information, convention institutions, and the role of nongovernmental organizations. The main focus of discussion was the cochair's single negotiating text, which helped to explore various concepts and options, concretize discussions, and elicit specific proposals from delegations for possible draft articles. Although discussions were not intended to be a drafting exercise, they did, in fact become that, with line-by-line reviews of the text.

Discussions began on scientific mechanisms, which served as a useful common starting point. There was widespread support for scientific cooperation and general endorsement of the need for an article on education, training, and public awareness, which Canada took the lead in drafting, as well as the need to include the social sciences, particularly economics, to address the technological and development aspects in the science section of the convention.

The discussion of institutions focused on decision-making procedures, verification and compliance, settlement of disputes, and final clauses. There was general acceptance of the need for a conference of the parties and a strong, independent secretariat. Although it was agreed that the former would be the supreme decision-making body, there was a divergence of views on the functions of the latter. France and Norway also proposed the establishment of an executive committee, a standing body with extensive authority under the convention. On the issue of verification, industrial countries strongly supported the concept of verification or review mechanisms to promote compliance with the convention, while emphasizing the need for a cooperative, nonconfrontational mechanism that would assist rather than penalize or judge countries. Developing countries were generally hostile to the proposal, because they saw it as infringing on national sovereignty, except when it came to reviewing the industrial countries' provision of financial and technical resources, which they favored. Some delegations suggested the need for differentiated reporting requirements between industrial and developing countries, as well as provision of requisite financial resources to developing countries to enable them to prepare reports.

Working Group II reviewed several options for dispute-settlement provisions in the convention, although the most appropriate mechanism depended upon the nature of the agreed obligations. The main point of contention was whether the dispute settlement procedure should be voluntary or compulsory. The group also discussed in some detail the concepts and language surrounding final clauses of the convention. The issue of how associated protocols would be treated in the convention was controversial, as was the matter of how the convention would come into force. Four options for entry into force were identified, based on ratification by an absolute number of states, by states accounting for a percentage of total global emissions, triggering by one or the other, or a requirement for both.

Financial and technology transfer mechanisms to implement commitment established in Working Group I were also the subject of extensive discussion. Two options emerged: under one, developing countries would receive assistance under a separate financial mechanism established under the authority of a conference of the parties and managed by an executive committee similar to the institutional mechanisms in the Montreal Protocol; the second option (supported by most industrial countries and opposed by virtually all developing countries) would use the existing World Bank/UNEP/UNDP Global Environment Facility, with some changes to its governing arrangements. Norway proposed a clearinghouse that would deal in emission credits as well as financial resources and technology. The concept of a clearinghouse, although supported by most delegations, received mixed reviews. The AOSIS countries proposed an insurance scheme, which was greeted politely but not with great enthusiasm or interest. The concept of a technology clearinghouse was also endorsed by the delegates, although many recognized the importance of referring to country studies as potentially contributing to the identification of appropriate technology needs.

Japan also offered a clarification of its concept of pledge-and-review, which had been made at the previous session. The Japanese statement emphasized that pledge-and-review was only a mechanism to ensure implementation of commitments. The pledge would come in the form of a public, national strategy and target or expectation of result. Subsequent reviews would be conducted by expert teams leading to a public report. The European Community took the view that a pledge would not be the same as a commitment, whereas the United States indicated that it had no position on pledge-and-review and that the concept required clarification. The Group of 77 response to pledge-and-review in the plenary was negative, on the grounds that it would lead to delay in reaching an agreement, and there was deep hostility to the possibility of reviews of its own programs and policies. The European Community tried to refine its own position on the concept and made a statement in an informal session of Working Group II that a pledge would be additional to general and specific obligations and would reflect a unilateral commitment, which would be translated into a national strategy.[46] All countries would make pledges, allowing for different approaches between industrial and developing countries. The EC statement provoked no discussion and was not welcomed by the other members of the group. The concept was set aside, with general acceptance that a pledge was no substitute for concrete commitments.

Round IV

Progress in the fourth round of the INC, held in Geneva, Switzerland, December 9–20, was minimal, because of continuing outstanding differences between the major players.[47] The working groups reviewed the texts prepared by the cochairs after the third INC meeting in Nairobi. There was continued strong pressure from developing countries to meet their development needs, with some countries arguing that industrial countries had a historic responsibility for climate change and an obligation to make deep cuts in GHG emissions to allow "head room" for increasing emissions by developing countries.[48] This would be over and above demands for massive financial and technology transfers. Industrial countries argued that although they accepted primary responsibility for limiting emissions, developing countries had to assume some responsibility, too, by adopting sensible development policies and protecting sinks. The United States stood firm on not accepting any targets and schedules to reduce GHG emissions but committed itself to tabling an effective national climate-change action plan within one year of signing the convention.[49] The Federal Republic of Germany reiterated its earlier pledge to reduce CO_2 emission by 25–30 percent by the year 2005. Some splits also emerged in the Group of 77 bloc over the common text on commitments, resulting in minority reports by different groups: a hard line group of twenty-four states led by China and India, and a more flexible group, led by the AOSIS states, willing to acknowledge some measures of commitment by developing countries. Although some compromises were achieved, the single negotiated text that emerged from the fourth session was strewn with options and heavily bracketed.

In Working Group I, the main points of contention centered on a differentiated approach to commitments, targets and schedules, and implementation.[50] Industrial countries were anxious to solicit some commitment from developing countries to GHG stabilization, while recognizing their need to grow economically. Views ranged from no required commitments until developing countries achieve economic parity with industrial countries to a no-regrets approach based on energy efficiency and good practices in the maintenance and enhancement of sinks. There was general support for a common but differentiated approach, with some developing countries endorsing the goals and general commitments of the convention while retaining the right to be excused from specific emission-control targets and schedules. The Eastern and Central European countries also appealed for special consideration because of their own economic difficulties and their dependence on fossil fuels. Their demands for economic assistance from industrial countries was resisted by developing countries fearful of a diversion of assistance from their needs. The AOSIS states also sought assistance but indicated their willingness to support commitments to some GHG reductions.

On the matter of targets and schedules, the United States continued to voice its strong opposition to specific targets and GHG reduction schedules in the convention. Similarly, though for different reasons, developing countries argued that specific commitments would constrain their capacity for economic development and thus were also inappropriate to them. Most of the other OECD countries favored some form of stabilization, at 1990 levels by the year 2000, or reductions. The key points of contention centered on whether the base year would be 1990 or some formulation that would allow for a three-year average; whether the commitment to a target could be expressed as a collective effort (the preference of the European Community) or a national one; whether the end point should be the year 2000 or some later time; whether the commitment would be based on sources alone or could be netted to include sinks; and whether CO_2 alone would be addressed or whether other greenhouse gases should be controlled under a comprehensive approach. On the last point, the European Community favored a CO_2-only approach, with stabilization to be achieved based on different levels of activity by individual members, across the European Community, by the year 2000. Canada, Australia, Japan, Norway, and Finland formed the core of those states in favor of a comprehensive approach, but there was a growing sense of isolation by these countries, even though informal meetings in the ad hoc OECD working group managed to bridge some differences. The United States generally stayed out of the debate, while indicating that for philosophical reasons it favored a comprehensive approach.

Implementation discussions centered on how to implement the convention in the most cost-effective and efficient manner. Some developing countries still pressed for preferential, concessional, and noncommercial transfers of technology, while others searched for compromise language that would recognize commercial property rights and also encourage technological innovation and access on preferential terms. Industrial countries stressed the importance of maintaining patent and property rights and emphasized the role of private industry. Developing countries also wanted to see the establishment of an independent climate change fund, but whereas some countries wanted no restrictions on funding, others sought to link financial and technological assistance to concrete commitments on climate change. There continued to be a split between industrial and developing countries on whether a climate change fund should rely on existing institutional mechanisms like the World Bank/UNEP/UNDP Global Environment Facility or should be based on new institutional mechanisms. Norway elaborated its concept for a clearinghouse under which developing country projects could be collected and accessed by industrial countries that would choose complementary matched projects for emission reduction or sink enhancement. Projects would be selected on the lowest marginal cost in order to maximize use of resources. Germany proposed a crediting system that would allow countries to implement a specified share of their domestic program to reduce emissions, by claiming a discounted share of the reduction implemented outside their borders. The proposal would apply to actions taken toward emissions-reduction targets (but not sinks).[51] Mexico proposed a centralized procurement mechanism to help developing countries negotiate technology acquisitions at the lowest cost by pooling needs lists and soliciting international tenders.

Working Group II was successful in reviewing the details of the text of the convention articles and annexes proposed by the cochairs, although many portions of the text continued to remain heavily bracketed, reflecting major points of disagreement. Although there was general agreement on the need for a conference of the parties as the supreme decision-making body of the convention, the powers and responsibilities of the body remained a matter of open discussion and debate. There was also a divergence of opinion on the need to establish subsidiary bodies beyond a secretariat to the conference of the parties. The cochairs proposed two subsidiary bodies: an advisory committee on science, which would be responsible for gathering and interpreting information on climate change; and an advisory committee on implementation, which would receive and study the national reports prepared by the parties to the convention. Developing countries were more enthusiastic about a scientific committee when it was proposed that the work of the committee should include matters of development. Developing countries were more strongly opposed to the implementation committee, preferring to leave questions of implementation to the open conference. France and Norway proposed an executive committee that would include the functions of implementation. Industrial countries and the small island states supported the concept of an advisory committee on implementation.

Four options were left on the table regarding the administrative mechanism for financial resources and technology transfer: the U.S. proposal designating the Global Environment Facility (GEF) as the sole mechanism through which financial assistance would be channeled and under which the conference of the parties could suggest general guidelines and specific proposals for funding; the United Kingdom's proposal, which also relied on the GEF but provided for arrangements between the conference of the parties and the GEF concerning the administration of the climate change fund; the cochairs' proposal for a specific fund for climate change, administered by the GEF, under specific guidelines and policy directives provided by the conference of the parties; and a proposal by India and a limited number of developing countries for the establishment of a separate International Climate Fund that would be completely independent of the GEF and controlled and administered by the conference of the parties.

Several options were also left on the table for dispute-settlement and resolution procedures under the convention. One involved a so-called friendly procedure for the settlement of disputes, with the objective of assisting the parties to implement the convention under which questions of procedure would be addressed by the conference of the parties. A second involved resort to bilateral mechanisms, including conciliation and arbitration, which could lead to binding decisions. A third option sought to merge the first two options by suggesting a two-step mechanism whereby questions would first be studied through the friendly mechanism; if the results were unsatisfactory, the parties would then resort to a bilateral dispute-settlement mechanism.

Round V

The fifth session of the INC was held in New York, February 18–28, 1992. It was marked by continuing divisions among the major players and little outward sign of compromise on outstanding issues. The divisions were more acute in Working Group I, and lack of progress there hindered progress in Working Group II. At the end of the session a trimmed-down text was distributed to the delegations to take back to their capitals in order to seek greater negotiating flexibility.[52] The most contentious issue had to do with section IV.2 of the draft text regarding specific commitments.[53] Among the OECD countries, the United States continued to resist specific targets and schedules, while the European Community pressed for firm CO_2 limitation targets and the CANZ-Nordic Group (Canada, Australia, New Zealand, Norway, Finland, and Sweden) advocated targets and schedules combined with maximum flexibility for implementation. India and China continued to slow the pace of negotiations with their demands for new financial resources and the notion of the historical responsibility of the industrial countries for anthropogenic global warming. These countries also resisted the idea of institutions and reporting procedures. Saudi Arabia, Kuwait, and Iran intervened frequently to weaken any commitments, particularly those addressing CO_2 emissions, as did institutions aimed at reviewing the convention. The oil-producing states, along with India and China, however, found themselves coming under criticism from more moderate members of the Group of 77—a split that had begun to emerge at the Geneva session.

Working Group I worked on the preamble to the convention and sections dealing with principles, objectives, and commitments.[54] The discussion about specific commitments was the most contentious, centering on a number of key issues, including stabilization commitment, net emissions, the comprehensive approach, joint implementation, financial resources, technology transfer, differentiation and special cases, and developing-country commitments. Of these, the paragraph on the stabilization commitment was the focus of the most heated debate among the OECD countries. The European Community pushed for a target stabilization of CO_2 at 1990 levels by the year 2000 and for a joint commitment for all twelve European Community members. The United States refused to accept any targets or schedules but stressed that countries pledge to take national actions to stabilize emissions. The CANZ-Nordic group together advocated a targets-and-schedules approach, combined with a flexible approach toward implementation. Norway led the group on joint implementation, Finland on net emissions, and Australia and Canada shared responsibility for developing the concept of a comprehensive approach.

The Finnish approach to net emissions came under some scrutiny from members of the European Community, Switzerland, and Sweden, who voiced concerns that there was a lack of proper inventories, and a poorly defined methodology for a crediting system based on net emissions. Similarly, the European Community attacked the concept of comprehensiveness on the grounds of a lack of science, even though this approach could serve as a long-term basis for the convention. Norway, Finland, and the United States joined Canada and Australia in arguing for a comprehensive approach sooner rather than later. India and the other Group of 77 countries were skeptical, viewing the comprehensive approach as a loophole to avoid more stringent CO_2 reductions. The Canadian delegation offered a draft paper suggesting how a country might implement its commitments in an integrated fashion, involving a mix of GHGs and their sources, which would be approved and updated by the conference on a regular basis.

Norway took the lead in defining a joint implementation mechanism by which countries could implement their commitment by taking credit for actions sponsored by other countries. This was the second most contentious item, next to stabilization commitments. The resulting text set out a process of three different transparency standards for three categories of joint implementation arrangements:

- countries sharing similar quantitative targets (e.g., stabilization by 2000) could implement their commitments jointly, and report how they did this as required under reporting requirements in the convention;
- developed countries working with Eastern European and former Soviet republics would only have to report on their cooperative arrangements but in accordance with criteria approved by the conference of the parties;
- developed countries working jointly with developing countries on implementation would have to do so in accordance with procedures and criteria approved and reviewed by the conference.

Some developing countries questioned the whole notion of standards, but others, notably the NICs (newly industrialized countries, like Thailand, Indonesia, and Korea) favored the scheme.

There was also debate over the technology transfer and whether the convention should refer only to traditional kinds of technology transfer or whether it should embrace a broader concept of technological cooperation. There were outstanding differences about whether the convention should mandate parties to promote technology transfer or to ensure that

technology is transferred; whether such transfer should be on concessional, preferential, or most favorable terms; whether intellectual property
rights should be adequately protected or whether they should not be permitted to hinder technology transfer.

Working Group II was charged with reviewing sections in the draft convention pertaining to institutions, procedures, final clauses and associated
annexes, and the section on science. Many major issues remained unresolved, resulting in a heavily bracketed text. On matters pertaining to science, research, information, and cooperation, disagreements related to attempts by developing countries to insert their priorities on development,
technology, funding, capacity building, and access to satellite data. A
coalition of industrial countries and small island states supported the creation of strong subsidiary institutional bodies under the convention; however, developing countries attempted to block the establishment of any
subsidiary bodies, except the secretariat and financial mechanisms, and
sought to weaken or eliminate procedures related to reporting requirements and review of implementation commitments. Developing countries
were opposed to establishment of an advisory committee on science, arguing that the convention should rely on or subsume the IPCC. A compromise package for an advisory committee on implementation, devised by
an informal working group led by the United States, was strongly opposed
by the Indian, Iranian, and Brazilian delegations.

Efforts to develop a compromise between those favoring an independent climate change fund and those seeking to place it under the control
of the GEF also floundered, leaving three options on the table: a fund
under the overall authority of the convention but administered by the
GEF (a proposal supported by Canada, the Nordic countries, Switzerland,
and Austria); a simple designation of the GEF as the unitary funding mechanism under loose control by the convention (the U.S. and EC proposal);
and an independent fund under the conference (supported by most developing countries). The issue of an insurance fund was also marked by major
differences: small island states supported the proposal, while recognizing
that it would be difficult to reach an agreement in the convention; African
countries sought to expand the concept to include desertification and
drought; hard-line countries rejected the concept because it would divert
funds available under the financial mechanism; and industrial countries
showed some flexibility by recognizing the threat of a sea-level rise to
small island states in the convention. Finally, as a result of informal work
done by New Zealand on the resolution of questions and dispute-settlement procedures, it was agreed to send two texts forward to the next session covering these issues.

Round VI

The last negotiating session, designated as a continuation of the fifth round, took place in New York on April 30–May 9, 1992.[55] The session began with the tabling of the chair's draft convention text, which sought to present a compromise package, bridging the different viewpoints expressed in the bracketed texts.[56] The draft text helped to focus the discussions on specifics, as did the creation of three informal working or "cluster" groups organized around different sections of the text. The first six days of the meeting were spent in informal consultations within these groups, which devoted most of their time to a line-by-line reading of the text. Bilateral and chair-initiated discussions helped to bring out key differences and pave the way toward a consensus. Once all the articles of the convention were reviewed, the chair met in closed session with a core group of representatives of thirty countries to prepare a revised text for final negotiation and adoption. These informal consultations ran for two days. A final set of plenary sessions was held on May 8–9 to achieve agreement on the finalized text. There was widespread recognition that the text represented a delicate balance and that to tamper with it might cause the whole package to unravel. At 6:12 P.M. eastern daylight time, the text was adopted by the INC by consensus and recommended for signature at the UNCED conference in Rio de Janeiro.

Discussions on the preamble, objective, and principles of the convention were marked by substantive conflicts between major industrial countries, particularly the United States, and many developing countries. Many of the expressed concerns were resolved by informal consultations with the conference chairman.

The commitments articles in the convention (Articles IV, XI, and XII) cover general commitments by industrial countries to limit GHG emissions and enhance sinks, financial commitments applying to industrial countries, and reporting requirements applying to all countries but in a differentiated manner. Under the accord, parties agree to prepare and publish inventories of GHG emissions and sinks; publish national strategies or measures to mitigate climate change and facilitate adaptation; promote and cooperate in developing technological applications, including technology transfer, promote and cooperate in the enhancement of sinks; and prepare for adaptation, especially in vulnerable areas. Developing countries' willingness to comply with the convention is to some extent dependent on financial resources and technology transfers from industrial countries. Industrial countries, however, agree to specific commitments, which include promoting and financing, as appropriate, technology transfer to developing countries; adopting national policies and measures to return

GHG emissions, by the end of the decade, to earlier levels; submitting detailed information, within six months of entry of the convention into force, and periodically thereafter, on national policies and measures as well as projected GHG emissions and sinks, taking into account the effects of such policies and measures aimed at returning GHG emissions to 1990 levels (including actions taken jointly with other countries); and coordinating the development of economic instruments as well as identifying and reviewing domestic policies that encourage higher GHG emissions.

Article XI of the convention provides a mechanism for the provision of financial resources and the transfer of technology. It is left up to the conference to decide what policies, program priorities, and eligibility criteria relate to the provision of resources. Interim operation of the mechanism is entrusted to the GHG. Industrial countries agreed to provide new and additional financial resources to meet the agreed full costs of the reporting requirement and any incremental costs of general commitments under the convention. Under the reporting requirements of the convention, all countries agree to provide a national inventory of GHG emissions and sinks, to provide a general description of measures taken to fulfill those commitments, and to provide this information within three years of entry into force of the convention. Industrial countries are further required to provide detailed descriptions of their policies, to provide specific estimates of the impact of these policies on GHG emissions and sinks, to describe their contributions to financial mechanisms, to provide such information within six months of the convention coming into force, and to provide technical and financial assistance to developing countries to assist them in compiling their reports.

Much of the debate in previous sessions of the INC had focused on the matter of commitments, and thus it was crucial to break the logjam on this issue in order to arrive at an agreement. The United States was consistently the most vigorous opponent to any targets and schedules in the convention, on the grounds that it did not want a commitment that Congress would view as a legally binding domestic target. Developing countries were also opposed to targets and schedules, if for different reasons, while other members of the OECD, like the EC and CANZ-Nordic countries, were on the record as being strongly in favor of such targets. The chair sought to find a middle ground on commitments that would be acceptable to the OECD countries and to developing countries. The chair's proposal in the draft text called for a vigorous and ongoing international review process that would give substance to the political commitments undertaken by the parties to the convention without actually setting targets and schedules. Although there was some attempt by Germany and Austria to introduce stronger language into the text, most countries realized that the United States would have to be accommodated if it was to remain part of the process, and they were therefore willing to go for a compromise. Argentina and the AOSIS (particularly Vanuatu and Nauru) were important voices of moderation among the developing countries and played a key role in reaching the final agreement on commitments. China also showed greater flexibility and was helpful in the discussions, although India, Bangladesh, Saudi Arabia, and Colombia were disruptive negotiating partners until the end.

On financial institutions, the chair's proposal was to establish a funding mechanism and then place it under the control of an existing institution. The European Community, with the support of the G-7, tabled an alternative text placing the mechanism under the control of the GEF. Developing countries did not want the GEF mentioned in the convention, and the final compromise named the GEF the financial mechanism on an interim basis, in a separate article in the convention on interim arrangements. The financial mechanism would be governed by the conference of the parties, which would set policy and determine program priorities. Meetings on the GEF, which took place in Washington on April 29 and 30, helped these discussions and the creation of a compromise package acceptable to developing countries.

The "cluster" group on institutions and final clauses met for five days. Discussions focused on the draft compromise text that had been prepared by Jean Ripert, the conference chair. The chair of the cluster group tried to isolate countries that were trying to stall discussion and produced a number of his own redrafts of the text to reflect consensus or competing points of view. There was substantial discussion about the entry in force provisions of the convention. Most countries wanted a simple numerical basis for entry into force, ranging from twenty signatures (Finland, and the AOSIS group) to approximately eighty (Saudi Arabia, China, and Iran). The United Kingdom suggested that entry into force should also be triggered by adherence of those countries representing two-thirds of global emissions as calculated in the *United Nations Energy Statistics Yearbook*. Austria supported the United Kingdom's position, but at a 50 percent level. The chair opted for Ripert's suggestion for fifty signatures, which was accepted by Canada, Australia, and the United States (even though they had favored a lower figure).

The provisions on settlement of disputes were also managed by the chair, with the assistance of New Zealand's delegation head. Venezuela, Chile, and Iran did not support the concept of dispute-settlement procedures being invoked by one country; industrial countries were also unhappy about the way the article was written, although ultimately the chair's proposal remained on the table. Developing countries also expressed reservations about the article on resolution of questions, although again the chair's interpretation held.

The most difficult questions involved articles dealing with the conference of the parties, the secretariat, and an implementation body. Developing countries, led by Iran, China, and India, initially sought to eliminate the article on an implementation body and then to confine its responsibilities to industrial countries' commitments. Industrial countries, led by Canada, the United States, France, and the Netherlands, supported the broader, generic nature of the body as set out in the chair's proposed text. The chair's proposal remained intact in spite of the strong objections of developing countries. Similarly, developing countries tried to add new language that would make it clear that the conference of the parties would have absolute authority over all subsidiary mechanisms, particularly funding mechanisms. The United States, supported by Canada, sought specific mention of the conference of the parties' responsibility to develop and refine methodologies for preparation of inventories and for evaluating the effectiveness of measures to limit emissions and enhance the removal of GHGs by sinks. This was accepted by the delegates. A joint American-British attempt to have the article on the conference secretariat refer specifically to the need for secretariat cooperation with the implementation body was rejected by developing countries, although the chair was successful in having the general thought incorporated in the generic language of the text.

Interim arrangements and a proposal that would authorize discussions to continue the period between signature of the convention and its entry into force also proved to be surprisingly controversial. Industrial countries wanted convention signatories to have a privileged place in these follow-on negotiations and to keep the process outside the U.N. General Assembly. Developing countries were opposed to both these positions. Under the final compromise, industrial countries accepted an extension of the INC under General Assembly authority in return for acceptance of a first session of the conference of the parties and provision for a first meeting on interim arrangements in 1992.

Explaining Outcomes

Critics of the climate change accords argue that U.S. opposition to targets and schedules effectively scuttled the possibilities of a substantive deal that would have had real teeth and led to concrete reductions in GHG emissions. Many of the NGOs attending the Rio conference expressed such disappointment; and several European countries, including the EC environment minister, made no secret of their unhappiness with the outcome and put much of the blame on the United States. Defenders of the accords argue that the convention provided more than a skeletal structure by setting forth an elaborate process of review and reporting and implementation mechanisms that would eventually pave the way to more concrete actions, once the science of climate change was better understood.[57] The creation of new financial mechanisms under the GEF to address developing country needs was also a major achievement. According to this point of view, half a loaf was better than none, and compromise was essential to secure the participation of major countries in the convention.

Whether the agreement is seen as a success or not depends very much on the expectations of the observer and the perceived urgency of the climate change problem. The agreement set out specific objectives and obligations, particularly on matters of reporting, financing, and scientific research and cooperation, and a commitment to continue and sustain negotiations. In this respect, the model of negotiations was not unlike those leading to the Vienna Convention for the Protection of the Ozone Layer (discussed in chapter 7) because it left specific control and GHG-limitation measures, including targets and schedules, to future negotiations and protocols.

Crisis

It is difficult to make the case that the prenegotiation phase of the climate change negotiations was marked by an acute or growing sense of crisis. Although a growing chorus in the scientific community pointed to the increasing dangers of climate change, the issue was not perceived by the public to have the same urgency as ozone depletion in the upper atmosphere, because the effects of climate change are long-term and are measured in decades, if not half-centuries. In spite of the active involvement by environmental nongovernmental organizations in the climate change issue, there are no obvious parallels to the ban-the-can movement in attitudes toward ozone depletion in the 1970s, which stirred public fears about skin cancer and other dangerous health effects of stratospheric ozone depletion. Whereas public opinion openly clamored for control on aerosols and CFCs well before scientists had reached definitive conclusions about the effects of CFCs, the same cannot be said about global warming. Public opinion surveys in some advanced industrial countries show global warming to be low on the list of environmental priorities and the link between energy consumption patterns and the accumulation of GHGs in the atmosphere to be poorly understood.[58]

International negotiations about climate change have also not been punctuated by dramatic new scientific revelations—as they were in the ozone case—of a looming environmental catastrophe of global proportions. There is no scientific or political analogy in climate change to the discovery of the ozone hole over Antarctica and of a general thinning of the ozone layer at higher latitudes. However, global climate change negotiations were the obvious beneficiaries of the large wave of ripening and maturing of environmental concerns in the late 1980s. Bureaucrats in UNEP and in the environmental ministries of various national bureaucracies (especially Canada, the Scandinavian countries, Germany, the Netherlands, and the United Kingdom) also carried the agenda forward. Moreover, climate change negotiators felt a sense of urgency resulting from politically imposed deadlines; in particular, the realization that tabling a convention on climate change was crucial to the success of the 1992 Rio Conference on the Environment and Sustainable Development.

Consensual Knowledge

The IPCC has been the principal vehicle for coordinating scientific assessments from around the world. It helped to develop the foundations for identifying both appropriate strategies to address climate change and points of consensus and divergence within the scientific community about the magnitude and scope of climate change. The IPCC underscored a growing consensus among scientists that without action to reduce emissions of GHGs, global warming will occur, although the "timing, magnitude, and regional patterns of climate change" are not yet fully understood.[59] However, the conventional wisdom linking GHG emissions to global warming has not gone unchallenged.[60] Moreover, the socioeconomic effects of climate change are poorly understood, and it is difficult to say who will be the real winners and losers. Some economists, for example, have suggested that the costs of adaptation to climate change, at least for some societies, will be lower than the costs of preventive responses that seek to curb GHG emissions, although this assertion has been hotly contested by others in the profession.[61] In the case of climate change, as perhaps with all issues of fundamental science, it may be more appropriate to speak of a majoritarian consensus, recognizing that the conventional wisdom has its critics.

Media reports undoubtedly sharpened (perhaps even exaggerated) differences of opinion within the scientific community about the consequences of climate change, while no doubt contributing to growing public confusion about its risks.[62] But there is no question that the international scientific consensus forged by the IPCC spurred governments to the negotiating table and laid the foundations for an international convention on climate change. (The creation of a new scientific advisory body that reports to the INC is intended to translate IPCC findings into advice for the convention itself and to keep IPCC an independent scientific advisory body.)

Science fell short in its inability to resolve thorny questions about how and when to act and what kinds of national and cooperative international strategies are relevant to addressing the climate change problem. As is evident from the third IPCC report on the formulation of response strategies and throughout the negotiations in the INC, international negotiations on climate change at the governmental level were plagued by major differences, not only between North and South on distributional questions but also between those advanced industrial nations seeking to move ahead on global warming and those seeking to avoid immediate action. At the heart of these divisions lie fundamental questions of equity, fairness, distribution, and economic competitiveness, as well as the assignment of moral and political responsibility for the climate change problem. These issues have been at the forefront of international negotiations and proved to be the most intractable, although all parties have recognized the need for more information and a better scientific basis for developing effective response strategies to the climate change problem.

Coalitions

The formation of coalitions was crucial to simplifying the negotiating process in the climate change negotiations, although it would be a mistake to characterize the fault lines as being too sharply drawn, since group membership varied across different issues in the negotiation. Negotiations were marked by a North-South split: whereas the North was primarily interested in addressing climate change as an environmental problem, the South saw it in development terms and as an opportunity to secure transfers of new financial and technological resources. Nonetheless, key divisions emerged, both in the South and in the North, on the matter of commitments in the convention, whether the convention should take a specific or comprehensive approach to sources and sinks, and institutions. On one hand, the presence of these fault lines made negotiations more difficult, particularly among advanced industrial countries, by introducing complexity, as there were multiple issues on the table that had to be resolved. On the other, divisions in the South, with some developing countries finding themselves in alliance with the position of industrial countries, helped to isolate hard-line states, like India, by creating a coalition of interests that crossed the North-South divide.

In the early sessions of the INC, the European Community, joined by Switzerland, Austria, and Finland, came out strongly in favor of commitments that would include specific targets and schedules for reducing emissions of GHGs. Most EC members wanted to tackle sources first, focusing on CO_2 emissions, leaving other GHGs and sinks until later. The "common concerns" group (Canada, Australia, New Zealand, the South Pacific

Island states, and the United States), however, favored a comprehensive approach to climate change that would treat sources and sinks together in a common package, on the grounds that this approach would be the most cost-effective and intellectually sound. Thus, at the outset of the talks there was a split among the advanced industrial states on how to tackle the climate change problem. In part, this split reflected the fact that most EC countries had already established domestic targets for CO_2 stabilization or reduction measures, whereas in the "common concerns" group some countries, notably Canada and the United States, had not. This tension in approaches was reflected in subsequent sessions, although Canada, Australia, and New Zealand supported the European Community's position on binding targets and schedules to limit GHG emissions—an approach that the United States continued to oppose and which became one of the most contentious issues in the negotiations. The U.S. position eventually shifted to one placing greater emphasis on independent national implementation measures that would ultimately stabilize GHG emissions by the year 2000, but the United States was unbending in its demand to leave concrete emission-stabilization and reduction targets out of the convention. By threatening not to go to Rio or sign the convention, it eventually forced the European Community to concede to its position. This was because the European Community and other countries clearly saw little value in a convention that the United States refused to sign and were willing to defer the issue to future discussions.

Developing countries made it clear at the outset of talks that they assigned moral and historical responsibility for climate change to the advanced industrial states, which, they argued, had the highest per capita emissions of greenhouse gases. They argued that industrial countries should provide new financial assistance to developing countries, over and above existing transfers, to help them meet their obligations under a climate change convention. For example, India argued for joint implementation provisions or tradable permits to assist developing countries. Some developing countries also argued for transfers of technology on favorable terms to assist them with emissions reduction, sinks enhancement, and development of alternative energy resources. However, in spite of widespread philosophical agreement on this point, the Group of 77 worked less and less effectively as a group as negotiations progressed. Although there was some effort to coordinate negotiating positions in the early round of negotiations, the group ceased to meet as a collectivity after the second INC session, because of growing disagreements between its members, particularly on the matter of commitments in the convention. At one extreme, the oil-producing states, led by Saudi Arabia and Kuwait, were opposed to any binding commitments in the convention because of fears about the impact CO_2 stabilization and reduction measures would have on oil prices. At the other end of the spectrum stood the AOSIS states, who supported concrete measures because of their concerns about the impact of temperature change on sea-level rise. Many of the other developing countries fell somewhere in between these two extremes.

The newly emerging democracies and market economies of Eastern Europe, supported by some of the NICs, argued for a differentiated approach between industrial and developing countries that would treat obligations differently, allowing states at lower levels of economic development to assume less stringent responsibilities under a climate change convention. Some countries, like the Commonwealth of Independent States (the former Soviet Union), did not foresee any great urgency for a climate convention, although virtually all Eastern European countries supported the concept of financial and technical assistance, technology transfer, and sharing of scientific information.

Representation

Certain states were also prominent in the negotiations by serving as spokespersons for particular regional interests. Among the developing countries, India and China were the most vociferous champions of the view that developing countries should not be required to undertake any commitments until they had reached an appropriate level of economic development comparable to that of the advanced industrial countries. Delegates from these two countries repeatedly argued, right up until the end, that climate change was a problem caused by advanced industrial countries, who bore sole moral and political responsibility for addressing the problem. These countries also strongly opposed placing the administrative mechanism for financial and technological transfers in the convention under the authority of the GEF. However, these countries (along with Iran and Brazil) increasingly found themselves in the minority, and their uncompromising approach to the negotiations was not shared by other developing countries, which saw greater gains to be achieved through a more flexible approach.

Among the industrial countries, Austria, the Netherlands, Switzerland, and Germany were the strongest supporters of a treaty that would impose targets and timetables and commit signers to stabilizing GHG emissions immediately. These countries made no secret of their unhappiness with the U.S. refusal to undertake specific commitments or to increase energy taxes, as had been suggested by the European Community. At the Earth Summit in Rio, the European Community adopted a joint statement setting targets and timetables for the reduction of carbon dioxide emissions to 1990 levels by the end of the century.[63]

Bridging and Bargaining Strategies

Brokers also emerged at critical junctures in the negotiation, offering important new proposals or ideas to bridge the gap between key actors and interests. During the early and middle phases of the negotiation, Japan tried to push (albeit unsuccessfully) a compromise formula, known as pledge-and-review, in an effort to narrow the outstanding differences between the European Community and the United States on GHG-reduction targets. Although several countries, notably the United Kingdom, France, Sweden, and Australia, also circulated pledge-and-review proposals, Japan proved to be the concept's strongest advocate. Ultimately, the concept failed to attract sufficient support because of differing interpretations about the nature of the pledge and mounting opposition from developing countries.

In the lead-up to the final negotiating session in New York, the United Kingdom's secretary of state for the environment, Michael Howard, played a key role in persuading the United States to join the treaty and designing language in the climate change agreement that the United States could accept. The chair of the INC negotiations, Jean Ripert, was also instrumental in developing compromise language that would gain the U.S. signature.[64] Smaller countries like Norway, Canada, and Finland also offered important suggestions for meeting targets and schedules that would be combined with a flexible approach to implementation in the fifth round of negotiations, although some of these items proved to be quite contentious. New Zealand also provided important input into the negotiations on dispute-settlement and resolution procedures in the convention.

Arguably, bridging formulas were less crucial to the outcome of the negotiations than the U.S. refusal to sign a treaty (coupled with President Bush's threat to boycott the Rio conference) containing timetables and emission limits. By threatening to walk away from a climate change treaty not to its liking, some argue that the United States forced the European Community and other countries to accept its position, because nobody wanted the conference to be judged a failure if the leader of the world's only remaining superpower (and major producer of GHGs) refused to sign the treaty.[65] But it would be a mistake to attribute the outcome solely to U.S. political (i.e., structural) power and its ability to wrest concessions from weaker negotiating partners, that is, to conclude that the United States had a better alternative to a negotiated agreement (BATNA) than its negotiating partners. There is strong evidence to suggest a greater flexibility in the U.S. negotiating position following Chief of Staff John Sunnunu's departure from the White House in December 1991.[66] Sunnunu made no secret of his contempt for the environmental movement and his own skepticism about the scientific basis for global warming.[67] His departure was coupled with growing concerns within the administration (notably from William Reilly, head of the EPA, and National Security Adviser Brent Scowcroft) that the president could not be seen standing against the entire world on climate change, particularly in light of the president's earlier commitments to clean up the environment. The reported quid pro quo was an informal U.S. offer to put into effect existing environmental programs that would reduce emissions of GHGs from 7 to 11 percent below what they would have been by the year 2000. In exchange, the Europeans agreed to drop their aim of formal long-term stabilization commitments in the convention.[68] Evidence for such a compromise is reflected in the text of the final agreement under which developed country signatories agreed to adopt national policies and measures to return GHG emissions, by the end of the decade, "to earlier levels."

Issue Decomposition and Sequencing Tactics

Issue decomposition and sequencing tactics were also crucial to the outcome of the negotiations. By separating the discussion of commitments and mechanisms into two working groups in the INC and addressing key items independently, issues where there was no apparent willingness to compromise were separated from those where there was a workable consensus. Although the slow progress of negotiations in Working Group I (commitments) threatened negotiations in Working Group II (mechanisms), by the same token early progress in Working Group II had a positive impact on Working Group I and contributed to a sense of momentum where there might have been none. The use of a single negotiating text (and bracketing of clauses where there were outstanding differences) was crucial to clarifying key points of agreement and disagreement among the parties. The tabling of the draft text, which had been prepared by the conference chair at the second round of the fifth session, also helped to focus discussion on specific points, as did the creation of several informal working or "cluster" groups working on different sections of the text. Bilateral and chair-initiated discussions helped to resolve outstanding differences and pave the way toward consensus. Informal meetings, particularly among the industrial countries in the OECD informal consultative group, contributed to flexibility in the negotiations, as did informal consultations headed by the conference chairman, Jean Ripert. These consultations were especially important in resolving key conflicts between the United States and the European Community and between industrial and developing countries.

Leadership

Leadership, defined as innovative thinking and constructive solving approaches to intractable problems, was evident throughout the negotiations. Conference chair Jean Ripert played a critical role in helping to devise a consensus document that would be acceptable to the major interests in the negotiation. In this he was ably assisted by the cochairs of the two working groups, Nobutoshi Akao, Edmundo de Alba-Alacaraz (Working Group I), and especially Elizabeth Dowdeswell and Robert van Lierop (Working Group II). Although some view the United States as the bad boy of the negotiations, American negotiators made a vital contribution to the development of a common methodology for country studies and other implementation mechanisms. Countries like Norway, Canada, New Zealand, Finland, Sweden, and the United Kingdom also played a constructive role in tabling proposals to address some of the more contentious technical aspects of the convention, as did countries like Argentina, Vanuatu, and Nauru, which proved to be important voices of moderation among developing countries.

Compliance and Verification

Compliance and verification provisions in the convention are similar to those of other environmental treaties. The effectiveness of the convention depends upon the willingness of the parties to comply with their formal obligation to submit to the conference of the parties a report containing information on national inventories of sources and sinks of all greenhouse gases not controlled by the Montreal Protocol and on strategies, policies, and activities adopted to reduce national GHG emissions. There are no formal verification provisions in the convention per se which, as one study notes, "would be unacceptable to almost all developing countries, and probably to many developed countries also." If formal targets or obligations to reduce GHGs are included in future protocols, compliance will depend upon "the generation and dissemination of information on the behavior of parties in relation to these obligations." This will require "an effective reporting system to provide a basis for national policy making and to influence state behavior toward compliance with the norms established in the Convention."[69]

In a real sense verification and compliance concerns were "dogs that didn't bark," because the treaty did not contain formal targets and schedules controlling GHG emissions. However, these issues are likely to become more important and increasingly contentious once protocols governing GHG emissions from the energy sector and protection of tropical rainforests, or forests in general, are adopted.[70]

The outcome of the climate change negotiations depended upon a number of critical factors. First, pressure from the international scientific community and the coordination of international scientific research results by the IPCC were crucial in bringing governments to the negotiating table to initiate discussions on a climate change convention. Without such pressure, it is unlikely that negotiations would have begun at all. Unlike the ozone case, however, there was not a groundswell of public concern about global warming. However, bureaucrats and scientists in a number of countries were able to push the issue to the forefront of their respective national agendas and garner sufficient international support to start negotiations. The sense of political urgency was by no means universally shared and contributed to the slow pace of negotiations and the obvious reluctance of some countries, notably the United States, to entertain specific stabilization targets and commitments in a climate change convention.

Second, once formal negotiations got underway, they were marked by conflicting attitudes toward substantive provisions regarding commitments and mechanisms in a climate change convention. Among the advanced industrial countries, Canada, the Nordic countries, Australia, New Zealand, and the members of the European Community were generally at the forefront of international efforts to push for a climate change convention that would contain detailed provisions and commitments to stabilize GHG emissions. In contrast, the United States favored what Daniel Bodansky calls a "process-oriented" convention that eschewed formal stabilization commitments but set in motion detailed implementation measures allowing for greater levels of scientific research, coordination, assessment, and implementation.[71] Developing countries sought exemption (or otherwise differentiated treatment) from commitments undertaken by industrial countries; they were generally hostile to the detailed implementation and procedural mechanisms sought by industrial countries but supportive of mechanisms that would create new institutions for financial and technology transfers. Agreement thus depended on the ability of negotiators to bridge the North-North and North-South split. Although developing countries were at the table and played a more important role throughout the climate change negotiations than they did in discussions leading to the Vienna Convention and Montreal Protocols on Protection of the Ozone Layer (where they were not key players), agreement between North and South on climate change obviously depended on the ability of the advanced industrial countries to secure agreement among themselves on what form commitments in the convention should take. Much of the hard bargaining was therefore between the United States and its European partners (with Japan situated somewhat ambiguously between the two).

Third, process variables played an important role in helping to bridge outstanding differences between these various groups. As noted above, the use of working groups, informal consultations, a single negotiating text, and incremental bargaining strategies that defined contentious issues while promoting agreement on those where a consensus could be reached helped to move the negotiations forward. At the same time, political leadership and the availability of third-party brokers or mediators in the negotiation also helped to break logjams and create winning coalitions. The fact that the Third World did not operate as a block also facilitated the possibilities of agreement between North and South on certain issues like institutional mechanisms and implementation procedures in the convention.

Fourth, the Rio conference deadline for tabling the convention created a political sense of urgency to the negotiations, which was skillfully exploited by a number of actors—perhaps most effectively by the United States, which threatened to boycott the conference if a satisfactory agreement on climate change could not be reached. At the same time, domestic political considerations and personnel changes in the Bush administration also allowed for greater flexibility in the U.S. position, demonstrating the importance of extranegotiatory influences to bargaining outcomes.

Finally, the climate change negotiations concluded in a convention that included a commitment to interim negotiations in the period between signature of the convention and its entry into force. This commitment left the door open to new measures that might give the convention more teeth, thereby following the pattern set in the ozone accords.

Science has played and will continue to play a crucial role in climate change diplomacy. The debates among diplomats and politicians have not been so much about science but about how to satisfy competing interests and values within the context of a new global regime on climate change. Political leadership (or its absence) and negotiating strategies have been crucial to this process and help to explain the shape and form of the climate change agreement.

V Conclusion

12 Understanding Multilateral
Negotiations: Lessons and Conclusions

The cases studied in this book address several common questions and themes. At the first level, prenegotiation, the key questions are: how do issues get to the table, and are prenegotiation processes similar or different for different kinds of issues? Once formal negotiations are underway, what are the procedures and institutional mechanisms for managing complexity, and do these mechanisms differ significantly from one issue area to another? Finally, what are the factors that facilitate agreement in multilateral negotiations, and are the apparent conditions or requisites for success similar or different across different issue areas?

In addressing these questions, this book argues that multilateral negotiation is, in essence, a coalition-building exercise involving states, nonstate actors, and international organizations. This process is essentially the same for any kind of negotiation, be it in arms control, trade, or the environment. Leadership, negotiating strategies and tactics, and formulas are directed at and related to the process of building coalitions (both across and within states) in order to achieve a consensus that will carry negotiations forward. Increasingly, the key players are of three types: (1) experts who define prenegotiation possibilities and the agenda for negotiations; (2) coalitions of smaller states or lesser powers who both sustain the momentum of negotiation and help devise bridging solutions when great powers are deadlocked; and (3) officials in international agencies who forge strategic alliances with their counterparts in national bureaucracies to move negotiations forward. Issue decomposition and sequencing tactics also serve to reduce complexity and advance negotiations.

Negotiations do not take place in a vacuum. They are shaped by their political environment. Learning, defined as a process of understanding means-ends relations and developing new forms of discourse about a problem, is crucial to the negotiation process, but unexpected events, like crises, often play a decisive role in reshaping political (and public) perceptions regarding the desirability of new international agreements. This study thus underscores the importance of outside triggers or catalytic events that bring issues to the negotiating table and to the forefront of the political agenda. It also stresses the importance of agency and the kinds of roles parties adopt in the multilateral setting in order to build coalitions, reduce complexity, simplify the bargaining process, and advance negotiations. Parties may play more than one role, and there may also be more than one turning point in the passage of negotiations from one stage to another. Zartman's characterization of the negotiation process as one of "ripening" is essentially correct.[1] But the metaphor is somewhat misleading, because international agreements typically do not fall off the branch of a tree like ripe fruit. Instead, the process is more like making wine, because different agents are involved in taking grapes from the orchard and turning them into wine.

Negotiations must pass through several stages or phases: prenegotiation, negotiation, agreement, and implementation. Issues and interests must be organized to facilitate bargaining processes when there are many parties and issues on the table. The shifting involvement of different actors and interests because of the protracted nature of such negotiations creates additional difficulties. In addition, decision-making procedures and rules for representing different interests must be devised. This chapter summarizes some of the principal findings from our case studies about how the bargaining process works.

"Old" versus "New" Multilateralism

Is there any difference between multilateral negotiation processes of the early postwar period and the "new" multilateralism of the 1980s and 1990s? Three cases were examined from the 1940s and the 1950s: in trade, negotiations leading to the formation of the General Agreement on Tariffs and Trade (GATT) and those that failed in the case of the International Trade Organization (ITO); in arms control, negotiations that led to the signing of the Limited Test Ban Treaty (LTBT) at the height of the Cold War. What is striking about all three cases is that they were all fundamentally "multilateral," involving a multiplicity of players who brought their own concerns and needs to the bargaining table. Moreover, lesser powers were not simply pawns of the great powers but played a key role in agenda setting, issue definition, and compromise. The fact that the great powers were at odds with one another gave lesser powers the opportunity to serve as intermediaries and help devise bridging solutions to seemingly intractable problems. Though not always successful, the presence of lesser powers in shaping negotiated outcomes is keenly evident.

In the origins of the GATT, although the United States and the United Kingdom were the key players and recognized as such, Canada, Australia, France, Argentina, India, and others played a crucial role in defining the issues, setting the agenda, and working out the necessary compromises. In part, this was because the United Kingdom worked closely with its former Dominions and kept them closely informed about negotiations. The close relationship Canada enjoyed with both the United Kingdom and the United States as a result of its wartime role also gave it special access to officials in London and Washington. However, access was only part of the key to influence. The other key was the high caliber of civil servants in these countries, who were well versed in the issues and could bring independent, professional expertise to the bargaining table.

Negotiations leading to the signing of the LTBT show a similar multilateral imprint. Although negotiations on a test ban were essentially trilateral in nature involving the United States, the Soviet Union, and the United Kingdom, when they moved to the Eighteen-Nation Disarmament Committee (ENDC) in Geneva, they became genuinely multilateral, as countries like Sweden, India, Canada, France, Italy, and others joined in. Some countries, notably Sweden, brought independent technical skills to the negotiations and were thus able to make a significant contribution to discussions about verification and compliance. Others, like India, took the moral high ground and used political suasion to pressure the United States and the Soviet Union not to break off negotiations as Cold War tensions heightened. The enlarged multilateral forum of the ENDC thus helped to maintain political momentum for negotiations and strengthened the hand of the president of the United States in dealing with domestic critics of a test ban.

It is argued by some contemporary scholars that one of the hallmarks of the new multilateralism is the growing involvement of citizens groups, experts, and epistemic communities, or consensual knowledge, in international negotiation and regime formation processes.[2] Our own review suggests that these processes are not new. The origins of the GATT can be traced to the epistemic influence of academic economists like Jacob Viner and Frank Taussig, who were on the staff of the U.S. Tariff Commission and provided much of the economic rationale for U.S. trade policy. Their ideas fitted in well with Cordell Hull's internationalist vision of open, nondiscriminatory markets. However, these ideas clashed with Keynesianism, which placed the onus on governments to stimulate demand and provide for full employment. The use of tariffs and quotas to safeguard the balance of payments was consistent with Keynesianism, which was generally skeptical of nondiscriminatory approaches to trade policy except in the most ideal circumstances. Keynesianism had its supporters and detractors on both sides of the Atlantic, and negotiators had to strike a middle ground between the philosophies of private enterprise and of state control.

Certainly, epistemic advice was crucial to the evolution of the whole postwar trading structure and architecture. But it would be a mistake to characterize this advice as consensual knowledge, because postwar economic thinking was marked by competing paradigms about how the new order should be constructed. In the absence of consensus, one of the main challenges for negotiators was to try to accommodate competing economic philosophies within a new international trading framework. The GATT solution was a series of measures that would reduce barriers to trade while allowing for discrimination in certain sectors, for example, agriculture, in order to promote economic development and full employment.

Similarly, in the case of the Limited Test Ban Treaty, epistemic advice was crucial to both the prenegotiation and negotiation phases. Scientists played a crucial role in raising public awareness about the dangerous health effects of nuclear testing in the atmosphere. Scientists were also at the forefront of discussions on verification and monitoring of a test ban, because these were highly technical issues. But again, it would be misleading to portray the role of the expert as a provider of consensual knowledge. Although scientists were pretty much in agreement about the harmful effects of continued atmospheric testing on human health, the scientific consensus on the verification requirements for a comprehensive test ban soon unraveled, as new evidence cast doubts on earlier assessments. In the highly charged atmosphere of the negotiating table, science found itself unable to resolve questions that were profoundly political and went right to the heart of the adversarial relationship between the two superpowers.

Multilateral diplomacy of the 1980s and 1990s shares some of the same characteristics of diplomacy in the previous era. The principal actors at the negotiation table continue to be states; cooperation among the great powers (what Kahler calls "minilateralism")[3] is essential for agreement, and the United States continues to exercise an important veto over any potential agreement. The contemporary international setting of multilateral diplomacy, however, is complicated by (1) the larger number of states that participate in international negotiations as a result of decolonization and the formation of new states resulting from the breakup of the Soviet empire; and (2) the increasing complexity of the issues themselves, such as in the areas of trade, environment, and even conventional arms control. There is also greater overlap between and among different issue areas. For example, national responses to ozone depletion in the upper atmosphere have had profound economic consequences, thus mobilizing industrial and other economic interests to become involved in negotiations. Trade policy is no longer concerned only with tariffs and quotas but now includes income support programs, product standards, and other matters hitherto viewed as exclusively domestic.

International negotiation processes are also increasingly affected by mobilized interest groups, including business, labor, nongovernmental organizations, and other actors, who see themselves as direct stakeholders and thus seek to affect outcomes by bringing pressure to bear on their national governments. Many of these groupings also have an international constituency. For example, many key environmental organizations have local chapters in many different countries, thus enabling them to mount effective campaigns at the national and international levels, as we saw in all three environmental cases.

Finally, the creation of international organizations as a direct result of earlier negotiations has introduced a new set of actors into the bargaining and negotiation process. The bureaucrats who staff international organizations have come to see themselves as having a direct stake in promoting the development and expansion of new international regimes associated with issue areas falling under their mandate. They have become actively involved in the negotiation process by forging strategic alliances with their counterparts in national bureaucracies, sponsoring and coordinating research, mobilizing technical expertise, raising public awareness, and playing a key leadership role at the bargaining table. This trend is most pronounced in trade and environment, as illustrated by the case studies in this volume. The corresponding lack of formal international organizational structures in arms control, with the exception of the International Atomic Energy Agency, has meant that transgovernmental cooperation takes place primarily at the national institutional level.[4]

Facilitating Factors in Negotiation

Does greater complexity, in terms of both parties and issues, pose an insurmountable barrier to international negotiation? The answer is surely no. This is because parties will respond to the negotiation challenge by assuming specialized roles, including bridging, brokering, and mediation, that facilitate the negotiation process and propel negotiations forward. Outside experts will help define prenegotiation and negotiation possibilities. The public will pressure political elites who must then decide whether cooperative solutions are called for. Catalytic events or crises can also prompt a change in attitudes (public as well as elite) and lead to new behaviors that involve the search for cooperative solutions. Taking each phase of the negotiation process in turn, our case studies reveal a number of common themes or patterns.

Prenegotiation

The prenegotiation phase is characterized as the period when the parties define the problem and develop a commitment to negotiate without undertaking the risks of formal negotiation. In prenegotiation, the parties will identify the problems, search for options, and decide upon the initial agenda of negotiations. Social learning, marked by the acquisition of greater understanding about the nature of a problem and means-ends relations, is thus crucial to prenegotiation. Two sets of factors were singled out for special examination of prenegotiation processes in our case studies. They were the roles of crises and consensual knowledge.

Crisis. Crises are important events in moving negotiations from the prenegotiation stage to the bargaining tale, thus underscoring the importance of contingency to the negotiation process. Crises were central to all three of the arms control cases examined in this volume. There are interesting parallels in the importance of human health concerns in nuclear arms control and global environmental problems. The calamity that befell the crew of the *Lucky Dragon* dramatized the consequences for human health of nuclear testing in the atmosphere and strengthened public demands for a halt to unrestricted nuclear testing. So too have health concerns been at the forefront of public demands for a ban on consumer and industrial products that contain CFCs and other ozone-harming substances. Public concerns about hazardous-waste dumping are also linked to health. In contrast, one of the reasons why climate change has not engaged public and media interest the same way ozone depletion has is that the potential health effects of global warming are less certain and much longer term.

Trade negotiations in the 1940s also took place against a background of economic crisis resulting from the protectionist excesses of the 1930s. The obvious desire of negotiators to avoid a repetition of previous mistakes was central to the prenegotiation, and subsequent negotiation, of the GATT. Crises, defined as sudden events or situations that threaten core values and beliefs of decision makers, are not so evident in the prenegotiation phase of the Uruguay Round of the GATT. But it can be said that the Uruguay Round was prompted by a growing realization that the GATT's current rules-based approach was inadequate for coping with the new challenges to the global economy brought about by the globalization of services and investment and by the new developments in communications technology and transportation. GATT rules were also weak in disciplining agriculture and trade in textiles and clothing, prompting additional demands for reform. The mismatch between a trade regime based on limiting tariffs and quotas and the growing threat of nontariff barriers to trade—what might be termed a "creeping crisis"—was a key factor in the start of the new round of multilateral trade negotiations in the 1980s. And a new GATT agreement was only grasped from the jaws of failure in 1993, when the public came to appreciate the depths of the international crisis that would result if the Uruguay Round failed.

All three issue areas also underscore the functional importance of prene-gotiation as a political risk-management strategy promising lower exit costs than formal negotiations. Prenegotiation was essential to setting boundaries to subsequent negotiations, setting the agenda and deciding upon the participants in formal negotiations. This was shown to have both positive and negative consequences for subsequent negotiations. On the one hand, the prenegotiation phase of the Stockholm Conference on Confidence- and Security-Building Measures (CSBMs) witnessed extensive jockeying between the United States and the Soviet Union on the agenda for the conference and an eventual agreement to deal only with CSBMs in Europe and not to interfere with the conventional arms negotiations that were taking place in the MBFR talks. This limited agenda contributed to the success of these talks. On the other hand, one of the reasons the agri-cultural concerns were a key stumbling block in the Uruguay Round of the GATT is that the issue surfaced very early in the prenegotiation phase and in such a way that the parties convinced themselves that it was important to achieve a critical success on agriculture. Agriculture was elevated to a position of such importance, as a make-or-break issue, that it handicapped progress on other issues once formal negotiations began.

Consensual Knowledge. The central importance of outside experts or epis-temic communities in prenegotiation is readily apparent on environmental issues. In the ozone case, a growing consensus in the scientific community about the CFC-ozone depletion link was key in identifying the problem and the need for controls. Scientific understandings about the link be-tween the buildup of greenhouse gases in the atmosphere and global warming were also crucial in laying the foundations for cooperative inter-national efforts to tackle the problems of global warming. Nonetheless, the impact of consensual knowledge is limited to issues characterized by high levels of uncertainty where professional risk assessments are needed. In the case of hazardous wastes, epistemic advice was less important than the well-publicized efforts of Greenpeace and other environmental groups to alert the global community to the dangerous dumping of hazardous wastes that was occurring in developing countries.

In contrast, arms control and trade have been marked by the changing nature, composition, and influence of epistemic communities in prenego-tiation and subsequent negotiation processes. As noted above, in early years, academic economists played a key role in helping to devise the in-ternational trade regime associated with the GATT, as did scientists in the case of arms control negotiations leading to the LTBT. However, the growth of national bureaucracies responsible for trade and arms control re-spectively has ensured that governments can now count on a wealth of internally generated analyses and advice and, therefore, have less need to rely on outside expertise. These bureaucracies are the product of earlier regime-building efforts that helped to create vested interests committed to preserving and expanding these regimes. Indeed, the institutional setting provides a basis for addressing issues and launching negotiations.

All three issue areas are marked by the growing judicialization of the negotiating process. To the extent that outside experts are called upon, they now tend to be lawyers and those with a legal background and training. Academic economists, who had a major influence in trade negotiations in the 1940s and 1950s, have become less influential, partly because their theories are too remote from the real world. Think-tank specialists and those with applied policy skills are correspondingly more influential because they are able to talk the language of the negotiators. This aspect of declining epistemic influence in formal negotiations is also evident on issues like climate change, where scientists were shunted aside in the INC (Intergovernmental Negotiating Committee) by the diplomats and senior bureaucrats who conducted the negotiations. Some of this change reflects the importance of process itself to the negotiation phase and the fact that bureaucrats and lawyers are experts in process management.

Negotiation

The negotiation phase is characterized by the construction of coalitions, the formal exchange of information, and negotiations between the parties on the actual details of an agreement. Negotiations usually move through a series of stages marked by the narrowing of the agenda, the establishment of limits to the issues under discussion, and the narrowing of differences between the parties, leading eventually to the formal execution of an agreement. As noted in chapter 2, this process may be thwarted in the multilateral setting by the large number of parties and issues in the negotiation; the presence or formation of blocking coalitions; intrinsic interests, belief systems, and ideology; process-generated stakes; and the actual rules and procedures governing the negotiating process itself. Given the vast number of potential roadblocks that stand in the way of agreement, it is perhaps surprising that multilateral negotiations ever succeed. But the fact that they do raises the obvious question: why? There is no simple answer to this question. However, our case studies point to the salience of a number of factors that appear to facilitate the negotiation process.

Coalitions. First, it is readily apparent that the formation of coalitions in multiparty bargaining situations is essential to simplifying the negotiating process. Coalitions reduce cognitive complexity and greatly facilitate the exchange of information by reducing the number of core positions and interests to a manageable number. Coalitions also choose representatives to speak for the group and bargain with other members. These representatives may be the most powerful members of the group, or they may possess special skills or technical expertise that are seen as desirable in advancing group interests.

However, the danger with any coalition is that group solidarity and coalition maintenance can become ends in themselves, leading to rigid and inflexible bargaining positions. This has happened on more than one occasion and was certainly characteristic of North-South negotiations in the 1970s.[5] The formation of flexible alliances that reduce the confrontational elements of multiparty bargaining by trading concessions on different issues is usually key to breaking such deadlocks. Such groupings, which typically straddle different coalitions, can be formal or informal. But flexibility is obviously the key to their success.

The Uruguay Round of the GATT, for example, witnessed the emergence of various coalitions, some of which cut across traditional North-South lines, thus marking an end to the sterile confrontations on trade of the 1960s and 1970s. These groupings included the Rio Group, the de la Paix Group, and various coalitions that rallied on specific issues, like the Cairns Group and the developing-countries caucus. Developing countries no longer behaved like a herd but joined forces with other players to advance their specific interests. These fluid alliances enabled smaller players to be some of the most dynamic and constructive participants in the negotiations. The formation of these various crosscutting and bridging coalitions moved negotiations along by drawing smaller countries into the process and increasing their stake in a positive outcome. They also formed a useful counterweight to the big three (the United States, Japan, and the European Community) whose own internal divisions were, for many years, a major obstacle to agreement.

Similarly, international negotiations on climate change were marked by the emergence of various coalitions, which helped to straddle some of the major fault lines that existed at the outset of talks. Small island states (the AOSIS), along with a number of Latin American countries, helped moderate traditional North-South antagonisms by creating a coalition of interests that crossed the North-South divide. As a result, hard-line states in the South, which took the view that climate change was primarily a problem for industrial countries, found themselves increasingly isolated as negotiations moved forward. The "common concerns" group favored a comprehensive approach to the climate change, although it was marked by a split among the advanced industrial states over how to approach the climate change problem.

In negotiations leading to the signing of the Montreal Protocol on ozone depletion and the subsequent London amendments, Latin American countries like Mexico played an important role in building support for financial and technology-transfer aid packages that would meet developing countries' interests while addressing the regulatory concerns of industrial countries. So too, in arms control, negotiations leading up to the Stockholm Agreement on CSBMs were facilitated by the presence of a third coalition, the neutral and nonaligned countries, which defined a new center of gravity in discussions and served as an important intermediary between NATO countries and those of the Warsaw Pact.

Leadership. A second important factor in multilateral negotiation is leadership, defined in Young's sense of the entrepreneur who has the skill to frame issues in ways that foster integrative bargaining and lead to the formation of crosscutting or bridging coalitions.[6] Innovative thinking is one important characteristic of this kind of leadership; another is the ability to broker and to make deals. Such leadership can be exercised by heads of international agencies, individual delegates, heads of state, and other politicians and diplomats.

Such roles were clearly evident in the Uruguay Round of the GATT. Delegates from smaller countries, both industrial and developing (notably Switzerland, Colombia, Canada, Australia, and ASEAN members), helped develop the agenda, define negotiating parameters, sequence and package issues, and thus determine the pace and progress of negotiations. These smaller countries also made unilateral concessions and thus built up bargaining credit, which they used advantageously later on. Arthur Dunkel, the director general of the GATT, also made effective use of his office to coax and cajole delegations on certain key issues, although agreement ultimately depended on a new director general, Peter Sutherland, who had the politician's skills to essentially bully the parties into making concessions.

Although the United States was a prime mover in both initiating the new round of talks and setting the pace of negotiations, it was increasingly hampered by its own domestic ambivalence about the value of multilateral trade rules. The slow growth of the U.S. economy in the late 1970s and early 1980s fostered protectionist impulses. American negotiators found themselves boxed in by Congressional hostility to concessions necessary for stimulating the interest of key trading partners. As a result, U.S. leadership was less effective than in previous GATT negotiations, with U.S. policies increasingly given to rhetoric about fairness, level playing fields, and the need for discipline. Collective leadership by the G-7, which was so evident in the Tokyo Round, was also undermined by the fact that the most intractable problems lay among its members.

Entrepreneurial leadership was also crucial to progress in arms control.

Starting with the Limited Test Ban Treaty, presidential leadership was a key to moving negotiations forward, particularly when they were in danger of stalling. Unlike his predecessor, President Kennedy was personally committed to concluding negotiations on a test ban. Leadership from the top also contributed to the success of the Stockholm Conference on CSBMs and the CFE Treaty several years later. Presidential leadership was necessary to make deals that could not be made by lower-level officials who lacked the requisite political authority to make key concessions. Such leadership also involved successful management of domestic policy-making processes to ensure that negotiations were not undermined by Congress, bureaucratic or interagency disputes, or blocking coalitions at the domestic level. Leadership was also extremely important on the Soviet side. For instance, President Gorbachev was prepared to make deals that his predecessors would have considered unthinkable.

Innovative thinking, inventiveness, and problem-solving skills were also crucial to the success of international environmental negotiations. In particular, UNEP's former executive director, Mostafa Tolba, had a major hand in structuring and shaping the agenda on a wide range of international environmental treaties, including those examined in this volume. Smaller states, like Austria, Canada, Norway, New Zealand, Sweden, and Switzerland, were also extremely influential because of the high caliber of their representatives at these negotiations. Conference chairs and cochairs also played a key role by using their authority to develop a consensus on major issues. This was especially evident in the climate change negotiations, where conference chair Jean Ripert was ably assisted by the cochairs of the two INC working groups.

Simple Solutions or Focal Points. A third requirement for success in multilateral negotiations is the identification of solutions or focal points that can serve as the basis for agreement and are based on concepts of fairness. Such solutions involve more than just compromise, but typically include what Zartman and Berman call a "simple definition or conception of an outcome."[7] However, they must also incorporate competing standards or definitions of justice in a way that is considered fair by the different parties to the negotiation. Typically, equity considerations, the sense that all parties have been treated fairly, are more important than efficiency or other allocative criteria in determining what constitutes a just outcome.

Several of the case studies illustrate the importance of this aspect of the negotiation process. Negotiations in the mutual and balanced force reduction (MBFR) talks, for example, were frustrated by the inability of the negotiators to find a relatively clear and simple resolving formula that would allow for reductions across asymmetrical force structures between NATO and the Warsaw Pact. Because of long-standing data disputes over the size and composition of current forces, the problem was made all the more difficult. In contrast, negotiations in the Conventional Forces, Europe (CFE) talks were greatly facilitated by (1) data exchanges that eliminated much of the uncertainty about force levels; and (2) the decision to pursue symmetrical reductions across different weapons categories, leaving negotiations on personnel strength, which were more problematic, to a second round. In establishing clear and equitable limits on certain categories of equipment and arms, CFE negotiators arrived at a relatively simple solution to conventional arms reductions that had eluded earlier negotiators.

The success of the Montreal Protocol and the subsequent London amendments to the Vienna Convention for the Protection of the Ozone Layer also reflected the importance of fairness in arriving at a compromise. The compromise formula on verification in the Montreal Protocol (production-plus-imports-minus-exports) successfully addressed the European Community's desire to focus CFC limits on production while also addressing the Toronto Group's demand for a level playing field in overseas markets that would not give the European Community an unfair advantage. So too, when parties met in London to discuss, among other things, the mechanisms and voting procedures for an ozone fund to help developing countries, the challenge was to find a formula that would bring developing countries into the protocol in a way that would not compromise their economic development. The establishment of an ozone fund and various procedures to help developing countries fulfill their treaty obligations addressed the important link between external assistance and the capability of developing countries to renounce usage of CFCs and other ozone-harming substances. At the heart of the bargain was the principle that industrial countries had an obligation to help developing countries fulfill their treaty obligations via technology transfer and financial assistance. In this instance, the just solution was also a distributive one.

Similarly, in international negotiations on climate change, the debate over a new financial mechanism that would operate under the collective authority of the contracting parties was based, in part, on competing notions of fairness and accountability between industrial and developing countries.

Issue Decomposition and Sequencing. Issue decomposition, sequencing, and participant and issue incrementalism are a fourth requirement for successful bargaining in negotiations on complex issues when many parties and interests are involved (both domestic and international). The careful sequencing of issues can build momentum in the direction of an agreement. Participant incrementalism, which restructures issues as small group problems in order to promote cooperation, works on the assumption that agreement is easiest among coalitions of the like-minded. Partial agreements are useful when basic value conflicts do not permit comprehensive solutions. But in the process of creating a limited zone of agreement, they may also freeze the possibilities of a more comprehensive settlement, because parties are wedded to the status quo or are unwilling to take further action.

Issue decomposition and sequencing tactics resulted in a limited, as opposed to comprehensive, test ban treaty, although, in this case, congressional pressures were also responsible for this partial result. Issue decomposition and sequencing tactics eventually closed the gap between the Western preference for a "functional" approach to CSBMs and the Soviet desire for a geographical approach. Issue decomposition and sequencing also led to rapid progress in services, intellectual property, and nontariff measures in the Uruguay Round of the GATT, despite the lack of progress on agriculture. Participant incrementalism underscored the approach behind the Vienna Convention and the subsequent Montreal Protocol on the ozone layer. Once advanced industrial countries had signed the protocol, the new challenge was to secure the participation of developing countries at the London Conference that followed. In contrast, negotiations on hazardous waste and climate change involved the early and full participation of developing countries, because of the growing recognition that international cooperation could not succeed without their involvement.

Negotiations in all three issue areas were also marked by the formation of working groups to address separate issues, the use of a single negotiating text highlighting the main points of agreement and disagreement, and bargaining strategies that sought to move from agreements on general principles to increasingly stringent and comprehensive regulatory controls. Agreements have also been tailored to respond and adapt to new information and the uncertainties associated with the issues. This is particularly true in the case of environmental agreements, which have sought to facilitate scientific research, promote the sharing of data, and develop institutional mechanisms to translate new scientific findings into workable policies.

Incremental approaches and partial solutions do not satisfy those who believe that nothing short of a radical restructuring of national and international institutions can effectively tackle the problems of climate change, ozone depletion, and conventional or nuclear war. There is also the danger that partial solutions end up satisfying no one, because they are the result of collective decisions.[8] This problem is reflected, in varying degrees, in all of the agreements examined in this volume, although it is perhaps most apparent in the Basel Convention on Hazardous Wastes, which has been roundly criticized by industrial and developing countries alike.

Compliance and Verification. Finally, the availability of verification measures and relatively straightforward compliance mechanisms has been important to the negotiation process, although more so in arms control than on trade and environmental issues. In part, this difference reflects the importance of the security dilemma to military and strategic issues and the obvious lack of trust between military and ideological rivals. However, all collective action problems suffer the problems of cheating and defection, and there is, thus, a need for clear-cut verification and compliance mechanisms. In the case of the GATT, verification and reporting matters are dealt with by the GATT disputes-settlement procedures as well as the new mechanisms for the review of trade policy. There are clear rules and penalties for noncompliance, although the application of such rules to nontariff trade barriers has proved problematic.

In the environmental arena, it is somewhat surprising, particularly in view of the growing of the environment as a security matter, that verification and compliance considerations have not been more central to negotiations. Does this mean that verification is easier in the environmental realm? The answer surely is no, given the obvious difficulties of verifying limits on production and consumption of various gases in both ozone and climate change. Indeed, the verification challenge is probably greater on environmental matters than in arms control, given the large number of industrial and consumer users whose behaviors have to be monitored. Weak formal obligations in the environmental treaties addressed here, especially in those involving hazardous wastes and climate change, have obviated the need for more stringent verification, reporting, and compliance requirements. However, when more effective agreements are negotiated, verification and compliance mechanisms will unquestionably have to be strengthened if these agreements are to have force. Efforts to build greater transparency, though, will run up against the usual barriers of national sovereignty and the private sectors' own desire for disclosure rules that do not undermine competitiveness. In this regard, the verification and compliance challenge for international environmental diplomacy has only just begun.

The Future of Multilateral Diplomacy

This book has argued that the large number of players and issues that are the subject of international negotiations in multilateral forums need not pose insurmountable barriers to international cooperation. There are, however, obvious disadvantages to this process, which tend to slow down decisions, restrict freedom of action, and frequently produce lowest-common-denominator results, as alluded to earlier. But the alternatives—little or no international cooperation or international regimes produced by great-power fiat—can be worse. Multilateral negotiation has in one sense become an exercise in participatory democracy at the international level. As such, it is subject to the limitations and deficiencies of any participatory exercise.

Ironically, the principal failings of this process come not so much from the enlarged forum of multilateral diplomacy as from the nature of the issues themselves. One of the problems in the Uruguay Round of the GATT, for example, was that the issues being discussed were enormously complex. This led to a growing gap between the experts, who were responsible for conducting these negotiations, and the politicians, who had to take the political risks on key decisions. The history of these negotiations demonstrated that practitioners are ill equipped to deal with the increasingly important public diplomatic dimension of GATT diplomacy. Although the agreements reached represented a major achievement in international legislation, this fact was not easily grasped or understood by either political decision makers or the public. As a result, the GATT became a whipping boy of narrow-based, parochial interests and was accused of everything from destroying the family farm to dismantling the national economy.

Similarly, international negotiations on global environmental issues were marked by competing and often contradictory advice and claims from experts. Ozone diplomacy is an exception, because the health consequences of ozone depletion in the upper atmosphere were quickly grasped by the public. Thus, politicians found a ready and eager public constituency willing to accept regulatory measures that would restrict production and consumption of ozone-harming chemicals. The same cannot be said about global warming, which did not elicit the same kind of public concern and, thus, led to a much weaker set of agreements and commitments.

For international negotiations to succeed, the ground has to be well prepared. Ideas must be tested and a public consensus built before agreements are negotiated. The failure of the ITO negotiations stands as a stark reminder that bureaucratic and epistemic priorities are not always the same as those held by politicians. In the ITO, bureaucrats and experts failed to translate ideas into pragmatic and politically realistic proposals. The compromises they reached were too far removed from core political values. In the absence of strong domestic support, critics were presented with an easy target, and while the negotiations may have formally succeeded, the result was never implemented.

At the same time, for international cooperation to succeed, the leading players themselves must agree to cooperate. What is clearly evident in recent trade and environmental negotiations is the continuing acrimony between the United States and the European Community. Ozone and climate change diplomacy suffered from this split. So too have negotiations about agriculture in the GATT. These divisions have had enormous consequences, not only for the progress of negotiations themselves but for international cooperation in general. Without West-West cooperation, there can be little or no North-South cooperation. For North and South to reach a new agreement on ozone depletion, there first had to be agreement between the United States and the European Community on the key elements of the Montreal Protocol. Similarly, in the GATT, a new regime on trade and services between North and South has been held up by continuing differences between the European Community and the United States on agriculture. Climate change was a near miss, because outstanding differences between the United States and the European Community over CO_2-reduction commitments threatened to scuttle negotiations right up to the eleventh hour.

These episodes suggest that multilateral negotiation processes continue to remain hostage to the interests and behaviors of the great powers. Negotiations can proceed in spite of great powers, but agreement is not possible without them. The United States continues to have an important veto power over negotiated outcomes in most settings. To an increasing extent, so too do the European Community and Japan. However, divisions between the great powers have created opportunities for lesser powers from both the North and South to serve as intermediaries, so that the negotiation process is not completely hostage to great power interests. New alliances that cross traditional North-South lines have been forged as smaller states have banded together in an effort to define agendas, develop negotiating parameters, and shape outcomes. Various transnational social and scientific groups have also made their presence felt, though most keenly in the prenegotiation phase of multilateral diplomacy. The process of international negotiation described in this book is thus consistent with what James Rosenau calls the new "turbulence" of international politics, which is marked, in part, by the emergence of a multicentric world order.[9] But it is a process that has old roots, in spite of the fact that it is becoming a more visible feature of international diplomacy as a result of the end of the Cold War.

Notes

Chapter 1: Multilateral Negotiations

1. Robert O. Keohane, "Multilateralism: An Agenda for Research," *International Journal* 45, no. 4 (1990): 731.

2. John Ruggie, "Multilateralism: The Anatomy of an Institution," *International Organization* 46, no. 3 (1992): 561–598.

3. I. William Zartman, *Many Are Called but Few Choose: Managing Complexity in Multilateral Negotiations,* Working Paper 14, Program of the Processes of International Negotiation (Cambridge, Mass.: American Academy of Arts and Sciences, 1988), p. 2.

4. See Joseph S. Nye Jr., *Bound to Lead: The Changing Nature of American Power* (New York: Basic Books, 1990).

5. Gilbert R. Winham, "Complexity in International Negotiation," in Daniel Druckman, ed., *Negotiations: Social-Psychological Perspectives* (Beverly Hills, Calif.: Sage, 1977), p. 348.

6. These theories are reviewed by Keohane in "Multilateralism," pp. 740–748.

7. See Ruggie, "Multilateralism"; James A. Caporaso, "International Relations Theory and Multilateralism: The Search for Foundation"; and Miles Kahler, "Multilateralism with Small and Large Numbers," *International Organization* 46, no. 3 (1992): 561–598, 599–632, and 681–708, respectively; and Lisa L. Martin, "Interests, Power, and Multilateralism," *International Organization* 46, no. 4 (1992): 765–792.

8. Gilbert R. Winham, "Negotiation as a Management Process," *World Politics* 30, no. 1 (1977): 111.

9. Jonathan Dean, "East-West Arms Control Negotiations: The Multilateral Dimension," in Leon Sloss and M. Scott Davis, eds., *A Game for High Stakes: Lessons Learned in Negotiating with the Soviet Union* (Cambridge, Mass.: Ballinger, 1986), p. 91.

10. Stephen Krasner, "Structural Causes and Regime Consequences," in Stephen Krasner, ed., *International Regimes* (Ithaca: Cornell University Press, 1983), p. 2.

11. I. William Zartman, "The Elephant and the Holograph: Toward a Theoretical Synthesis and a Paradigm," in I. William Zartman, ed., *International Multilateral Negotiation: Approaches to the Management of Complexity* (San Francisco: Jossey-Bass, 1994), p. 222.

12. Alexander Wendt, "Anarchy Is What States Make of It: The Social Construction of Power Politics," *International Organization* 46, no. 2 (1992): 417. Emphasis added.

13. Zartman, *Many Are Called but Few Choose,* p. 1.

14. Some of the more recent treatments of multilateral negotiations include Victor A. Kremenyuk, ed., *International Negotiation: Analysis, Approaches, Issues* (San

Francisco: Jossey-Bass, 1991); Frances Mautner-Markhof, ed., *Processes of International Negotiation* (Boulder, Colo.: Westview, 1989); I. William Zartman, *Positive Sum: Improving North-South Negotiations* (New Brunswick, N.J.: Transaction Books, 1987); and Bruce Bueno de Mesquita, "Multilateral Negotiations: A Spatial Analysis of the Arab-Israeli Dispute," *International Organization* 44, no. 3 (1990): 317–340.

15. See, for example, Krasner, *International Regimes;* and Robert O. Keohane, *After Hegemony: Cooperation and Discord in the World Political Economy* (Princeton: Princeton University Press, 1984).

16. As Keohane writes, "incentives to form international regimes depend most fundamentally on the existence of shared interests . . . [which] may reflect the gains to be obtained from exploiting others more effectively . . . [or] on a mutual desire to increase the efficiency of the exchanges in which they engage." Keohane, *After Hegemony,* p. 79.

17. Oran R. Young, "The Politics of International Regime Formation: Managing Natural Resources and the Environment," *International Organization* 34, no. 3 (1989): 356.

18. Gilbert R. Winham, "Multilateral Economic Negotiation," *Negotiation Journal* 3, no. 2 (1987): 175.

19. For a variety of different approaches to classifying the negotiation literature, see, for example, Jacob Bercovitch, "Problems and Approaches in the Study of Bargaining and Negotiation," *Political Science* 36, no. 2 (1984): 125–144; John S. Murray, "Understanding Competing Theories of Negotiation," *Negotiation Journal* 2, no. 2 (1986): 179–186; Margaret A. Neale and Max B. Bazerman, "Perspectives for Understanding Negotiation," *Journal of Conflict Resolution* 29, no. 1 (1985): 33–55; and I. William Zartman, "Common Elements in the Analysis of the Negotiation Process," *Negotiation Journal* 4, no. 1 (1988): 31–43.

20. For various discussions and critiques of realism, see Robert O. Keohane, *Neorealism and Its Critics* (New York: Columbia University Press, 1986).

21. Stephen D. Krasner, *Structural Conflict: The Third World against Global Capitalism* (Berkeley: University of California Press, 1985), pp. 268–271.

22. Joseph M. Greico, *Cooperation among Nations: Europe, America, and Non-Tariff Barriers to Trade* (Ithaca: Cornell University Press, 1990), p. 35. Also see Joseph M. Greico, "Anarchy and the Limits of Cooperation: A Realist Critique of the Newest Liberal Institutionalism," *International Organization* 42, no. 3 (1988): 485–508.

23. Samuel B. Bacharach and Edward J. Lawler, "Power Dependence and Power Paradoxes in Bargaining," *Negotiation Journal* 2, no. 1 (1986): 167–174.

24. This is the thrust of some of the classic studies of deterrence and bargaining and negotiation. See, for example, Thomas Schelling, *The Strategy of Conflict* (Cambridge: Harvard University Press, 1960), esp. pp. 173–204; Glenn H. Snyder and Paul Diesing, *Conflict among Nations: Bargaining, Decision Making, and System Structure in International Crises* (Princeton: Princeton University Press, 1977), pp. 118–129; and I. William Zartman, "Negotiating from Asymmetry: The North-South Stalemate," *Negotiation Journal* 1, no. 2 (1985): 121–138.

25. See I. William Zartman and Maureen R. Berman, *The Practical Negotiator* (New Haven: Yale University Press, 1982), pp. 205–207.

26. See Zartman, "Negotiating from Asymmetry."

27. R. Harrison Wagner, "Economic Interdependence, Bargaining Power, and Political Influence," *International Organization* 42, no. 3 (1988): 461–483.

28. See Jeffrey Rubin and Bert Brown, *The Social Psychology of Bargaining and Negotiation* (New York: Academic, 1975), pp. 244–247; and Zartman, "Common Elements in the Analysis of the Negotiating Process," p. 33.

29. Robert L. Rothstein, "Regime-Creation by a Coalition of the Weak: Lessons from the NIEO and the Integrated Program for Commodities," *International Studies Quarterly* 28, no. 3 (1984): 307–328.

30. Zartman, "Common Elements in the Analysis of the Negotiation Process," p. 33.

31. Bercovitch, "Problems and Approaches in the Study of Bargaining and Negotiation," 134. Also see David A. Baldwin, "Power Analysis and World Politics," *World Politics* 31, no. 2 (1979): 161–194.

32. Zartman, *Many Are Called but Few Choose,* p. 5.

33. See, for example, Richard A. Higgott and Andrew Fenton Cooper, "Middle Power Leadership and Coalition Building: Australia, the Cairns Group, and the Uruguay Round of Trade Negotiations," *International Organization* 44, no. 4 (1990): 591–632.

34. This is the argument in Robert O. Keohane and Joseph S. Nye, *Power and Interdependence: World Politics in Transition,* 2d ed. (Boston: Scott, Foresman, 1989). The importance of transnational actors and groupings in multilateral negotiations on the environment is the subject of several recent works. See, for example, Peter M. Haas, "Do Regimes Matter? Epistemic Communities and Mediterranean Pollution Control," *International Organization* 43, no. 3 (1989): 377–404; Peter M. Haas, *Saving the Mediterranean: The Politics of International Environmental Cooperation* (New York: Columbia University Press, 1990); Peter M. Haas, "Obtaining International Environmental Protection through Epistemic Consensus," *Millennium: Journal of International Studies* 19, no. 3 (1990): 347–364; Young, "Politics of International Regime Formation"; and Oran R. Young, *International Cooperation: Building Regimes for Natural Resources and the Environment* (Ithaca: Cornell University Press, 1989).

35. Robert D. Putnam, "Diplomacy and Domestic Politics: The Logic of Two-Level Games," *International Organization* 42, no. 3 (1988): 427–460.

36. For discussions and applications of game-theoretic models of bargaining, see Daniel Ellsberg, "Theory of the Reluctant Duelist"; John F. Nash, "The Bargaining Problem"; John F. Nash, "Two-Person Cooperative Games"; John C. Harsanyi, "Bargaining and Conflict Situations in the Light of a New Approach to Game Theory"; and Robert L. Bishop, "Game-Theoretic Analyses of Bargaining," in Oran R. Young, ed., *Bargaining: Formal Theories of Negotiation* (Urbana: University of Illinois Press, 1975).

37. Duncan Snidal, "The Game Theory of International Politics," in Kenneth A. Oye, ed., *Cooperation under Anarchy* (Princeton: Princeton University Press, 1986), pp. 52–53.

38. See, for example, Robert Axelrod, *The Evolution of Cooperation* (New York: Basic Books, 1984); and Duncan Snidal, "Coordination versus Prisoners' Dilemma: Implication for International Cooperation and Regimes," *American Political Science Review* 79, no. 4 (1985): 923–942.

39. Bueno de Mesquita, "Multilateral Negotiations," pp. 319–320.

40. The classic study of coalitions is William Riker, *The Theory of Political Coalitions* (New Haven: Yale University Press, 1962). Also see Howard Raiffa, *The Art and Science of Negotiation* (Cambridge: Harvard University Press, 1982), pp. 257–274.

41. Kenneth A. Oye, "Explaining Cooperation under Anarchy," in Oye, *Cooperation under Anarchy*, p. 21.

42. Knut Midgaard and Arild Underdal, "Multiparty Conferences," in Druckman, *Negotiations*, p. 332. Emphasis in original.

43. Bercovitch, "Problems and Approaches in the Study of Bargaining and Negotiation," p. 139.

44. James K. Sebenius, *Negotiating the Law of the Sea: Lessons in the Art and Science of Reaching Agreement* (Cambridge: Harvard University Press, 1984), p. 114.

45. For a discussion of these models, see Raiffa, *The Art and Science of Negotiation*, pp. 275–287.

46. See Sebenius, *Negotiating the Law of the Sea*, pp. 182–217; and James K. Sebenius, "Negotiation Arithmetic: Adding and Subtracting Issues and Parties," *International Organization* 37, no. 2 (1983): 281–317.

47. These problems were all too evident in the Law of the Sea negotiations. For a further discussion, see Ann L. Hollick, *U.S. Foreign Policy and the Law of the Sea* (Princeton: Princeton University Press, 1981); and Sebenius, *Negotiating the Law of the Sea*, esp. pp. 7–39.

48. Raiffa, *The Art and Science of Negotiation*, p. 274.

49. See Dean G. Pruitt, *Negotiation Behavior* (New York: Academic, 1981), pp. 19–56.

50. For a review and discussion of different concession strategies, see W. Clay Hamner and Gary A. Yukl, "The Effectiveness of Different Offer Strategies in Bargaining," in Druckman, *Negotiations*, pp. 137–160.

51. See Winham, "Multilateral Economic Negotiations"; and Gilbert R. Winham, "Complexity in International Negotiation," in Druckman, *Negotiations*, pp. 347–366.

52. See Herbert A. Simon, "Rationality in Psychology and Economics," in Robin M. Hogarth and Melvin A. Reder, eds., *Rational Choices: The Contrast between Economics and Psychology* (Chicago: University of Chicago Press, 1986), pp. 25–40.

53. Ibid., p. 26.

54. A useful overview of the process-oriented model of negotiation is to be found in P. H. Gulliver, *Disputes and Negotiations: A Cross-Cultural Perspective* (New York: Academic, 1979), esp. pp. 81–178.

55. On the difference between integrative and distributive bargaining, see Richard E. Walton and Robert B. McKersie, *A Behavioral Theory of Labor Negotiations: An Analysis of Social Interaction Systems* (New York: McGraw-Hill, 1965), pp. 11–57, 126–143.

56. Young, "The Politics of International Regime Formation," pp. 360–366.

57. Ibid., pp. 367–373.

58. See I. William Zartman, "Ripening Conflict, Ripe Moment, Formula, and Mediation," in Diane B. Bendahmane and John W. McDonald Jr., eds., *Perspectives on Negotiation* (Washington, D.C.: Foreign Service Institute, U.S. Department of State, 1986), pp. 205–228; and I. William Zartman, *Ripe for Resolution: Conflict and Intervention in Africa* (New York: Oxford University Press, 1985).

59. Daniel Druckman, "Stages, Turning Points, and Crises: Negotiating Military Base Rights, Spain and the United States," *Journal of Conflict Resolution* 30, no. 2 (1986): 329. William Zartman and Maureen Berman identify three stages: the "diag-

nostic stage," the "formula phase," and the "detail phase." See Zartman and Berman, *The Practical Negotiator.*

60. See Daniel Druckman, "Turning Points in the INF Negotiations," *Negotiation Journal* 7, no. 1 (1991): 55–68.

61. See Bercovitch, "Problems and Approaches in the Study of Bargaining and Negotiation," 136–137; and Rubin and Brown, *The Social Psychology of Bargaining and Negotiation,* esp. pp. 19–42.

62. Winham, "Complexity in International Negotiation"; and Winham, "Multilateral Economic Negotiation."

63. See Janice Gross Stein, "International Negotiation: A Multidisciplinary Perspective," *Negotiation Journal* 4, no. 3 (1988): 227.

64. See David V. J. Bell, "Political Linguistics and International Negotiation"; and Deborah Welch Larson, "The Psychology of Reciprocity in Diplomatic Negotiations," *International Negotiation* 4, no. 3 (1988): 233–246, and 281–302, respectively.

65. Ernst B. Haas, *When Knowledge Is Power: Three Models of Change in International Organization* (Berkeley: University of California Press, 1990), pp. 41–42.

66. See Peter Haas, "Do Regimes Matter?"; and Peter Haas, *Saving the Mediterranean.*

67. Ernst Haas, *When Knowledge Is Power,* p. 128.

68. See Joseph S. Nye Jr., "Nuclear Learning and U.S.-Soviet Security Regimes," *International Organization* 41, no. 2 (1987): 371–402. This is by no means intended to detract from the important work conducted on the role of international regimes and international organization in social learning. See, for example, Alexander L. George, Philip J. Farley, and Alexander Dallin, eds., *U.S.-Soviet Security Cooperation: Achievements, Failures, Lessons* (New York: Oxford University Press, 1988); Ernst Haas, *When Knowledge Is Power;* and Ernst B. Haas, Mary Pat Williams, and Don Babai, *Scientists and World Order* (Berkeley: University of California Press, 1977).

69. Jeffrey Z. Rubin, introduction to Jeffrey Z. Rubin, ed., *Dynamics of Third Party Intervention: Kissinger in the Middle East* (New York: Praeger, 1981), pp. 28–43; James Laue, "The Emergence and Institutionalization of Third Party Roles in Conflict"; Marie A. Dugan, "Intervenor Roles and Conflict Pathologies"; and Thomas Colosi, "A Model for Negotiation and Mediation," in Dennis J. D. Sandole and Ingrid Sandole-Staroste, eds., *Conflict Management and Problem Solving: Interpersonal to International Applications* (London: Frances-Pinter, 1987), pp. 17–29, 57–61, and 86–99, respectively.

70. See, for example, Saadia Touval, *The Peace Brokers: Mediators in the Arab-Israeli Conflict, 1948–79* (Princeton: Princeton University Press, 1982), pp. 321–331.

71. Lawrence Susskind and Jeffrey Cruikshank, *Breaking the Impasse: Consensual Approaches to Resolving Public Disputes* (New York: Basic Books, 1989), pp. 143–145.

72. See Saadia Touval and I. William Zartman, eds., *International Mediation in Theory and Practice* (Boulder, Colo.: Westview, 1985).

73. See Saadia Touval, "Biased Intermediaries: Theoretical and Historical Considerations," *Jerusalem Journal of International Relations* 1, no. 1 (1977): 51–87.

74. For a further discussion of the similarities and differences between formal decision-making approaches to negotiation and more practically oriented or "process-driven" explanations, see Geoffrey R. Martin, "The 'Practical' and the 'Theoretical' Split in Modern Negotiation Literature," *Negotiation Journal* 4, no. 1 (1988): 45–54.

75. On the role of mediators in complex, multiparty, multi-issue negotiations, see, for example, C. R. Mitchell, "The Motives for Mediation," in C. R. Mitchell and K. Webb, eds., *New Approaches to International Mediation* (New York: Greenwood, 1988); C. R. Mitchell, *Peacemaking and the Consultants' Role* (New York: Nichols, 1981); Abie M. Davis and Howard Gadlin, "Mediators Gain Trust the Old-Fashioned Way—We Earn It!" *Negotiation Journal* 4, no. 1 (1988): 55–62; Loraleigh Keashley and Ronald J. Fisher, "Towards a Contingency Approach to Third Party Intervention in Regional Conflict," *International Journal* 45, no. 2 (1990): 425–453; Touval and Zartman, *International Mediation in Theory and Practice;* and Zartman, *Ripe for Resolution.*

76. Martin, "The 'Practical' and the 'Theoretical' Split in Modern Negotiation Literature," p. 52.

77. This approach is consistent with the emphasis placed on role differentiation, simplification, structuring, and leadership as discussed in I. William Zartman's introduction and conclusion to *Many Are Called but Few Choose.*

78. Alexander L. George, "Case Studies and Theory Development: The Method of Structured, Focused Comparison," in Paul G. Lauren, ed., *Diplomacy: New Approaches in History, Theory, and Policy* (New York: Free Press, 1979), p. 54. This is also akin to the method of synchronic-diachronic analysis suggested by historian John Lewis Gaddis in "Expanding the Data Base: Historians, Political Scientists, and the Enrichment of Security Studies," *International Security* 12, no. 1 (1987): 3–21.

79. George, "Case Studies and Theory Development," p. 60.

Chapter 2: Barriers to Negotiation and Requisites for Success

1. See Miles Kahler, "Multilateralism with Small and Large Numbers," *International Organization* 46, no. 3 (1992): 681–708.

2. Mancur Olson, *The Logic of Collective Action* (New York: Schocken, 1968); Russell Hardin, *Collective Action* (Baltimore: Johns Hopkins University Press, 1982). Buckley and Casson have also shown that all cooperative ventures are subject to strong and weak cheating pressures, and ventures that start without trust and good will are likely to fail. See Peter Buckley and Mark Casson, "A Theory of Cooperation in International Business," in Farok Contractor and Peter Lorange, eds., *Cooperative Strategies in International Business* (Lexington, Mass.: Lexington Books, 1988), pp. 31–53; Kenneth A. Oye, "Explaining Cooperation under Anarchy," in Kenneth A. Oye, ed., *Cooperation under Anarchy* (Princeton: Princeton University Press, 1986), pp. 1–24; Robert O. Keohane, *After Hegemony: Cooperation and Discord in the World Political Economy* (Princeton: Princeton University Press, 1984); and Robert O. Keohane, "The Demand for International Regimes," in Stephen Krasner, ed., *International Regimes* (Ithaca: Cornell University Press, 1983), pp. 141–172.

3. See, for example, Keohane, *After Hegemony;* Alexander L. George, "Factors Influencing Security Cooperation," in Alexander L. George, Philip, J. Farley, and Alexander Dallin, eds., *U.S.-Soviet Security Cooperation: Achievements, Lessons, Failures* (New York: Oxford University Press, 1988); and Joseph S. Nye Jr., "Nuclear Learning and U.S.-Soviet Security Regimes," *International Organization* 41, no. 2 (1987): 371–402.

4. Kahler, "Multilateralism with Small and Large Numbers," p. 685; and Duncan Snidal, "The Limits of Hegemonic Stability Theory," *International Organization* 39, no. 4 (1985): 579–615. Also see Joanne Gowa, "Rational Hegemons, Excludable

Goods, and Small Groups: An Epitaph for Hegemonic Stability Theory?" *World Politics* 41, no. 3 (1989): 307–324.

5. Kahler, "Multilateralism with Small and Large Numbers," p. 685.

6. Timothy Devine, "A Preemptive Approach in Multilateral Negotiation," *Negotiation Journal* 6, no. 4 (1990): 369–381.

7. William R. Pendergast, "Managing the Negotiation Agenda," *Negotiation Journal* 6, no. 2 (1990): 135–145.

8. See, for example, Janice Gross Stein, ed., *Getting to the Table* (Baltimore: Johns Hopkins University Press, 1990).

9. To focus exclusively on one level of analysis to the exclusion of other levels is to fall prone to two different kinds of error: the fallacy of creeping determinism, confusing underlying causes with final consequences, and the error of contingency, believing that "final" or "proximate" causes have sufficient explanatory power to explain political outcomes without attention to underlying structures. For a useful discussion of different levels of causation in international relations theory, see Richard Ned Lebow, *Between Peace and War: The Nature of International Crises* (Baltimore: Johns Hopkins University Press, 1981), pp. 1–7.

10. Daniel Druckman, Jo L. Husbands, and Karin Johnston, "Turning Points in the INF Negotiations," *Negotiation Journal* 7, no. 1 (1991): 56.

11. Harold Saunders, "We Need a Larger Theory of Negotiation: The Importance of Prenegotiation Phases," *Negotiation Journal* 1, no. 3 (1985): 250.

12. I. William Zartman and Maureen R. Berman, *The Practical Negotiator* (New Haven: Yale University Press, 1982), pp. 47–48.

13. Louis Kriesberg, ed., *Timing and De-Escalation in International Conflict* (Syracuse: Syracuse University Press, 1990).

14. I. William Zartman, "Prenegotiation: Phases and Functions," in Stein, *Getting to the Table,* p. 4.

15. Brian W. Tomlin, "The Stages of Prenegotiation: The Decision to Negotiate North American Free Trade," in Stein, *Getting to the Table,* pp. 21–22.

16. These four phases are outlined in ibid., pp. 22–24.

17. Janice Gross Stein, "Getting to the Table: The Triggers, Stages, Functions, and Consequences of Prenegotiation," in Stein, *Getting to the Table,* pp. 252–257.

18. Fen Osler Hampson, "Headed for the Table: United States Approaches to Prenegotiation," in Stein, *Getting to the Table,* pp. 129–173.

19. Saadia Touval, "Multilateral Negotiation: An Analytic Approach," *Negotiation Journal* 5, no. 2 (1989): 162.

20. Daniel Druckman, "Stages, Turning Points, and Crises: Negotiating Military Base Rights, Spain and the United States," *Journal of Conflict Resolution* 30, no. 2 (1986): 331.

21. Zartman and Berman, *The Practical Negotiator,* pp. 95, 147.

22. P. H. Gulliver, *Disputes and Negotiations: A Cross-Cultural Perspective* (New York: Academic, 1979), pp. 122–178.

23. Touval, "Multilateral Negotiation," p. 163.

24. See Gilbert R. Winham, "The Prenegotiation Phase of the Uruguay Round," *International Journal* 44, no. 2 (1989): 280–303.

25. Knut Midgaard and Arild Underdal, "Multiparty Conferences," in Daniel Druckman, ed., *Negotiations: Social-Psychological Perspectives* (Beverly Hills, Calif.: Sage, 1977), p. 334.

26. Gilbert R. Winham, "Multilateral Economic Negotiations," *Negotiation Journal* 3, no. 2 (1987): 176.

27. Jeffrey Z. Rubin and Bert R. Brown, *The Social Psychology of Bargaining and Negotiation* (New York: Academic, 1975), p. 64.

28. I. William Zartman, "Conclusions: Importance of North-South Negotiations," in I. William Zartman, ed., *Positive Sum: Improving North-South Negotiations* (New Brunswick, N.J.: Transaction Books, 1987), p. 295; and Rubin and Brown, *Social Psychology of Bargaining and Negotiation,* pp. 67–80.

29. Ian Bellany, "Negotiating Arms Control," *Arms Control* 10, no. 3 (1989): 209.

30. On the positive role played by crosscutting coalitions in the Third United Nations Conference on the Law of the Sea, see Robert L. Friedheim, "The Third United Nations Conference on the Law of the Sea: North-South Bargaining Issues," in Zartman, *Positive Sum,* pp. 73–114; and Ann L. Hollick, *U.S. Foreign Policy and the Law of the Sea* (Princeton: Princeton University Press, 1981).

31. James K. Sebenius, "Designing Negotiations Toward a New Regime: The Case of Global Warming," *International Security* 15, no. 4 (1991): 127.

32. Zartman, "Conclusions," p. 279.

33. See Robert L. Rothstein, "Commodity Bargaining: The Political Economy of Regime Creation," in Zartman, *Positive Sum,* pp. 15–47; and Robert L. Rothstein, "Regime-Creation by a Coalition of the Weak: Lessons from the NIEO and the Integrated Program for the Commodities," *International Studies Quarterly* 28, no. 3 (1984): 307–328.

34. David A. Lax and James K. Sebenius, *The Manager as Negotiator: Bargaining for Cooperation and Competitive Gain* (New York: Free Press, 1986), p. 71.

35. Ibid., p. 73.

36. Helmut Sonnenfeldt, "Soviet Negotiating Concept and Style," in Leon Sloss and M. Scott Davis, eds., *A Game for High Stakes: Lessons Learned in Negotiating with the Soviet Union* (Cambridge, Mass.: Ballinger, 1986), p. 24.

37. Gilbert R. Winham, "Complexity in International Negotiation," in Druckman, *Negotiations,* pp. 353, 364.

38. Steve Rayner, "A Cultural Perspective on the Structure and Implementation of Global Environmental Agreements," *Evaluation Review: A Journal of Applied Science and Research* 15, no. 1 (1991): 75–102.

39. Ype H. Poortinga and Erwin C. Hendriks, "Culture as a Factor in International Negotiations: A Proposed Research Project from a Psychological Perspective," in Victor A. Kremenyuk, ed., *International Negotiation: Analysis, Approaches, Issues* (San Francisco: Jossey-Bass, 1991), pp. 204, 206.

40. Ronnie Lipschutz, "Bargaining among Nations: Culture, History, and Perceptions in Regime Formation," *Evaluation Review: A Journal of Applied Research* 15, no. 1 (1991): 54.

41. Arild Underdal, "The Outcome of Negotiation," in Kremenyuk, *International Negotiation,* p. 106. Emphasis in original.

42. Sebenius, "Designing Negotiations Toward a New Regime," p. 143.

43. Underdal, "The Outcome of Negotiation," p. 107.

44. This discussion is based on Guennadi K. Yefimov, "Developing a Global Negotiating Machinery," in Frances Mautner-Markhof, ed., *Processes of International Negotiation* (Boulder, Colo.: Westview, 1989), pp. 62–64.

45. Ibid., p. 63.

46. Midgaard and Underdal, "Multiparty Conferences," p. 339.

47. These different definitions of learning in international politics are discussed in Nye, "Nuclear Learning and U.S.-Soviet Security Regimes."

48. Stein, *Getting to the Table*, p. 264.

49. For a discussion of these different approaches to learning, see Deborah Welch Larson, *Origins of Containment: A Psychological Explanation* (Princeton: Princeton University Press, 1985), pp. 24–62.

50. Quoted in Glenn H. Snyder and Paul Diesing, *Conflict among Nations: Bargaining, Decision Making, and System Structure in International Crises* (Princeton: Princeton University Press, 1977), pp. 9–10.

51. Stein, *Getting to the Table*, p. 265.

52. Oran Young, "The Politics of International Regime Formation: Managing Natural Resources and the Environment," *International Organization* 43, no. 3 (1989): p. 371.

53. Arthur Lall, *Modern International Negotiation: Principles and Practice* (New York: Columbia University Press, 1966), p. 3.

54. Richard N. Haass, *Conflicts Unending: The United States and Regional Disputes* (New Haven: Yale University Press, 1990), pp. 141–142.

55. Druckman, "Stages, Turning Points, and Crises," p. 333.

56. Farley notes that formal negotiations leading to the SALT I treaties were delayed for almost a year by the crisis in the East-West relations provoked by the Soviet invasion of Czechoslovakia in August 1968. See Philip J. Farley, "Strategic Arms Control, 1967–87," in George, Farley, and Dallin, *U.S.-Soviet Security Cooperation*, pp. 215–253. The crisis brought about the discovery of the Soviet brigade in Cuba. Subsequently, the Soviet invasion of Afghanistan also prevented Senate ratification (though not implementation) of the provisions of SALT II. See Gloria Duffy, "Crisis Mangling and the Cuban Brigade," *International Security* 8, no. 1 (1983): 67–87.

57. Crises can also be "redistributive," a subset of distributive bargaining. As Snyder and Diesing explain, distributive bargaining "refers to bargaining over the division of a good that is mutually desired. Redistributive bargaining is a subclass: the objects at issue are already possessed or in the process of being acquired by one of the parties; the other party tries to force the possessor to give up all or part of it, or to stop acquiring it." See Snyder and Diesing, *Conflict among Nations*, p. 23. For the purposes of simplification, distributive and redistributive crises are treated together in this study as part of the same set.

58. For a useful discussion about the difference between distributive and integrative bargaining situations, see Richard E. Walton and Robert B. McKersie, *A Behavioral Theory of Labor Negotiations: An Analysis of a Social Interaction System* (New York: McGraw-Hill, 1965), pp. 1–183.

59. James K. Sebenius, *Negotiating the Law of the Sea: Lessons in the Art and Science of Reaching Agreement* (Cambridge: Harvard University Press, 1984), p. 73.

60. BATNA is defined as "the subjective expected utility of alternatives to negotiated agreement," i.e., "the minimum worth required of an acceptable agreement" or the "reservation value" or "reservation price" of agreement. See Lax and Sebenius, *The Manager as Negotiator*, p. 51.

61. Gulliver, *Disputes and Negotiations*, p. 83.

62. Robert L. Rothstein, "Consensual Knowledge and International Collabora-

tion: Some Lessons from Commodity Negotiations," *International Organization* 38, no. 4 (1984): 734, 735.

63. Peter M. Haas, "Do Regimes Matter? Epistemic Communities and Mediterranean Pollution Control," *International Organization* 43, no. 3 (1989): 380.

64. Stephan Haggard and Beth A. Simmons, "Theories of International Regimes," *International Organization* 41, no. 3 (1987): 511.

65. For discussions about the role of risk in decision making, see William W. Lowrance, *Of Acceptable Risk: Science and the Determinant of Safety* (Los Altos, Calif.: William Kaufmann, 1976); and Mary Douglas and Aaron Wildavsky, *Risk and Culture: An Essay on the Selection of Technical and Environmental Dangers* (Berkeley: University of California Press, 1982).

66. Ernst B. Haas, *When Knowledge Is Power: Three Models of Change in International Organizations* (Berkeley: University of California Press, 1990), p. 41.

67. Peter M. Morrisette, "The Evolution of Policy Responses to Stratospheric Ozone Depletion," *Natural Resources Journal* 29, no. 3 (1989): 749–820.

68. See Stephen H. Schneider, *Global Warming: Are We Entering the Greenhouse Century?* (San Francisco: Sierra Club Books, 1989).

69. Underdal, "The Outcome of Negotiation," pp. 105–106.

70. Edward A. Parson and Richard J. Zeckhauser, "Cooperation in the Unbalanced Commons," paper, Harvard University, Cambridge, Mass., 1993.

71. Klaus L. Aurisch, "The Art of Preparing a Multilateral Conference," *Negotiation Journal* 5, no. 3 (1989): 285.

72. Touval, "Multilateral Negotiation," p. 164.

73. This discussion on "logrolling" and "bridging" is drawn from Dean G. Pruitt, *Negotiation Behavior* (New York: Academic, 1981), pp. 153–155.

74. Zartman, "Conclusions," p. 296.

75. Pruitt, *Negotiation Behavior*, p. 154.

76. Richard A. Higgott and Andrew Fenton Cooper, "Middle Power Leadership and Coalition Building: Australia, the Cairns Group, and the Uruguay Round of Trade Negotiations," *International Organization* 44, no. 4 (1990): 628.

77. In this respect, they are *not* members of what Duncan Snidal calls the "k" group, i.e., states that are large and powerful and contribute to provision costs of a public good. See Snidal, "The Limits of Hegemonic Stability Theory."

78. On the rewards, risks, and costs of mediation, see Christopher R. Mitchell, "The Motives for Mediation," in C. R. Mitchell and K. Webb, eds., *New Approaches to International Mediation* (New York: Greenwood, 1988), pp. 29–51.

79. Zartman, "Conclusions," pp. 296–297; and Touval, "Multilateral Negotiation," pp. 164–165.

80. Jonathan Dean, "East-West Arms Control Negotiations: The Multilateral Dimension," in Sloss and Davis, *A Game for High Stakes*, p. 92.

81. Oran R. Young, "Political Leadership and Regime Formation: On the Development of Institutions in International Society," *International Organization* 45, no. 3 (1991): 293–294.

82. These conditions associated with different kinds of market failure are stressed in functionally based literature on international regimes. See Keohane, *After Hegemony*; and Krasner, *International Regimes*.

83. Devine, "A Preemptive Approach in Multilateral Negotiation," p. 380.

84. Alexander L. George, "Factors Influencing Security Cooperation," in George, Farley, and Dallin, *U.S.-Soviet Security Cooperation*, p. 673.

85. Barbara Kellerman, introduction to Barbara Kellerman and Jeffrey Z. Rubin, eds., *Leadership and Negotiation in the Middle East* (New York: Praeger, 1988), p. 4.

86. Zartman and Berman, *Practical Negotiator*, pp. 95–109.

87. Young, "The Politics of International Regime Formation," p. 368.

88. Zartman, "Conclusions," p. 284.

89. Kenneth A. Oye, "Explaining Cooperation under Anarchy: Hypotheses and Strategies," in Oye, *Cooperation under Anarchy*, pp. 19–20.

90. Young, "The Politics of International Regime Formation," p. 371.

91. For a discussion of this problem, see Gloria Duffy, "Conditions that Affect Arms Control Compliance," in George, Farley, and Dallin, *U.S.-Soviet Security Cooperation*, pp. 276–277.

92. Sebenius, "Designing Negotiations Toward a New Regime," pp. 134–137.

93. Zartman, "Conclusions," pp. 290, 292–293.

94. Alexander L. George, Philip J. Farley, and Alexander Dallin, "Research Objectives and Methods," in George, Farley, and Dallin, *U.S.-Soviet Security Cooperation*, pp. 13, 14.

95. Sebenius, "Designing Negotiations Toward a New Regime," p. 138.

96. Bellany, "Negotiating Arms Control," p. 215. Emphasis in original.

97. Pendergast, "Managing the Negotiation Agenda," pp. 136–140.

98. Milgaard and Underdal, "Multiparty Conferences," p. 336.

99. See Harry Eckstein, "Case Study and Theory in Political Science," in Fred I. Greenstein and Nelson W. Polsby, eds., *Strategies of Inquiry: Handbook of Political Science*, vol. 7 (Reading, Mass.: Addison-Wesley, 1975), pp. 113–123; and Alexander L. George, "Case Studies and Theory Development: The Method of Structured, Focused Comparison," in Paul G. Lauren, ed., *Diplomacy: New Approaches in History, Theory, and Policy* (New York: Free Press, 1979), pp. 50–51.

100. This is the same cautionary advice given by Deborah Welch Larson to case-study analysts. See *Origins of Containment*, pp. 58–59.

101. George, "Case Studies and Theory Development," p. 63.

Chapter 3: The Limited Test Ban Treaty

1. For contemporary accounts of the issues associated with the test ban negotiations, see Richard Scott, "A Ban on Nuclear Tests: The Course of the Negotiations, 1958–1962," *International Affairs* 38, no. 4 (1962): 501–510; Hedley Bull, "The Arms Race and the Banning of Nuclear Tests," *Political Quarterly* 30, no. 4 (1959): 344–356; Harold K. Jacobson, "The Test-Ban Negotiations: Implications for the Future," *Annals of the American Political Science Association*, no. 351 (January 1964): 91–101; and Henry A. Kissinger, "Nuclear Testing and the Problem of Peace," *Foreign Affairs* 37, no. 1 (1958): 1–18. On issues surrounding a comprehensive test ban, see National Academy of Sciences, *Nuclear Arms Control: Background and Issues* (Washington, D.C.: National Academy Press, 1985), pp. 187–223.

2. Scott, "A Ban on Nuclear Tests," p. 501.

3. For a useful history of these and other early arms control initiatives, see Coit D. Blacker and Gloria Duffy, eds., *International Arms Control: Issues and Agreements*, 2d ed. (Stanford: Stanford University Press, 1984), pp. 94–147.

4. Glenn T. Seaborg, *Kennedy, Khrushchev, and the Test Ban* (Berkeley: University of California Press, 1981), p. 10. Emphasis in original.

5. Quoted in ibid., p. 12.

6. The following account of these negotiations is based on Harold Karan Jacobson and Eric Stein, *Diplomats, Scientists, and Politicians: The United States and the Nuclear Test Ban Negotiations* (Ann Arbor: University of Michigan Press, 1971).

7. Soviet endorsement of a test ban was viewed suspiciously by its ally, the People's Republic of China. The test ban ultimately became a source of major tension in relations between Moscow and Peking, because the latter viewed it as an attempt to keep it out of the nuclear club. See Walter C. Clemens Jr., "The Nuclear Test Ban and Sino-Soviet Relations," *Orbis* 10, no. 3 (1966): 152–183.

8. Nikita Khrushchev, *Khrushchev Remembers: The Last Testament* (Toronto: Little, Brown, 1974), pp. 69–71.

9. Quoted in ibid., pp. 373, 374.

10. Ibid., p. 376.

11. Ibid., pp. 381–382.

12. Ibid., p. 388.

13. Ibid., p. 410.

14. For various accounts of the Cuban missile crisis, see Graham T. Allison, *Essence of Decision: Explaining the Cuban Missile Crisis* (Boston: Little, Brown, 1971); James G. Blight and David A. Welch, *On the Brink: Americans and Soviets Reexamine the Missile Crisis* (New York: Hill and Wang, 1989); and McGeorge Bundy, *Danger and Survival: Choices about the Bomb in the First Fifty Years* (New York: Random House, 1988), pp. 391–462.

15. Quoted in Seaborg, *Kennedy, Khrushchev, and the Test Ban*, p. 176. Also see *U.S. and USSR Exchange of Views on Nuclear Test Ban (Exchange of Letters between Kennedy and Khrushchev)*, Bulletin 48 (Washington, D.C.: U.S. Department of State, 1963), pp. 198–202.

16. Theodore C. Sorensen, *Kennedy* (New York: Harper and Row, 1965), pp. 727–728.

17. The United States' position on nuclear testing and its willingness to accept a limited test ban in lieu of a comprehensive ban was explained by U.S. Ambassador to the United Nations Adlai E. Stevenson. See Adlai E. Stevenson, *United States Position on Nuclear Testing Explained to the United Nations*, Bulletin 47 (Washington, D.C.: U.S. Department of State, 1962), pp. 635–641.

18. Quoted in Alistaire Horne, *Macmillan, 1957–1986* (London: Macmillan, 1989), p. 505.

19. For a discussion of the history and origins of the Skybolt crisis, see Richard E. Neustadt, *Alliance Politics* (New York: Columbia University Press, 1970).

20. See "Administration in Center of Test-Ban Crossfire," *Congressional Quarterly*, no. 21 (March 1, 1963), pp. 263–272.

21. Jacobson and Stein, *Diplomats, Scientists, and Politicians*, p. 444.

22. Quoted in Seaborg, *Kennedy, Khrushchev, and the Test Ban*, p. 193.

23. Quoted in Harold W. Chase and Allen W. Lerman, eds., *Kennedy and the Press: The News Conferences* (New York: Thomas Y. Crowell, 1965), p. 410.

24. Seaborg, *Kennedy, Khrushchev, and the Test Ban*, p. 182. On the history of China's nuclear program, see John Wilson Lewis and Xue Litai, *China Builds the Bomb* (Stanford: Stanford University Press, 1988).

25. Horne, *Macmillan,* pp. 506–507.

26. Ibid., pp. 508–509.

27. See Robert F. Kennedy, *Thirteen Days: A Memoir of the Cuban Missile Crisis* (New York: W. W. Norton, 1969).

28. Horne, *Macmillan,* p. 510.

29. Arthur M. Schlesinger, Jr. *A Thousand Days: John F. Kennedy in the White House* (Boston: Houghton Mifflin, 1965).

30. Jacobson and Stein, *Diplomats, Scientists, and Politicians,* p. 448.

31. Ronald J. Terchek, *The Making of the Test Ban Treaty* (The Hague: Martinus Nijhoff, 1970), pp. 82–83.

32. Ibid., pp. 115–116, 119.

33. Ibid. pp. 42–43, 37–38.

34. Seaborg, *Kennedy, Khrushchev, and the Test Ban,* pp. 227–229.

35. For various examinations of the Senate debate on ratification of the Limited Test Ban Treaty, see James Hubert McBride, *The Test Ban Treaty: Military, Technological, and Political Implications* (Chicago: Henry Regnery, 1967); and Ivo H. Daalder, "The Limited Test Ban Treaty," in Albert Carnesale and Richard N. Haass, eds., *Superpower Arms Control: Setting the Record Straight* (Cambridge, Mass.: Ballinger, 1987), pp. 9–40.

Chapter 4: The Stockholm Conference

1. James E. Goodby, "The Stockholm Conference: Negotiating a Cooperative Security System for Europe," in Alexander L. George, Philip J. Farley, and Alexander Dallin, eds., *U.S.-Soviet Security Cooperation: Achievements, Failures, Lessons* (New York: Oxford University Press, 1988), p. 152.

2. For a useful discussion on the origins of the CSCE, see Stephen J. Flanagan, "The CSCE and the Development of Detente," in Derek Leebaert, ed., *European Security: Prospects for the 1980s* (Lexington, Mass.: Lexington Books, 1979), pp. 189–232.

3. Quoted in John Borawski, *From the Atlantic to the Urals: Negotiating Arms Control at the Stockholm Conference* (Washington, D.C.: Pergamon-Brassey's, 1988), p. 12.

4. Ibid., pp. 12, 13.

5. Ibid., p. 13.

6. Ibid., p. 16.

7. Quoted in John Borawski, Stan Weeks, and Charlotte E. Thompson, "The Stockholm Agreement of September 1986," *Orbis* 30, no. 4 (1987): 645.

8. Ibid., p. 646.

9. On the Madrid CSCE Conference, see Jan Sizoo and Rudolf Th. Jurrjens, *CSCE Decision-Making: The Madrid Experience* (The Hague: Martinus Nijhoff, 1984), especially pp. 23–45 and 84–106. For a more general discussion of the relationship between the CSCE process and European security, see Reimund Deidelmann, "European Security and the CSCE Process," *Review d'Integration Europeene/Journal of European Integration* 9, nos. 2–3 (1986): pp. 209–242.

10. On the role and function of confidence-building measures, see James Macintosh, "Confidence-Building Measures—A Conceptual Exploration"; and Johan Jorgen Holst, "A CBM Regime in Europe—Nineteen Interrelated Propositions," in R. B. Byers, F. Stephen Larrabee, and Allen Lynch, eds., *Confidence-Building Measures and International Security* (New York: Institute for East-West Security Studies, 1987), pp. 9–30 and 31–28. A useful comparison of the two types of arms control—confidence-

374 Notes to Pages 83–91

building measures and conventional force reductions—is found in Richard E. Darilek, "The Future of Conventional Arms Control in Europe, A Tale of Two Cities:
Stockholm, Vienna," *Survival* 29, no. 1 (1987): pp. 5–20.

11. In addition to Borawski's detailed and extremely useful discussion of these
negotiations, see Carl C. Krehbiel, *Confidence- and Security-Building Measures in Europe: The Stockholm Conference* (New York: Praeger, 1989), esp. pp. 1–24 and 219–301.

12. On Soviet goals and interests in the CDE, see Mark A. Cichock, "Soviet Goal
Articulations and Involvement at the European Disarmament Conference," *Coexis-
tence* 23, no. 3 (1986): pp. 189–207.

13. Goodby, "The Stockholm Conference," p. 151.

14. Ibid., p. 152.

15. Ibid., p. 153.

16. Ibid., p. 154.

17. Quoted in Borawski, *From the Atlantic to the Urals,* p. 63.

18. Quoted in Goodby, "The Stockholm Conference," p. 156.

19. Canadian Institute for International Peace and Security (CIIPS), *A Guide to
Canadian Policies on Arms Control, Disarmament, Defence and Conflict Resolution* (Ottawa, 1986), p. 52.

20. Quoted in Borawski, *From the Atlantic to the Urals,* p. 92.

21. For in-depth discussions of the accords, see James E. Goodby, "Reducing the
Risks of War: The Stockholm Achievement," *Disarmament* 9, no. 3 (1986): 53–77;
James E. Goodby, *The Stockholm Conference: Negotiating a Cooperative Security System
for Europe,* Occasional Paper 6 (Washington, D.C.: Center for the Study of Foreign
Affairs, 1986); Borawski, Weeks, and Thompson, "The Stockholm Agreement"; John
Borawski, "Accord at Stockholm," *Bulletin of Atomic Scientists* 42, no. 10 (1986):
34–36; and John Borawski, "Confidence and Security Building Measures in Europe,"
Parameters: Journal of the War College 16, no. 4 (1986): 68–83.

22. "Document of the Stockholm Meeting on Security," *New York Times,* September 22, 1986; and *Reuters News Reports,* Items 855, 879, September 22, 1986.

23. Goodby, "The Stockholm Conference," p. 160.

24. James Macintosh, "Multilateral Regional Negotiations: The View of the Allies," in Fen Osler Hampson, Harald von Riekhoff, and John Roper, eds., *The Allies
and Arms Control* (Baltimore: Johns Hopkins University Press, 1992), p. 58.

25. Goodby, "The Stockholm Conference," p. 166.

26. Ulf Lindell, "The Consensus Rule in Two International Conferences," *Cooperation and Conflict* 22, no. 2 (1987): p. 129.

27. Karl E. Birnbaum, "The Neutral and Non-Aligned States in the CSCE Process,"
in Bengt Sundelius, ed., *The Neutral Democracies and the New Cold War* (Boulder,
Colo.: Westview, 1987), p. 150. Emphasis in original.

28. Ibid., p. 153.

29. Ibid., p. 154.

30. C. A. Namiesniowski, *The Stockholm Agreement: An Exercise in Confidence Building,* Background Paper 14 (Ottawa: Canadian Institute for International Peace and
Security, 1987), p. 4.

31. Ljubovije Acimovic, "The Role of the Neutral and Non-Aligned Countries in
the Process of the CSCE," *Review of International Affairs* 38 (January 20, 1987): 8.

32. Goodby, "The Stockholm Conference," p. 166.

33. Ibid., pp. 165–166.

34. Quoted in Borawski, *From the Atlantic to the Urals*, pp. 29–30.

35. Sverre Lodgaard, "The Building of Confidence and Security at Negotiations in Stockholm and Vienna," in Stockholm International Peace Research Institute, *SIPRI Yearbook, 1986: World Armaments and Disarmament* (New York: Oxford University Press, 1986), p. 425.

36. Namiesniowski, "The Stockholm Agreement," p. 6.

37. Goodby, "The Stockholm Conference," p. 162.

Chapter 5: Conventional Arms Control

1. Christopher Coker, *A Farewell to Arms Control: The Irrelevance of CFE*, Occasional Paper 49 (London: Institute for European Defence and Strategic Studies, 1991), p. 11.

2. For various discussions of the historical background to these negotiations, see Christoph Bertram, *Mutual Force Reductions in Europe: The Political Aspects*, Adelphi Paper 84 (London: International Institute of Strategic Studies, 1972); Ian Smart, *MBFR Assailed: A Critical View of the Proposed Negotiation on Mutual and Balanced Force Reductions in Europe*, Occasional Paper 3 (Ithaca: Cornell University Peace Studies Program, 1972); Joseph Harned, "CSCE and Negotiations on MBFR," *Atlantic Community Quarterly* 11, no. 1 (1973): 29–43, 46–51; Hans-George Wieck, "Perspectives on MBFR in Europe," *Aussenpolitik* 23, no. 1 (1972): 36–40; and Robin Ranger, "MBFR: Political or Technical Arms Control," *World Today* 30, no. 10 (1974): 411–418.

3. On the early history of MBFR, see J. G. Keliher, *The Negotiations on Mutual and Balanced Force Reductions: The Search for Arms Control in Central Europe* (New York: Pergamon, 1980); Abbott Brayton, "MBFR and Conventional Forces Reductions in Europe," *World Today* 40, no. 12 (1984): 497–507; Richard F. Starr, "The MBFR Process and Its Prospects," *Orbis* 27, no. 4 (1984): 999–1009; and Lowther Ruehl, *MBFR's Lessons and Problems*, Adelphi Paper 176 (London: International Institute of Strategic Studies, 1982).

4. See Robert D. Blackwill, "Conceptual Problems of Conventional Arms Control," *International Security* 12, no. 4 (1988): 28–47; John Borawski, "Toward Conventional Stability," *Washington Quarterly* 10, no. 4 (1987): 13–30; Jonathan Dean, "Will Negotiated Force Reductions Build Down the NATO–Warsaw Pact Confrontation?" *Washington Quarterly* 11, no. 2 (1988): 69–84; Roger Hill, *Are Major Conventional Force-Reductions in Europe Possible?* Aurora Paper 7 (Ottawa: Canadian Centre for Arms Control and Disarmament, 1988); and Jack Snyder, "Limiting Offensive Conventional Forces: Soviet Proposals and Western Options," *International Security* 12, no. 4 (1988): 48–77.

5. Coit D. Blacker, "Negotiating Security: The MBFR Experience," *Arms Control* 7, no. 3 (1986): 232–233.

6. See Hans Rattinger, "MBFR—Stagnation and Further Prospects," *Aussenpolitik* 30, no. 3 (1979): 336–343; Richard Darelik, "Separate Process, Converging Interests MBFR and CBMs," in Clarke Branch, ed., *Decisionmaking for Arms Limitation* (Cambridge, Mass.: Ballinger, 1983), pp. 237–257; and David C. Skaggs, "MBFR," *Military Review* 67, no. 1 (1987): 85–94.

7. Quoted in Richard Darilek, "The Failure of Conventional Arms Control in Europe," *Survival*, 24, no. 1 (1988): 16.

8. Ernst F. Jung, "Conventional Arms Control in Europe in Light of the MBFR Experience," *Aussenpolitik* 39, no. 2 (1988): 151–152. Also see David S. Yost, "Beyond MBFR: The Atlantic to the Urals Gambit," *Orbis* 31, no. 1 (1987): 99–134.

9. Thomas J. Marshall, "New Openings for Conventional Arms Control," *Parameters: Journal of the U.S. Army War College* 19, no. 2 (1989): 75–85.

10. See Robert D. Blackwill, "Conventional Stability Talks: Specific Approaches to Conventional Arms Control in Europe," *Survival* 30, no. 5 (1988): 429–447; John Toogood, *Conventional Arms Control in Europe: Western Opening Position,* Working Paper 15 (Ottawa: Canadian Institute for International Peace and Security, 1988).

11. U.S. Department of State, *To Strengthen Stability and Security: CFE Negotiation on Conventional Armed Forces in Europe* (Washington, D.C.: USIA, 1989), pp. 4–5.

12. Jonathan Dean, "Cutting Back the NATO–Warsaw Treaty Confrontation," *Disarmament* 12, no. 2 (1989): 19. Dean also argues that the conclusion and successful implementation of the Stockholm Document of September 1986, which expanded the provisions of the Helsinki Accord on prenotification and observation of military activities in the area from the Atlantic to the Urals, also had a positive influence on the CFE talks.

13. For a discussion of how these developments affected the growing enthusiasm for conventional arms control, see Lawrence Freedman, "The Politics of Conventional Arms Control," *Survival* 31, no. 5 (1989): 387–396. Also see Klaus Wittman, *Challenges of Conventional Arms Control,* Adelphi Paper 239 (London: International Institute of Strategic Studies, 1989).

14. See Jack Mendelsohn, "Borgachev's Preemptive Concession," *Arms Control Today* 19, no. 2 (1989): 10–15.

15. Critics argue that issues of military strategy and doctrine should have been included in these and subsequent negotiations. See Manfred R. Hamm and Hartmut Pohlman, "Military Strategy and Doctrine: Why They Matter to Conventional Arms Control," *Washington Quarterly* 13, no. 1 (1990): 185–198. For other critical perspectives on these negotiations, see Gyula Horn, "Reduction of Conventional Armed Forces and Armaments in Europe"; Jean Desazars de Montgailhard, "Conventional Disarmament in Europe"; Heinz Vetschera, "Reduction of Conventional Armed Forces in Europe: Problems and Prospects," *Disarmament* 12, no. 2 (1989): 34–40, 51–59, and 70–80.

16. The historical discussion of these negotiations that follows is drawn from Jane M. O. Sharp, "Conventional Arms Control in Europe," *SIPRI Yearbook, 1989: World Armaments and Disarmament* (Oxford: Oxford University Press, 1989), pp. 372–402; Jane M. O. Sharp, "Conventional Arms Control in Europe," *SIPRI Yearbook, 1990: World Armaments and Disarmament* (Oxford: Oxford University Press, 1990), pp. 478–501; Paul Dunay, *The CFE Treaty: History, Achievements and Shortcomings,* Report 24 (Frankfurt: Peace Research Institute, Frankfurt, 1991); and Canadian Institute for International Peace and Security (CIIPS), *Guide to Canadian Policies on Arms Control, Defence, and Conflict Resolution* (Ottawa: 1989), pp. 51–58; CIIPS, *Guide to Canadian Policies on Arms Control, Defence, and Conflict Resolution* (Ottawa, 1990), pp. 69–84; and CIIPS, *Guide to Canadian Policies on Arms Control, Defence, and Conflict Resolution* (Ottawa, 1991), pp. 23–30.

17. North Atlantic Treaty Organization (NATO), *A Comprehensive Concept of Arms Control and Disarmament,* Press Communiqué M-1 (89) 20 (Brussels: NATO Press Service, 1989); *A Declaration of the Heads of Government Participating in the Meeting of the North Atlantic Council in Brussels,* Press Communiqué (89) 21 (Brussels: NATO Press Service, 1989).

18. NATO, *A Declaration of the Heads of Government.*

19. These were based on Bush's earlier proposals. See Michael Mecham and Patricia Gilmartin, "Bush Includes Combat Aircraft Cuts in NATO Arms Proposals," *Aviation Week and Space Technology* 130, no. 23 (1989): 16–21.

20. R. W. Apple, "Bush Calls on Soviets to Join in Deep Troop Cuts for Europe as Germans See Path to Unity," *New York Times*, February 1, 1991.

21. R. Jeffrey Smith, "U.S. Allies Ease Terms on Arms Verification," *Washington Post*, March 14, 1990.

22. Andrew Slade, "Europe's Troubles Stall Vienna Talks," *Jane's Defence Weekly* 13, no. 13 (1990), p. 580.

23. Michael R. Gordon, "Baker Has New Arms Deal for Moscow, Officials Say," *New York Times*, May 18, 1990.

24. "Message from Turnberry," *NATO Review* 38, no. 3 (1990): 28–29.

25. Theresa Hitchens, "NATO Gives Negotiators Improved Flexibility," *Defense News*, June 11, 1990, pp. 3, 39.

26. Serge Schemann, "Shevardnadze Seeks Curbs on Forces in New Germany," *New York Times*, June 23, 1990.

27. "London Declaration on a Transformed North Atlantic Alliance," *NATO Review* 38, no. 4 (1990): 32.

28. Article 2 of the North Atlantic Treaty (1949) states that: "The Parties will contribute toward the further development of peaceful and friendly international relations by strengthening their free institutions, by bringing about a better understanding of the principles on which these institutions are founded, and by promoting conditions of stability and well-being. They will seek to eliminate conflict in their international economic policies and will encourage economic collaboration between any or all of them."

29. *Extract for Transcript of a Press Conference, July 18, 1990*, News Release 203 (Ottawa: British Information Services, 1990).

30. The discussion of how these outstanding issues were resolved is drawn from Jane M. O. Sharp, "Conventional Arms Control in Europe," *SIPRI Yearbook, 1991: World Armaments and Disarmament* (Oxford: Oxford University Press, 1991), pp. 412–421.

31. See Patricia M. Lewis, "The Conventional Forces in Europe Treaty," in J. B. Poole, ed., *Verification Report 1991: Yearbook on Arms Control and Environmental Agreements* (London: VERTIC, 1991), pp. 55–66.

32. For various assessments of the agreement (prospective and retrospective), see Jonathan Dean, "The CFE Negotiations, Present and Future," *Survival* 32, no. 4 (1990): 313–324; Coker, *A Farewell to Arms Control;* Lynn M. Hansen, "Towards an Agreement on Reducing Conventional Forces in Europe," *Disarmament* 13, no. 3 (1990): 61–76; Jonathan Dean, "Defining Long-term Western Objectives in CFE," *Washington Quarterly* 13, no. 1 (1990): 169–184; Jonathan Dean and Randall Watson Forsberg, "CFE and Beyond: The Future of Conventional Arms Control," *International Security* 17, no. 1 (1992): 76–121; James M. Garrett, "CFE II: A Quest for Stability," *Armed Forces and Society* 18, no. 1 (1991): 51–79; Jenonne Walker, "New Thinking about Conventional Arms Control," *Survival* 23, no. 1 (1991): 53–65; and Gilles Andreani, Michael Moodie, and Tadeusz Strulak, "The Conventional Armed Forces Europe Treaty," *Disarmament* 14, no. 2 (1991): 1–31.

33. For further discussions of the CFE ratification process and the problems that

subsequently surfaced see Jane M. O. Sharp, "Conventional Arms Control in Europe: Development and Prospects in 1991"; Zdzislaw Lachowski, "Implementation of the Vienna Document 1990 in 1991"; and Zdzislaw Lachowski, "The Second Vienna Seminar on Military Doctrine," in *SIPRI Yearbook, 1992: World Armaments and Disarmament* (Oxford: Oxford University Press, 1992), pp. 459–479, 480–495, 496–505.

34. See Jane M. O. Sharp, "The CFE Treaty and the Dissolution of the Union of Soviet Socialist Republics," in J. B. Poole and R. Guthrie, eds., *Verification Report 1992: Yearbook on Arms Control and Environmental Agreements* (London: VERTIC, 1992), pp. 25–37.

35. Paval K. Baev, "Farewell to Arms Control? A View from Russia," *Bulletin for Arms Control,* no. 7 (1992): 10.

36. Lee Feinstein, "Nations Sign CFE Follow-On," *Arms Control Today,* 22, no. 6 (1992): 29.

37. Jane M. O. Sharp, "New Roles for the CSCE," *Bulletin for Arms Control,* no. 7 (1992): 16–17.

Chapter 6: The 1947–1948 United Nations Conference on Trade and Employment

1. The most detailed account of the negotiations can be found in William Adams Brown, *The United States and the Restoration of World Trade* (Washington: Brookings Institution, 1950). See also Richard N. Gardner, *Sterling-Dollar Diplomacy: The Origins and the Prospects of Our International Economic Order* (New York: McGraw-Hill, 1969); Clair Wilcox, *A Charter for World Trade* (New York: Macmillan, 1948); and L. S. Pressnell, *External Economic Policy Since the War,* vol. 1: *The Post-War Financial Settlement* (London: Her Majesty's Stationery Office, 1986).

2. J. M. Letiche, *Reciprocal Trade Agreements in the World Economy* (Morningside Heights, N.Y.: King's Crown, 1948).

3. For an indication of what U.S. officials learned about commercial negotiations, see Harry Hawkins, *Commercial Treaties and Agreements: Principles and Practice* (New York: Rinehart, 1951).

4. J. M. Keynes, "National Self-sufficiency," *Yale Review* (June 1933), p. 758.

5. See Pressnell, *The Post-War Financial Settlement,* pp. 16–25.

6. See William Diebold Jr., *The End of the I.T.O.* (Princeton: Princeton University Press, 1952), p. 13. More generally, see Robert Hudec, *Developing Countries in the GATT Legal System* (London: Trade Policy Research Centre, 1988); and Jacob Viner, *International Trade and Economic Development* (Glencoe, Ill.: Free Press, 1952).

7. Deepak Lal, *The Poverty of "Development Economics"* (Cambridge: Harvard University Press, 1985).

8. Gerard Curzon, *Multilateral Commercial Diplomacy: The General Agreement on Tariffs and Trade and Its Impact on National Commercial Policies and Techniques* (London: Michael Joseph, 1965), p. 29.

9. In *A Life in Our Times: Memoirs* (Boston: Houghton Mifflin, 1981), John Kenneth Galbraith describes the arrival of Keynes at Harvard and his influence on New Deal thinking. He and others of similar persuasion had, of course, already struck out in similar directions and questioned the orthodoxies of classical economics.

10. Harry Hawkins's scornful dismissal of Keynesian thinking was typical. See his *Commercial Treaties and Agreements,* pp. 58–59.

11. See, for example, the introduction to Clair Wilcox's *A Charter for World Trade:* "But the world we live in is not, as yet, a world at peace. Its peoples are not one. They do not speak the same language. They do not attach the same meaning to the same words." p. xv.

12. Lionel Charles Robbins tells of both his criticism of Keynesian thinking and their wartime collaboration in his memoirs, *Autobiography of an Economist* (London: Macmillan, 1971). His earlier criticism of the trade policy implications of Keynes's thinking can be found in *Economic Planning and International Order* (London: Macmillan, 1937).

13. Kenneth Dam, *The GATT: Law and the International Economic Organization* (Chicago: University of Chicago Press, 1970), p. 13.

14. See Gardner, *Sterling-Dollar Diplomacy,* pp. 4–12.

15. Clair Wilcox's apologia for the Havana Charter, *A Charter for World Trade,* provides a contemporary explanation of the failure of policy as well as a clear picture of the determination of officials not to repeat the same mistakes.

16. See Notter, *Postwar Foreign Policy Preparation 1939–1945,* Publication 3580 (Washington, D.C.: U.S. Department of State, 1950). Pressnell, *The Post-War Financial Settlement,* pp. 67–74, documents the extent of British preparations.

17. R. Warren James, *Wartime Economic Cooperation: A Study of Relations between Canada and the United States* (Toronto: Ryerson, 1949), provides a detailed overview of some of this planning activity.

18. See E. F. Penrose, *Economic Planning for the Peace* (Princeton: Princeton University Press, 1953).

19. Norman Robertson, Canada's undersecretary of state for external affairs, in an April 1943 memorandum to the prime minister, wrote: "Their approach, on the basis of a multilateral Convention of Commerce providing for tariff reductions and the removal of other barriers to the exchange of goods, is the only really sound and comprehensive method of securing satisfactory conditions of trade." Document 586, *Documents on Canadian External Relations,* vol. 9: *1942–1943* (Ottawa: Department of External Affairs, 1980), p. 640.

20. The integrated approach to postwar planning being pursued by American officials is evident, for example, in the paper presented by Secretary Hull to the Moscow Conference on October 20, 1943. See Notter, *Postwar Foreign Policy Preparation,* p. 560.

21. Robbins, *Autobiography of an Economist,* pp. 186–212; and Gardner, *Sterling-Dollar Diplomacy,* p. 4.

22. The text is reproduced in J. G. Crawford, *Australian Trade Policy 1942–1966: A Documentary History* (Canberra: Australian National University, 1968), p. 9.

23. Pressnell, *The Post-War Financial Settlement,* pp. 373–380, reproduces various drafts of the fourth point.

24. April 21, 1944, quoted in Crawford, *Australian Trade Policy 1942–1966,* pp. 10–11. See Gardner, *Sterling-Dollar Diplomacy,* p. 62. Pressnell, *The Post-War Financial Settlement,* pp. 384–386, reproduces Churchill's handwritten comments on a telegram to Roosevelt, which clearly sets out his personal views along these lines. The telegram was never dispatched.

25. See Penrose, *Economic Planning for the Peace,* pp. 20–21. The Conservative Party had been divided on the benefits of imperial preferences. It had been the policy of Chamberlain in the United Kingdom, Bennett in Canada, and Bruce in Aus-

tralia. None of these leaders still held office. Canada's Mackenzie King, for example, saw their utility mainly as bargaining ammunition rather than as an end to be defended.

26. Pressnell, *The Post-War Financial Settlement*, pp. 46ff., suggests the extent to which Article VII was part of State Department orthodoxy, which was not necessarily shared by Roosevelt and others (pp. 50–51).

27. Pressnell, *The Post-War Financial Settlement*, pp. 28–65, describes the detailed discussions of the Consideration, including the conflicting views in the British cabinet.

28. See Documents 559–561, *Documents on Canadian External Relations, 1942–1943*, pp. 604–608. Some of the drama of the discussions is captured by Dean Acheson, *Present at the Creation: My Years in the State Department* (New York: W. W. Norton, 1969), pp. 27–34.

29. The final language is reproduced as appendix 8, in Notter, *Postwar Foreign Policy Preparation*, p. 463. Pressnell, *The Post-War Financial Settlement*, pp. 381–389, clearly illustrates Churchill's personal distaste for U.S. arm-twisting.

30. Penrose, *Economic Planning for the Peace*, pp. 32–34.

31. Ibid., pp. 32–40.

32. Ibid., pp. 34–37. Pressnell, *The Post-War Financial Settlement*, pp. 66–115, provides detail on the 1942–43 planning and informal discussions.

33. For a full discussion of these themes and how they were approached by the planners, see Lionel Robbins, *Autobiography of an Economist* (London: Macmillan, 1971), pp. 190–195. Robbins was a member of the Cabinet War Office planning staff and had worked with Keynes before the war as well as being part of the wartime planning discussions. See also Pressnell, *The Post-War Financial Settlement*, pp. 67–74.

34. Robbins, *Autobiography of an Economist*, p. 194.

35. Ibid., p. 200.

36. Penrose, *Economic Planning for the Peace*, p. 40. Penrose suggests further, however, that there was a wide range of ideas being discussed in London, Ottawa, and Washington, many of them based on ideas that had been discussed at various League of Nations meetings. He finds it difficult to pin the origin of any specific idea to any particular individual. In the United States, for example, Percy W. Bidwell of the Council on Foreign Relations was a passionate exponent of this approach in a series of articles and books written during the war, material with which both British and American planners were familiar, starting with "Controlling Trade after the War," *Foreign Affairs* 21, no. 2 (1943): 297–311. In this article Bidwell advocates establishment of an international trade "authority."

37. The debate is carefully tracked in Pressnell, *The Post-War Financial Settlement*, pp. 99–109. See also Penrose, *Economic Planning for the Peace*, pp. 87–96.

38. For the agenda and a report on that meeting, see documents 567 and 575 in *Documents on Canadian External Relations, 1942–1943*, pp. 617, 627–629.

39. Penrose, *Economic Planning for the Peace*, p. 95.

40. An outline of the Meade proposal had been circulated to the dominions in an April 22 telegram (document 585). A May 14 detailed report to the Canadian cabinet analyzing the proposal is reproduced as document 589. Document 605 provides a detailed report on the meeting by the Canadian delegation, and document 607 reproduces the revised proposal. See *Documents on Canadian External Relations,*

1942–1943. At that time, Canada's Norman Robertson told an American diplomat that if the U.S. side was bold and prepared to lower its high tariffs, preferences could be abolished, but if multilateralism failed, Canada would seek a bilateral deal with the United States and stay out of any protectionist British schemes. See also Robert Bothwell and John English, "Canadian Trade Policy in the Age of American Dominance and British Decline, 1943–1947," *Canadian Review of American Studies* 8, no. 1 (1977): 54–65.

41. Documents 601–603, *Documents on Canadian External Relations, 1942–1943*, pp. 678–679. Pressnell, *The Post-War Financial Settlement*, pp. 124–125, indicates that throughout the September–October 1943 U.S.-U.K. discussions in Washington, British officials briefed Commonwealth officials.

42. Penrose, *Economic Planning for the Peace*, p. 34.

43. Gardner, *Sterling-Dollar Diplomacy*, p. 103. Notter's semi-official account of the meeting can be found in Notter, *Postwar Foreign Policy Preparation*, pp. 190–194. Pressnell, *The Post-War Financial Settlement*, pp. 116–126.

44. See Penrose, *Economic Planning for the Peace*, pp. 63–86, for a detailed discussion of postwar planning regarding trade in raw materials.

45. Robert E. Hudec, *The GATT Legal System and World Trade Diplomacy*, 2d ed. (Salem, N.H.: Butterworth, 1990), p. 9.

46. Pressnell, *The Post-War Financial Settlement*, pp. 83–84.

47. Hudec, *The GATT Legal System and World Trade Diplomacy*, p. 5.

48. Robbins, *Autobiography of an Economist*, pp. 200–204; and Penrose, *Economic Planning for the Peace*, pp. 96–103.

49. An official American version of what had been accomplished during the discussions can be found in the paper presented by Secretary Hull at the Moscow Conference on October 20, 1943. It is reproduced as appendix 30 in Notter, *Postwar Foreign Policy Preparation*, pp. 560–564. An abridged U.K. version of the agreed minutes is reproduced as appendix 13 in Pressnell, *The Post-War Financial Settlement*, pp. 390–396.

50. Pressnell, *The Post-War Financial Settlement*, pp. 129–137, discusses the extent of British division and unease. Robbins reports that British officials were "forbidden to say anything to our American opposite numbers." See *Autobiography of an Economist*, p. 203.

51. See A. F. W. Plumptre, *Three Decades of Decision: Canada and the World Monetary System, 1944–75* (Toronto: McClelland and Stewart, 1977). Plumptre was a Canadian participant in these discussions. Many of the documents reproduced in *Documents on Canadian External Relations, 1942–1943* and *1944–1945* (vol. 11) (Ottawa: Department of External Affairs, 1990) also indicate the extent of Canadian involvement.

52. Notter, *Postwar Foreign Policy Preparation 1939–1945*, pp. 194–199.

53. A summary of the report is reproduced as appendix 45, ibid., pp. 622–624.

54. Ibid., pp. 193–194.

55. See Bothwell and English, "Canadian Trade Policy 1943–1947."

56. An agreed summary report on the meetings can be found annexed to Document 48 in *Documents on Canadian External Relations, 1944–1945*, pp. 70–78.

57. Bothwell and English, "Canadian Trade Policy 1943–1947," pp. 148–150. Document 49, in *Documents on Canadian External Relations, 1944–1945*, provides a

Canadian synopsis of the course of events up until then and Canadian interests and participation in the discussions.

58. Penrose, *Economic Planning for the Peace*, pp. 83–86.

59. Pressnell, *The Post-War Financial Settlement*, pp. 201–211, describes the U.K.-U.S.-Canada discussions, indicating the extent to which Canada played a mediating role that was carefully calibrated to achieve its own objectives—that the United States remain faithful to its multilateral impulses and not go down bilateral routes that would cut Canada out of the action.

60. See Notter, *Postwar Foreign Policy Preparation 1939–1945*, for some of the detail of this planning and its results.

61. Document 69 in *Documents on Canadian External Relations, 1944–1945*, pp. 114–118, reproduces notes by Bank of Canada Governor Graham Towers dated November 5, 1945, reporting on his conversations with Lord Keynes on the U.S.-U.K. financial and commercial policy discussions in the fall of 1945.

62. Robbins, *Autobiography of an Economist*, pp. 209–210.

63. Penrose, *Economic Planning for the Peace*, pp. 114–115.

64. The text is reproduced as appendix 47, in Notter, *Postwar Foreign Policy Preparation 1939–1945*, pp. 626–641. It can also be found in *Bulletin* 13, no. 337 (Washington, D.C.: U.S. Department of State, 1945), along with statements by Will Clayton, assistant secretary of state for economic affairs, and Secretary of State James Byrnes.

65. Canada also published its own version, together with the U.K.-U.S. financial agreement and related documents, with explanation and commentary immediately after they were received in order to promote their discussion. See *Conference Series*, no. 3 (Ottawa: Department of External Affairs, 1945). The Canadian Institute of International Affairs sought to stimulate debate by asking V. W. Bladen to give a generally favorable review of these provisions in its new publication, "The Proposals for the Expansion of World Trade and Employment," *International Affairs* 1, no. 2 (1946): 164–172.

66. Clair Wilcox, for example, suggested in 1948 that increasing economic woes in the United Kingdom strengthened the views of the various schools of British thought on its trading problems and made it very difficult for the United Kingdom to accede to U.S. demands. He was clearly aware of the difference between long-term interests and the political necessity of some short-run myopia. See *A Charter for World Trade*, pp. 28–30.

67. Documents 593–604, *Documents on Canadian External Relations, 1946* (vol. 12) (Ottawa: Department of External Affairs, 1977), pp. 1032–1066, spell out Canadian preparation for and participation in the London meeting and indicate the extent to which the U.S. proposals were now the only focus for discussion.

68. These principles are discussed in detail by one of the architects of the proposals, Clair Wilcox, in his *A Charter for World Trade*, pp. 15–21.

69. Ibid., pp. 23–24.

70. Ibid., p. 39.

71. Ibid., p. 40. The background to the U.S. proposal is set out in a series of January 1946 telegrams from Assistant Secretary of State Dean Acheson to U.S. Ambassador Winant in London. See *Foreign Relations of the United States, 1946*, vol. 1 (Washington, D.C.: GPO, 1972), pp. 1267–1273. The ECOSOC resolution is reproduced on pp. 1278–1280. The Soviet Union was among the original fifteen countries

433

invited by the United States. Intense diplomatic efforts, however, were unable to overcome the Soviet conviction that these talks addressed issues of concern only to capitalist countries. As a result, the preparatory committee was limited to seventeen members.

72. Some of the diplomatic correspondence is excerpted in *Foreign Relations of the United States, 1946,* vol. 1, pp. 1290ff.

73. *Suggested Charter for an International Trade Organization of the United Nations,* Publication 2598, Commercial Policy Series 93 (Washington, D.C.: U.S. Department of State, 1946). A box on the cover describes it as "an elaboration of the United States *Proposals for Expansion of World Trade and Employment* prepared by a technical staff within the Government of the United States and presented as a basis for public discussion." For British misgivings, see the memorandum handed by British officials to the American ambassador in London, July 6, 1946, *Foreign Relations of the United States, 1946,* vol. 1, pp. 1328–1330.

74. Wilcox, *A Charter for World Trade,* pp. 40–41.

75. John Jackson, *World Trade and the Law of the GATT* (Indianapolis: Bobbs-Merrill, 1969), p. 40.

76. Hudec, *The GATT Legal System and World Trade Diplomacy,* p. 17.

77. For a general discussion of these postwar monetary problems, see W. M. Scammel, *The International Economy since 1945,* 2d ed. (London: Macmillan, 1983), pp. 19–38.

78. At the 1946 London preparatory meeting, the American delegation insisted that the multilateral agreement "should deal with these subjects in precise detail so that the obligations of member governments would be clear and unambiguous. Most of these subjects readily lend themselves to such treatment. Provisions on such subjects, once agreed upon, would be self-executing and could be applied by the governments concerned without further elaboration or international action." U.N. Doc. E/PC/T/C.II/PV.2 (Geneva, 1946), p. 8, as quoted in Ernst-Ulrich Petersmann, "Strengthening the Domestic Legal Framework," in Petersmann and Meinhard Hilf, eds., *The New GATT Round of Multilateral Trade Negotiations: Legal and Economic Problems* (Boston: Kluwer, 1988), p. 56.

79. Wilcox, *A Charter for World Trade,* p. 33. Document 55, *Documents on Canadian External Relations, 1944–1945,* p. 92, reproduces a letter from Canada's High Commissioner to Australia T. C. Davis to Norman Robertson, seeking an explanation of Canada's policy on these matters so that he can be better placed to discuss the Australian preoccupation with full-employment policies. Robertson's detailed reply is reproduced as Document 56, pp. 92–94.

80. Document 602, *Documents on Canadian External Relations, 1946,* pp. 1056–1062, reporting on a meeting between the Canadian delegation to the London meeting and visiting cabinet minister Brooke Claxton, provides a candid assessment of the issues and the protagonists at the meeting and indicates the extent to which Canada shared U.S. perspectives.

81. Wilcox, *A Charter for World Trade,* pp. 42–43. The report on the preparatory meeting can be found in U.N. Doc. E/PC/T/33 (London: His Majesty's Stationery Office, 1946). A confidential U.S. report from Clair Wilcox to Secretary of State Marshall setting out what was accomplished at the London meeting can be found in *Foreign Relations of the United States, 1946,* vol. 1, pp. 1360–1366.

82. The U.S.-sponsored resolution can be found in the report of the London

meeting, U.N. Doc. E/PC/T/33, pp. 47–48, and the memorandum setting out the approach at pp. 48–52. U.S. planning for a two-track approach is clearly evident in background memorandum prepared in State's Division of Commercial Policy at the beginning of February 1946, which sets out how the United States would advance discussions on both the charter and a protocol excerpted from the charter and covering preliminary tariff negotiations. See *Foreign Relations of the United States, 1946,* vol. 1, pp. 1280–1290.

83. Wilcox, *A Charter for World Trade,* p. 43.

84. The report of the Lake Success meeting can be found in U.N. Doc. E/PC/T/34 of March 5, 1947. The draft GATT can be found on pp. 65–80.

85. Hudec, *The GATT Legal System and World Trade Diplomacy,* pp. 20–21.

86. Wilcox, *A Charter for World Trade,* p. 44. The draft charter as it stood at the end of the Geneva session is reproduced in the report of the committee adopted on August 22, 1947, as U.N. Doc. E/PC/T/186, 1947.

87. Wilcox, *A Charter for World Trade,* pp. 44–47.

88. The difficulty of this task and the complexity of the negotiations can be gleaned from the diplomatic correspondence excerpted in *Foreign Relations of the United States, 1947,* vol. 1, pp. 915ff.

89. See, e.g., Prime Minister King's December 9, 1947, report. Dominion of Canada, *Official Report of Debates, House of Commons,* 4th sess., 20th Parliament, 11–12 George V, 1948, vol. 1 (Ottawa: King's Printer, 1948).

90. John W. Evans, *The Kennedy Round in American Trade Policy* (Cambridge: Harvard University Press, 1971), pp. 9–11. John C. Campbell provides figures on the potential economic effect of the Geneva tariff cuts made by the United States and assesses the political astuteness of the U.S. negotiators. The United States made virtually no concessions on wheat and only reluctantly agreed to some on wool, without which Australia and some of the developing countries would have walked out. See *The United States in World Affairs 1947–1948* (New York: Harper and Brothers, for the Council on Foreign Relations, 1948), pp. 246–259.

91. The mercantilist nature of U.S. bargaining comes out clearly in a memo, prepared by a member of the U.S. team, reporting on a conversation between William Adams Brown of the Brookings Institution and James Hellmore, head of the British delegation, which outlines British frustration with American efforts to negotiate a code that would lead to a minimum of trade restrictions while making as few concessions of their own as possible. See *Foreign Relations of the United States, 1947,* vol. 1 (Washington, D.C.: GPO, 1973), pp. 937–941.

92. The text of the General Agreement as adopted in Geneva on October 30, 1947, can be found in 55 U.N. Treaty Series 188. A typescript of the text as brought home by the Canadian delegation is kept by the Historical Division of the Department of External Affairs in Ottawa.

93. The result was substantially less than the United States had hoped for and more than the United Kingdom and the dominions had been prepared to consider, given the unwillingness of the United States to accept either a ceiling or deeper cuts in its own tariffs. The extent of the difference between the two sides and the depth of U.S. frustration with imperial preferences are evident in an impassioned statement made by Clair Wilcox to representatives of the British Commonwealth on September 15, when progress on the tariff negotiations was stalled. See *Foreign Relations of the United States, 1947,* vol. 1, pp. 983–993.

94. John H. Jackson, *Restructuring the GATT System* (London: Pinter Books, 1990), pp. 10–12.

95. The American delegation's report on the conclusion of the Geneva negotiations, *Foreign Relations of the United States, 1947*, vol. 1, pp. 1021–1025, indicates that it was well satisfied with what had been achieved, particularly in concluding the General Agreement.

96. Even Canada, which had been the staunchest ally of the United States in preparing a draft charter that had the mettle to stand the test of time and provide a basis for more secure and more open trade, did not find it necessary to send the same delegation to Havana as it had sent to London and Geneva. Some of its most senior members were replaced by their assistants, to the initial chagrin and frustration of Dana Wilgress, the head of delegation. See Michael Hart, "Almost But Not Quite: The 1947–48 Bilateral Canada-U.S. Negotiations," *American Review of Canadian Studies* 19, no. 1 (1989): 25–58.

97. See W. M. Scammel, *The International Economy since 1945*, 2d ed. (London: Macmillan, 1983), for a general discussion of the deteriorating financial and economic situation in Western Europe.

98. The preparatory committee had been made up of eighteen members, but the Soviet Union never showed up; fifty-six countries participated in the Havana conference, six of whom had already participated in the Geneva tariff negotiations and had signed the General Agreement.

99. Wilcox, *A Charter for World Trade*, p. 47. Sir Eric Wyndham-White, the U.N. official who was secretary to the conference and the GATT's first secretary general, concluded: "There was a head-on collision between those who were wedded to the idea of a free, multilateral trading system on the one hand, and those who placed the whole emphasis on full-employment policies on a national basis." Quoted in Curzon, *Multilateral Commercial Diplomacy*, p. 31.

100. Wilcox, *A Charter for World Trade*, pp. 47–49.

101. "The Charter was the longest, most detailed, most complex, and probably the most comprehensive international economic agreement ever made." Campbell, *The United States in World Affairs 1947–1948*, pp. 272–273.

102. Diebold, *The End of the I.T.O.*, provides a detailed description of the debate in the United States and elsewhere on the merits of the charter. In short, American critics thought the charter too flexible, while British critics thought it was not flexible enough.

103. Hudec, *The GATT Legal System and World Trade Diplomacy*, p. 57.

104. See Jan Tumlir, *Protectionism: Trade Policy in Democratic Societies* (Washington, D.C.: American Enterprise Institute, 1985), pp. 26–27.

105. In the preparatory phase of the financial discussions, for example, Keynes had suggested the establishment of an organization—the Clearing Union—to promote international monetary stability. American negotiator Harry Dexter White had preferred a stabilization fund administered by central banks. The Canadian compromise plan also involved a fund administered by an international organization. Plumptre, in *Three Decades of Decision*, writes: "an overriding Canadian objective was to build a durable international *institution* which the Americans and British would find acceptable in terms of initial legislation and also workable in terms of continuing operation" (p. 39).

106. See Jackson, *World Trade and the Law of the GATT*, pp. 39–41; and Hudec, *The*

GATT Legal System and World Trade Diplomacy, pp. 59–61, for a discussion of some of the congressional hearings. Diebold, *The End of the I.T.O.,* also reports on the tenor of these hearings.

107. The difficulties imposed by these conflicting goals is clearly captured by a series of lead articles in the *Economist* over a period of eight weeks in January and February 1944. Scammel concludes that the failure of the charter to come into being "is part of the story of the change which took place in Anglo-American relations in the early postwar years. The trade proposals must not be seen in isolation but as part of the unfolding problem of British economic weakness and suspicion of the Americans on the one hand and the single-minded American thrust for multilateralism, embodying in this case an all-out attack on Imperial Preferences, on the other. . . . It is clearly, in retrospect, too much to expect that in 1948 wide agreement was possible upon the early application of a principle which one country believed had redounded to its detriment and which the other had pursued too ruthlessly." See *The International Economy since 1945,* p. 43.

108. Scammel notes that the single-minded pursuit of nondiscrimination by the United States "had expressed much that was admirable and constructive in the American vision, but the methods of its pursuit had been often ill-conceived, had at best been frequently ill-timed and over-pressed until to the rest of the world the aim itself was like a wine that had soured by the time it was ready for use." *The International Economy since 1945,* p. 45.

Chapter 7: The GATT Uruguay Round, 1986–1993: The Setting and the Players

1. The annual GATT survey of developments in international trade provides a continuously updated picture of the importance of trade in the global economy. The latest survey, GATT, *International Trade 1993–94* (Geneva, 1994), provides information up to the middle of 1994.

2. The GATT had 92 members by the end of 1986. There were 117 signatories by the end of 1993, not all of whom participated actively in the round. Throughout the round, at least 100 countries participated, with a core of some 45–50 participating actively.

3. It is still too early for any serious comprehensive analytical work to have emerged on the Uruguay Round. The most convenient source of information on the issues and progress on them is the annual volume prepared by the GATT Secretariat, *GATT Activities.* These can be supplemented by the continuing series of booklets prepared by Sidney Golt, such as *The GATT Negotiations 1986–1990* (Toronto: C. D. Howe Institute, 1988) for the British-American Committee; and Alan Oxley's *The Challenge of Free Trade* (London: Harvester Wheatsheaf, 1990). Oxley was Australia's ambassador to the GATT from 1985 to 1989 and chairman of the Contracting Parties in 1988. An excellent guide to the issues is the handbook developed for developing country participants by the World Bank, under the direction of J. Michael Finger and Andrzej Olechowski, *The Uruguay Round: A Handbook on the Multilateral Trade Negotiations* (Washington, D.C.: World Bank, 1987). See also Patrick Low, *Trading Free: The GATT and U.S. Trade Policy* (New York: Twentieth Century Fund Press, 1993). National interests and priorities can be gleaned from the burgeoning trade policy literature in the United States, the European Community, Canada, Australia, and elsewhere, much of which is noted in the list of references.

4. Following the original GATT negotiations in 1947, the GATT sponsored six more multilateral trade negotiations or rounds: at Annecy (1949), Torquay (1950–51), Geneva (1955–56), Geneva (the 1961–62 Dillon Round), Geneva (the 1964–67 Kennedy Round), and Geneva (the 1973–79 Tokyo Round). The Uruguay Round is thus counted as the eighth general multilateral trade negotiations. As a result of these rounds, virtually all industrial tariffs maintained by OECD countries have been "bound" against increase and reduced to relatively low rates. These conferences, particularly the Kennedy and Tokyo rounds, also provided opportunities to clarify, enlarge, and strengthen the rules. Unlike the media image of each negotiation leading to a new agreement, therefore, these rounds succeeded in ensuring that the GATT was a dynamic and constantly expanding code governing the trade policies of its member states and in ensuring steady progress toward freer trade. On the early rounds, see Gerard Curzon, *Multilateral Commercial Diplomacy: The General Agreement on Tariffs and Trade and Its Impact on National Commercial Policies and Techniques* (London: Michael Joseph, 1965). For the later rounds, see John W. Evans, *The Kennedy Round in American Trade Policy* (Cambridge: Harvard University Press, 1971); Ernest H. Preeg, *Traders and Diplomats: An Analysis of the Kennedy Round of Negotiations under the General Agreement on Tariffs and Trade* (Washington, D.C.: Brookings Institution, 1970); and Gilbert R. Winham, *International Trade and the Tokyo Round Negotiation* (Princeton: Princeton University Press, 1986).

5. Martin Wolf, "A European Perspective," in Robert M. Stern, Philip H. Trezise, and John Whalley, eds., *Perspectives on a U.S.-Canadian Free Trade Agreement* (Washington, D.C.: Brookings Institution, 1987).

6. See, for example, Miriam Camps and William Diebold Jr., *The New Multilateralism: Can the World Trading System Be Saved?* (New York: Council on Foreign Relations, 1983, 1986); and Rodney de C. Grey, "The General Agreement after the Tokyo Round," in John Quinn and Philip Slayton, eds., *Non-Tariff Barriers after the Tokyo Round* (Montreal: Institute for Research on Public Policy, 1982).

7. Robert Gilpin, *The Political Economy of International Relations* (Princeton: Princeton University Press, 1987), p. 3.

8. Gerard Curzon and Victoria Curzon, "The Multi-Tier GATT System," in Otto Hieronomi, ed., *The New Economic Nationalism* (London: Macmillan, 1980).

9. John H. Jackson, "Strengthening the International Framework of the GATT-MTN System: Reform Proposals for the new GATT Round," in Ernst-Ulrich Petersmann and Meinhard Hilf, eds., *The New GATT Round of Multilateral Trade Negotiations: Legal and Economic Problems* (Boston: Kluwer, 1988), p. 11.

10. See Patrick Low, *Trading Free*, pp. 9–33, for an up-to-date treatment of the GATT's strengths and weaknesses.

11. Gary Hufbauer and Jeffrey Schott, *Trading for Growth: The Next Round of Trade Negotiations* (Washington, D.C.: Institute for International Economics, 1985), provides a robust version of the conventional wisdom among multilateralists in the United States about what a new round should seek to accomplish. A more cautious appraisal is provided in Royal Commission on the Economic Union and Development Prospects for Canada (Macdonald Commission), *Final Report*, vol. 1 (Ottawa: Supply and Services Canada, 1985), pp. 279–296.

12. Given the extent and longevity of these problems, there is no shortage of literature analyzing both the problems and potential solutions. The most extensive work has been done by the OECD. Its annual volume, *Agricultural Policies, Markets,*

388   Notes to Pages 176–179

and Trade, provides a continuously updated series, which is supplemented by individual country studies, like *National Policies and Agricultural Trade: Country Study— Canada.*

13. There is a growing literature on the changing nature of the global economy. A good introduction is provided by Robert Reich, *The Work of Nations* (New York: Knopf, 1991); Michael Porter, *The Competitive Advantage of Nations* (New York: Free Press, 1990); and Kenichi Ohmae, *The Borderless World: Power and Strategy in the Interlinked World Economy* (New York: Harper Business, 1990). Each provides insight on the sometimes conflicting changes taking place. Daniel Drache and Meric S. Gertler, eds., *The New Era of Global Competition: State Policy and Market Power* (Montreal and Kingston: McGill–Queen's University Press, 1991), is an attempt to provide an analysis of some of the policy implications from a left-wing perspective. Sylvia Ostry in *Governments and Corporations in a Shrinking World* does so from a more conventional trade policy perspective (New York: Council on Foreign Relations, 1990).

14. Some of this analysis was pursued in the context of the Canada-U.S. bilateral negotiations. See, for example, Michael Hart, "The Mercantilists's Lament: National Treatment and Modern Trade Negotiations," *Journal of World Trade* 21, no. 6 (1987): 37–61. Rodney de C. Grey, *Concepts of Trade Diplomacy and Trade in Services* (London: Harvester Wheatsheaf, for the Trade Policy Research Centre, 1990), which builds on a number of earlier articles, provides a detailed critique of the pitfalls that might be encountered in efforts to negotiate general rules about services.

15. The GATT's rules of nondiscrimination involve most-favored-nation and national treatment, i.e., nondiscrimination in the application of a country's import policy among member states and nondiscrimination between domestic and imported goods once the GATT-sanctioned import regime has been satisfied.

16. The GATT's bargaining strategy, however, made more political than economic sense, particularly for the developing countries. The habit of gaining many concessions and giving few meant that smaller countries took on fewer binding self-denial ordinances and thus maintained much higher levels of protection. In the case of developing countries, it meant that many never had to undergo the policy discipline of internalizing a set of external obligations.

17. In a series of articles starting soon after the conclusion of the Tokyo Round, Canadian negotiator Rodney Grey warned of the problems created for the trading system by the rise in contingency protection measures. See his *United States Trade Policy Legislation: A Canadian View* (Montreal: Institute for Research on Public Policy, 1982). Others subsequently took up this theme, and in a number of articles and studies analysts like Michael Finger, at the World Bank, and Brian Hindley, at the Trade Policy Research Centre, indicated the extent of the problem. Finger went so far as to suggest that by putting rule-writing ahead of liberalization, the Uruguay Round had created a recipe that was bound to fail. See "That Old GATT Magic No More Casts Its Spell (How the Uruguay Round Failed)," *Journal of World Trade* 25, no. 2, (1991): 19–22.

18. The complexity of the issues involved is well illustrated by the U.S.-Japan Structural Impediments Initiative (SII). Conflicting views of how to approach domestic and international economic issues were explored at a level of detail that at times bordered on the bizarre. Both sides complained about the different values and priorities of the other side, with the United States strongly suggesting that if Japan were prepared to become more American, many of the trade frictions would disap-

pear. Such discussions are difficult enough bilaterally; they are even more difficult multilaterally and suggest the need for careful preparation regarding both substance and technique. See Amelia Porges, "U.S.-Japan Trade Negotiations: Paradigms Lost," in Paul Krugman, ed., *Trade with Japan: Has the Door Opened Wider?* (Chicago: University of Chicago Press, 1991); and Michael Mastanduno, "Framing the Japan Problem: The Bush Administration and the Structural Impediments Initiative," *International Journal* 47 (spring 1992): 235–264. Jagdish Bhagwati in *The World Trading System at Risk* (Princeton: Princeton University Press, 1991) also explores some of the complexities of negotiating rules about the new issues.

19. Preliminary discussion of some of the issues involved can be found in Michael Hart, "After NAFTA: Trade Policy and Research Challenges for the 1990s," in William G. Watson, ed., *North American Free Trade Area* (Kingston, Ont.: John Deutsch Institute for the Study of Economic Policy, 1992); and Michael Hart, "The End of Trade Policy?" in Christopher Maule and Fen Hampson, eds., *Global Jeopardy: Canada among Nations 1993–1994* (Ottawa: Carleton University Press, 1993).

20. Michael Aho and Jonathan Aronson characterize the difficulties that would need to be surmounted in concluding a successful new round as follows: "Growing interdependence, the decline in the ability and will of the United States to dictate terms, the proliferation of industrial policies and the emergence of excess capacity in many sectors at a time when world economic growth is slowing puts profound pressure on negotiators. In addition, negotiations will be difficult because traditional sectoral distinctions are breaking down, global corporate competition is changing, new types of trade barriers have replaced tariffs as the focus of attention, services need to be addressed, and product life cycles are shortening as the pace of change accelerates. These challenges make it more difficult to build domestic coalitions favoring trade liberalization, particularly because employment and adjustment problems are critical everywhere and are related to broad domestic reforms which ultimately will determine whether trade can be liberalized." *Trade Talks: America Better Listen!* (New York: Council on Foreign Relations, 1985), p. 158.

21. The macroeconomic sources of U.S. protectionism are examined by Richard G. Lipsey and Murray G. Smith, *Global Imbalances and U.S. Responses: A Canadian Perspective* (Toronto: C. D. Howe Institute, 1987); Alan S. Blinder, *Hard Heads Soft Hearts: Tough-Minded Economics for a Just Society* (Reading, Mass.: Addison-Wesley, 1987); Benjamin M. Friedman, *Day of Reckoning: The Consequences of American Economic Policy under Reagan and After* (New York: Random House, 1988); and Paul Krugman, *The Age of Diminished Expectations* (Cambridge: MIT Press, 1992).

22. The various strains in American trade policy, including the new fascination with bilateralism, are examined in William A. Dymond, *Lord Ronald and United States Trade Policy,* Occasional Paper 91-4 (Ottawa: Centre for Trade Policy and Law, 1991). See also Aho and Aronson, *Trade Talks,* pp. 87–102; and Low, *Trading Free,* pp. 53–140.

23. Both Hufbauer and Schott, *Trading for Growth,* and Aho and Aronson, *Trade Talks,* provide clear statements of multilateral orthodoxy.

24. Hufbauer and Schott, *Trading for Growth,* translates the U.S. litany of complaints into the comprehensive vision of a "Growth Round." Its emphasis on both free and fair trade, however, stamps it as vintage U.S. trade policy aimed at having one's cake and eating it too.

25. For insight on U.S. trade policy in the 1980s, see, for example, I. M. Destler,

American Trade Politics: System under Stress (Washington, D.C.: Institute for International Economics, 1986): Robert E. Baldwin, *The Political Economy of U.S. Import Policy* (Cambridge: MIT Press, 1985); Bhagwati, *The World Trading System at Risk*; Robert Z. Lawrence et. al., *An American Trade Strategy: Options for the 1990s* (Washington, D.C.: Brooking Institution, 1990); and Robert Kuttner, *The End of Laissez-Faire: National Purpose and the Global Economy after the Cold War* (Philadelphia: University of Pennsylvania Press, 1991). For the impact on the round of declining U.S. leadership, see Oxley, *The Challenge of Free Trade*, pp. 18–22; Sidney Golt, *The GATT Negotiations, 1986–90*, pp. 54–61; and Aho and Aronson, *Trade Talks*, pp. 25–27.

26. For a discussion of developments in Europe in the 1980s, see Dennis Shaw, *The Economics of the Common Market*, 7th ed. (London: Penguin, 1992). Gary C. Hufbauer, ed., *Europe 1992: An American Perspective* (Washington, D.C.: Brookings Institution, 1990), provides a detailed sectoral analysis, while Robert O. Keohane and Stanley Hoffman, eds., *The New European Community: Decision-making and Institutional Change* (Boulder, Colo.: Westview, 1991), focuses on the political dimension.

27. For a balanced assessment of the implications of the drive toward a more integrated European market, see Michael Callingaert, *The 1992 Challenge from Europe: Development of the European Community's Internal Market* (Washington, D.C.: National Planning Association, 1988); Shaw, *The Economics of the Common Market;* and Hufbauer, *Europe 1992*.

28. See Oxley, *The Challenge of Free Trade*, pp. 74–87, and Aho and Aronson, *Trade Talks*, pp. 77–82, for a discussion of EC interests in the round and the nature of its participation. A more academic approach can be found in Meinhard Hilf, F. G. Jacobs, and Ernst-Ulrich Petersmann, eds., *The European Community and GATT* (Boston: Kluwer, 1986).

29. Michael M. Hart, *Canadian Economic Development and the International Trading System* (Toronto: University of Toronto Press, 1985), p. 48. The enigma of Japan has fascinated Western scholars for many years. One of the most arresting pictures of the Japanese economic challenge is provided by Karel van Wolferen, first in "The Japanese Problem," *Foreign Affairs* 65, no. 2 (1987): 288–303, and subsequently expanded into a full-length book, *The Enigma of Japanese Power: People and Politics in a Stateless Nation* (New York: Knopf, 1989). More recent specimens of the more traditional Japan-bashing literature are Lester Thurow, *Head to Head: The Coming Battle among Japan, Europe, and America* (New York: Morrow, 1992); and Clyde Prestowitz, *Trading Places: How We Are Giving Our Future to Japan and How to Reclaim It* (New York: Basic Books, 1989). A more balanced view emerges in Edward J. Lincoln, *Japan's Unequal Trade* (Washington, D.C.: Brookings Institution, 1990).

30. See Oxley, *The Challenge of Free Trade*, pp. 94–95; and Aho and Aronson, *Trade Talks*, pp. 82–89.

31. For consideration of the intellectual deficiency of development economics and the role of developing countries in the GATT, see Deepak Lal, *The Poverty of "Development Economics"* (Cambridge: Harvard University Press, 1985); Robert Hudec, *Developing Countries in the GATT Legal System* (London: Trade Policy Research Centre, 1988); Martin Wolf, "Differential and More Favorable Treatment of Developing Countries and the International Trading System," *World Bank Economic Review* 1, no. 4 (1987): 647–666; and John Whalley, *The Uruguay Round and Beyond: The Final Report from the Ford Foundation Project on Developing Countries and the Global Trading System* (London: Macmillan, 1989). Gerald M. Meier and Dudley Seers, eds., *Pioneers*

in Development (New York: Oxford University Press for the World Bank, 1984) contains papers by many of the theorists who first developed the contours of development economics.

32. See Low, *Trading Free,* for a description of GATT activities in the 1980s.

33. A good indication of the changing ideological fashion is provided by the World Bank, *The Challenge of Development: World Development Report, 1991* (Washington, D.C.: World Bank, 1991).

34. Oxley observes that "the Uruguay Round is the first multilateral trade negotiation in which developing countries have participated wholeheartedly. They helped shape its agenda, they bargained over the political compact which underpins it and they have helped to keep it on course." *The Challenge of Free Trade,* p. 101. See also Aho and Aronson, *Trade Talks,* pp. 95–114.

35. See Michael Hart, *A North American Free Trade Agreement: The Strategic Implications for Canada* (Ottawa: Centre for Trade Policy and Law, 1990).

36. Oxley, *The Challenge of Free Trade,* pp. 111–123, provides a detailed description of the origins and interests of the Cairns Group.

37. The kind of analytical work that would have prepared the secretariat for this kind of advice was in fact being done in Paris at the OECD. See Geza Feketekuty, *The New Trade Agenda,* (Washington, D.C.: Group of Thirty, 1993).

38. See William R. Cline, ed., *Trade Policy in the 1980s* (Cambridge: MIT Press, 1984). For a 1986 update on the thinking of *Trade Policy in the 1980s* contributors, see R. H. Snape, ed., *Issues in World Trade Policy: GATT at the Crossroads* (New York: St. Martin's, 1986), indicating the international character of much of this thinking.

39. Martin Wolf, "Fiddling while the GATT Burns," *World Economy* 9, no. 1 (1986): 1–2.

40. See, for example, Camps and Diebold, *The New Multilateralism;* and Hufbauer and Schott, *Trading for Growth.*

41. Finance officials, for example, brought their own values and priorities to the financial services discussions, while patent and trademark officials similarly thought trade officials had little to teach them about negotiating intellectual property rules.

42. For example, the first systematic treatment of the GATT in the United States was entirely the work of legal scholars such as John Jackson, Robert Hudec, and Kenneth Dam, all of whom analyzed GATT as a legal regime. By way of contrast, contemporary systematic treatments by European scholars such as Gerard Curzon and Karin Kock looked upon the GATT largely as a diplomatic regime. Legal periodicals remain one of the best sources of information on GATT issues in the United States.

43. The broader interests, priorities, and values of the international legal community are admirably represented in Petersmann and Hilf, *The New GATT Round of Multilateral Trade Negotiations.* Similarly, there are now textbooks on the GATT available from Canadian and European legal scholars such as Robert Paterson, J.G. Castel, Edmond Montgomery, and Edwin Vermulst.

44. See, for example, John H. Jackson, *Restructuring the GATT System* (London: Frances-Pinter, 1990).

45. A number of the chapters in Petersmann and Hilf, *The New GATT Round of Multilateral Trade Negotiations,* focus on this potential.

46. Interestingly, much of that effort was balanced by economists whose analysis focused on the extent to which these remedies made little economic sense. See, for

example, the contrast between John H. Jackson and Edwin Vermulst, eds., *Anti-dumping Law and Practice* (Ann Arbor: University of Michigan Press, 1989), and Richard Boltuck and Robert E. Litan, eds., *Down in the Dumps: Administration of the Unfair Trade Laws* (Washington, D.C.: Brookings Institution, 1991). The former was written under the direction of legal scholars, the latter at the behest of economists.

47. The 1990 draft text at Brussels was more than 400 pages, the 1991 Dunkel text approached 500 pages, and the final product is equally long. Some of this length, of course, is the result of laborious drafting that papers over differences with studied ambiguity; other reasons include the need to anticipate the devilish capacity of governments to work their way around new obligations, as well as the increasing preoccupation with transparency and due process.

48. See, for example, Elhanan Helpman and Paul R. Krugman, *Trade Policy and Market Structure* (Cambridge: MIT Press, 1991).

49. See Paul Krugman, ed., *Strategic Trade Policy and the New International Economics* (Cambridge: MIT Press, 1987), for a discussion of this literature. In "Does the New Trade Theory Require a New Trade Policy?" *World Economy* 15, no. 4 (1992): 423–441, Krugman considers the trade policy implications of the new theories of international trade. While interesting, it offers little in the way of pertinent advice. To be fair, the work of academic political scientists, concentrated on regimes and hegemonies, realism and functionalism, also seems stylized and irrelevant. See, for example, Stephen D. Krasner, ed., *International Regimes* (Ithaca: Cornell University Press, 1983), which provides a good introduction to this kind of literature.

50. Studies and polemic literature on the issues in the round come from such diverse think tanks as the Council on Foreign Relations and the Institute for International Economics in the United States, the Trade Policy Research Centre and the Royal Institute for International Affairs in the United Kingdom, the Kiel Institute in Germany, the Graduate School at the University of Geneva, the Centre for Trade Policy and Law and the Institute for Research on Public Policy in Canada, the Centre for International Economics in Australia, the Institute for South East Asian Studies in Singapore, and the Getulio Vargas Foundation in Rio de Janeiro.

51. Various studies by Jagdish Bhagwati, for example, are helpful in explaining the benefits of a fixed-rule multilateral trade system to special interest groups on both sides of the Atlantic. See his *Protectionism* (Cambridge: MIT Press, 1988), and *The World Trading System at Risk.*

52. Typical is Hufbauer and Schott, *Trading for Growth,* which goes so far as to suggest that the Tokyo Round codes be amended to cover services. To be fair, there were some think-tank scholars with broad policy backgrounds who appreciated that more fundamental thinking was required. See, for example, Grey, *Concepts of Trade Diplomacy,* which built on earlier essays along these lines. More typical are Bhagwati, *The World Trading System at Risk,* and Aho and Aronson, *Trade Talks,* both of which recognize the difficulties that would need to be surmounted but do not appear to appreciate the magnitude of the change from a regime based on negative prescriptions to one based on normative rules.

53. See, for example, Robert Z. Lawrence and Robert E. Litan, "The World Trading System after the Uruguay Round," *Boston University International Law Journal* 8, no. 2 (1990): 247–276.

54. See, for example, Finger and Olechowski, *The Uruguay Round.*

55. In the United States, for example, the administration is mandated by Con-

gress to seek the views of the Advisory Committee on Trade Negotiations (ACTN) as well as Industry Sector Advisory Committees (ISACs) (Trade Act of 1974, section 135). See Destler, *American Trade Politics,* pp. 94–95. In Canada, the federal government in 1986 established an International Trade Advisory Committee (ITAC) as well as some fifteen Sectoral Advisory Groups on International Trade (SAGITs) as formal vehicles for consulting the private sector.

56. Agricultural economists have been particularly active, cranking out a wide variety of literature; among the most interesting and persuasive are Institute for International Economics, *Reforming World Agricultural Trade: A Policy Statement by Twenty-nine Professionals from Seventeen Countries* (Washington, D.C., 1988); and D. Gale Johnson, Kenzo Hemmi, and Pierre Lardinois, *Agricultural Policy and Trade: Adjusting Domestic Programs in an International Framework—A Report to the Trilateral Commission* (New York: New York University Press, 1985). See, also, studies by individual agricultural economists, such as J. C. Gilson, *World Agricultural Changes: Implications for Canada* (Toronto: C. D. Howe Institute, 1989); and William M. Miner and Dale E. Hatheway, eds., *World Agricultural Trade: Building a Consensus* (Halifax: Institute for Research on Public Policy, 1988). On trade in services, see Raymond J. Krommenaker, *World Traded Services: The Challenge for the Eighties* (London: Dedham, 1984); Grey, *Concepts of Trade Diplomacy,* and *The Services Agenda* (Halifax: Institute for Research on Public Policy, 1990).

57. Sylvia Saborio, *The Premise and the Promise: Free Trade in the Americas* (Washington, D.C.: Overseas Development Council, 1992), provides an overview of Latin American interest in a WHFTA.

58. Jeffrey J. Schott, ed., *Free Trade Areas and U.S. Trade Policy* (Washington, D.C.: Institute for International Economics, 1989), provides a comprehensive overview of the growing fascination with regionalism. Andrew Stoeckel, David Pearce, and Gary Banks, *Western Trade Blocs: Game, Set, or Match for Asia-Pacific and the World Economy?* (Canberra: Centre for International Economics, 1990), provides an anxious Australian perspective.

59. Hufbauer and Schott's suggestion, in *Trading for Growth,* for a "Growth Round" never captured politicians' imaginations. While it may have appealed to some globally oriented firms, too many interest groups in the 1980s saw retrenchment, rather than growth, as the defining characteristic of the period. Such firms proved more adept at spooking politicians than global firms in translating their advocacy of an ambitious round into politically acceptable concessions. Sir Leon Brittan's effort to rekindle the growth flame in a speech to the European Chambers of Commerce in Washington, D.C., February 12, 1993, similarly had little impact.

Chapter 8: The GATT Uruguay Round, 1986–1993: The Negotiations

1. Contemporary Canadian appreciations of the various elements of the GATT's work program can be found in Department of External Affairs, *A Review of Canadian Trade Policy* (Ottawa: Supply and Services, 1983), pp. 180–187; and W. Frank Stone, *Canada, the GATT, and the International Trade System,* (Halifax: Institute for Research on Public Policy, 1984), pp. 202–213.

2. Michael M. Hart, *Canadian Economic Development and the International Trading System* (Toronto: University of Toronto Press, 1985), pp. 109–138.

3. On the nature of the "new protectionism" generally, see Brian Hindley and Eric Nicolaides, *Taking the New Protectionism Seriously,* Thames Essay 34 (London:

Trade Policy Research Centre, 1983); and Jan Tumlir, *Protectionism: Trade Policy in Democratic Societies* (Washington, D.C.: American Enterprise Institute, 1985).

4. General Agreement on Tariffs and Trade (GATT), *Basic Instruments and Selected Documents (BISD)*, 28th supplement (Geneva, 1982), p. 15.

5. The Ministerial Declaration is reproduced in GATT, *BISD*, 29th supplement (Geneva, 1983), pp. 9–23, and described in GATT, *Activities 1982: An Annual Review of the Work of the GATT* (Geneva, 1983), pp. 7–26. See also Michael Aho and Jonathon Aronson, *Trade Talks: America Better Listen!* (New York: Council on Foreign Relations, 1985), pp. 20–21; and Sidney Golt, *The GATT Negotiations, 1986–1990* (Toronto: C. D. Howe Institute, 1988), pp. 9–13.

6. At any one time, Congress has before it dozens of trade bills proposed by individual members of Congress and senators. These had turned into a flood during the 1981–82 recession and were now gaining the attention of the congressional leadership. See Stephen L. Lande and Craig vanGrasstek, *The Trade and Tariff Act of 1984: Trade Policy in the Reagan Administration* (Lexington, Mass.: D. C. Heath, 1986).

7. See Lande and vanGrasstek, *The Trade and Tariff Act of 1984*.

8. Sylvia Ostry, *Governments and Corporations in a Shrinking World* (New York: Council on Foreign Relations, 1990), p. 13.

9. Robert E. Hudec, *Developing Countries in the GATT Legal System* (London: Trade Policy Research Centre, 1988).

10. Fritz Leutwiler et al., *Trade Policies for a Better Future: Proposals for Action* (Geneva: GATT, 1985).

11. Gilbert R. Winham, *International Trade and the Tokyo Round Negotiations* (Princeton: Princeton University Press, 1986), p. 75.

12. Aho and Aronson, *Trade Talks*, p. 13; and Golt, *The GATT Negotiations 1986–1990*, p. 12.

13. The period 1980–86 at the GATT is well covered in Patrick Low, *Trading Free: The GATT and U.S. Trade Policy* (New York: Twentieth Century Fund Press, 1993), pp. 189–207.

14. Alan Oxley, *The Challenge of Free Trade* (London: Harvester Wheatsheaf, 1990), pp. 100–110, discusses participation of developing countries in the GATT during the negotiations that led to Punta del Este.

15. See Oxley, *The Challenge of Free Trade*, pp. 84–87, on evolving EC attitudes toward the round.

16. UNCTAD's penchant for long speeches, dreary meetings, and highly negotiated political statements full of rhetoric and weasel words had been alien to the GATT before the 1980s. The decline in UNCTAD's attractiveness as a forum for political negotiations had led to a new fascination with the GATT and the introduction to GATT meetings of UNCTAD's preoccupation with procedure, texts, and agenda. While delegates from OECD countries generally operate on the basis of very specific instructions from their capitals, it is not uncommon for delegations from developing countries to operate on the basis of very broad, general mandates. The result is a Geneva or New York mentality that is more fascinated by gamesmanship than by genuine policy discussion, a mentality that began to show up at GATT meetings in the 1980s.

17. Aho and Aronson, *Trade Talks*, pp. 22–23.

18. GATT, *BISD*, 32d supplement (Geneva, 1986), pp. 9, 10.

19. Golt, *The GATT Negotiations, 1986–1990*, pp. 14–16.

20. Oxley, *The Challenge of Free Trade*, pp. 133–134.

21. GATT, *BISD*, 32d supplement, pp. 14–15.

22. Low, *Trading Free*, pp. 209–212, describes the details of the preparatory discussions.

23. GATT, *Activities 1986*, p. 7.

24. Gilbert R. Winham, "The Prenegotiation Phase of the Uruguay Round," *International Journal* 44, no. 2 (1989): 280–303.

25. See Low, *Trading Free*, pp. 206–207, 209–212.

26. See Oxley, *The Challenge of Free Trade*, p. 137.

27. Ibid., pp. 137–138.

28. Ibid., pp. 138–140.

29. Ibid., p. 140.

30. GATT, *Activities 1986*, p. 9. Low, *Trading Free*, pp. 212–215, discusses the Punta del Esta meeting.

31. Winham, "The Prenegotiation Phase of the Uruguay Round."

32. See John W. Evans, *The Kennedy Round in American Trade Policy* (Cambridge: Harvard University Press, 1971); and Gilbert R. Winham, *International Trade and the Tokyo Round Negotiation* (Princeton: Princeton University Press, 1986).

33. GATT, *BISD*, 33d supplement, pp. 22–23.

34. The Punta del Este Declaration is reproduced in ibid., pp. 19–28.

35. Ibid., pp. 19, 27, 28.

36. The decision of January 28, 1987, can be found in ibid., pp. 31–52.

37. Complaints were launched against Japan (regarding various agricultural products), the Nordics (apples and pears), the European Community (apples), Canada (ice cream and yoghurt), Korea (beef), and Thailand (cigarettes).

38. Ingrid Nordgren, "The GATT Panels during the Uruguay Round: A Joker in the Negotiating Game," *Journal of World Trade* 25, no. 4 (1991): 57–72, examines the use of dispute settlement to gain negotiating leverage.

Not to be outdone, the European Community demonstrated that it had also learned the utility of the GATT complaints procedure and launched claims against the United States on its Superfund tax, its customs user fee, and its section 337 procedures (unfair methods of competition, usually involving patent issues). Japan found itself at the receiving end of complaints about the distribution of alcoholic beverages and its agreement with the United States on trade in semi-conductors. It then turned around and complained about the EC's use of dumping duties to get at so-called screwdriver assembly plants. Other countries followed suit, so that the period 1986–90 proved one of the busiest in the GATT's history.

For its first thirty years, with the exception of a series of cases at the beginning that laid the foundation for the procedures, the GATT's dispute settlement procedures had been used sparingly. Starting in the late 1970s, however, the United States rediscovered them, followed soon thereafter by the European Community. The resultant flurry of activity erased the Europeans' traditional difference in attitude toward the GATT. The European Community now amended its view that the GATT was primarily a diplomatic instrument and accepted that it had utility as a legal instrument.

39. GATT, *International Trade 89–90*, vol. 1, pp. 5–6.

40. GATT, *Activities 1988*, p. 19. Oxley's point spoke more directly to the smaller than the larger countries and was more a professional than a political sentiment.

41. GATT, *Activities 1988*, p. 22.

42. Oxley, *The Challenge of Free Trade*, pp. 158–159.

43. GATT, *Activities 1988*, pp. 22–23.

44. Oxley, *The Challenge of Free Trade*, pp. 161–164.

45. At both the Venice (1987) and Toronto (1988) summits, the leaders under-lined the importance of making progress on agriculture and at Venice went so far as to commit their delegations to tabling detailed proposals before the end of the year. Oxley, *The Challenge of Free Trade*, pp. 161–162.

46. GATT, *Activities 1988*, pp. 23. Low, *Trading Free*, discusses the midterm review on pp. 215–218.

47. Oxley, *The Challenge of Free Trade*, pp. 166–169.

48. Ibid., p. 169.

49. GATT, *Activities 1988*, pp. 24–25. The texts adopted are reproduced on pp. 138–167.

50. Yeutter was named secretary of agriculture in the new administration and was replaced at USTR by Carla Hills, a lawyer with extensive experience as an an-titrust litigator.

51. The TPRM decision is reproduced in GATT, *BISD*, 36th supplement, pp. 403–409, the streamlined dispute settlement procedures, ibid., pp. 61–67. For a crit-ical examination of the TPRM, see Gary Banks, "Transparency, Surveillance, and the GATT System," in Hart and Steger, *In Whose Interest?* pp. 55–85. William J. Davey, "GATT Dispute Settlement: The 1988 Montreal Reforms," in Richard Dearden, Michael Hart, and Debra Steger, eds., *Living with Free Trade: Canada, The Free Trade Agreement, and the GATT* (Ottawa: Centre for Trade Policy and Law, 1989), pp. 167–185, provides a critical overview of the dispute settlement reforms.

52. Detailed descriptions of the issues in the negotiations and progress on them can be found in GATT, *Activities 1989*, pp. 37–75; and GATT, *Activities 1990*, pp. 27–54. For an analysis of many of the critical issues, see Jeffrey J. Schott, ed., *Completing the Uruguay Round: A Results-Oriented Approach to the GATT Trade Negotiations* (Washington, D.C.: Institute for International Economics, 1990).

53. GATT, *Activities 1989*, pp. 39–41; and GATT, *Activities 1990*, pp. 29–30.

54. A number of international agreements and organizations address intellectual property issues, including the World Intellectual Property Organization (WIPO) in Paris. None, however, include the dispute settlement provisions and contractual commitments characteristic of the GATT.

55. GATT, *Activities 1989*, pp. 62–66; and GATT, *Activities 1990*, pp. 44–46.

56. The detail of the agricultural negotiations can be traced in GATT, *Activities 1989*, pp. 49–52; and GATT, *Activities 1990*, pp. 33–36. Given the central place of these negotiations in the round as a whole, there is a wide variety of commentary available on the issues, some of which is listed in references. See also Dale E. Hathe-way, "Agriculture," in Schott, *Completing the Uruguay Round*, pp. 51–62.

57. GATT, *Activities 1989*, pp. 68–70; and GATT, *Activities 1990*, pp. 48–49.

58. GATT, *Activities 1989*, pp. 34–35; and GATT, *Activities 1990*, pp. 20–21.

59. GATT, *Activities 1990*, p. 21.

60. Ibid., p. 22. For an explanation of the fast-track procedures, see I. M. Destler, *American Trade Politics: System under Stress* (Washington, D.C.: Institute for Interna-tional Economics, 1986).

61. Low, *Trading Free*, pp. 219–222, discusses the Brussels meeting.

62. GATT, *Activities 1990,* pp. 22–23.

63. Ibid., pp. 16–27.

64. Since the draft text of the Final Act was still incomplete and the all-important negotiations on market access were far from complete, it may be somewhat disingenuous to speak of a "package." Nevertheless, the negotiators under Dunkel's direction had made the judgment that the contours of the agreements being developed in each of the groups, plus the market access elements that they anticipated, did constitute a useful package. See Schott, *Completing the Uruguay Round,* for an assessment on that "package."

65. GATT, *Activities 1991,* p. 19.

66. Ibid., p. 20.

67. Progress reports on the work pursued in each of the seven groups are outlined in ibid., pp. 22–47.

68. GATT, "Draft Final Act Embodying the Results of the Uruguay Round of Multilateral Trade Negotiations," MTN.TNC/W/FA, December 20, 1991 (The "Dunkel Text"). The text is described in some detail in GATT press release NUR 055 of December 3, 1992.

69. Statement by Arthur Dunkel to the TNC, as quoted in GATT, *Activities 1991,* p. 5.

70. "GATT's Trade Talks—Final Sprint or Stumble?" *Economist,* January 18, 1992; and GATT, *Activities 1992,* p. 15.

71. GATT, *Activities 1991,* pp. 69–71; and GATT, *Activities 1992,* pp. 15–18. The director general concluded at meetings of the TNC in April and September that the round was losing momentum. "At root, it has become a question of timing—rightly or wrongly, the political winds were never quite right, never blowing in the same direction for everyone." GATT, *Activities 1992,* p. 3.

72. "Endgame," *Economist,* November 14, 1992.

73. GATT, *Activities 1992,* p. 18; "The Uruguay Round: Coup de Grace, Coup de Foudre," *Economist,* November 28, 1992.

74. Hills's accomplishments as a negotiator are well captured in "The Fairest Trader of Them All," *Economist,* November 14, 1992.

75. GATT, *Activities 1992,* p. 20. The Swedish ambassador to the GATT and chair of the Contracting Parties, Lars Anell, in his opening address to the annual meeting of the Contracting Parties, claimed: "As never before, we appear to have both an opportunity to conclude the Round and, at the highest levels of government, a substantial political will to settle. It is also clear that a successful conclusion would give—both for psychological and economic reasons—a much-needed boost to the world economy now when it is still possible to save us from a worsening of the already gloomy economic situation." GATT, *Activities 1992,* p. 11.

76. "Uruguay Round Unraveling," *Economist,* December 26, 1992.

77. "The Uruguay Round . . . and Round," *Economist,* January 23, 1993.

78. Notes the *Economist:* "Opponents of liberal trade all over the world long for the United States to grow tough on trade. What they dread is a shrewdly accommodating America—one that presses for a quick conclusion for the Uruguay round, to bank what has been achieved, and then calls for a new round to keep those bicycle wheels spinning. That was the United States' old trade diplomacy. It worked much better than the new, steel-shod approach will—as the world, including America, may find to its costs." "The New Threats to Open Trade," February 27, 1993.

79. Press reports of visits to Washington by Canadian Prime Minister Brian Mulroney and Minister for International Trade Michael Wilson and EC Trade Commissioner Sir Leon Brittan in the first half of February spelled out the tough new line being taken in Washington but also a willingness to pursue the round. See, for example, "Mr. Kantor's Trade Folly," *Economist,* February 6, 1993; and "Clinton to Request Fast-Track Extension," *Toronto Globe and Mail,* February 12, 1993.

80. In the Canada-U.S. context, for example, Kantor made it quite clear that he was in no way impressed with either the letter or the spirit of the GATT or the FTA. What he was interested in was the art of the deal—he was prepared to give something of value only in return for receiving something, preferably of greater value. In the case of NAFTA, he indicated that he wanted side deals on labor, the environment, and safeguards, without which he was unprepared to suggest to the president that he put the agreement before the Democratic Congress.

81. Noted Canada's ambassador to the GATT, Gerry Shannon: "He [Dunkel] has been very creative and carried a lot of us on his back." Quoted by Neville Nankivell in the *Financial Post,* April 10, 1993.

82. The profiles of the new director general set out in the media all stressed these characteristics. See, for example, *Times* of London, July 17, 1993; *Financial Times* of London, October 8, 1993; and *European,* December 23, 1993.

83. Noted summit veteran and former chief negotiator for Canada, Sylvia Ostry: "All the delays in the GATT negotiations were getting to be a serious political embarrassment. So what could the G-7 leaders do to give a positive signal? They chose what was most feasible, most workable and most politically easy—market access." Quoted in *Maclean's,* July 19, 1993.

84. Reading newspaper clippings for the period from mid-June to mid-July is a study in the art of media manipulation. While something substantial had in fact been agreed at Tokyo, more importantly, briefings—on and off the record—had carefully built and resolved crises that served the purpose of restoring momentum to the negotiations. All this flimflammery is well captured in *Economist,* July 10, and in Frances Williams, "General Agreement to End All the Talk," *Financial Post* of London, July 9, 1993.

85. See Samuel Brittan, "Where GATT's $200bn really comes from," the *Financial Post* of London, October 4, 1993; and Frances Williams, "General in the War for Free Trade," *Financial Post,* October 8, 1993.

86. See David Crane, "GATT Chief Sutherland is Real Hero of Trade Deal," *Toronto Star,* December 20, 1993; and *Financial Post,* October 8, 1993, for some of the detail.

87. See "The Eleventh Hour Has Arrived"; and "Endgame in the GATT," in *Financial Post* of London, September 24 and 29, 1993.

88. *A Vision for APEC: Towards an Asia-Pacific Economic Community,* Report of the Eminent Persons Group (Singapore: Asia-Pacific Economic Cooperation, 1993).

89. See, for example, reports in the *Financial Post* and the *Times* of London as well as the *Wall Street Journal* in the second half of September, 1993, for some of the ongoing jockeying with the EC.

90. Annex 1A to the GATT 1994 lists twelve separate codes covering trade in agriculture, sanitary and phytosanitary measures, textiles and clothing, technical barriers to trade, trade-related investment measures, antidumping measures, customs valuation, preshipment inspection, rules of origin, import licensing procedures,

subsidies, and countervailing measures and safeguards. GATT, *Final Act Embodying the Results of the Uruguay Round of Multilateral Trade Negotiations* (Geneva, 1994).

Understandings were reached on the interpretation of Articles II:1(b), XVII, XXIV, XXV, XXVIII, and XXXV, as well as on dispute settlement and the trade policy review mechanism. A total of twelve "decisions" further clarify or amplify various aspects of the agreements and understandings.

91. Pietro S. Nivola, *Regulating Unfair Trade* (Washington, D.C.: Brookings Institution, 1992), provides a balanced and up-to-date assessment of the problems raised by the growth in the trade remedy system and the sometimes bizarre rules that have been developed to address the problems of so-called unfair trade, a concept that may have some political but little economic validity.

92. "New Threats to Free Trade," *Economist,* February 27, 1993.

Chapter 9: The Ozone Accords

1. See Peter M. Haas, "Obtaining International Protection through Epistemic Consensus," *Millennium: Journal of International Studies* 19, no. 3 (1990): 347–364.

2. The following discussion of the stakeholders in the negotiations is drawn from Chris Granada, "The Montreal Protocol on Substances That Deplete the Ozone Layer," in Lawrence E. Susskind, Esther Siskind, and J. William Breslin, eds., *Nine Case Studies in International Environmental Negotiation* (Cambridge, Mass.: MIT-Harvard Public Disputes Program, 1990), pp. 31–33.

3. Allan S. Miller and Irving M. Mintzer, *The Sky Is the Limit: Strategies for Protecting the Ozone Layer,* Research Report 3 (Washington, D.C.: World Resources Institute, 1986), p. 3. For various discussions about the early history and scientific theories about ozone depletion, see Sharon L. Roan, *Ozone Crisis: The 15-Year Evolution of a Sudden Global Emergency* (New York: John Wiley, 1989); and Lydia Dotto and Harold Schiff, *The Ozone War* (New York: Doubleday, 1978).

4. Peter M. Morrisette, "The Evolution of Policy Responses to Stratospheric Ozone Depletion," *Natural Resources Journal* 29, no. 3 (1989): 800.

5. Ibid., p. 804.

6. Peter S. Thacher, "International Agreements and Cooperation in Environmental Conservation and Resource Management" (paper prepared for the Workshop on Managing the Global Commons: Decision Making and Conflict Resolution, Washington D.C., August 1, 1989), p. 9.

7. Miller and Mintzer, *The Sky Is the Limit,* p. 21.

8. Quoted in Thacher, "International Agreements and Cooperation in Environmental Conservation and Resource Management," p. 14.

9. Jim MacNeill, "The Greening of International Relations," *International Journal* 45, no. 1 (1989–90): 26.

10. Quoted in Morrisette, "The Evolution of Policy Responses to Stratospheric Ozone Depletion," p. 812.

11. Roan, *Ozone Crisis,* p. 156.

12. Quoted in ibid., pp. 190–191.

13. Quoted in Morrisette, "The Evolution of Policy Responses to Stratospheric Ozone Depletion," p. 813.

14. See U.S. House Committee on Foreign Affairs, Subcommittee on Human Rights and International Organization, *U.S. Participation in International Negotiations on Ozone Protocol,* Report 87-395-P, 100th Cong., 1st sess., 1987, pp. 1–24.

15. Haas, "Obtaining International Protection through Epistemic Communities," p. 356.

16. Richard Elliot Benedick, *Ozone Diplomacy: New Directions in Safeguarding the Planet* (Cambridge: Harvard University Press, 1991), pp. 68–69.

17. Ibid., p. 70.

18. John Eberlee, "Ozone Layer and Warming CFCs," *International Perspectives* (July/August 1987): 23.

19. Haas, "Obtaining International Environmental Protection through Epistemic Communities," p. 356.

20. Quoted in Benedick, *Ozone Diplomacy,* p. 72.

21. *Preserving the Ozone Layer: A First Step,* A Report for Meeting Canada's Obligations Under the Montreal Protocol (Ottawa: Environment Canada, May 1988), pp. 4–5.

22. Benedick, *Ozone Diplomacy,* p. 77.

23. This formula worked as follows, as Benedick explains: "If a CFC-importing country's traditional supplier raised prices excessively or cut back on exports, the importing nation could meet the shortfall either by substituting its own production or by turning to another CFC producer from among the protocol parties. In turn, a producing country could increase its own production (and exports) to meet such needs without having to reduce its domestic consumption. Beginning in 1992, however, exports to nonparties could no longer be subtracted but would have to be counted against domestic consumption (Article 3). This prospect would serve as an added incentive for importing countries to join the protocol, lest they lose access to suppliers. It would also stimulate current exporters (the EC) to encourage their customers to join." Ibid., pp. 8–81.

24. Ibid., p. 81.

25. Ibid., p. 85.

26. Quoted in ibid., p. 96.

27. Edward A. Parsons, "Stratospheric Ozone and CFCs: The Evolution and Impact of International Institutions," International Environmental Institutions Project, Harvard University, Cambridge, Mass., November 24, 1991.

28. Quoted in *Preserving the Ozone Layer,* pp. 2–3.

29. Morrisette, "The Evolution of Policy Responses to Stratospheric Ozone Depletion," pp. 815–816.

30. U.S. ratification came in 1988. See U.S. Senate Committee on Foreign Relations, *Ozone Protocol,* Executive Report 100-14, 100th Cong., 2d sess., 1988, pp. 1–72.

31. United Nations Environment Programme (UNEP), *Helsinki Declaration on the Protection of the Ozone Layer,* U.N. Doc. OzL.Pro.1/L.1/App. 1, 1989.

32. UNEP, *Report of the First Meeting of the Parties to the Montreal Protocol on Substances that Deplete the Ozone Layer,* U.N. Doc. OzL.Pro.1/1/Add. 1, 1989, p. 1.

33. Ibid., p. 3.

34. UNEP, *Synthesis Report,* U.N. Doc.OzL.Pro. WG11(1)/4, 1989.

35. A detailed discussion of the debates and discussions surrounding the phaseout of CTs, MCs, and hydrochlorofluorocarbons (HCFCs) is found in Benedick, *Ozone Diplomacy,* pp. 128–147.

36. Ibid., pp. 159–160.

37. Ibid., p. 174.

38. Government of Canada, "Exchange of Letters Constituting an Interim Agreement between Canada and the United Nations of the Headquarters of the Montreal Ozone Secretariat," Treaty Series 1990, no. 38, Montreal, December 17, 1990.

39. See U.S. House Committee on Science, Space, and Technology, Subcommittee on Natural Resources, Agriculture Research, and Environment and the Subcommittee on International Scientific Cooperation, *CFC Reduction—Technology Transfer to the Developing World,* Hearing 149, 101st Cong., 2d sess., 1990, pp. 1–175.

40. Benedick, *Ozone Diplomacy,* pp. 188–189.

41. Quoted in ibid., p. 196.

42. Ibid., p. 198.

43. UNEP, *Report of the First Meeting of the Parties to the Montreal Protocol,* p. 3.

44. For a further discussion of the verification and compliance aspects of the Montreal Protocol and London amendments, see Owen Greene, "Ozone Depletion: Implementing and Strengthening the Montreal Protocol," in J. B. Poole and R. Guthrie, eds., *Verification Report 1992: Yearbook on Arms Control and Environmental Agreements* (London: VERTIC, 1992), pp. 265–274.

45. J. Alan Beesley, "Protection of the Atmosphere: The Law" (paper prepared for the Conference on the Protection of the Atmosphere: International Meeting of Legal and Policy Experts, Ottawa, February 22, 1989), p. 13.

Chapter 10: Hazardous Wastes

1. These cases are described in Brian Wynne, "The Toxic Waste Trade: International Regulatory Issues and Options," *Third World Quarterly* 11, no. 3 (1989): 124–128.

2. United Nations Environment Programme (UNEP), preamble to *Basel Convention on the Control of Transboundary Movements of Hazardous Wastes and Their Disposal,* U.N. Doc. IG.80/3, 1989.

3. Organization for Economic Cooperation and Development (OECD), *Monitoring and Control of Transfrontier Movement of Hazardous Wastes,* Environmental Monograph 34 (Paris, 1990), p. 8.

4. Ibid., p. 9.

5. Quoted in ibid., p. 10.

6. Ibid., p. 18.

7. Ibid., p. 19. Governments should also ensure that regulations on imported chemicals are not more restrictive than those applied to domestically produced chemicals or those imported from other countries, according to the guidelines. Information provided to the register is treated as confidential, and governments are encouraged to work on facilitating the exchange of scientific information and technical, economic, and legal information concerning their management of chemicals.

8. "Issue of Prior Informed Consent Reopens as Result of Action by Third World Nations," *International Environmental Reporter* 10, no. 9 (1987): 435–436; "Third World Countries Feel Unprotected under Dangerous Chemical Export Guidelines," *International Environmental Reporter* 10, no. 11 (1987): 589–590.

9. "Hazardous Wastes," *Environmental Policy and Law* 18, nos. 1–2 (1988): 2–3.

10. "Working Group Makes Progress on Treaty to Control Transboundary Wastes Movement," *International Environmental Reporter* 11, no. 2 (1988): 131.

11. "UNEP Working Group Reaches Agreement on Question of 'Prior Informed Consent,'" *International Environmental Reporter* 11, no. 3 (1988): 165.

12. Ibid.

13. Ibid.

14. "Waste Shipment Incidents Spur Interest in UNEP Agreement to Deal with Problem," *International Environmental Reporter* 11, no. 9 (1980): 471.

15. "Transboundary Movements of Hazardous Wastes," *Environmental Policy and Law* 18, no. 4 (1988): 103–105.

16. "Developed, Developing Countries Disagree over Elements of Waste Shipment Agreement," *International Environmental Reporter* 11, no. 7 (1988): 376–377; "Transfrontier Waste 'A Difficult Issue' Despite Caracas Conference, Long States," *International Environmental Reporter* 11, no. 7 (1988): 377.

17. "Differences Said to Remain on Accords Being Developed Separately by OECD, UNEP," *International Environmental Reporter* 11, no. 11 (1988): 567–568.

18. "Declaration of the Inter-Parliamentary Conference on Health—A Basis for Development in Africa, Brazzaville, Congo, 27 June to 1 July, 1988," *Environmental Policy and Law* 18, no. 4 (1988): 133–134.

19. "Progress in Hazardous Waste Negotiations," *Environmental Policy and Law* 18, no. 6 (1988): 194–195; "Delegates of 50 Countries Fail to Agree on Draft Covering Movement of Toxic Wastes," *International Environmental Reporter* 12, no. 2 (1989): 49–50; "Waste Convention: Negotiations Bogged Down," *Environmental Policy and Law* 19, no. 1 (1989): 5.

20. Wynne, "The Toxic Waste Trade," p. 138.

21. Kathleen Howard, "The Basel Convention: Control of Transboundary Movements of Hazardous Wastes and Their Disposal," *Hastings International and Comparative Law Review* 14, no. 1 (1990): 232.

22. Barbara D. Huntoon, "Emerging Controls on Transfers of Hazardous Waste to Developing Countries," *Law and Policy in International Business* 21, no. 1 (1989): 265–266; and Michelle M. Vilchek, "The Control on the Transfrontier Movement of Hazardous Waste from Developed to Developing Nations: The Goal of a 'Level Playing Field,'" *Northwestern Journal of International Law and Business* 11, no. 3 (1991): 659–666.

23. "Basel Convention: Legitimizing Toxic Terrorism Worldwide," in Jim Valleetee and Heather Spalding, eds., *The International Trade in Wastes: A Greenpeace Inventory,* 5th ed. (Washington, D.C.: Greenpeace U.S.A., 1990), pp. 14, 15.

24. Wynne, "The Toxic Waste Trade," p. 139.

25. Michelle M. Vilchek, "The Controls on the Transfrontier Movement of Hazardous Wastes from Developed to Developing Nations: The Goal of a Level Playing Field," *Northwestern Journal of International Law and Business* 11, no. 3 (1991): 671–672.

26. "Toxic Waste Convention," *Africa Research Bulletin* (Economic Series) 26, no. 3 (1989): 9493.

27. "Basel Convention: Liability and Compensation: Elements for a Protocol," *Environmental Policy and Law* 21, no. 2 (1991): 83–84.

28. "Liability and Compensation: Progress on Protocol," *Environmental Policy and Law* 21, no. 2 (1991): 49–50.

Chapter 11: Climate Change and Global Warming

1. See World Meteorological Organization and International Council of Scientific Unions, *Global Climate Change: A Scientific Review* (Geneva: World Meteorological

Organization, 1990); Thomas E. Graedel and Paul J. Crutzen, "The Changing Atmosphere"; and Stephen H. Schneider, "The Changing Climate," in *Scientific American* 261, no. 3 (1989): 58–69, 70–79; C. Beem, W. Furler, and N. Quinn, "Greenhouse: International and Policy Questions," in G. I. Perman, ed., *Greenhouse: Planning for Climate Change* (Canberra: CSRO Division of Atmospheric Research, 1987); F. Kenneth Hare, "The Global Greenhouse Effect"; Robert T. Watson, "Atmospheric Ozone"; Irving Mintzer, "Our Changing Atmosphere: Energy Policies, Air Pollution, and Global Warming"; and Jill Jaeger, "The Changing Atmosphere: Conference Background Paper," in *The Changing Atmosphere: Implications for Global Security* (Geneva: Secretariat of the World Meteorological Organization, 1989), pp. 59–69, 70–92, 117–139, and 384–404, respectively; Dean Edwin Abrahamson, *The Challenge of Global Warming* (Washington, D.C.: Island Press for the Natural Resources Defense Council, 1989), pp. 3–70; Jessica Tuchman Mathews, "Redefining Security," *Foreign Affairs* 68, no. 2 (1989): 162–177; Norman Myers, "Environment and Security," *Foreign Policy*, no. 74 (Spring 1989), pp. 3–22; Michael Renner, *National Security: The Economic and Environmental Dimension* (Washington, D.C.: Worldwatch Institute, 1989); Irving M. Mintzer, *A Matter of Degrees: The Potential for Controlling the Greenhouse Effect*, Research Report 5 (Washington, D.C.: World Resources Institute, 1987); Irving M. Mintzer, "Living in a Warmer World: Challenges for Policy Analysis and Management," *Journal of Policy Analysis and Management* 7, no. 2 (1988): 445–459; U.S. Senate Committee on Environment and Public Works, *Ozone Depletion, the Greenhouse Effect, and Climate Change: Hearings Before the Subcommittee on Environmental Pollution*, Hearing 99-723, 99th Cong., 2d sess., 1986; Joel B. Smith and Dennis A. Tirpak, *The Potential Effects of Global Climate Change on the United States* (Washington, D.C.: U.S. EPA, 1988); "The Greenhouse Effect: How It Can Change Our Lives," *EPA Journal* 15, no. 1 (1989); J. Titus, ed., *Effects of Changes in Stratospheric Ozone and Global Climate Change* (Washington, D.C.: U.S. EPA and UNEP, 1986); and Michael H. Glantz, ed., *Societal Responses to Regional Climate Change* (Boulder, Colo.: Westview, 1988).

2. On the problem of different time scales for decision making, see J. S. Maini, "Forests: Barometers of the Environment and Economics," in Constance Mungall and Digby J. McLaren, *Planet Under Stress* (Toronto: Oxford University Press, 1990), p. 201.

3. On the difficulties of cost-benefit analysis for calculating long-term environmental effects, see Roefie Hueting, "The Use of the Discount Rate in a Cost-Benefit Analysis for Different Uses of a Humid Tropical Forest Area," *Ecological Economics* 3, no. 1 (1991): 43–57. Also see R. Repetto, W. Magrath, M. Wells, C. Beer, and F. Rossini, *Wasting Assets: National Resources in the National Income Accounts* (Washington, D.C.: World Resources Institute, 1989); and Peter O. Johannsson, *The Economic Theory and Measurement of Environmental Benefits* (Cambridge, Eng.: Cambridge University Press, 1987).

4. See A. Agarwal and S. Narain, *Global Warming in an Unequal World—A Case of Environmental Colonialism* (New Delhi: Center for Science and Environment, 1990); People's Republic of China, *Beijing Ministerial Declaration on Environment and Development* (Beijing, 1991); and Alvaro Umana Quesada, "Greenhouse Economics: Global Resources and the Political Economy of Climate Change," *Environmental Policy and Law* 19, no. 5 (1989): 154–161.

5. U.N. General Assembly, *Report of the Intergovernmental Negotiating Committee for*

a Framework Convention on Climate Change on the Work of the Second Part of Its Fifth Session, Held at New York from 30 April to 9 May, U.N. Doc. A/AC.237/18 (Part II)/Add. 1, 1992.

6. Steven Raynor, Wolfgang Negeli, and Patricia Lund, *Managing the Global Commons: Decision Making and Conflict Resolution in Response to Climate Change,* ORNL/TM-11619 (Oak Ridge, Tenn.: Oak Ridge National Laboratory, 1990), p. 28.

7. Quoted in Ian Rowlands, "The Security Challenges of Global Environmental Change," *Washington Quarterly* 14, no. 1 (1991): 108.

8. Ibid., pp. 107–108.

9. Quoted in Jill Jaeger, *Developing Policies for Responding to Climate Change* (Stockholm: Beijer Institute, 1988), p. 3.

10. World Climate Programme, *Report of the International Conference on the Assessment of the Role of Carbon Dioxide and of Other Greenhouse Gases on Climate Variations and Associated Impacts,* WMO 661 (Geneva: World Meteorological Organization, 1986).

11. Jaeger, *Developing Policies for Responding to Climate Change,* p. 35.

12. "Conference Statement," in *The Changing Atmosphere,* pp. 293–296.

13. Ibid., p. 295.

14. See "Protection of the Atmosphere," Statement of the International Meeting of Legal and Policy Experts, Ottawa, February 22, 1989. Some delegates expressed a preference for a comprehensive umbrella convention to protect the atmosphere. This preference came out of the recommendations of the Toronto Conference and the belief that a comprehensive approach would achieve a better result by linking together the different dimensions of atmospheric pollution and global warming. However, Dr. Mostafa Tolba, UNEP executive director, convinced the delegates that it would take too long to negotiate such a convention and that attention should be focused on the development of a framework convention to address the immediate problems of climate change.

15. "Declaration of The Hague," March 11, 1989.

16. "Key Sections of the Paris Communiqué by the Group of Seven," *New York Times,* July 17, 1989.

17. For example, the Regional Conference on Global Warming and Sustainable Development, sponsored by the University of Sao Paulo and the Woods Hole Research Center, Sao Paulo, June 18–20, 1990; the International Conference on Global Warming and Sustainable Development, sponsored by the Thailand Development Research Institute, the Institute for Research and Public Policy, and the Woods Hole Research Center, Bangkok, June 10–11, 1991; the International Conference on Global Warming and Climate Change, sponsored by the African Centre for Technology Studies and the Woods Hole Research Center, Nairobi, May 2–4, 1990; the International Conference on Global Warming and Climate Change, sponsored by the Tata Energy Research Institute, the Woods Hole Research Center, UNEP, and the World Resources Institute, New Delhi, February 21–23, 1989; the ASEAN Workshop on Scientific, Policy, and Legal Aspects of Global Climate Change, sponsored by the Government of Thailand and the Woods Hole Research Center, Bangkok, September 19–20, 1990; and the International Workshop on Climate Change and Energy Policies in Developing Countries, sponsored by the Human Dimensions Global Change Program (IFIAS, ISSC, UNU, UNESCO), Montebello, Quebec, July 29–August 1, 1990.

18. *Report of the First Session of the WMO/UNEP Intergovernmental Panel on Climate Change*, TD 267 (Geneva: World Climate Programme, 1988), p. 2; and *National Climate Change Program*, U.S. IPCC News, no. 1 (Rockville, Md.: U.S. Department of Commerce, 1989).

19. Intergovernmental Panel on Climate Change, *Scientific Assessment of Climate Change*, report from WGI to IPCC, June 1990; Intergovernmental Panel on Climate Change, *Potential Impacts of Climate Change*, report from WGII to IPCC, June 1990; and Intergovernmental Panel on Climate Change, *Formulation of Response Strategies*, report from WGIII to IPCC, June 1990; and Intergovernmental Panel on Climate Change and World Meteorological Organization, *First Assessment Report: Overview* (Geneva, 1990).

20. The report stated that "industrialized countries should adopt domestic measures to limit climate change by adapting their own economies in line with future agreements to limit emissions," while arguing for a "flexible and progressive approach." *Formulation of Response Strategies*, p. ii.

21. "The Great Sky Greenhouse," *Nature* 345, no. 6274 (1990): 371, 373; "Hot Air—or What?" *Nature* 345, no. 6276 (1990): 562; "IPCC's Climate Change Mindset," *Nature* 348, no. 6296 (1990): 9.

22. Jim MacNeill, Pieter Winsemius, and Taizo Yakushiji, *Beyond Interdependence: The Meshing of the World's Economy and the Earth's Ecology* (New York: Oxford University Press, 1991), p. 77.

23. "Disarray over Declaration," *Nature* 347, no. 6295 (1990): 702; and "Two Declarations at Odds," *Nature* 348, no. 6297 (1990): 98.

24. Quoted in MacNeill, Winsemius, and Yakushiji, *Beyond Interdependence*, p. 77.

25. Quoted in ibid., p. 78.

26. *Report of the 8th Session of Scientific Advisory Committee of the World Climate Impact Assessment and Response Strategies Programme* (Budapest, October 1991), p. 9.

27. Canadian government official, interview by author, Ottawa, Canada, August 22, 1992.

28. Results of Round I negotiations can be found in U.N. General Assembly, *Report of the Intergovernmental Negotiating Committee for a Framework Convention on Climate Change on the Work of Its First Session. Held at Washington, D.C., from 4 to 14 February 1991*, U.N. Doc. A/AC.237/6, 1991.

29. The following discussion is drawn from *Summary of Perspectives Noted in Country Statements at the Beginning of the Negotiations on a Climate Change Convention* (Ottawa: Environment Canada, 1991); *Positions of Countries and Regional Groups at the Beginning of the Negotiating Session* (Ottawa: Environment Canada, 1991); and Canadian Delegation Report, *Intergovernmental Negotiation Committee for a Framework Convention on Climate Change* (Ottawa: Environment Canada, 1991); and "INC Climate Change Convention: First Discussions," *Environmental Policy and Law* 21, no. 2 (1991): 50–53. For an excellent legal analysis and interpretation of the negotiation and subsequent convention, see Daniel Bodansky, "The United Nations Framework Convention on Climate Change: A Commentary," *Yale Journal of International Law* 18, no. 2 (1993): 451–558.

30. A source is defined as any process or activity that releases a greenhouse gas, aerosol, or a precursor of a greenhouse gas into the atmosphere. Sink refers to any process, activity, or mechanism that removes a greenhouse gas or a precursor of a greenhouse gas from the atmosphere, e.g., forests.

31. A large number of NGOs attended the INC negotiations, with some being allowed to attend plenary and other special sessions of the INC. The list of organizations in consultative status with the U.N. Economic and Social Council includes the International Chamber of Commerce, the International Council of Women, the World Federation of U.N. Associations, Greenpeace International, the International Council of Environmental Law, the International Council of Scientific Unions, the International Petroleum Industry Environmental Conservation Association, the World Coal Institute, the World Resources Institute, Friends of the Earth, the International Organization of Automobile Manufacturers, the International Studies Association, the National Audubon Society, and the National Resources Defense Council. Other nongovernmental organizations represented include such groups as the Alliance for Responsible CFC Policy, the American Forestry Association, the Center for Clean Air Policy, the Environmental Defense Fund, the Forum of Brazilian NGOs to UNCED, the World Wildlife Fund, etc.

32. Michael R. Deland, *America's Climate Change Strategy: An Agenda for Action* (Washington, D.C.: White House, 1991).

33. Results of Round II negotiations can be found in U.N. General Assembly, *Report of the Intergovernmental Negotiating Committee for a Framework Convention on Climate Change on the Work of its Second Session, Held at Geneva from 19 to 28 June 1991,* U.N. Doc. A/AC.237/9, 1991.

34. Intergovernmental Negotiating Committee for a Framework Convention on Climate Change, *Preparation of a Framework Convention on Climate Change: Set of Informal Papers Provided by Delegations, Related to the Preparation of a Framework Convention on Climate Change, Second Session, Geneva, 19–28 June 1991,* U.N. Doc. A/AC.237/Misc.1./Add.1, 1991; Intergovernmental Negotiating Committee for a Framework Convention on Climate Change, *Preparation of a Framework Convention on Climate Change: Set of Informal Papers provided by Delegations, Related to the Preparation of a Framework Convention on Climate Change, Second Session, Geneva, 19–28 June 1991,* U.N. Doc. A/AC.237/Misc.1./ Add.2,1992; Intergovernmental Negotiating Committee for a Framework Convention on Climate Change, *Preparation of a Framework Convention on Climate Change: Set of Informal Papers Provided by Delegations, Related to the Preparation of a Framework Convention on Climate Change, Second Session, Geneva, 19–28 June 1991,* U.N. Doc. A/AC.237/Misc.1./Add. 3, June 1991; Intergovernmental Negotiating Committee for a Framework Convention on Climate Change, *Preparation of a Framework Convention on Climate Change: Set of Informal Papers Provided by Delegations, Related to the Preparation of a Framework Convention on Climate Change, Second Session, Geneva, 19–28 June 1991,* U.N. Doc. A/AC.237/ Misc.1./Add. 5, 1991.

35. Canadian Delegation Report, *Intergovernmental Negotiating Committee for a Framework Convention on Climate Change,* 2d sess. (Ottawa: Environment Canada, 1991); Sebastian Oberthur, "Climate Negotiations: Progress Slow," *Environmental Policy and Law* 21, no. 5–6 (1991): 193–195.

36. Intergovernmental Negotiating Committee for a Framework Convention on Climate Change, *Preparation of a Framework Convention on Climate Change: Set of Informal Papers Provided by Delegations, Related to the Preparation of a Framework Convention on Climate Change, Second Session, Geneva, 19–28 June 1991,* U.N. Doc. A/AC.237/ Misc.1./Add. 6, 1991; Intergovernmental Negotiating Committee for a Framework Convention on Climate Change, *Preparation of a Framework Convention on Climate*

Change: Set of Informal Papers Provided by Delegations, Related to the Preparation of a Framework Convention on Climate Change, Second Session, Geneva, 19–28 June 1991, U.N. Doc. A/AC.237/Misc.1./Add. 7, 1991.

37. Results of Round III negotiations can be found in U.N. General Assembly, *Report of the Intergovernmental Negotiating Committee for a Framework Convention on Climate Change on the Work of Its Third Session, Held at Nairobi from 9 to 20 September 1991,* U.N. Doc. A/AC.237/12, 1991.

38. Canadian Delegation Report, *Intergovernmental Negotiating Committee for a Framework Convention on Climate Change,* 3d sess. (Ottawa: Environment Canada, 1991).

39. Norwegian Delegation, "Convention on Climate Change/Cost-Effective Implementation of Commitments Across National Borders/Proposal for a new Partnership in Development Funding related to the Financial Mechanism," and "Commitments on Financial Resources, Transfer of and Cooperation on Technology," papers prepared for INC 3d sess., September 1991.

40. "Intervention by the Presidency on Behalf of the European Community and Member States," paper prepared for INC 3d sess., September 1991.

41. United States Delegation, "U.S. Statement on Sources and Sinks," paper prepared for INC 3d sess., September 1991, p. 2.

42. Government of Canada, "Canadian Position on Net Emissions," paper prepared for INC 3d sess., September 1991, p. 1.

43. Government of Norway, "Commitments on Financial Resources, Transfer of Cooperation and Technology," paper prepared for INC 3d sess., September 1991, p. 4. Emphasis in original.

44. United States Delegation, "U.S. Statement on Technology Transfer and Financial Assistance," paper prepared for INC 3d sess., September 1991, p. 1.

45. United States Delegation, "Proposed Country Study Process (Elements of a Methodology)," draft, paper prepared for INC 3d sess., September 1991.

46. Intervention by The Netherlands on behalf of the European Community and Its Member States, "The Structure and Implementation of the Convention," paper prepared for INC 3d sess., September 1991.

47. Results of Round IV negotiations can be found in U.N. General Assembly, *Report on the Intergovernmental Negotiating Committee for a Framework Convention on Climate Change on the Work of its Fourth Session, Held at Geneva from 9 to 20 December 1991,* U.N. Doc. A/AC.237/15, 1991.

48. "Joint Statement of the Group of 77 made by its Chairman, Ghana, at the Fourth Session of the Intergovernmental Negotiating Committee for a Framework Convention on Climate Change," paper prepared for INC 4th sess., December 1991.

49. United States Delegation, "U.S. Statement on General Commitments," and "U.S. Statement on Specific Commitments," papers prepared for INC 4th sess., December 1991.

50. Canadian Delegation Report, *Intergovernmental Negotiating Committee for a Framework Convention on Climate Change,* 4th sess. (Ottawa: Environment Canada, 1992).

51. Federal Republic of Germany, "Joint Implementation of Commitments Contained in a Global Climate Convention (Emission Reduction Crediting System), paper prepared for INC 4th sess., December 1991.

52. Results of Round V negotiations can be found in U.N. General Assembly, *Re-*

port on the Intergovernmental Negotiating Committee for a Framework Convention on Climate Change on the Work of the First Part of its Fifth Session, Held at New York from 18 to 28 February 1992, U.N. Doc. A/AC.237/18 (pt. 1), 1992. Also see Bert Bolin, "Report to the Fifth Session of the Intergovernmental Negotiating Committee for a Framework Convention on Climate Change," (New York, February 1992).

53. U.N. General Assembly, Intergovernmental Negotiating Committee for a Framework Convention on Climate Change, *Completion of a Framework Convention on Climate Change, Draft Proposed by the Chairman, Addendum 2, Article 4, Commitments,* U.N. Doc. A/AC.237/L.14Add.2*/1992.

54. Canadian Delegation Report and Text of Framework Convention on Climate Change, *Intergovernmental Negotiating Committee for a Framework Convention on Climate Change,* (Ottawa: Environment Canada, 1992).

55. Results of Round VI negotiations can be found in U.N. General Assembly, *Report on the Intergovernmental Negotiating Committee for a Framework Convention on Climate Change on the Work of the Second Part of Its Fifth Session* U.N. Doc. A/AC.237/18(part 2)/Add. 1, 1992; and Canadian Delegation Report, *Intergovernmental Negotiating Committee for a Framework Convention on Climate Change,* 5th sess. (Ottawa: Environment Canada, 1992).

56. This text was drafted by the chair at the request of the Extended Bureau, composed of a select group of INC bureau and working group officials who met in Paris in April to discuss various aspects of the convention in an effort to surmount the outstanding differences that still remained on the core issues of targets and timetables and financial commitments and mechanisms.

57. Rose Gutfeld, "Accord on Climate Change Launches Modest Effort to End Global Warming," *Wall Street Journal,* May 11, 1992.

58. Willett Kempton, "Lay Perspectives on Global Climate Change," *Global Environmental Change* 1, no. 3 (1991): 183–208.

59. Second World Climate Conference, *Final Conference Statement, Scientific/Technical Sessions* (Geneva: WMO and UNEP, 1990).

60. See, for example, Olker A. Mohnen, Walter Goldstein, and Wei Chyung Wang, "The Conflict Over Global Warming: The Application of Scientific Research to Policy Choices," *Global Environmental Change* 1, no. 2 (1991): 109–123; Robert C. Balling Jr., *The Heated Debate: Greenhouse Predictions vs. Climate Reality* (San Francisco: Pacific Research Institute for Public Policy, 1992); Robert J. Swart and Monique J. M. Hootsmans, "A Sound Footing for Controlling Climate Change," *International Environmental Affairs* 3, no. 2 (1991): 124–136; Vaclav Smil, "Planetary Warming: Realities and Responses," *Population Development and Review* 16, no. 1 (1990): 1–30.

61. See William D. Nordhaus, "The Cost of Slowing Climate Change: A Survey"; William W. Hogan and Dale W. Jorgenson, "Productivity Trends and the Cost of Reducing CO_2 Emissions"; John Whalley and Randall Wigle, "Cutting CO_2 Emissions: The Effects of Alternative Policy Approaches"; and David Pearce and Edward Barbier, "The Greenhouse Effect: A View From Europe," *Energy Journal* 12, no. 1 (1991): 37–66, 67–86, 87–108, 147–160. A useful review of the debates among economists is also to be found in Chris Green, "Economics and the 'Greenhouse Effect,'" Department of Economics and Centre for Climate and Global Change Research, McGill University, May 1991. For useful discussions about the relation between energy policy and the greenhouse effect, see Michael Grubb, *Energy Policies and the Greenhouse*

Effect, vol. 1, Policy Appraisal (Brookfield, Vt.: Dartmouth for the Royal Institute of International Affairs, 1990); and Michael Grubb, Peter Brackley, Michele Ledic, Ajay Mathur, Steve Raynor, Jeremy Russell, and Akira Tanabe, *Energy Policies and the Greenhouse Effect: Volume Two: Country Studies and Technical Options* (Brookfield, Vt.: Dartmouth, for the Royal Institute of International Affairs, 1991).

62. This follows a well-known pattern of public perceptions of risk when scientific and technical issues are involved. See Aaron Wildavsky, *Searching for Safety* (New Brunswick, N.J.: Transaction Books, 1988); and Sheila Jasanoff, *Risk Management and Political Culture* (New York: Russell Sage Foundation, 1986). For a provocative discussion on the need for new concepts of risk management for climate change, see Timothy O'Riordan and Steve Rayner, "Risk Management for Global Environmental Change," *Global Environmental Change* 1, no. 2 (1991): 91–108.

63. "U.S. Reluctance to Reduce CO_2 Is Sharply Criticized by Germany," *New York Times*, May 21, 1992; James Brooke, "To Protect Bush, U.N. Will Limit Access to Talks," *New York Times*, June 8, 1992; Paul Lewis, "U.S. at the Earth Summit: Isolated and Challenged," *New York Times*, June 10, 1992.

64. Mark Stevens, "Compromise Offered at U.N. on Greenhouse Gas Emissions," *New York Times*, May 2, 1992; and Rose Gutfeld, "How Bush Achieved Global Warming Pact with Modest Goals," *Wall Street Journal*, May 27, 1992.

65. Gutfeld, "How Bush Achieved Global Warming Pact."

66. William K. Stevens, "Washington May Change Its Position on Climate," *New York Times*, February 18, 1992; Rose Gutfeld, "White House Figures Indicate Cutting Greenhouse Gases Could Be Fairly Easy," *Wall Street Journal*, April 27, 1992.

67. Matthew Paterson and Michael Grubb, "The International Politics of Climate Change," *International Affairs* 68, no. 2 (1992): 302.

68. Paul Lewis, "U.S. Informally Offers to Cut Rise in Climate-Warming Gases," *New York Times*, April 29, 1992; William K. Stevens, "Accord on Limits on Gas Emissions Is Reported Near," *New York Times*, May 8, 1992; William K. Stevens, "Compromise Offered at U.N. on Greenhouse Gas Emissions," *New York Times*, May 2, 1992; Rose Gutfeld, "Bush Caught in Earth Summit Crossfire," *Wall Street Journal*, April 7, 1992.

69. Virginia Ferreira, "Implementing the Framework Convention on Climate Change," in J. B. Poole and R. Guthrie, eds., *Verification Report 1992: Yearbook on Arms Control and Environmental Agreements* (London: VERTIC, 1992), p. 279. Ferreira notes that, although compliance and verification issues have been raised in the INC, verification of a country's CO_2 emissions from the energy sector is no easy matter and "only roughly reliable."

70. See Wolfgang Fisher, "Update: Verification of a Greenhouse Gas Convention," in ibid., pp. 283–285. Also see W. Fischer, J. S. di Primio, and G. Stein, "A Convention on Greenhouse Gases: Towards the Design of a Verification System" report Jül=2390 (Forschungszentrum Jülich Gimbl, Programmgruppe Technologiefolgenforschung, Jülich, Federal Republic of Germany, October 1990).

71. Daniel Bodansky, "The United Nations Framework Convention on Climate Change, *Yale Journal of International Law* 18, no. 2 (1993): 496.

Chapter 12: Understanding Multilateral Negotiations

1. For a discussion of the concept of "ripening" in international negotiation and mediation processes, see I. William Zartman, *Ripe for Resolution: Conflict and Interven-*

tion in Africa (New York: Oxford University Press, 1985); and I. William Zartman, "Ripening Conflict, Ripe Moment, Formula, and Mediation," in Diane B. Bendahmane and John W. McDonald Jr., eds., *Perspectives on Negotiation* (Washington, D.C.: Foreign Service Institute, U.S. Department of State, 1986), pp. 205–228. The concept of ripeness is also used in Richard N. Haass, *Conflicts Unending: The United States and Regional Disputes* (New Haven: Yale University Press, 1990).

2. See, for example, Gareth Porter and Janet Welsh Brown, *Global Environmental Politics: Dilemmas in World Politics* (Boulder, Colo.: Westview, 1991); John E. Carroll, ed., *International Environmental Diplomacy* (Cambridge: Cambridge University Press, 1988); James N. Rosenau and Ernset-Otto Czempiel, eds., *Governance Without Government: Order and Change in World Politics* (Cambridge: Cambridge University Press, 1992); and Peter M. Haas, *Saving the Mediterranean: The Politics of International Environmental Cooperation* (New York: Columbia University Press, 1990).

3. Miles Kahler, "Multilateralism with Small and Large Numbers," *International Organization* 46, no. 3 (1992): 681–708.

4. This is due to the security dilemma, which was heightened by the U.S.-Soviet rivalry during the Cold War. See Alexander L. George, "Factors Influencing Security Cooperation," in Alexander L. George, Philip J. Farley, and Alexander Dallin, eds., *U.S.-Soviet Security Cooperation: Achievements, Failures, Lessons* (New York: Oxford University Press, 1988), pp. 655–678.

5. See, for example, Stephen D. Krasner, *Structural Conflict: The Third World against Global Capitalism* (Berkeley: University of California Press, 1985); and Robert L. Rothstein, "Regime-Creation by a Coalition of the Weak: Lessons from the NIEO and the Integrated Program for Commodities," *International Studies Quarterly* 28, no. 3 (1984): 307–328.

6. Oran R. Young, "Political Leadership and Regime Formation: On the Development of Institutions in International Society," *International Organization* 45, no. 3 (1991): 293–294.

7. I. William Zartman and Maureen Berman, *The Practical Negotiator* (New Haven: Yale University Press, 1982), p. 93.

8. This problem is the subject of Kenneth Arrow's classic study, *Social Choice and Individual Values* (New York: John Wiley, 1961).

9. James N. Rosenau, *Turbulence in World Politics: A Theory of Change and Continuity* (Princeton: Princeton University Press, 1990).

Index

Hampson, Fen Osler,
    Multilateral negotiations : lessons from arms control, trade, and the
environment / by Fen Osler Hampson, with Michael Hart.
        p.   cm.
    Includes bibliographical references and index.
    ISBN 0-8018-4999-3 (alk. paper)
    1. Negotiation. 2. Arbitration, International.   I. Hart, Michael, 1944–   .
II. Title.
BF637.N4H36   1995
302.3—dc20   94-40826